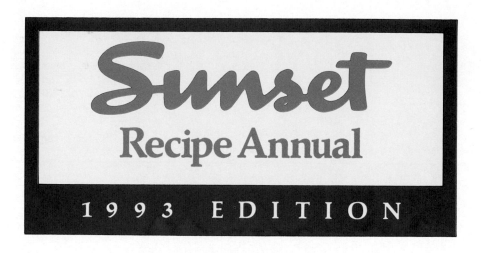

Sunset
Recipe Annual

1993 EDITION

Every *Sunset Magazine* recipe and
food article from 1992

By the *Sunset* Editors

Blueberry Tart (page 123)

Sunset Publishing Corporation ■ **Menlo Park, California**

An Annual Tradition

Artichokes with Thai Shrimp Salsa (page 224)

Once again we invite you to join us in what has become a *Sunset* tradition—our annual gathering of every food article from the past year's issues of *Sunset Magazine*.

If you've enjoyed previous editions, you already know that a banquet awaits you. This year's book offers hundreds of recipes to meet all your cooking needs, whether you're looking for family entrées, party ideas for casual gatherings, or great suggestions for holiday entertaining.

Here's just a sampling of this year's treats: seafood Caesar salad, skewered appetizer tidbits for the barbecue, citrus surprise salads, tropical sorbets in delicate cookie "tulips", pepper-crusted barbecued salmon, salad-salsas, chocolate brownie cake made with fresh raspberries, tailgate picnic dishes, lightened-up versions of *Sunset* favorites, and holiday specialties.

You'll also find our popular features—*Sunset's Kitchen Cabinet*, *Chefs of the West*, and *Menus*—along with a new one, *Why?*, which offers answers to readers' cooking questions.

Front cover: Peppered Salmon (recipe on page 136). Photography by Kevin Sanchez. Design by Susan Bryant. Food and photo styling by Susan Massey.

Back cover: Bear Lake Raspberry Shake (recipe on page 163). Photography by Peter Christiansen.

Sunset Magazine
    Editor: William R. Marken

Sunset Books
    Editor: Elizabeth L. Hogan

First printing March 1993

All material in this book originally appeared in the 1992 issues of *Sunset Magazine* and was created by the following editors, illustrators, photographers, and photo stylists:

Senior Editor (Food and Entertaining)
Sunset Magazine
Jerry Anne Di Vecchio

Food Writers
Sunset Magazine
Linda Lau Anusasananan,
    Senior Writer
Betsy Reynolds Bateson
Paula Smith Freschet
Bernadette Hart
Elaine Johnson
Karyn I. Lipman
Christine B. Weber

Illustrations
David Broad (*Chefs of the West*)
Alice Harth (*Sunset's Kitchen Cabinet*)
Pete Collins
Lucy I. Sargeant

Photography
Glenn Christiansen
Peter Christiansen
Norman A. Plate
Darrow M. Watt
(See page 280 for individual credits)

Photo Styling
Carol Hatchard Goforth
Dennis W. Leong

Recipe Annual was produced by *Sunset Books*.

Contributing Editors
Cornelia Fogle
Helen Sweetland

Design
Williams & Ziller Design

Contents

A Letter from Sunset

DEAR READER,

As we plan and develop stories for your use through the year, much attention is devoted to recipes. But memorable meals, as you well know, depend on more than the menu. Other needs must be met, and we learn about them by listening to you—in person, on the phone, through your letters, and even by fax, these days.

To answer questions that don't fit the how-to nature of recipes, we've introduced a new column, *Why?* It appears several times in this year's *Recipe Annual*—starting in May, with an explanation of why green and red vegetables change color when cooked. Later, in December, we tell you why mashed potatoes turn to glue in the food processor. To help us address your queries in straightforward, everyday language, we've enlisted the aid of food technologist George York.

You want to serve attractive meals that, now and then, offer pleasant little surprises. Suggestions are found regularly in each month's *Menus*. A section headlined "The Details" focuses on simple flourishes that dress up both the food and the table, provide unexpected variety, or just bring a smile. This year's extra touches include luminarias to brighten a Southwestern New Year's party in January; carrot slices cut as hearts for a Valentine Day's dinner in February; and a simple icer of nested bowls to keep salads cold in August. You'll find similar ideas in other articles, too; for example, a November feature tells you how to create fresh produce centerpieces that look like still-life paintings.

You like good value and know that one way to get it is to use fresh foods in season. This keeps us working a year ahead, so you'll have the facts at the right time. Learn ways to serve citrus fruits in lively salads in February; in December, use short-season cranberries for brilliant red vinegar to give as gifts or enjoy at home all year long.

The seasons bring other demands: you need meals to match festive occasions. November's holiday entertaining section focuses on a big bird and all the trimmings, while that month's *Menus* include a dinner you

In our test kitchens, food writers and editors gather regularly to evaluate recipes and article ideas: (left to right) Elaine Johnson, Betsy Bateson with Amanda Marie, Jerry Di Vecchio, Bernadette Hart, Karyn Lipman, Linda Anusasananan, and Christine Weber.

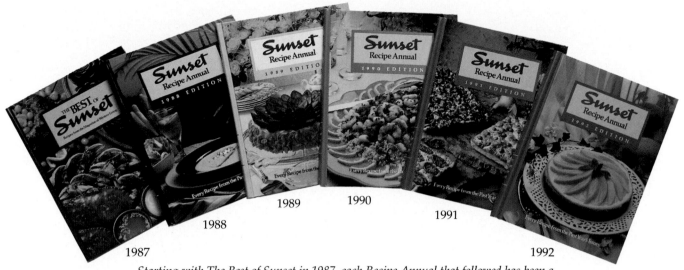

Starting with The Best of Sunset in 1987, each Recipe Annual that followed has been a keepsake edition of the previous year's food articles and recipes from Sunset Magazine.

1987 1988 1989 1990 1991 1992

can't manage with a normal turkey—a breast roast and *four* roasted drumsticks. We've also designed a potluck appetizer party tailor-made for busy people who want to share the work as well as the fun. Christmas dinner comes up twice. In November, we tell you how to cook a magnificent crown pork roast; December offers an impressive (and impressively manageable) feast starring a grand beef roast.

For Passover, try April's rhubarb cobbler and Matzo Meal Cookies. Both treats meet dietary laws and are delicious on any occasion.

Big Game time is highlighted in September, with tailgate-party favorites from campuses around the West.

You want news about food. In January, we update you on the status of summer fruits imported from Chile during our winter months; in April, we identify Hawaiian fish now becoming more widely available on the Mainland—and share Hawaiian chefs' ideas for cooking them. In August, seven basic market varieties of watermelon are pictured, described, and presented in an assortment of cut-and-serve dishes.

Sometimes, our news concerns old favorites that have returned to the limelight. In February, we rediscover coffee as a denser, darker, richer, and better brew—and give you a scientific (but simple) method for making that perfect cup. The revival of California-made olive oils inspired an October story. You'll learn the nutritional benefits of this ancient food and how to interpret some confusing label information.

Cutting down on fat is a goal we all share. Our efforts to lighten up *Sunset* classics continue, but now you've joined in the game. In January, we present a reader's trimmed down version of a chilies rellenos recipe we first published in 1973.

Perhaps this is the best place to emphasize that our fat-trimming efforts aren't limited to special features or articles. Leaf through the pages of this book and note the many recipes—both ours and yours!—with fat-reducing techniques built right in. One favorite method, called braise-deglazing, uses vegetables browned without fat as a starting point for soups, braised

...A Letter from Sunset

dishes, stews, and sauces. Similar techniques are used to cut fat in roasted foods. In all cases, the ingredients are everyday, no engineered foods are required, and the finished dishes are actually more flavorful than their richer counterparts might be.

Because increasing the day's consumption of complex carbohydrates makes it easier to balance fats, you're interested in more ideas for grains, legumes, pasta, and all-vegetable main dishes. We respond to your requests with meals like the Indian dal dinner in February and eggs scrambled with bulgur in March.

Are sinfully rich treats entirely off limits? Certainly not. We know you still want to bake your cake—and then eat it, too. That's why we offer desserts like ginger-caramel macadamia pie in November.

Of course, you may wonder how you can fit these frankly fattening foods into a nutritious diet. The answer is simple: consider them not just on their own, but in relation to your total caloric and fat intake over a day or two. To get the big picture, add up a day's worth of fat grams and total calories (aiming to meet your personal requirements), then do your arithmetic. Multiply total fat grams x 9, then divide that number by total calories x 100 —and you have the percentage of calories from fat. When you balance high-fat foods with those that have little fat but are calorie-rich (such as complex carbohydrates), you can still meet the goal today's nutritionists recommend: 30 percent or less of the day's calories from fat. When you want that wedge of Chocolate-Raspberry Brownie for dessert, just focus on complex carbohydrates and low-fat dishes the rest of the day. To calculate, use the nutritional information with each of our recipes.

This year's *Recipe Annual* continues to bring you a good supply of what you've come to expect: simple ways to entertain, buy-and-serve parties, lots of quick and easy dishes, ample activity on the barbecue, ethnic discoveries that bring new taste adventures, and more.

In this book, as in its five predecessors, recipes are grouped by the month in which they appeared in *Sunset Magazine*. For help in locating particular recipes easily, consult the three indexes on pages 269 to 280: an index of article titles, one of recipe names, and a longer, general index.

Enjoy, and keep in touch!

Jerry Anne Di Vecchio
Senior Editor (Food and Entertaining)
Sunset Magazine

Seattle Seafood Caesar salad (page 12)

Join our midwinter food
discovery trip to summertime in Chile, where we gather
recipes that use fresh fruits with Latin American
flair. In Seattle we discover an elegant version of Caesar
Salad; with the addition of shrimp, crab, or other seafood,
this perennial favorite becomes a handsome main-dish salad.
Experiment with fresh pickled beets in creamy borscht,
piquant salad, or zesty relish. Other articles highlight
a lightened-up chili relleno casserole and a handsome
Dutch apricot treat for midmorning coffee or dessert.

7

From Chile to Your Market & Table

GOLDEN CALIFORNIA POPPIES *gleam beside the road, tattered eucalyptus shade the way, and wild briers studded with ripe blackberries drape over fences. All are sights you would expect to see on a summer drive along California's Central Coast. But this is January, and you are on the bottom half of the world. Stretching 2,700 miles long and 110 miles at its widest point, Chile uncannily mirrors our Pacific coast, with agricultural areas reversed.*

In northern Chile, where it's hot and dry, barren land responds as fruitfully to water as does the Southern California desert (both are grape-growing areas). In the central regions, stone fruits, berries, apples, and pears flourish. South, toward Patagonia, the land is lush and green, its vines and bushes laden with raspberries, blackberries, and blueberries.

Over the last two decades, Chileans have made a Herculean effort to develop an agricultural program to serve a world market, and to capitalize upon their reverse-season advantage. Chile's summer is our winter, and nothing more vividly makes this point than the summer fruits from Chile now in our markets. Because of their country's climatic and geographic similarities to California, Oregon, and Washington, Chileans invited agriculture experts from these states to guide variety choices, planting, cultivation, harvesting, packing, and transport of produce familiar to North Americans.

As Chilean fruit has gained acceptance, plantings have increased. Exports have grown from 161 million pounds in 1976 to more than 1.8 billion pounds in 1991— about half to the United States and Canada. More than half of that bounty was grapes. By bridging California's harvests, Chile has turned grapes into a year-round commodity in North America. From late November through April, look for Flame, Ruby, and Thompson (all seedless), and Ribier varieties.

Similarly, blackberries, blueberries, and raspberries (4.5 million pounds) arrive from late November through April. Mid-December through early January brings apricots (1.7 million pounds). December into mid-January, keep an eye out for cherries (3.5 million pounds); Bings are here now. Continuing to arrive from mid-December to mid-March are nectarines (58 million pounds). Late December to mid-March brings plums (57.5 million pounds). The season for peaches (43 million pounds) runs from late December to early April.

Besides conforming to USDA and FDA requirements for fruits and vegetables, Chilean exporters must meet regulations set by various states for domestic produce.

Through cooperative effort, much fruit is inspected in Chile by the USDA; it may be inspected again upon arrival in this country. Earliest fruits, available in November, are often shipped by air. Berries regularly arrive by air freight, but most fruits make a 10- to 12-day ocean voyage in refrigerated ships, then arrive at your market in refrigerated trucks.

On a visit to Chile last winter, we gathered recipes for summer fruits from good cooks we met. Here we share two choices, a cake and a tart, from Hacienda Los Lingues, a 400-year-old estate about 80 miles south of Santiago; the estate not only produces fruit, but breeds horses and accepts guests. The last recipe is for manjar (delicacy), Chile's version of one of Central and South America's most popular sweets—milk boiled with sugar to form a rich, smooth caramel.

PEACH BREAKFAST CAKE

- ½ cup (¼ lb.) butter or margarine
- ½ cup sugar
- 1 teaspoon grated orange peel
- ¼ teaspoon almond extract
- 2 large eggs
- ¾ cup all-purpose flour
- 3 large (about 3-in. diameter, or 1¾ lb. total) firm-ripe peaches, peeled, halved, and pitted
  Topping (recipe on page 10)
  Cinnamon sugar (optional)

With a mixer or food processor, beat or whirl butter, sugar, peel, and almond extract until blended. Add eggs, 1 at a time, mixing well. Add flour; whirl or beat until smoothly mixed. Spread batter in a buttered, flour-dusted 9-inch cheesecake pan with removable rim.

Arrange peach halves, cut side down, on batter. Bake in a 350° oven until cake is lightly browned and just begins to pull from pan sides, about 1 hour. Remove from oven and, quickly and neatly, spoon cream topping around fruit. Bake 10 minutes longer. Cool on a rack at least 30 minutes; serve warm or cool. If made ahead, cool, cover, and let stand up to 3 hours at room temperature, or chill up to 8 hours.

Run a knife between pan rim and cake. Remove rim and set cake on a

(Continued on page 10)

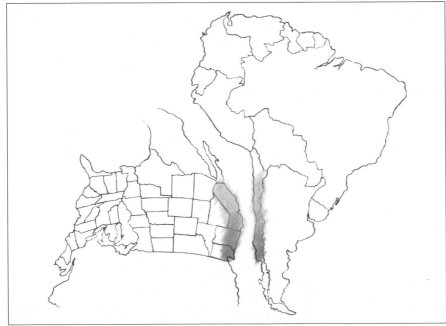

Chile's rich agricultural areas resemble those of our West Coast, upside down with seasons reversed. Farmland ranges from irrigated desert to regions with ample natural rainfall.

Fruit desserts join Chile's leading export items—copper, lapis lazuli, and cut flowers. Peach cake, on copper plate, overlaps brim of a huaso, the Chilean cowboy hat. Manjar, the ubiquitous native favorite, is a thick caramel to serve on fruit. Red tart combines poached plums and fresh raspberries.

Near Osorno, in central Chile, raspberries and other berries are ripe now.

Summer fruit arrives in our winter markets within hours by air, days by sea.

platter; sprinkle top lightly with cinnamon sugar. Makes 8 or 9 servings.

PER SERVING: 295 calories, 4.2 g protein, 33 g carbohydrates, 11 g fat (10 g saturated), 85 mg cholesterol, 138 mg sodium

Topping. Beat to blend 1 cup **sour cream,** ¼ cup **sugar,** 1 **large egg white,** and ¼ teaspoon **almond extract.**

RED FRUIT TART

- ⅓ **cup sugar**
- 1 **envelope (2 teaspoons) unflavored gelatin**
- ¾ **cup rosé wine**
- ¼ **cup port**
- 3 **or 4 strips orange peel, orange part only, 3 to 4 inches long**
- ½ **cup orange juice**
- 4 **large (about 2½-in. diameter, or 1 lb. total) firm-ripe, dark red-skinned plums, rinsed, pitted, and each cut into 8 wedges**
  Baked pastry (recipe follows)
  About 1 cup rinsed and drained raspberries or pitted cherries

In a 2- to 3-quart pan, mix sugar and gelatin. Add wine, port, peel, and juice. Bring to a rolling boil on high heat. Add plums; simmer until fruit begins to soften slightly, 3 to 5 minutes. Remove from heat. With a slotted spoon, transfer fruit to plate; discard peel. Chill fruit.

Chill poaching liquid in uncovered pan in the refrigerator—or, to speed chilling, set pan in a large bowl of ice. Stir often until it begins to thicken slightly.

Quickly arrange plum slices in pastry; set raspberries decoratively on plums. When poaching liquid is slightly jelled but still soft enough to pour smoothly, ladle over fruit (if mixture gets too thick, warm to soften, then chill to thicken). Chill tart until gelatin is set, at least 1 or up to 8 hours; cover airtight after 1 hour. Remove pan rim and set tart on a platter. Makes 8 to 10 servings.

PER SERVING: 244 calories, 3.8 g protein, 35 g carbohydrates, 10 g fat (5.9 g saturated), 46 mg cholesterol, 103 mg sodium

Baked pastry. In a food processor or bowl, combine 1½ cups **all-purpose flour;** ¼ cup **sugar;** and 6 tablespoons **butter** or margarine, cut into chunks. Whirl or rub with your fingers until fine crumbs form. Add 1 **large egg** and whirl or stir with a fork until dough holds together. Firmly pat dough into a ball, then break into large chunks into an 8- by 11-inch tart pan with removable bottom, or a 9-inch cake pan with removable bottom. Press dough firmly and evenly over pan bottom and flush with rim.

Bake in a 350° oven until golden brown (don't worry if crust cracks), about 35 minutes; cool on a rack. Remove pan rim and slip a long spatula under pastry to release, but leave in place; set back in rim. If made ahead, cover airtight up until next day.

MANJAR

Spoon onto fresh grapes, raspberries, peaches, apricots, or plums. For a cool, tart accent, accompany with sour cream.

You'll find manjar in any food store in Chile, but to make it at home, even the best cooks start with this one ingredient.

- 1 **can (14 oz.) sweetened condensed milk**

Remove can top; cover can tightly with foil. Bake or pressure-cook, as follows.

To bake. Set covered can in a 5- by 9-inch loaf pan. Place on rack in a 350° oven. Add boiling water to pan to within 1 inch of rim. Using insulated mitts to protect hands, cover pan tightly with foil. Bake until milk is a golden caramel color, about 3 hours. (For a richer caramel flavor, bake until a darker color, about 4 hours.) When checking color, open foil carefully to avoid hot steam.

To pressure-cook. Set covered can on rack in a 4- to 6-quart pressure cooker. Add 1½ inches water. Cover pan with lid and bring to pressure according to manufacturer's directions. Cook at 15 pounds pressure for 45 minutes for golden caramel color, 1 hour for a darker color. Release pressure quickly as manufacturer directs.

Hold hot can with insulated mitts and scrape milk into a blender or food processor; whirl until very creamy and smooth. Serve hot, warm, or cold (manjar thickens as it cools; beat to thin, adding a little water to thin more, if desired). If made ahead, cover and chill airtight up to 1 month. Makes 1¼ cups.

PER TABLESPOON: 64 calories, 1.6 g protein, 11 g carbohydrates, 1.7 g fat (1.1 g saturated), 6.7 mg cholesterol, 25 mg sodium

Fresh Pickled Beets

COOKING FRESH BEETS *in a pungent pickling mixture counters their natural earthy flavor with a sweet tartness.*

Enjoy the beets as pickles, or use them (or canned ones) for a quick borscht, a salad, or a lively relish.

FRESH PICKLED BEETS

    4 small (about 2½-in. diameter)
      beets, about 1½ pounds total,
      untrimmed
 1½ cups water
  ¼ cup red wine vinegar
    2 tablespoons sugar

Trim tops and roots from beets. Reserve tender leaves for another use or discard. Peel beets. In a 1½- to 2-quart pan, combine water, vinegar, and sugar. Bring to a boil. Add beets; cover and simmer, turning often, until tender when pierced, 30 to 45 minutes. Cool. (If made ahead, cover and chill up to 3 days.) Serve, or use in the following recipes. Makes about ¾ pound.

PER 3 OUNCES (DRAINED): 38 calories, 0.8 g protein; 9 g carbohydrates, 0.1 g fat, 0 mg cholesterol, 42 mg sodium

To make about 1½ pounds pickled beets (4 cups drained, 5 cups with liquid). Use a 3- to 4-quart pan. Double amounts of beets, water, vinegar, and sugar.

CREAMY BEET BORSCHT

    About 1½ pounds fresh pickled
      beets (recipe precedes), sliced, or
      2 cans (16 oz. each) whole or sliced
      pickled beets
    About 1 quart unflavored nonfat
      yogurt
    1 cup regular-strength chicken
      broth
    Fresh dill sprigs
    Pepper

Drain beets; reserve 1½ cups juice. Combine beets, juice, 1 quart yogurt, and broth. In a food processor or blender, smoothly purée about ⅓ at a time. Mix together. (If made ahead, cover and chill up to 1 day.)

Serve borscht cool or cold in wide bowls. Garnish with dill. Offer additional yogurt and pepper to add to taste. Makes 6 to 8 servings.

PER SERVING: 141 calories, 7.7 g protein, 27 g carbohydrates, 0.5 g fat (0.2 g saturated), 2.3 mg cholesterol, 392 mg sodium

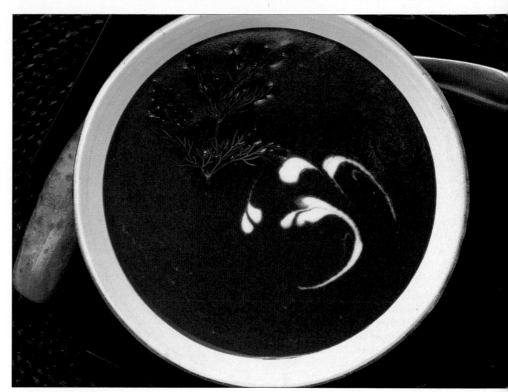

Sweet-tart pickled beets intensely color and flavor this lean borscht. Serve soup in wide bowls, each topped with a decorative swirl of yogurt and a sprig of fresh dill.

SEEDED BEET SALAD

    ½ teaspoon *each* mustard seed and
      cumin seed
    About 1½ pounds fresh pickled
      beets (recipe precedes), or 2 cans
      (16 oz. each) whole or sliced
      pickled beets
    2 tablespoons red wine vinegar
    1 tablespoon salad oil
    ½ teaspoon pepper
    ½ cup thinly sliced green onions,
      including tops
    2 large (about 1 lb. total) tart green
      apples
    Salt

In a 6- to 8-inch frying pan over medium heat, shake mustard and cumin seed often until fragrant, 5 to 6 minutes. Set aside.

Drain beets; save ¼ cup juice. Thinly slice whole beets. In a bowl, mix mustard and cumin seed, beets, reserved juice, vinegar, oil, pepper, and onions.

Core and dice apples; mix with beets. Add salt to taste. Serve, or cover and chill up to 1 hour. Makes 8 servings.

PER SERVING: 141 calories, 1.4 g protein, 31 g carbohydrates, 2.3 g fat (0.3 g saturated), 0 mg cholesterol, 343 mg sodium

KUMQUAT-BEET RELISH

    About ¾ pound fresh pickled
      beets (recipe precedes), or 1 can
      (16 oz.) whole or sliced pickled
      beets
    6 kumquats (about 1½ oz. total),
      seeded and thinly sliced
    1 tablespoon red wine vinegar
    1 tablespoon minced fresh ginger
    1 fresh jalapeño chili, stemmed,
      seeded, and minced
    1 to 3 teaspoons sugar

Drain beets; put 2 tablespoons juice in a bowl. Mince beets; mix with juice, kumquats, vinegar, ginger, and chili; add sugar to taste. Serve, or cover and chill up to 2 days; stir occasionally. Makes about 1½ cups, 6 servings.

PER SERVING: 55 calories, 0.7 g protein, 14 g carbohydrates, 0.1 g fat (0 g saturated), 0 mg cholesterol, 200 mg sodium

Seattle Caesar

SEAFOOD REACHES *new heights in Seattle's version of Caesar salad. This showy salad, often assembled at the table, takes on aristocratic airs with the addition of Northwest seafood to the original combination. Use one or more of the seafood choices, and serve the salad as a first course or main dish.*

Classic Caesar salad uses a coddled egg, olive oil, lemon juice, anchovies, and garlic to dress crisp romaine. Because of the concern about salmonella in raw eggs, we offer three dressings that are traditional in flavor but completely safe.

The egg white dressing uses lemon juice to acidify the whites for at least 48 hours, eliminating the possibility of salmonella. This dressing tastes remarkably similar to the original.

The other two options require less advance planning. One uses a hard-cooked egg to add body to the dressing, while the other omits the egg completely and uses sour cream as a base.

As an alternative to anchovies, consider a Southeast Asian condiment—fish sauce (nuoc mam or nam pla). It's made from anchovies, salt, and water and has a more delicate flavor. Look for it in some supermarkets and Asian grocery stores.

Serve small spears of crisp romaine whole. Or tear larger spears into bite-size pieces, or cut into fine shreds. Each presentation offers a slightly different texture and look.

SEATTLE SEAFOOD CAESAR SALAD

If you plan to use only the tender inner leaves of the romaine, buy the larger amount of lettuce. Choose smaller heads so more of the leaves can be used.

- 2 to 4 small (1¾ to 2 lb. total) heads romaine lettuce
- ¼ cup freshly grated parmesan cheese
- Croutons (recipe follows)
- About 1 pound Seattle seafood (choices follow)
- Caesar dressing (choices and recipes follow)
- Freshly ground pepper

Rinse the lettuce well and drain. Wrap loosely in towels, enclose in plastic bags, then chill until lettuce is crisp, at least 30 minutes or up until the next day.

Use whole tender inner leaves to make about 3 quarts (reserve coarse outer leaves for another salad, or discard). Or tear enough leaves into bite-size pieces or cut crosswise into thin shreds to make about 2½ quarts.

Place lettuce in a large bowl. Arrange cheese, croutons, seafood, and dressing in separate containers. Bring to the table and pour dressing over lettuce; mix gently to coat greens. Add the cheese, croutons, seafood, and pepper to taste; mix gently and serve. Makes 4 or 5 main-dish, 6 or 7 first-course servings.

PER FIRST-COURSE SERVING WITH 2 OUNCES SHRIMP AND NO DRESSING: 142 calories, 16 g protein, 7.9 g carbohydrates, 5 g fat (1.3 g saturated), 114 mg cholesterol, 258 mg sodium

Croutons. Mix 1½ tablespoons **olive oil** and 1 small clove **garlic,** pressed or minced. Cut about 2½ ounces **French bread** into ¾-inch cubes to make about 2 cups. Stir garlic-oil mixture with bread to coat.

In a 10- by 15-inch rimmed pan, spread out bread cubes. Bake in a 325° oven until cubes are crisp and golden brown, 25 to 30 minutes. If made ahead, cool, wrap airtight, and store up until the next day.

Seattle seafood choices. Offer 1 to 4 of the following seafoods: **tiny cooked shelled shrimp; cooked shelled crab; smoked salmon, sturgeon,** or **trout,** cut into thin slivers; **cooked bay scallops** (recipe follows); or **fried oysters** (recipe follows).

Cooked bay scallops. Rinse and drain ½ to 1 pound **bay scallops.** In a 3- to 4-quart pan, bring about 2 quarts **water** to a boil. Stir in scallops. Tightly cover pan and remove from heat. Let stand until scallops are opaque in thickest part (cut to test), 3 to 4 minutes. Drain. Cool, cover, and chill until cold, at least 1 hour or up until the next day.

PER 2 OUNCES: 50 calories, 9.5 g protein, 1.3 g carbohydrates, 0.4 g fat (0.1 g saturated), 19 mg cholesterol, 91 mg sodium

Fried oysters. Mix ⅓ cup **all-purpose flour,** 3 tablespoons **yellow cornmeal,** and ⅛ teaspoon **pepper.** Beat 1 **large egg** to blend. Drain 1 jar (10 oz.) shucked fresh **small Pacific oysters,** cut in halves. Coat in egg, then in flour mixture; set aside in a single layer.

Pour about ½ inch **salad oil** into a deep 10- to 12-inch frying pan. Place over high heat. When oil reaches 350° on a thermometer, place oysters slightly apart in pan. Cook, turning once, until golden and crisp, about 3 minutes. Remove with a slotted spatula; drain on towels. Add **salt** to taste. Serve hot.

PER 2 OUNCES: 206 calories, 7.9 g protein, 13 g carbohydrates, 13 g fat (2 g saturated), 74 mg cholesterol, 73 mg sodium

Egg white Caesar dressing. Mix 2 **large egg whites** and ¼ cup **lemon juice.** Cover and chill at least 48 hours or up to 4 days.

Whisk egg white mixture to blend with ¼ cup **olive oil;** 3 or 4 **canned anchovy fillets,** drained and chopped, or 2 to 3 tablespoons fish sauce (*nuoc mam* or *nam pla*); and 1 to 2 cloves **garlic,** pressed or minced. If made ahead, cover and chill up to 1 hour. Makes ⅔ cup.

PER TABLESPOON: 63 calories, 1.6 g protein, 1.1 g carbohydrates, 5.9 g fat (0.8 g saturated), 0.7 mg cholesterol, 56 mg sodium

Cooked-egg Caesar dressing. In a blender or food processor, smoothly purée 6 tablespoons **olive oil;** 1 **large hard-cooked egg,** shelled and cut up; 4 to 6 drained and chopped **canned anchovy fillets** or 2 to 3 tablespoons of fish sauce (*nuoc mam* or *nam pla*); ¼ cup **lemon juice;** and 1 to 2 cloves **garlic.** If made ahead, cover and chill up until next day. Makes about ¾ cup.

PER TABLESPOON: 77 calories, 1.3 g protein, 0.9 g carbohydrates, 7.6 g fat (1.1 g saturated), 18 mg cholesterol, 55 mg sodium

No-egg Caesar dressing. In a blender or food processor, purée ⅔ cup **light** or regular **sour cream,** 4 to 6 drained **canned anchovy fillets** or 2 to 3 tablespoons fish sauce (*nuoc mam* or *nam pla*), 2 tablespoons **lemon juice,** and 1 to 2 cloves **garlic.** If made ahead, cover and chill up until next day. Mix well. Makes ¾ cup.

PER TABLESPOON: 32 calories, 1.7 g protein, 1.6 g carbohydrates, 2.2 g fat (1 g saturated), 5.2 mg cholesterol, 50 mg sodium

Assembled at the table, showy Seattle Caesar salad features Northwest seafood. Mix traditional Caesar salad elements—crisp inner leaves of romaine, freshly grated parmesan cheese, and crunchy garlic croutons—with new egg-safe dressing and your choice of seafood.

A Cross Between Coffee Cake & Pie

DUTCH CHOCOLATE *and Dutch tulips are justifiably famous. But what about Dutch vlaai? Chances are you've never heard of this cross between pie and coffee cake, a specialty of the Limburg region in the southern part of the Netherlands.*

Frans Knaapen bakery in the town of St. Geertruid, near Maastricht, makes an

apricot vlaai like this one. Limburgers enjoy its yeast crust and slightly sweet filling with morning coffee; it's also good for breakfast or a not-too-sweet dessert.

The recipe's royal designation alludes to the orange color of the apricots and to the Dutch royal family's surname, van Oranje.

Poached apricots shine in sugar-dusted yeast-crust pie, a traditional favorite in the Netherlands. Serve it for breakfast, with midmorning coffee, or for dessert.

QUEEN'S VLAAI

   Sweet yeast dough (recipe
   follows)
3 cups (about 1 lb.) dried apricots
½ cup granulated sugar
1½ cups water
   Powdered sugar

Let dough rise in a warm place until about doubled, 1 to 1¼ hours.

Meanwhile, combine apricots, granulated sugar, and water in a 2- to 3-quart pan; bring to a boil over high heat. Reduce heat and simmer, uncovered, occasionally stirring gently, until apricots are tender when pierced, 5 to 10 minutes.

With a slotted spoon, transfer apricots to a bowl to cool. Boil syrup, uncovered, over high heat until reduced to ⅓ cup, about 5 minutes (watch closely); set aside.

Heavily butter a 10- to 11-inch-diameter plain or fluted tart pan with a removable rim. Punch down dough in bowl to expel air. On a lightly floured board, pat dough into an 8-inch round. Lift dough into center of pan, then pat out evenly over bottom and ¾ inch up on pan rim.

Arrange apricots (slightly overlapping) in dough-lined pan. Evenly pour syrup over fruit. Gently press dough edge to flatten flush with fruit. Bake on lowest rack of a 375° oven until the crust is deep brown, about 40 minutes.

Loosen pie from pan side with a knife. Protecting hands, remove pan rim. Serve warm, or, if made ahead, let cool, cover, and store up until next day. Just before serving, sift powdered sugar over top of vlaai, or just around rim. Makes 10 servings.

PER SERVING: 301 calories, 4.2 g protein, 60 g carbohydrates, 6.5 g fat (3.8 g saturated), 16 mg cholesterol, 125 mg sodium

Sweet yeast dough. In a bowl, soften 1 package **active dry yeast** in ½ cup warm **water** (110°). Stir in ⅓ cup **butter** or margarine (at room temperature), ¼ teaspoon **salt,** and ¼ cup **sugar.** Stir in 1 cup **all-purpose flour** and beat until dough is stretchy. Stir in another ¾ cup all-purpose flour.

Scrape dough onto a lightly floured board; knead until smooth and elastic, 8 to 10 minutes, adding just enough flour to prevent dough from sticking. Place dough in a greased bowl, turn over, and cover with plastic wrap.

LIGHTENING UP SUNSET CLASSICS: Chili Relleno Casserole

THIS PUFFY CHILI *relleno casserole has long ranked high with readers. One reason for its popularity is its ease of preparation.*

In the original recipe, canned green chilies were filled with jack cheese, covered with a flour and egg mixture, then sprinkled with cheddar cheese. When baked, the topping puffed like a soufflé.

Debbie Pleis of Colorado tried her hand at lightening up this recipe and sent her revision to us to share with you. She reduced the cheese in the filling by about 25 percent, then added much leaner tofu. (Another way to cut fat slightly is to use a reduced-fat natural cheese—check the label to be sure.) To trim fat and cholesterol further, she also used more egg whites and fewer whole eggs.

The reaction of Sunset's taste panel? The lightened-up casserole maintains much of the original's flavor despite omitting half the fat and two-thirds the cholesterol.

LIGHTENED-UP CHILIES RELLENOS WITH MARINARA SAUCE

To serve 4, cut this recipe in half and bake in a shallow 1- to 1½-quart casserole.

- **About 1 pound soft tofu, rinsed**
- 2 **cans (7 oz. each) whole green chilies**
- 1½ **cups (6 oz.) shredded natural (reduced-fat or regular) jack cheese**
- 6 **large egg whites**
- 2 **large eggs**
- ⅔ **cup nonfat or low-fat milk**
- 1 **cup all-purpose flour**
- 1 **teaspoon baking powder**
- 1¼ **cups (5 oz.) shredded natural (reduced-fat or regular) cheddar cheese**
- 1 **can (about 15 oz.) marinara sauce**
  Sliced black ripe olives

Coarsely mash tofu with a fork or hands; drain in a colander at least 10 minutes.

Meanwhile, cut a slit down the side of each chili. In a bowl, mix tofu and jack cheese. Fill chilies equally with tofu mixture and arrange side by side in a lightly oiled, shallow 2½- to 3-quart casserole.

In a bowl, whip egg whites and whole eggs on high speed until thick and foamy. Add milk, flour, and baking powder; beat until smooth. Fold in half the cheddar cheese. Pour egg mixture over chilies; sprinkle with remaining cheddar.

Bake, uncovered, in a 375° oven until top is a rich, golden brown, 25 to 30 minutes.

Meanwhile, occasionally stir marinara sauce in a 1- to 1½-quart pan over low heat until hot. Or heat sauce in a microwave-safe bowl in a microwave oven at full power (100 percent) until hot; check at 1-minute intervals.

Scatter sliced olives over casserole; spoon onto plates and accompany with marinara sauce. Makes 8 servings.— *Debbie Pleis, Fort Collins, Colo.*

PER REVISED SERVING: 291 calories, 21 g protein, 24 g carbohydrates, 12 g fat (4.8 g saturated), 81 mg cholesterol, 1,022 mg sodium

PER ORIGINAL SERVING (FEBRUARY 1973, PAGE 162): 407 calories, 24 g protein, 21 g carbohydrates, 26 g fat (12 g saturated), 270 mg cholesterol, 962 mg sodium

Pour foamy batter over tofu- and cheese-filled chilies; bake until puffed and golden. Casserole has half the fat and a third the cholesterol of original version.

More January Recipes

OTHER ARTICLES IN JANUARY *included a popular Mexican soup featuring canned cactus and a hearty multigrain bread.*

SOPA DE NOPALES

Cactus looks forbidding. Stripped of its prickly points, however, it is a mild-mannered vegetable with a slightly tart flavor. Look for easy-to-use canned cactus (sold as nopales or nopalitos) in supermarkets and Mexican groceries.

- 1 **tablespoon olive or salad oil**
- 1 **large (about 8 oz.) onion, chopped**
- 1 **pound (about 16 medium-size) tomatillos, husks removed, rinsed and coarsely chopped**
- 6 **cups regular-strength chicken broth**
- 1 **large jar (33 oz.) sliced cactus (nopales or nopalitos) packed in water, drained and rinsed**
- 2 **tablespoons lime juice**
- 2 **tablespoons minced fresh cilantro (coriander) leaves**
   About 2 ounces panela cheese or feta cheese, crumbled
   Lime wedges (optional)

In a 4- to 5-quart pan over medium heat, stir oil and onion often until onion is golden, about 15 minutes. Add tomatillos; stir often just until soft, about 6 minutes. Add broth; bring to a boil over high heat. Stir in cactus, lime juice, and cilantro. Cook until hot. Ladle soup into a tureen. Offer cheese to add to taste. Accompany with lime wedges. Makes 6 to 8 servings.

PER SERVING: 86 calories, 4.6 g protein, 9 g carbohydrates, 4 g fat (0.5 g saturated), 2.5 mg cholesterol, 234 mg sodium

Cilantro and cheese float on slices of tender-crisp cactus. Garnish with limes.

Tear chunks of warm bread from hearty multigrain loaf to eat with butter and jam. Or slice fine-textured loaf for aromatic, crisp toast.

HONEY MULTIGRAIN HEARTH BREAD

Fat, round, and flavorful, this surprisingly fine-textured bread contains a variety of grains.

If you have trouble finding soy flour in a supermarket, check health-food stores.

- 1 **package active dry yeast**
- 1½ **cups warm water (110°)**
- 3 **tablespoons honey**
- ¾ **cup milk, at room temperature**
   About 1½ cups stone-ground whole-wheat flour or graham flour
   About 3¾ cups all-purpose flour
- 3 **tablespoons yellow cornmeal**
- 3 **tablespoons regular rolled oats**
- 3 **tablespoons soy flour**
- 3 **tablespoons salad oil**
- ½ **teaspoon salt**

In a large bowl, combine yeast, 1 cup water, and honey; let stand 5 minutes to soften yeast. Add milk, whole-wheat flour, and ¾ cup all-purpose flour; stir until moistened. Cover and keep in a warm place 1 to 2 hours.

Meanwhile, in a small bowl, combine remaining ½ cup warm water, cornmeal, and oats; let stand until grains soften, 1 to 2 hours. Add cornmeal mixture to yeast mixture along with 2¾ cups all-purpose flour, soy flour, oil, and salt.

By hand. Beat dough until stretchy; scrape onto a board lightly coated with all-purpose flour. Knead dough (add flour to prevent sticking) until smooth and elastic, about 10 minutes. Rinse, dry, and oil large bowl; turn dough over in bowl to oil top.

With a dough hook. Beat on high speed until dough pulls from sides of bowl, 5 to 8 minutes. If dough clings to bowl or is sticky, mix in all-purpose flour, 1 tablespoon at a time, as needed.

Cover dough in bowl with plastic wrap; let rise in a warm place until doubled, about 1 hour. Knead on a lightly floured board or beat with hook to release air.

Shape dough into a ball and set on an oiled 12- by 15-inch baking sheet. Pat into a 7-inch-wide round. Lightly cover with plastic wrap and let rise until puffy, 15 to 20 minutes; uncover.

Bake in a 350° oven until deep golden brown, about 50 minutes. Cool on a rack at least 10 minutes. Serve hot, warm, or cool. If made ahead, wrap airtight when cool; hold up until next day or freeze to store longer. Makes 1 loaf, about 3 pounds.—*Hennie Wooldridge, Portland.*

PER OUNCE: 64 calories, 1.9 g protein, 12 g carbohydrates, 1.1 g fat (0.2 saturated), 0.5 mg cholesterol, 25 mg sodium

Chefs of the West®
Adventures with Food

Like the Roman god *Janus, cornmeal wears two faces. Served as mush, it's about as classy as a chrome-plated boat on a blue mirror coffee table. But serve it as polenta and you will get accolades.*

Grits, lacking any detectable continental equivalent, remain just grits.

But grits are moving north and west and going upscale.

They can, like their cousin cornmeal, make a splendid foundation for all sorts of casseroles. Retired Colonel Sam Roberts sends us his formula for a cheddar- and jalapeño-enhanced preparation that just may bite back.

HOT GRITS WITH JALAPEÑOS & CHEESE

    5   cups water
    1¼ cups quick-cooking grits
    1   pound sharp cheddar cheese,
        shredded
    1   to 2 canned jalapeño chilies,
        minced
        Salt
    4   large eggs, beaten to blend
        Cayenne (optional)

In a 3- to 4-quart pan over high heat, gradually stir water into grits. Stirring over high heat, bring to a boil; reduce heat and simmer, stirring often, for 10 minutes.

Add 3 cups cheese to grits and stir until cheese is smoothly melted. Add jalapeños and salt to taste.

Beat about ½ cup hot grits into eggs, then stir egg mixture into the remaining grits. Scrape mixture into a greased 2- to 2½-quart shallow casserole. Top with remaining cheese and dust very lightly with cayenne.

Bake, uncovered, in a 350° oven until mixture is set when lightly touched, 40 to 45 minutes. Let stand 10 minutes before serving. Makes 10 to 12 servings.

PER SERVING: 234 calories, 13 g protein, 13 g carbohydrates, 14 g fat (8.5 g saturated), 111 mg cholesterol, 274 mg sodium

Sam A. Roberts

Salt Lake City

Russian cuisine is *notable for its soups. Borscht—either with beets or with cabbage, and richly endowed with thick sour cream—is the most familiar. Bill Lilken re-created this remembered favorite from a Russian restaurant (no longer in existence) on San Francisco's Clement Street.*

RUSSIAN SPINACH SOUP

    1   tablespoon butter or margarine
    1   large (¼ lb.) carrot, chopped
    1   large (½ lb.) onion, chopped
    2   tablespoons all-purpose flour
    6   cups or 1 can (49½ oz.) regular-
        strength chicken broth
    2   dried bay leaves
    ¼   teaspoon ground nutmeg
    2   packages (10 oz. each) frozen
        chopped spinach, thawed
        Salt and pepper
        Unflavored nonfat yogurt, or
        sour cream
        Chopped hard-cooked eggs
        (optional)

Melt butter in a 4- to 5-quart pan over medium heat; add carrot and onion and stir often until onion is limp, about 10 minutes. Stir in flour. Remove from heat and smoothly blend in broth; add bay and nutmeg. Stirring, bring to a boil on high heat; simmer, covered, for 10 minutes to blend flavor.

Meanwhile, in a blender or food processor, whirl spinach until smoothly puréed.

Remove bay leaves from soup and stir in spinach. Ladle into bowls, adding to taste salt, pepper, yogurt, and chopped egg. Makes 8 cups; allow 1 to 2 cups per serving.

PER 1 CUP: 77 calories, 4.5 g protein, 9.2 g carbohydrates, 2.9 g fat (1.2 g saturated), 3.9 mg cholesterol, 113 mg sodium

Bill Lilken

Fort Collins, Colo.

Costliest of spices, *saffron is not the sort of ingredient you pick up at your neighborhood convenience store. Indeed, markets that sell it may display it in a locked case. Fortunately, a little goes a long way. Tom Visel, king of the potluck chefs at the Idyllwild School of Music and the Arts, uses a practical, therefore limited, amount to create a marinade and glaze for baked chicken.*

SAFFRON & HONEY CHICKEN

    ⅔   cup regular-strength chicken
        broth
    2   tablespoons lime juice
    2   tablespoons honey
    ¼   teaspoon saffron threads
    1   teaspoon white Worcestershire
    2   teaspoons curry powder
    ½   teaspoon dried oregano leaves
    ¼   teaspoon paprika
    ⅛   teaspoon pepper
    2   teaspoons soy sauce
    2   tablespoons white rice flour
        blended with 4 tablespoons water
    6   *each* chicken drumsticks and
        thighs (about 3¼ lb. total), skin
        and fat removed
        Chopped parsley

In a 1½- to 2-quart pan on high heat, boil broth, lime juice, honey, saffron, Worcestershire, curry, oregano, paprika, pepper, and soy until reduced to ½ cup. Stir occasionally. Stir in rice flour mixture; stir over high heat until boiling.

Rinse chicken pieces and arrange in a 9- by 13-inch pan. Spoon sauce over chicken; cover pan with foil. Bake in a 375° oven until meat at thigh bone is no longer pink, about 35 minutes. Lift chicken onto plates; stir sauce and spoon over meat. Add chopped parsley. Makes 6 servings.

PER SERVING: 225 calories, 31 g protein, 9.8 g carbohydrates, 6.1 g fat (1.5 g saturated), 121 mg cholesterol, 259 mg sodium

Tom Visel

Idyllwild, Calif.

"Cornmeal wears two faces."

Hearty soda bread with sunflower seed complements a hot winter soup.

SUNFLOWER SODA BREAD

2½ cups all-purpose flour
1 cup *each* whole-wheat flour and yellow cornmeal
½ cup unsalted dry roasted sunflower seed
⅓ cup sugar
2 teaspoons baking powder
1 teaspoon baking soda
½ teaspoon salt
2 cups buttermilk
1 large egg

In a large bowl, mix all-purpose flour, whole-wheat flour, cornmeal, sunflower seed, sugar, baking powder, soda, and salt.

Add buttermilk and egg; beat until dough is thoroughly moistened and stretchy, about 2 minutes.

Spoon dough in 2 equal mounds, each on center of a greased 10- by 15-inch pan. With floured hands, pat each portion into an 8-inch round. With a floured sharp knife, cut a ½-inch-deep cross on top of each round. Bake in a 375° oven until golden brown, 25 to 30 minutes; switch pan positions after 15 minutes. Serve warm or cool, cut into wedges. To store, wrap airtight when cool; hold at room temperature up until next day, or freeze. Makes 2 loaves, each about 1⅓ pounds.—*Nancy Kisner, Anacortes, Wash.*

PER OUNCE: 71 calories, 2.3 g protein, 13 g carbohydrates, 1.2 g fat (0.2 g saturated), 5.5 mg cholesterol, 80 mg sodium

Herb-stuffed trout, baked, is topped with aromatic balsamic sauce.

SICILIAN TROUT WITH BALSAMIC SAUCE

⅓ cup *each* chopped green bell pepper and chopped green onion
2 tablespoons *each* currants, minced parsley, and drained canned capers
1 clove garlic, minced or pressed
4 boned whole trout (each about ½ lb.)
3 tablespoons *each* balsamic vinegar and minced fresh basil leaves (or more parsley)
1 tablespoon extra-virgin olive oil
Lemon wedges

Mix bell pepper, green onion, currants, parsley, capers, and garlic. Rinse fish, pat dry, and open, skin side down. Spoon an equal portion of vegetable mixture onto 1 side of each fish. Fold fish to enclose filling. Lay trout in a lightly oiled 10- by 15-inch pan.

Bake fish in a 400° oven until flesh is opaque but still moist-looking in thickest part when prodded with a knife tip, about 20 minutes. Meanwhile, mix vinegar, basil, and oil. Place fish on platter or individual plates. Serve sauce with fish and add lemon to taste. Makes 4 servings.—*Roxanne E. Chan, Albany, Calif.*

PER SERVING: 324 calories, 39 g protein, 5.5 g carbohydrates, 16 g fat (2.6 g saturated), 107 mg cholesterol, 208 mg sodium

Stir-fried beef is seasoned by orange and ginger; serve with rice.

CITRUS BEEF STIR-FRY

2 large (about 1 lb. total) oranges
3 tablespoons *each* dry sherry and soy sauce
2 tablespoons minced fresh ginger
1 pound boneless, fat-trimmed lean beef, such as top sirloin
2 teaspoons cornstarch
2 tablespoons salad oil
3 stalks celery, thinly sliced
1 cup bean sprouts
1 cup Chinese pea pods, ends and strings removed

Grate peel from 1 orange. Squeeze juice from oranges into a large bowl; mix in peel, sherry, soy, and ginger.

Slice meat ⅛ inch thick across grain. Stir into bowl. Let stand at least 5 minutes, or cover and chill up until next day; stir several times. Drain marinade and mix with cornstarch.

Place a wok or 12- to 14-inch frying pan on high heat. When pan is hot, add 2 teaspoons oil and half the meat. Stir-fry until meat is tinged with brown, then pour meat into another bowl. Repeat to cook remaining meat. Heat remaining oil; add celery, sprouts, and peas. Stir until peas turn brighter green, about 1 minute. Add marinade; stir until boiling. Mix in meat. Makes 4 servings.—*Astrid Churchill, Cliff, N. Mex.*

PER SERVING: 297 calories, 27 g protein, 16 g carbohydrates, 12 g fat (2.6 g saturated), 69 mg cholesterol, 869 mg sodium

BUTTER BEAN SALAD

    2 cans (15 oz. each) butter beans
    2 tablespoons olive or salad oil
    ⅓ cup lemon juice
    ½ cup minced parsley
    ½ cup thinly sliced green onions
    2 large (about ½ lb. total) Roma-
      type tomatoes, cored and diced
      About 1 teaspoon pepper
    ⅓ cup packed feta cheese
    1 or 2 green onions, ends trimmed

Drain beans, rinse with cool water, and
drain well. In a bowl, mix beans with
oil, lemon juice, parsley, sliced green
onions, tomatoes, and enough pepper
to make salad slightly hot to taste. If
made ahead, cover and chill up to 4
hours; mix and continue.

Crumble cheese onto salad; garnish
with the whole onions. Makes 5 cups,
4 to 6 servings.—*Nadya Malconian,
Westlake Village, Calif.*

PER SERVING: 184 calories, 9 g protein, 23 g carbohydrates, 7.6 g fat
(2.3 g saturated), 10 mg cholesterol, 577 mg sodium

*Creamy butter beans make a lively salad with
tomatoes and feta cheese.*

PARADISE PASTA WITH PINE NUTS

    ⅓ cup pine nuts
    1 pound mushrooms
    1 medium-size (5 to 6 oz.) onion
    4 cloves garlic, minced or pressed
    1 tablespoon salad oil
    1 teaspoon *each* dried basil leaves
      and dried oregano leaves
    4 cups broccoli flowerets
    1 small (about 4 oz.) red bell
      pepper, stemmed, seeded, and
      thinly sliced
    1½ cups regular-strength chicken
      broth
      About 4 cups hot cooked angel
      hair pasta (about ½ lb. dried,
      uncooked), drained
      About ½ cup freshly shredded
      parmesan cheese
      Salt and pepper

In a 10- to 12-inch frying pan over
medium heat, stir pine nuts often until
golden, about 8 minutes; pour from pan
and set aside.

Rinse, drain, and thinly slice mushrooms. Finely chop the onion. In frying
pan, combine mushrooms, onion, garlic,
oil, basil, and oregano. Cover and cook
over high heat, stirring often, until liquid accumulates. Uncover and stir often
until vegetables are lightly browned,
about 8 minutes. Add broccoli, bell
pepper, and broth. Bring to a boil and
cook, covered, until broccoli is just
tender when pierced, about 5 minutes.

Pour pasta into a large shallow bowl.
Pour vegetables and juices onto pasta;
sprinkle with pine nuts and parmesan.
Add salt and pepper to taste. Makes 4
servings.—*Julie Hoiland, Paradise, Calif.*

PER SERVING: 461 calories, 24 g protein, 63 g carbohydrates, 16 g fat
(4 g saturated), 10 mg cholesterol, 289 mg sodium

*Garden-patch vegetable collection becomes
sauce for angel hair pasta.*

FRESH APPLE CAKE

    3 cups all-purpose flour
    1 cup sugar
    1 teaspoon baking soda
    ¼ teaspoon salt
    1 cup chopped almonds or walnuts
    2 large eggs
    ¾ cup (⅜ lb.) butter or margarine,
      melted and cooled
    2 tablespoons lemon juice
    1 tablespoon vanilla
    3 cups diced, unpeeled tart green
      apples (about 2 large, 1 lb. total)

In a large bowl, mix flour, sugar, soda,
salt, and nuts.

In another bowl, beat to blend eggs,
butter, lemon juice, and vanilla; mix in
apples. Stir into flour mixture until batter is evenly moistened. Scrape batter
into a buttered and floured 10- to 11-
inch (10-cup) tube pan. Bake in a 350°
oven until cake begins to pull from pan
sides, feels firm when lightly touched
in the center, and is a rich brown, about
1 hour.

Let cake stand until warm; tip out
onto a rack. Invert a platter onto cake;
holding platter and rack, flip cake over.
Serve warm or cool. Makes 10 to 12
servings.—*Elaine Shanafelt, Mt. Ashland Inn, Ashland, Oreg.*

PER SERVING: 382 calories, 6.6 g protein, 48 g carbohydrates, 18 g fat
(8.3 g saturated), 66 mg cholesterol, 243 mg sodium

*Fruit cake, dense with almonds and fresh
apples, bakes in a tube pan.*

January Menus

START THE YEAR *with Southwestern and Italian flavors in meals the whole family will enjoy. Even when time is short, these menus dress up easily.*

Gather a group of six for a New Year's enchilada party with make-ahead components. Use decorative Southwestern touches—red chili lights, potted cacti, luminarias, and a piñata. Buy or make party favors. At midnight, blindfolded guests strike the piñata and open the favor-filled "crackers."

Pasta and almond liqueur carry out the Italian theme in the baked chicken dinner. This hurry-up meal for four features chicken and a colorful mélange of vegetables—zucchini, mushrooms, and tomatoes—that bake together in just 20 minutes. Serve with hot ribbons of spinach fettuccine.

SOUTHWEST FAMILY NEW YEAR'S

Chili Popcorn
Fiesta Enchiladas
Citrus Salad
Black Beans
Salsa   Sour Cream
Anise Cookies
Margaritas or Limeade

A day ahead, make the pork filling for the enchiladas and buy or make cookies with anise flavoring.

Up to 2 hours before serving, assemble the enchiladas; pop the popcorn and season with butter, chili powder, and salt.

To accompany the mild pork enchiladas, drain 3 pounds canned black or pinto beans; heat (on the range or in a microwave oven) with a little water until steaming. For brave diners, provide hot salsa.

Mix salad greens with grapefruit wedges, avocado slices, almonds, and sliced nopales (canned cactus, sold in supermarkets and Mexican markets).

Greet the New Year with a Southwestern buffet. Fiesta enchiladas, citrus salad, black beans, and other dishes are arranged buffet style for easy serving.

FIESTA ENCHILADAS

1⅔ **pounds boned pork butt or shoulder, fat trimmed**
1 **large (10 oz.) onion, chopped**
2 **large cloves garlic, chopped**
3 **tablespoons chili powder**
2 **teaspoons dried oregano leaves**
1 **quart regular-strength beef broth**
12 **corn tortillas (6- to 7-in. size)**
1½ **cups (6 oz.) shredded jack cheese**
1 **large can (7 oz.) chopped green chilies**
1 **large can (15 oz.) tomato sauce**
   About 1 jar or can (10 to 12 oz.) enchilada sauce
   Fresh cilantro (coriander) sprigs

Cut pork into 1½-inch chunks. Place meat, onion, garlic, and ½ cup water in a 5- to 6-quart pan. Cover and simmer on medium-high heat for 20 minutes, stirring occasionally. Uncover; stir often until the juices evaporate, begin to brown, and stick to pan, 10 to 15 minutes.

THE DETAILS

Margaritas. Serve from a variety of festive glasses; offer limeade as an alternative.

Luminarias. For Southwestern lamp, cut design in bag. Add sand and candle.

Crackers. Buy or make favors: gift-wrapped paper tubes filled with candies, trinkets.

Piñata. Fill paper animal with candy or toys. Blindfolded guests vie to break it apart.

Stir in chili powder, oregano, and beef broth; scrape browned bits free.

Cover and simmer gently until the meat is very tender when pierced, 1 to 1½ hours.

Uncover; stir over high heat, breaking meat into shreds, until the mixture is reduced to 3 cups, 6 to 8 minutes. (If made ahead, chill airtight up to 1 day; stir over medium heat until juices are bubbling.)

Into a bowl of very hot water, immerse 1 tortilla at a time until pliable, 5 to 15 seconds; drain. Spoon a scant ¼ cup pork filling along 1 tortilla edge; roll to enclose.

Set enchilada, seam down, in a greased 10- by 15-inch pan. Repeat, fitting enchiladas close together in 1 layer. Cover pan tightly with foil. (If made ahead, chill up to 2 hours.)

Bake in a 350° oven until enchiladas are hot in center, about 15 minutes (about 25 minutes if chilled). Uncover and sprinkle with cheese; bake until cheese melts, 8 to 10 minutes longer.

Meanwhile, in a 2- to 3-quart pan over medium-high heat, mix together chilies, tomato sauce, and enchilada sauce to taste (use all for mildly spiced sauce); stir until hot, about 5 minutes. Spread sauce on a warm rimmed platter. Set enchiladas in sauce; scatter with cilantro sprigs. Makes 6 servings.

PER SERVING: 475 calories, 31 g protein, 45 g carbohydrates, 20 g fat (2.9 g saturated), 85 mg cholesterol, 1,447 mg sodium

Flavorful, lean juices of vegetables and chicken season spinach fettuccine.

EASY ITALIAN CHICKEN DINNER

Patrizio's Chicken & Vegetables
Spinach Fettuccine
Vanilla Ice Cream with Amaretto
Zinfandel

While chicken bakes, cook 6 to 8 ounces dried spinach fettuccine in boiling water; drain well. Use juices from the chicken, well flavored by vegetables and herbs, to season the hot pasta. Serve with a young and fruity Zinfandel or a chianti with the main course.

For dessert, pour almond flavor liqueur over scoops of ice cream; for the younger constituency, crumble almond macaroons onto the ice cream.

(Continued on next page)

PATRIZIO'S CHICKEN & VEGETABLES

4 chicken breast halves (2 lb. total), skinned

½ pound mushrooms, rinsed and sliced

3 medium-size (about 1 lb. total) zucchini, rinsed and ends trimmed, sliced

2 tablespoons olive oil

1 teaspoon freshly ground pepper

1 teaspoon fennel seed, crushed

1 tablespoon dried basil leaves

1 can (14 oz.) tomatoes with basil and oregano

Parsley sprigs

Grated parmesan cheese

Place chicken, mushrooms, and zucchini in a 12- by 15-inch broiler pan. Drizzle with oil. Sprinkle with pepper, fennel, and basil; mix to coat.

Cover pan tightly with foil. Bake in a 425° oven for 15 minutes. Break up tomatoes, then stir into pan. Bake, covered, until meat is no longer pink at bone (cut to test), 3 to 8 minutes longer. Spoon onto plates; garnish with parsley. Add parmesan to taste. Makes 4 servings.—*Patrick McEvoy, Palo Alto, Calif.*

PER SERVING: 291 calories, 38 g protein, 15 g carbohydrates, 9.1 g fat (1.5 g saturated), 86 mg cholesterol, 450 mg sodium

FEBRUARY

Pink Grapefruit & Shrimp Salad (page 26)

Eat right and exercise"
dictates the life style of the 1990s. This month we explore
creative and delicious, yet sensible, ways to eat well in dishes
ranging from snacks and salads to pasta and desserts.
What makes a great cup of coffee? In a feature article, you'll
learn about various coffee beans and their flavors,
how to figure out what you like, and how to reproduce
it cup after cup. Informal entertaining ideas include
an easy lasagne buffet party for a crowd and a block party
to help you get better acquainted with your neighbors.

Light & Healthy: 30 Percent or Less

FAT! IT'S IMPORTANT to regulate the amount you consume. If only the butter on your bread counted, that would be a snap, but most foods include fats in combination with carbohydrates and proteins. The chore is to add up those less obvious fats.

The amount of fat you need is based on your age, size, and level of activity. Specifics are easy to locate on National Research Council charts (in your library), or your doctor can advise you. For example, a physically active middle-aged female whose ideal weight is 138 pounds needs 2,000 to 2,200 calories a day, of which about 30 percent, or 67 to 73 grams, can come from fat. This is roughly 4½ to 5 tablespoons pure fat.

Aids for tallying fat include recipes with nutritional information, as given in Sunset; nutrient charts, as in USDA Agricultural Handbook 456, Nutrient Value of American Foods in Common Units (from the library or Government Printing Office); and, sometimes, food labels.

Fat is usually measured by weight, typically as grams (100 grams is about 3½ ounces). Or it's measured by the percentage of calories it contributes to a food. Experts favor using percentage because it is constant, regardless of your caloric requirements.

The way to calculate percentage is shown for each of these recipes. Both dinners featured here are under the 30 percent limit. They taste great—and prove it's not so difficult to eat well and healthfully at the same time.

Although protein portions are limited to the recommended 4 ounces raw weight, the grains and vegetables fill the plates with appetite-satisfying volume.

As for that 138-pound female, the chicken dinner contains 22 to 25 percent of her daily recommended calories and 10 percent of the fat, leaving 4 to 4½ tablespoons fat for other meals.

Total calories and grams of fat on plate:

	cal.	g fat
Chicken	177	4.5
Rice	269	1.5
Chinese pea pods	44	0.9
Total	**490**	**6.9**

Oriental chicken with pea pods and rice   **Total calories: 490**
Calories from fat: *6.9 grams fat × 9 =* **62.1** *(1 gram of fat has 9 calories)*
Percent of calories from fat: *(62.1 ÷ 490) × 100 =* **13**

Oriental Chicken with Pea Pods & Rice

- 2 teaspoons sesame seed
- ¾ pound Chinese pea pods
  About 3 cups regular-strength beef broth
- ⅓ cup sake or dry sherry
- 3 tablespoons sugar
- 2 tablespoons soy sauce
- 2 cloves garlic, minced or pressed
- 1⅓ cups long-grain white rice
- 1 cup thinly sliced mushrooms
- ½ cup minced green onions
- 8 small (each about 2 oz., 1 lb. total) boned and skinned chicken thighs

In a 3- to 4-quart pan over medium-high heat, stir sesame seed until golden, 4 to

6 minutes. Remove sesame seed from pan and set aside.

Remove ends and strings from pea pods. In pan, bring 3 inches water to boiling; add peas. Cook, uncovered, just until peas are a brighter green, about 3 minutes. Drain; quickly immerse in ice water. When peas are cold, drain. If made ahead, cover and chill up until next day.

Mix ⅓ cup broth, sake, sugar, soy, and garlic. Reserve ¼ cup mixture for rice. Mix mushrooms, ¼ cup onions, and 1 tablespoon of remaining broth mixture.

Rinse chicken; pound with a flat mallet between sheets of plastic wrap until ⅛ inch thick. Mound mushroom mixture equally in center of each thigh. Fold meat over filling to enclose. Set thighs, folded sides down, about 1 inch apart in a 9- by 13-inch pan. If made ahead, cover and chill up to 8 hours.

Brush some of the remaining broth mixture over chicken. Bake, uncovered, in a 450° oven until meat is white in thickest part (cut to test), 25 to 30 minutes. Brush chicken occasionally with remaining broth mixture, using all. If pan drippings begin to burn, add 4 to 6 tablespoons water; scrape dark bits free.

In the pan used for seed, combine reserved ¼ cup broth mixture and 2¾ cups broth. Add rice and bring to a boil over high heat. Cover, reduce heat, and simmer until liquid is absorbed, about 20 minutes; keep rice warm until chicken is ready.

Mix remaining onion and rice; spoon onto a platter with chicken and peas. Pour any pan juices onto rice. Sprinkle with sesame seed. Makes 4 servings.— *Mickey Strang, McKinleyville, Calif.*

PER SERVING: 490 calories (13 percent from fat), 32 g protein, 69 g carbohydrates, 6.9 g fat (1.7 g saturated), 94 mg cholesterol, 661 mg sodium

FISH WITH POLENTA

4⅓ cups regular-strength chicken broth
1 cup polenta
½ teaspoon cumin seed

Fish with polenta   **Total calories: 318**
Calories from fat: *10 grams fat* × 9 = **90** *(1 gram of fat has 9 calories)*
Percent of calories from fat: *(90 ÷ 318) × 100* = **28**

1 pound boned and skinned orange roughy or sole fillets (4 pieces, 4 oz. each)
1 can (4 oz.) diced green chilies
1 small (about 5 oz.) red bell pepper, stemmed, seeded, and minced
1 tablespoon fresh cilantro (coriander) leaves
Lime wedges and salt

In a 3- to 4-quart pan, mix broth smoothly into polenta and add cumin; set on medium heat.

Quickly rinse and drain fish. Arrange pieces in a 9- by 13-inch pan. Bake, uncovered, in a 475° oven until thickest part of fish is opaque but still moist-looking (cut to test), 6 to 8 minutes.

Meanwhile, increase heat under polenta to high; stir often with a long-handled spoon (mixture spatters) until boiling. Reduce heat; simmer gently, stirring often, until polenta tastes creamy, about 8 minutes. Mix in chilies.

If fish is done before polenta, keep warm.

Spoon polenta equally onto 4 dinner plates. Top each portion with a piece of fish; sprinkle with bell pepper and cilantro. Add lime and salt to taste. Makes 4 servings.

PER SERVING: 318 calories (28 percent from fat), 23 g protein, 32 g carbohydrates, 10 g fat (0.7 g saturated), 23 mg cholesterol, 305 mg sodium

A DOUBLE DOSE *of citrus and some lean Asian seasonings inject a fresh liveliness into these salads. Serve them as the starter course for dinner or as light main dishes for lunch.*

Try kumquats mixed with chicken and a Vietnamese lemon-mint dressing. Pink grapefruit and shrimp take on Thai flavors with coconut and a tart-hot lime dressing. Southeast Asian seasonings also spice orange slices with peppery browned pork bits in cilantro-spiked lemon juice.

Look for pickled ginger and fish sauce in supermarkets or Asian food stores.

CHICKEN SALAD WITH KUMQUATS

1½ **pounds chicken breast halves, rinsed**
   Ginger-mint dressing (recipe follows)

¾ **cup (5 oz.) kumquats, thinly sliced, seeds and ends discarded**
1 **small (about 8 oz.) cucumber**
8 **to 10 large (6 to 8 oz. total) radicchio leaves or 16 to 20 Belgian endive spears, rinsed and crisped**
   Fresh mint sprigs (optional)

In a 5- to 6-quart pan, bring about 2 quarts water to a boil. Add chicken. Return to a boil. Cover pan tightly and remove from heat. Let stand until chicken is white in thickest part (cut to test), 20 to 24 minutes.

Remove chicken from pan and cool. Reserve water to make broth, or discard. Remove and discard skin and bones. Tear cool chicken into bite-size shreds. (If done ahead, cover and chill up until next day.)

In a large bowl, combine dressing and kumquats. Trim ends off cucumber. Cut cucumber in half lengthwise; thinly slice crosswise. Mix cucumber and chicken with kumquats. On each of 4 or 5 salad or dinner plates, place 2 radicchio leaves or 4 endive spears. Mound equal portions of salad onto leaves. Garnish with mint sprigs. Makes 4 or 5 servings.

PER SERVING: 169 calories (9.1 percent from fat), 22 g protein, 17 g carbohydrates, 1.7 g fat (0.4 g saturated), 52 mg cholesterol, 72 mg sodium

Ginger-mint dressing. Mix ½ cup **lemon juice,** ¼ cup finely shredded **fresh** or 2 tablespoons dried **mint leaves,** 2 tablespoons finely chopped **crystallized ginger,** 2 tablespoons **water,** 2½ teaspoons **sugar,** and 1 tablespoon **fish sauce** (*nuoc mam* or *nam pla*) or soy sauce.

PINK GRAPEFRUIT & SHRIMP SALAD

¼ **cup sweetened shredded dried coconut**
4 **large (about 4 lb. total) ruby or pink grapefruit**
½ **pound shelled cooked tiny shrimp**
   Tart-hot dressing (recipe follows)
10 **to 18 large (6 to 10 oz.) butter lettuce leaves, rinsed and crisped**

In a 6- to 8-inch frying pan, stir coconut over medium-low heat until golden, about 5 minutes. Remove coconut from pan and set aside.

Cut peel and white membrane off grapefruit. Over a bowl, cut between inner membranes and lift out grapefruit sections; place sections in the bowl. Squeeze juice from membranes into bowl. (If done ahead, cover and chill up to 4 hours.)

Gently drain juice from grapefruit; reserve juice for another use. Add shrimp and dressing to fruit; gently mix. On each of 5 or 6 salad or dinner plates, arrange 2 or 3 lettuce leaves. Mound equal portions of grapefruit mixture onto leaves; sprinkle with coconut. Makes 5 or 6 servings.

PER SERVING: 120 calories (17 percent from fat), 10 g protein, 16 g carbohydrates, 2.2 g fat (1.1 g saturated), 74 mg cholesterol, 143 mg sodium

Sliced fresh kumquats, with sweet edible skin and tart centers, accent cucumber and chicken. Moisten salad with ginger-mint dressing; garnish with fresh mint.

Tart-hot dressing. Mix ¼ cup minced **shallots,** ¼ cup **lime juice,** 2 tablespoons **shredded pickled ginger,** 2 tablespoons **fish sauce** (*nuoc mam* or *nam pla*) or soy sauce, 2 teaspoons **sugar,** and ½ to ¾ teaspoon (add to taste) **crushed dried hot red chilies.**

HOT SPICED PORK ON ORANGES

  5 **large (about 3 lb. total) oranges**
30 **large (about 3 oz. total) spinach leaves, rinsed and crisped**
 ¾ **pound pork tenderloin or loin, fat trimmed**
  1 **teaspoon salad oil**
  1 **tablespoon minced garlic**
  1 **teaspoon ground coriander**
  1 **teaspoon coarsely ground pepper**
     Dressing (recipe follows)
     About 2 teaspoons fish sauce (nuoc mam or nam pla) or soy sauce
     Fresh cilantro (coriander) sprigs

Cut peel and white membrane off oranges. Cut fruit crosswise into thin slices. (If done ahead, cover and chill up to 4 hours.) Drain off juice; save for another use.

Arrange ⅙ of spinach and oranges on each of 6 salad or dinner plates.

Cut pork into ½-inch cubes; whirl in food processor until coarsely ground, or finely chop with a knife.

Pour oil into a 10- to 12-inch frying pan over high heat. Add pork, garlic, coriander, and pepper. Stir until pork is crumbly and brown film forms in pan, about 5 minutes. Add dressing, and add fish sauce to taste; stir to free film. Spoon hot mixture equally over oranges. Garnish with cilantro. Makes 6 servings.

PER SERVING: 179 calories (14 percent from fat), 14 g protein, 27 g carbohydrates, 2.8 g fat (0.7 g saturated), 31 mg cholesterol, 44 mg sodium

Dressing. Mix ½ cup **lemon juice,** 2 tablespoons **sugar,** and ¼ cup chopped **fresh cilantro** (coriander).

Thinly sliced fresh oranges on spinach leaves cool the hot, peppery bite of spiced pork. Finely chopped meat is quickly sautéed with garlic, coriander, and pepper.

V EGETABLES STAR *in these satisfying main dishes. High in fiber, carbohydrates, vitamins, and minerals, yet low in fat and cholesterol, they provide flavorful, healthful alternatives to meals based on animal protein.*

For a colorful entrée, roast cherry tomatoes and shallots to concentrate their sweetness, *then mix with pasta and broccoli. Or steep aromatic seeds in broth, then add a potpourri of winter vegetables and lentils for main-dish soup. A generous portion of spices seasons potato curry.*

ROASTED TOMATO & SHALLOT PASTA

Serve with a green salad.

- 1 pound (2 to 3 cups) cherry tomatoes, stemmed, cut in half
- 1 pound shallots, cut in half
- 1 tablespoon olive oil
- 1 pound broccoli
- 12 ounces dried ziti, zitoni, or other short-tube pasta
- 1½ cups regular-strength chicken broth
- 2 cloves garlic, pressed or minced
- 1 tablespoon drained canned capers
- 1 tablespoon dried basil leaves
- ¼ teaspoon crushed dried hot red chilies
  - Grated parmesan cheese
  - Salt and pepper

Roasted cherry tomatoes and shallots have concentrated flavors that season pasta and bite-size flowerets of broccoli. High in fiber and nutrients, low in fat and cholesterol, this hearty dish makes a satisfying entrée for a no-meat meal.

In a deep 10- by 15-inch roasting pan, combine tomatoes, shallots, and oil. Bake in a 425° oven until vegetables are browned, 50 to 60 minutes; stir vegetables occasionally.

Trim tough ends off broccoli. Peel stems; thinly slice. Cut flowerets into 1-inch pieces.

Shortly before tomatoes are done, bring about 3 quarts water to boiling in a 5- to 6-quart covered pan on high heat. Add pasta; cook, uncovered, 8 minutes. Add broccoli; boil until pasta and broccoli are barely tender to bite, 3 to 5 minutes longer. Drain. Pour into a serving bowl; keep warm.

Add broth, garlic, capers, basil, and chilies to roasting pan. Stir over high heat to free browned bits and vegetables and until liquid boils. Pour over pasta; mix. Add cheese, salt, and pepper to taste. Makes 4 servings.

PER SERVING: 487 calories (11 percent from fat), 19 g protein, 93 g carbohydrates, 6 g fat (0.1 g saturated), 0 mg cholesterol, 133 mg sodium

WINTER VEGETABLE LENTIL CHOWDER

If you like, supplement soup with hearty bread and cheese such as regular or reduced-fat jarlsberg or lappi.

- 2½ **quarts regular-strength chicken broth**
- 1 **teaspoon white peppercorns**
- 1 **teaspoon coriander seed**
- ½ **teaspoon whole allspice**
- 3 **strips lemon peel (each about ½ by 3 in., yellow part only)**
- 1 **cup (6 oz.) lentils**
- 3 **large (about 1 lb. total) leeks**
- 1½ **pounds banana squash**
- ¾ **pound Swiss chard**
   Salt and pepper

In a 5- to 6-quart pan, combine broth, peppercorns, coriander, allspice, and peel. Bring to a boil on high heat; cover and simmer 20 to 30 minutes to blend flavors.

Sort and discard debris from lentils; rinse lentils. Trim dark tops and root ends off leeks. Split in half lengthwise, rinse well, and slice thin. Peel squash and cut into ½-inch cubes.

Add lentils to broth; simmer, covered, for 15 minutes. Add squash and leeks. Cover and simmer until both are tender to bite, about 15 minutes. Meanwhile, cut chard into ¼-inch strips; rinse and drain. Add chard to broth; simmer, uncovered, until wilted, about 5 minutes. Add salt and pepper to taste. Makes 6 servings.

PER SERVING: 214 calories (14 percent from fat), 16 g protein, 33 g carbohydrates, 3.3 g fat (0.8 g saturated), 0 mg cholesterol, 213 mg sodium

POTATO CURRY

Accompany with hot cooked brown rice.

   Spices (list follows)
   About 5 cups regular-strength chicken broth
- 2 **large (about 1 lb. total) onions, chopped**
- 4 **cloves garlic, pressed or minced**
- 2 **tablespoons minced fresh ginger**
- ¼ **teaspoon coconut extract**
- 3 **large (about 1½ lb. total) russet potatoes**
- 2 **large (about 1½ lb. total) sweet potatoes or yams**
- 1 **cup nonfat milk**
- 1 **package (10 oz.) frozen petite peas, thawed**
- ½ **cup fresh cilantro (coriander) leaves**
- 2 **cups unflavored nonfat yogurt**
   Salt

In a 5- to 6-quart pan, stir spices over medium-low heat until fragrant, about 5 minutes. Remove spices.

To pan, add ½ cup broth, onions, garlic, and ginger. Cook, uncovered, over high heat, stirring often until liquid evaporates and brown film sticks to pan, 10 to 12 minutes. Deglaze by stirring in ⅓ cup broth to release film; boil and stir until brown film forms again. Repeat deglazing step until onions are richly browned, about 3 more times. Add spices. Repeat deglazing step 1 more time.

Winter vegetables and lentils enrich aromatic broth in this chowder.

Add 3 cups broth and coconut extract. Peel russet potatoes and sweet potatoes, cut into 1½- to 2-inch chunks, and add to broth. Cover and simmer until potatoes are very tender when pierced, 40 to 45 minutes. Stir in milk and peas; simmer, uncovered, stirring occasionally, just until hot. Pour into a serving bowl. Sprinkle with cilantro leaves. Offer yogurt and salt to add to taste. Makes 6 servings.

PER SERVING: 226 calories (7.6 percent from fat), 11 g protein, 42 g carbohydrates, 1.9 g fat (0.4 g saturated), 1.7 mg cholesterol, 157 mg sodium

Spices. Combine 2 tablespoons **ground coriander**, 1 tablespoon **ground cumin**, ½ teaspoon *each* **ground turmeric** and **cayenne**, and ¼ teaspoon **ground cinnamon**.

LIGHT & HEALTHY: Slim Snacks

INDULGE WITHOUT GUILT *in these party appetizers and snacks. Low in fat, they provide healthful nibbling.*

Nonfat yogurt is the base for a handsome cheese torta appetizer. Drain the yogurt overnight to make a soft, creamy cheese, then layer cheese with a pesto made from dried tomatoes. For a simpler choice, offer barley seasoned like sushi to eat in lettuce leaves or nori.

YOGURT CHEESE & TOMATO TORTA

Yogurt cheese (recipe follows)
Tomato pesto (recipe follows)
Fresh rosemary sprigs
Toasted baguette slices or bite-size pieces of raw vegetables

Smoothly line a tall, wide-mouth 2-cup container (such as a bowl; basket without a finish or dye; or clean, unused flowerpot) with dry muslin or a double layer of cheesecloth. Press ¼ of the yogurt cheese evenly into bottom of container. Evenly distribute ⅓ of the tomato pesto onto cheese; repeat layers, ending with cheese. Fold edges of cloth over cheese. Press gently to compact. If using a basket, set in a rimmed pan to catch liquid. Cover airtight and chill at least 1 hour or up to 6 hours; occasionally pour off liquid as it accumulates.

Fold back cloth; invert torta onto plate. Lift off cloth. Garnish with rosemary sprigs. Spread onto bread or vegetables. Makes 8 to 10 two-cup servings.

PER TABLESPOON: 18 calories (10 percent from fat), 1.6 g protein, 2.6 g carbohydrates, 0.2 g fat (0.1 g saturated), 0.3 mg cholesterol, 19 mg sodium

Yogurt cheese. Line a fine strainer with a single layer of muslin or a double layer of cheesecloth. Set strainer over a deep bowl (bottom of strainer should sit at least 2 in. above bottom of bowl). Spoon 1 quart **unflavored nonfat yogurt** into cloth. Cover airtight. Chill until yogurt is firm, at least 12 hours or up to

Handsome look of layered appetizer torta belies its low-fat profile. Serve the chilled tomato pesto–yogurt cheese mold to spread onto bread or crisp vegetables.

2 days (pour off drained liquid occasionally). Gently press cheese to remove excess liquid.

Tomato pesto. Soak 1 cup (about 2¼ oz.) **dried tomatoes** in boiling **water** to cover until soft, about 10 minutes. Drain; squeeze out excess liquid. With a food processor or knife, finely chop tomatoes. Mix with 2 tablespoons grated **parmesan cheese**, 1 clove **garlic** (pressed or minced), and 1 teaspoon minced **fresh** or ½ teaspoon crumbled dried **rosemary leaves**. Add **salt** to taste.

BARLEY SUSHI SCOOPS

¾ **cup pearl barley**
1 **large (about ¼ lb.) carrot, finely diced**
⅓ **cup seasoned rice vinegar (or distilled white vinegar with 2 tablespoons sugar)**
1 **small (about ½ lb.) cucumber, finely diced**
⅓ **cup sliced green onions**
2 **tablespoons drained pickled ginger, chopped**
¼ **pound shelled cooked tiny shrimp**
Fish sauce (nuoc mam or nam pla) or salt
1 **green onion, ends trimmed**
3½ **to 4 dozen medium-size (about 1½ lb. total) butter lettuce leaves, rinsed and crisped; or toasted nori squares (each about 4 in.)**

Rinse barley in a fine strainer. In a 1½- to 2-quart pan, bring 2 cups water to a boil. Add barley; cover and cook 20 minutes over low heat. Sprinkle carrot over barley. Continue cooking, covered, until barley is tender to bite, about 10 minutes. Drain; cool in pan.

Mix barley, vinegar, cucumber, sliced onions, ginger, shrimp, and fish sauce to taste. Spoon into a bowl. Garnish with whole onion. Spoon mixture onto lettuce and enclose to eat. Makes 10 to 12 appetizer servings.

PER SERVING: 77 calories (4.7 percent from fat), 4.2 g protein, 15 g carbohydrates, 0.4 g fat (0.1 g saturated), 18 mg cholesterol, 52 mg sodium

THE EASIEST *lean desserts start with naturally lean fruit. All three of these warm fruit creations have fewer than 150 calories per serving, with no more than 7 percent of them coming from fat.*

PINEAPPLE COMETS

1½ to 2 cups frozen vanilla yogurt
1½ cups frozen, lightly sweetened raspberries, thawed
1 tablespoon water
1½ teaspoons cornstarch
1 medium-size pineapple, peeled and cored (1⅓ lb. peeled; 3 lb. with peel and crown)

Scoop frozen yogurt into 6 balls; place in the freezer in a metal pan. Smoothly purée raspberries and water in a blender. Rub through a fine strainer into a 1- to 1½-quart pan. Mix in cornstarch. Stir over high heat until boiling, 2 to 3 minutes. Scrape into a zip-lock plastic freezer bag and seal.

Cut pineapple into 6 equal rounds. Place in a 10- by 15-inch pan. Broil about 3 inches below heat until tinged brown, 5 to 7 minutes. Turn slices over; broil until tinged brown, 4 to 5 minutes more.

Put slices on 6 dessert plates; let cool slightly. Top each slice with a scoop of frozen yogurt. Quickly snip a ⅛-inch hole in 1 corner of raspberry sauce bag; squeeze sauce in a zigzag over desserts. Makes 6 servings.

PER SERVING: 131 calories (6.9 percent from fat), 2.6 g protein, 29 g carbohydrates, 1 g fat (0 g saturated), 2.5 mg cholesterol, 29 mg sodium

SPICED BAKED APPLES

3 cups apple cider
1 tablespoon lemon juice
3 cinnamon sticks (3 in. each)
12 whole cloves
12 whole allspice
6 whole star anise (optional)
4 large (about 2 lb. total) Rome Beauty or Golden Delicious apples
Light sour cream and brown sugar (optional)

In a 2- to 3-quart pan, bring cider, lemon juice, cinnamon, cloves, allspice, and anise to a boil. Cover and simmer for 10

Zigzag design of puréed raspberries decorates pineapple slice topped by scoop of frozen vanilla yogurt. Do-ahead steps make final assembly of dessert very simple.

minutes. Core apples; slice into ¼-inch rounds into a shallow 2½- to 3-quart casserole. Pour cider mixture over apples.

Bake, uncovered, in a 350° oven until apples are tender when pierced, 15 to 20 minutes; baste several times.

Spoon fruit and cider into bowls. Add sour cream and sugar to taste. Makes 6 servings.

PER SERVING: 143 calories (4.4 percent from fat), 0.4 g protein, 36 g carbohydrates, 0.7 g fat (0.1 g saturated), 0 mg cholesterol, 4.9 mg sodium

SPARKLING JEWELS FRUIT SOUP

Mixed fruit (suggestions following)
2 tablespoons lemon juice
2 cups white grape juice
2 tablespoons minced crystallized ginger
3 tablespoons orange-flavor liqueur
Mint sprigs (optional)

Place fruit in a large bowl and mix gently with lemon juice. If made ahead, cover and chill up to 2 hours.

In a 1- to 1½-quart pan over high heat, bring grape juice and ginger to a boil. Add liqueur; pour over fruit. Ladle into bowls and garnish with mint. Makes 4 to 6 servings.

PER SERVING: 121 calories (2.2 percent from fat), 0.5 g protein, 27 g carbohydrates, 0.3 g fat (0 g saturated), 0 mg cholesterol, 12 mg sodium

Mixed fruit. Try this combination, or others (2½ cups *total*): 1 large (¼ lb.) firm-ripe **kiwi fruit,** peeled and thinly sliced; ½ cup diced firm-ripe **nectarine** or peeled peach; ⅓ cup fresh or frozen **blueberries;** ⅓ cup thinly sliced **strawberries;** and ⅓ cup paper-thin slices firm-ripe **plum.**

Coffee Reconquers the West

I'LL HAVE A HALF DOUBLE *decaffeinated half caff, with a twist of lemon," burbled Steve Martin in the movie L.A. Story.*

It's easy to laugh at Martin's spoof of the Los Angeles coffee scene, but in fact the array of options facing coffee drinkers today is no joke. Never has there been as wide a choice of beans, roasts, grinds, and brewing methods. And never has the process of making and drinking coffee promised such rewards.

A good cup depends on what goes into it. In recent years, the availability of specialty coffees—high-quality, locally roasted beans—has increased rapidly. To match general consumer demand for better-quality foods and beverages, coffee purveyors have sought to provide finer beans and more skillful roasts.

A burgeoning crop of coffeehouses is introducing more people to the joys of great coffee and engendering a desire to get equally flavorful results at home.

On these pages, we'll tell you how to figure out what you like and how to reproduce it cup after cup.

THE WEST'S OWN COFFEE ROOTS & HISTORY

Good coffee in the West goes back to 1850, when The Pioneer Steam Coffee and Spice Mills set up shop in San Francisco. It had three assets.

One was fresh beans, shipped directly from the Pacific coasts of Central and South America. The second was coffee roasted and ground on the premises—a real convenience to the gold-hungry, mostly male population that until then could buy only whole green beans.

The third asset was an ambitious teenager named J. A. Folger. He took Pioneer's coffee directly to the goldfields, made a tidy profit, and went on to own the company.

Hills Bros. was another member of the San Francisco vanguard. Around the turn of the century, it popularized vacuum-packing and paved the way for mass-marketed coffee. Until that process was used, beans didn't keep long once roasted, so roasters were almost as much a part of the local commercial scene as the corner druggist.

These days, the local coffee roaster is making a comeback. Some trace its revival to Berkeley in 1966, when Peet's Coffee & Tea started selling whole beans, dark-roasted on the premises. It was a welcome change from the standardized taste of most canned coffee.

Coffee connoisseurs all over the West developed a taste for the dark-roasted Bay Area style. New purveyors, passionate about their product, set up their own stores. They are still eager to educate consumers in how to get the most out of the finest coffee available.

Seattle now claims the title of coffee-craziest city, sporting a multitude of coffee bars, espresso stands, coffee drive-throughs—even a dental office serving espresso.

Coffee is catching on rapidly in Southern California, too. Hip cafes are popping up, vying for high counts of celebrity sightings. In fact, most Western cities can offer up their own tales of coffee popularity.

THE WORLD'S FAMOUS COFFEE CLANS

A great cup of coffee starts on the land. Like wine grapes, coffee beans from different soils and climates have varying characteristics. So, depending on what flavors you like, you can choose beans from one part of the world or another.

Coffee is divided into three basic clans.

From the Americas. These coffees are generally light bodied and smooth—although flavors range from light (Mexico) to full bodied (Colombia)—with clean, straightforward tastes. They share a lively crispness, or acidity. (In coffee terms, acidity means a sparkling flavor, not sourness; see the box on page 34 to learn coffee tasters' lingo.)

These coffees carry the names of their origins, such as Colombia, Costa Rica, Guatemala, Mexico, Panama.

This clan includes Kona, the only coffee grown in the United States.

It also includes Jamaica Blue Mountain—sweet, aromatic, and fuller bodied than others in the clan. The real thing is expensive and in short supply; Japan gets most of the crop. Watch out for impostors (often other beans of the Americas) labeled Blue Mountain–style.

From East Africa, Arabia. Coffees from this vast region have medium body with distinctive flavors and aromas of berries, citrus, flowers, spices, or red wine. Common names you'll see are Tanzania and Zimbabwe. The rarest and costliest is Yemen Mocha, a complex coffee with a chocolatelike aftertaste.

Kenya has snappy acidity. Ethiopia's lowland-grown Harrar has full body and winy flavor and is known as poor man's Yemen Mocha. Highland-grown Ethiopian Yergecheffe is mellower. Both Ethiopian coffees may be tough to find.

From the Indonesian region. Coffees are full bodied, earthy, nutty, and lower in acidity than coffees of the Americas. Some, such as Sumatra and Java, are popular for their syrupy body. Other regional names to look for include Indonesia, Sulawesi (Celebes), and Papua New Guinea.

(Continued on page 34)

In Seattle. *Neon lights and sleek decor invite coffee lovers to coffee store.*

In Los Angeles. *Sip coffee or browse the shelves at Big & Tall Books.*

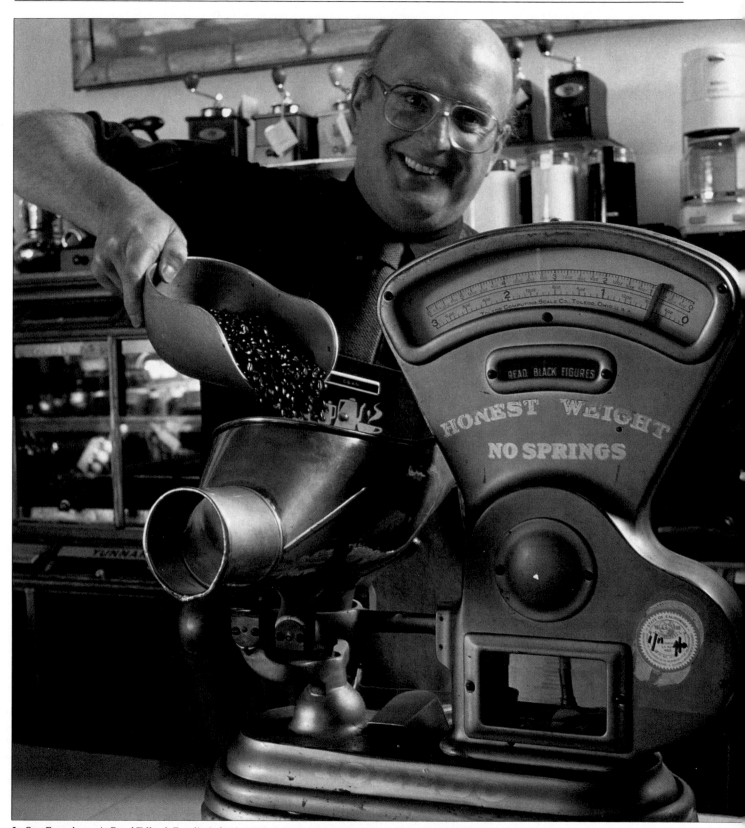

In San Francisco. *At Freed Teller & Freed's, in business since 1899, today's popular roasts are weighed out with old-fashioned friendliness.*

FROM GREEN TO BROWN— THE ROASTER'S ROLE

Until coffees rush out of the roaster in a smoking mountain of motion, they have none of the qualities we know and love. Green, unroasted beans are actually khaki- to straw-colored and smell a lot like green grass.

Roasting is a variable process. The same beans in the hands of five roasters may yield five very different results. A roastmaster roasts beans just long enough to achieve maximum flavor according to customers' preferences.

In a large drum, up to 500 pounds of beans are exposed to air approaching 450°. In the course of 15 minutes or so, beans crackle and swell, lose moisture, then suddenly begin to darken. Oils rise to the bean surface. As sugars and starches caramelize, beans develop toasted flavors.

Coffees labeled *dark roasted* look dark and taste very rich, toasted, and bittersweet, with fewer of the subtle nuances of lighter roasts.

Dark coffee is tagged with names like French roast, Italian, Viennese, and Continental (none suggests geographical origin). Sometimes *espresso* also indicates this roasting style.

Remember, what is pleasantly inky to one taster may seem unpleasantly carbonized to another. You'll need to try different companies' selections to find what suits you.

Green beans will last up to a year. Once roasted, beans stay fresh at room temperature only about one week, because the oils that carry the coffee flavors are perishable. For best home-brewing results, buy from a company that roasts frequently and has a high turnover. (See tips on home bean storage, explained on facing page.)

HOW TO MAKE A PERFECT CUP OF COFFEE

Amid often-conflicting advice, just how *do* you make a great cup at home every time you brew?

To test conventional coffee do's and don'ts, we conducted a series of taste tests with a panel of coffee aficionados.

Coffee Talk—Learn the Language of Professional Tasters

IN THE BEGINNING, coffee was hot, it was caffeinated, and we drank it. Period. These days, coffee is so hot it has its own lingo, but you don't need to be left in the cold. Read a few definitions and you, too, can be among the initiated.

The first three terms are botanical, the rest qualitative.

Arabica. Coffee species that grows at elevations from about 3,000 to 6,000 feet. These high-quality beans with refined flavors go into nearly all specialty coffees.

Robusta. Coffee species that grows from sea level up to about 3,000 feet. The hardy plants deliver higher yield and harsher flavor. Robusta is the primary ingredient of commercial (nonspecialty) coffees.

Peaberry. Round beans, borne one to a coffee berry. (Most beans grow two to a berry, with one flat side.) Some think peaberries have more concentrated flavor.

Acidity. An often-misunderstood term describing the sort of liveliness that you would find in a well-balanced wine and that is caused by the same compounds that give fruits their sparkle. Don't confuse it with the sourness that develops when coffee sits too long over heat.

Kenyan and Guatemalan coffees are especially noted for *lively* acidity. Lower-acid coffee is *mellow*. Coffee lacking acidity is *flat*.

Aged. Green beans stored one to two years to develop more complexity.

Aroma. Coffee's fragrance.

Body. Mouth feel, from watery to syrupy. Body is a result of the ratio of grounds to water and the beans' inherent qualities (Indonesian coffees, for example, are *heavy* or *full* bodied; coffees from the Americas are generally *light.*)

Body that is too light is *thin* or *weak*, lacking concentrated flavors. It may result from a low grounds-to-water ratio or from water temperature that's too low (see the middle column of facing page).

Flavor. Aroma and taste. May be acidic, bittersweet, chocolatelike, floral, nutty, rich, spicy, toasted, or winy.

Full flavored means you got the water temperature and water-to-beans ratio just right. It also means beans were good to start with and were roasted optimally. *Strong* suggests you used so many grounds you can stand a spoon in your cup (a highly individual call).

Mild describes delicate, straightforward flavors, as found in coffees of the Americas.

Rich describes complex flavors, typical of coffees from Indonesia and Africa. Often synonymous with *full*.

Bitter describes the unpleasantness that develops when coffee is *overextracted*—brewed too slowly because grinds are too fine for brewing method. Not to be confused with *bittersweet*, the sought-after flavor of dark-roasted coffees.

Earthy means robust, pleasingly unrefined. Typical of Indonesian coffees.

Flavored refers to regular beans infused with natural or artificial flavorings: vanilla, mint, butter pecan.

Muddy. Grounds in the cup. A little muddiness is unavoidable when using gold-plated filters and plunger pots. Some believe the advantage is more flavor-carrying oils.

Organic. Coffee grown without pesticides or commercial fertilizers. Both farm and processors must be certified organic. Higher price reflects lower yields than with conventional farming techniques.

Starting with batches of whole beans, we tested two types of grinder, three grinds of differing coarseness, three brewing methods, three types of filter, and three ranges of water temperature.

We rated aroma, flavor, and appearance (consistency, sediment). Overall responses varied widely; each taster had favorites.

There is not one absolutely correct way to make coffee, but the following guidelines, compiled from our tests, can help you in your quest to produce the perfect cup. Factors that most affect flavor are coarseness of grind, brewing method, and water temperature.

Buy top-quality beans. Once you have found the variety or blend of beans that you like, buy only from stores that sell freshly roasted beans. If a store does not do its own roasting, or if you are unsure of the beans' freshness, ask how often the coffee is delivered. Beans should not be more than a few days out of the roaster.

Store beans properly. Always store beans in an airtight, moistureproof container. If you plan to use them within a week, you can keep them in the refrigerator or in a dark place at a cool room temperature (around 60°) without significant flavor loss. For longer storage, freeze beans, then use them directly from the freezer (do not thaw) as you need them. Otherwise, they get stale and develop rancid flavors.

Grind just before brewing. Since flavor and aroma components begin to dissipate as soon as beans are ground, grind coffee just before you plan to brew it, and only grind as much as you need.

Match the grind to your brewing method. The coarseness of the grounds can affect flavor. With a very coarse grind, water flows through the coffee quickly and does not have time to extract much flavor. This produces a light, weaker-bodied brew.

A very fine grind will clog the filter somewhat, keeping water in contact with coffee longer. The longer the coffee steeps, the richer tasting and fuller bodied the brew—up to a point; extended extraction brings out bitter or sharp flavors, unpleasant to most people.

Read the following section to find out which grinds our tasters preferred for various brewing methods.

Use fresh-tasting water. Any off-flavors in your water will come through in coffee. If you dislike your tap water, you may want to use bottled water for brewing.

Use a ratio of coffee to water that suits you. No single ratio is correct, because desired strength is a matter of preference. The ratio also depends on variety and roast of beans.

A general guideline for medium-strength coffee is 2 level tablespoons of grounds for 6 ounces of water. For a stronger brew, use more grounds; for weaker coffee, use less. You will need to experiment to find pleasing proportions.

Pay attention to water temperature. The hotter the water, the more flavor components that are extracted. For optimum flavor and acid balance, use water between 195° and 205° (just below boiling).

Our taste panel found that this range produced the best, most well-rounded flavor. Coffee brewed with water below 190° was much weaker and less flavorful, whereas coffee that was brewed with boiling water had a very strong, bitter, and harsh taste.

With an electric drip coffee maker, of course, you have no control over water temperature. If yours is not brewing coffee to your taste, check the water temperature; you may need to buy a new coffee maker.

Drink right away. If you are not serving all your coffee immediately, do not keep it over heat. Prolonged exposure to heat can produce bitter or burnt flavors. If you need to hold it more than a few minutes, transfer it to a thermos.

WHICH WAY TO GRIND? WHICH WAY TO BREW?

There are two types of coffee grinders (see drawings above right) and three home brewing methods.

Burr-type mills contain small ring-shaped mechanisms, or burrs, that crush beans. Mills are either manual or electric.

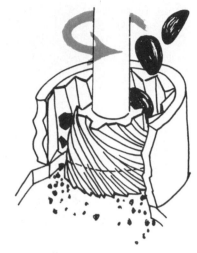

Notched burrs turn in two directions to crush beans against chamber wall.

Rapidly rotating blade turns in one direction to cut beans to desired coarseness.

Blade-type grinders are electric and have a rotating blade, which cuts beans.

Purists usually prefer burr-type mills because they make it easier to get a completely even grind. However, burr mills cost significantly more.

We tested grind coarseness with the commonest home brewing methods: *electric drip, filter-cone drip,* and *plunger pot* (French press). Here are our taste panel's top-rated combinations of grind coarseness and brewing method.

Coarse. Grounds resemble a coarse meal, such as polenta or cracked pepper. Best for plunger pot method.

(Continued on next page)

Staging the cupping party. *To set it up: grind coffee, measure ¼ cup into a bowl, and label. To each bowl, add 12 ounces of water at 195° to 205°. Let stand 1 to 2 minutes, then stir. Next step: sample the aroma. How is it—sweet or rich? Spicy or sour? Last step: slurp, but don't swallow. Swish a spoonful around in your mouth. How is the flavor? Weak to full, flat to lively, smooth to bitter? Does it feel thin or syrupy? The goal is finding coffee with just the right flavors and strength for you.*

Medium. Grounds have a consistency similar to that of regular cornmeal. Best for electric drip and plunger pot methods.

Fine. Grounds have the consistency of a smooth powder, like cocoa. Best for the filter-cone drip method.

ANOTHER CHOICE— WHICH FILTER?

Our taste panel tested the three types of filter commonly used for filter-cone drip brewing: *chlorine-bleached* (white) paper filters, *unbleached* (brown) paper filters, and *gold-plated* filter cones. The first two are disposable, while the third never wears out.

We found significant flavor differences. While we noticed no off-flavors from the bleached filters, the unbleached filters gave the coffee a distinct papery, musty taste. The gold filter produced the best flavor, although it did allow more grounds to end up in the brew.

INVITE FRIENDS FOR A CUPPING PARTY

Miss Manners might be horrified, but most of us would take childish delight in an invitation to slurp and spit. Coffee, that is. Professionals use this technique, called cupping, to evaluate quality and flavor.

All you do is pour hot water over various ground coffees in bowls, then smell and taste to discern differences. To aerate the coffee so it hits all your taste receptors at once, slurp from a spoon, sucking in some air at the same time. This helps you get the full flavor. Then spit out coffee so your palate stays fresh for the next taste. The process is shown above.

You might want to set a theme for tasting. Try one coffee from each of the regions discussed on page 32, or several from the same region. Or compare how several coffee companies treat one style of coffee, such as French roast.

Consider making your own measured blends, combining coffees by the spoonful and noting proportions.

If you want to compare brewing equipment, as we did, round up an assortment of gear from friends. Once coffee is made, keep each kind hot in a thermos and sample different brews from individual cups.

To stage a cupping, you'll need:

Beans (each guest might bring ½ pound of a different type), **grinder, white bowls** (one for each kind of bean, another for each brewed coffee), **drip coffee maker** or **plunger pot, filter cones** (for drip brewing), **measuring tablespoon, measuring cup, kettle, thermometer, thermoses, labels** for bowls and thermoses, **cups** (one per person), **spoons** (several per person), **container** for discarding tastes, **notepaper,** and **pencils.**

With or Without?...Caffeine, That Is

FOR SOME, the great value of coffee is the familiar jolt of caffeine that helps them start the day. Others, however, want the flavor without the jolt, accounting for the increased popularity of decaffeinated coffee.

It's important to realize that all methods of decaffeination disrupt the beans' chemical structures. Thus, there is always some flavor change when caffeine is removed.

Over the last few years, the technology of decaffeination has greatly advanced. Methods affect flavor to differing degrees. To try to experience differences, taste side by side the same variety of coffee decaffeinated in different ways.

Terminology can be confusing. First, *decaffeinated* does not actually mean caffeine-free, but about 97 percent caffeine-free.

All decaffeination processes start by either soaking or steaming green beans until they swell and the caffeine comes to the bean surface. Then a chemical or nonchemical solvent removes the caffeine.

Chemical decaffeination. The most widely used chemical solvent is methylene chloride. It removes caffeine with the least damage to flavor components in the beans.

The solvent is applied in one of two ways. In the *direct* method, coffee goes through repeated methylene chloride rinses, then beans are steamed for 8 to 12 hours to evaporate the solvent.

The *indirect* method is sometimes called the European water process, or simply water process (not to be confused with the patented nonchemical Swiss Water process). Beans are soaked in water until caffeine—and water-soluble flavor components—leaches into the water. Once water is drained off, it is treated with methylene chloride to remove caffeine.

This first batch of beans is discarded, but the decaffeinated water—retaining flavor elements—is used to decaffeinate subsequent batches of beans. The flavor-saturated water allows *only* caffeine, not flavor, to escape the beans.

Most plants using methylene chloride are in Europe and in Central and South America. Concern over the chemical's possible carcinogenic effects is answered by the argument that, since the solvent evaporates at 103° and coffee is roasted at nearly 450°, there's little chance of residue remaining in the final product.

The second most common chemical decaffeination process uses ethyl acetate. This is sometimes called a natural process because minute quantities of ethyl acetate occur naturally in some fruits.

The procedures are almost identical to those for methylene chloride. Ethyl acetate decaffeination is used mainly by large commercial producers, although some specialty coffee brokers are beginning to offer beans decaffeinated this way.

Chemical-free decaffeination. Of nonchemical methods, best known is the Swiss Water process, patented by Nabob Foods Limited of Vancouver, British Columbia. Steps are like those of the indirect methylene chloride method.

Caffeine is removed from the beans' soaking water by granular activated charcoal that has been treated to absorb *only* caffeine and *not* water-soluble flavor compounds.

The technique, developed in Nabob's Vancouver plant, has greatly improved flavor. (The company's Swiss plant uses an older process, which returns the flavor-bearing water to each batch of beans for reabsorption of flavor compounds. This technique is less successful in retaining flavor.)

A second nonchemical decaffeination agent in common use is supercritical carbon dioxide (carbon dioxide that has been pressurized until it liquifies). Carbon dioxide, added to beans, removes caffeine, then evaporates as beans dry. This method was developed for mass-produced coffee, but beans decaffeinated this way are increasingly seen in specialty stores.

A third, relatively new nonchemical method is the coffee-oil decaffeination process. It uses coffee oil, refined from ground caffeinated coffee, to remove caffeine in steps similar to those of the indirect methylene chloride process. Coffee decaffeinated this way is not yet widely available.

(And what happens to all the caffeine removed from coffee? Much of it is sold to pharmaceutical manufacturers and soft drink companies.)

Block Party!

WHAT'S THE BIG DEAL?" *my husband, Larry, wondered. "We already know their children from playing street soccer and buying Girl Scout cookies."*

"But I would like to get to know my neighbors," I said. "No one even says hello when I wave."

Meeting my neighbors was something I had wanted to do for a long time. What if someone's house alarm went off or there was a fire? What if I needed help? I wouldn't know anyone to call. More to the point, I was a little hurt. The neighborhood life I had imag-ined—OK, fantasized—for myself just wasn't coming true.

In 1990, Larry and I moved to the Hampton Place subdivision in Fremont, California. It's a great starter neighborhood—Honda in every driveway, the works.

Newly acquainted Hampton Place residents gather for a group photo during informal neighborhood party.

But when no one rang the doorbell to say hello, and no Welcome Wagon greeted us, all I could think about was how every time my mother moved to a new house in the Chicago suburbs, someone came by to offer a basket of goodies, important phone numbers,

shopping hints. It was a comforting rite of passage I had looked forward to in my own home.

But in Fremont, the neighbors seemed to keep to themselves. Like us, most are young couples (many with children and grandparents all under the same roof). From the number of For Sale signs, a lot of them appear on their way somewhere else.

Many of the families in the neighborhood are immigrants, and I was afraid language would be a barrier. I guess that's why it took me so many months to get the nerve to cross the street and ask the Datts if they thought it would be crazy to have a neighborhood party.

"What a great idea," said Shavila Datt, a native of India, whom I had met before only because her husband had dented my brand-new car. "I know others would want to meet each other."

Having lost my last excuse not to stumble ahead, I typed up a simple questionnaire asking who would like to attend a party and when they might be available. Larry and I were still timid enough when we dropped the questionnaire into each mailbox that we didn't even give our names—anything to avoid the prospect of having an entire neighborhood ducking our invitation and our gaze.

But Shavila Datt had not exaggerated. Within days, 14 of 20 households on our block popped filled-in questionnaires in our mailbox. And many attached nice notes. I was dumbfounded. Our neighborhood of nonwavers was genuinely happy that someone was organizing a party.

Quickly, Larry and I picked a date and typed up an invitation. To try to get each family involved (and also to attract foods from the amazing number of native lands represented), we asked everyone to bring a different dish, which started a flurry of notes and visits.

Evelyn and David Miramontes stopped by to ask how they could help. The Rees family offered to bring utensils and supplies for the entire party in addition to their buffet dish—a contribution far beyond their assignment.

The Parasos, from the Philippines, announced that they had swapped their assignment of rice, pasta, or bread with the Phans, from Vietnam, so they could bring their specialty, beef lumpia. At a minimum, the party had everyone speaking the same language of food, recipes, and entertaining. The night before, Michael Teymouri even invited us to his jazz club nearby. Larry went. I stayed up late cooking.

For me the day of the party was very much a blur. The Miramontes helped, all right; they surprised everyone by bringing tables with benches, a great improvement over the curbside seating I'd planned. By 3:45, 60 people, most of whom had never met each other, filled the street.

The Miramontes's music box blared sounds of the Temptations and Hall & Oates. The children, herded into games by 11-year-old Jennifer Paraso and 9-year-old Andrea Davila, were well behaved. People from other blocks even wandered over to sample the food.

As for me, I ran around so much making sure the lemonade pitcher was full and the children all had lollipops that I hardly had a chance to do what had motivated me in the first place: talk with my neighbors. So when I retired into our house around 6:30, I had no idea whether the party had been a success.

I got my answer pretty quickly. At 8:30 I looked out the window and saw a handful of neighbors still gathered, talking and playing in the street. My mother would have been proud.

I can't say exactly how my life has changed in the intervening months. But the other day I recognized and said hello to a neighbor at Safeway, where he is a manager, and noticed 5-year-old Natalie Miramontes leaving her ballet recital, which her mother, Evelyn, said had gone well.

I also spent several evenings sharing recipes and tasting specialties prepared by Shavila Datt in her home. Small steps, perhaps, but enough to confirm for me that Larry was wrong. Neighbors are a big deal.

(Continued on next page)

Dishes from around the world appear on buffet table at block party. Arrange foods by type: appetizers, salads, breads, rice and pasta, main dishes, and desserts.

PAKORAS (INDIA)

You can find split pea flour in an Indian or international food market.

- 1½ cups yellow split pea flour or homemade flour (directions follow)
- ½ teaspoon *each* baking soda and salt
- ¼ teaspoon *each* cayenne, ground turmeric, cumin seed, and caraway seed
- 1 package (10 oz.) frozen chopped spinach, thawed and squeezed dry
- 1 medium-size (5 to 6 oz.) onion, finely chopped
- 5 cloves garlic, minced or pressed
- 2 tablespoons minced fresh ginger
- 1 tablespoon lemon juice
  Salad oil
  Tomato chutney and unflavored yogurt

In a bowl, mix pea flour, soda, salt, cayenne, turmeric, cumin, and caraway seed. Mix in ½ cup water, spinach, onion, garlic, ginger, and lemon juice until moistened.

In a deep 3- to 4-quart pan over medium-high heat, bring 1½ to 2 inches oil to 350°. Drop batter into oil, 1 table-spoon at a time (do not crowd), and turn until golden, about 2 minutes. Adjust heat to maintain temperature. Drain pakoras on towels. Serve hot. If made ahead, let cool, cover, and hold up to 1 day. To reheat, arrange in a 10- by 15-inch pan and bake at 350° until hot to touch, about 5 minutes.

To eat, dip pakoras into chutney or yogurt. Makes 12 to 14 appetizer serv-ings.—*Shavila Datt, Fremont, Calif.*

PER SERVING WITHOUT DIPS: 117 calories, 5.9 g protein, 15 g carbohy-drates, 4.2 g fat (0.5 g saturated), 0 mg cholesterol, 126 mg sodium

Homemade flour. Sort 1½ cups **yellow split peas** and discard debris. Whirl in a blender on high speed, about half at a time, until powdery like stone-ground whole-wheat flour, at least 5 minutes. Measure 1½ cups flour (you will have extra flour).

Shavila Datt offers crisp pakoras from her native India for block party buffet.

CHICKEN & SHRIMP PANSIT (PHILIPPINES)

- 6 **ounces dry thin rice noodles (mai fun or rice sticks)**
- 1 **large (about 8 oz.) onion, finely chopped**
- 4 **green onions**
- 4 **cups finely shredded cabbage**
- 2 **cups diced, cooked, skinned chicken**
- 1 **cup thinly sliced carrot**
- ½ **cup regular-strength chicken broth**
  About 3 tablespoons oyster sauce, or 2 tablespoons soy sauce
  About 2 tablespoons rice vinegar
- 1 **tablespoon minced fresh ginger**
- 4 **cloves garlic, minced or pressed**
- ¼ **teaspoon pepper**
- ½ **pound shelled cooked tiny shrimp**
- 1 **or 2 hard-cooked eggs, shelled, cut lengthwise into wedges (optional)**

In a bowl, soak noodles in warm water to cover until just tender to bite, about 20 minutes; drain well.

In a 12-inch frying pan or 5- to 6-quart pan, cook chopped onion with 2 tablespoons water over high heat, stirring often until liquid evaporates and browned bits stick in pan. Deglaze by adding ¼ cup water and scraping browned bits free. Stir often until liquid evaporates and browned bits form again. Repeat the deglazing step, using ¼ cup water each time, until onion is richly browned, about 3 more times, about 15 minutes total.

Meanwhile, trim green onion ends; thinly slice 2.

To cooked onion, add noodles, cabbage, chicken, carrot, broth, oyster sauce, vinegar, ginger, garlic, and pepper. Stir mixture often, until liquid evaporates and browned bits stick in pan, about 10 minutes. Add ¼ cup water, off the heat; scrape browned bits free.

Pour noodle mixture onto a platter; top with shrimp and sliced onions. Garnish with remaining green onions and eggs. Makes 6 main-dish servings.—*Janet Iringan, Fremont, Calif.*

PER SERVING: 291 calories, 26 g protein, 33 g carbohydrates, 5.1 g fat (1.4 g saturated), 151 mg cholesterol, 517 mg sodium

KIWI FRUIT & ORANGE CHEESE PIE (U.S.)

- 1 **envelope (2 teaspoons) unflavored gelatin**
- 2 **large packages (8 oz. each) neufchâtel (light cream) cheese, or cream cheese**
- ½ **cup sugar**
- 1 **teaspoon vanilla**
- ¾ **cup nonfat milk**
  Graham cracker crust (recipe follows)
- 2 **large (about ½ lb. total) kiwi fruit, peeled and thinly sliced**
- ¼ **cup fresh orange segments (membrane removed), or drained, canned mandarin orange segments**

In a 1- to 1½-quart pan, sprinkle gelatin over ¼ cup water. Let stand to soften, about 3 minutes; stir over low heat until dissolved.

In a large bowl, beat cheese, sugar, and vanilla with a mixer until blended. Gradually add gelatin mixture and milk, beating until smooth. Pour into crust. Chill until filling is set just enough to support a topping, 20 to 30 minutes.

Decoratively arrange kiwi slices and orange segments on pie, gently pressing to adhere to filling. Cover and chill until firm enough to cut, at least 4 hours or up until next day. Makes 8 or 9 servings.—*Jennifer Chen, Fremont, Calif.*

PER SERVING: 381 calories, 7.8 g protein, 35 g carbohydrates, 23 g fat (14 g saturated), 66 mg cholesterol, 438 mg sodium

Graham cracker crust. In a 10-inch pie pan, mix 1½ cups **graham cracker crumbs,** ½ cup (¼ lb.) melted **butter** or margarine, and 2 tablespoons **sugar.** Press over pan bottom and sides. Bake in a 350° oven until a slightly darker brown, about 10 minutes. Cool. If made ahead, cover and chill up until next day.

Lazy Lasagne

LASAGNE AS A MAKE-AHEAD *casserole is a long-time winner, but time consuming. We think you'll find it more fun— and more relaxing—to let your guests do the work. No need to worry about taste preferences or portion size; those decisions are made by each person while layering ingredients from the lasagne bar onto his or her own plate. The bar offers pasta, roasted and boiled vegetables, several cheeses, cooked meat, and an aromatic tomato sauce.*

There's no baking of the lasagne, but you do need to provide a system for keeping most of its components hot or a way to reheat the assembled lasagne right on the plate.

The challenge is easily met. Keep ingredients hot on electric warming trays, over hot water in chafing dishes, or in an oven at lowest setting.

Exceptions are the pasta and broccoli; they hold best unheated but, swished in hot water, warm quickly.

If you have a microwave oven, you can present all the elements cold and zap portions one at a time (about 3 minutes is adequate for a 2-cup-size serving). Stagger arrival times at the buffet so waiting is minimal.

The lasagne bar makes for dining at a leisurely, flexible pace and is ideal for informal occasions when guests are apt to show up over a period of time, or when other diversions are scheduled, such as a movie or game to watch on TV.

LASAGNE BAR BUFFET FOR 20

Lasagne Pasta
Roasted Vegetables
Cheeses to Layer
Cooked Italian Sausage
Broccoli Buds
Herbed Tomato Sauce
Grated Parmesan Cheese
Green Salad
with Add-Your-Own Dressing
Baguettes
Chianti & Frascati Wines
Lemon Cookies   Espresso

---

*In addition to the following elements for lasagne, you will need about 4½ pounds **Italian turkey** or pork **sausage**, crumbled, lightly browned, and drained (if cooked ahead, cover and chill up until next*

day); 10 cups cooked and chilled **broccoli flowerets;** and 3 cups grated **parmesan cheese.**

To reheat pasta and broccoli (if lasagne ingredients are hot), have a large pan of simmering water on the range or on a portable burner. Dunk pasta and broccoli, a portion at a time, in water for about ½ minute; use a skimmer ladle, a slotted spoon, or tongs to retrieve.

Round out the menu with crisp salad greens and a selection of dressings. Buy or make your favorite lemon cookies. Offer with coffee.

LASAGNE PASTA

2 pounds dried lasagne, broken into 4- to 5-inch lengths

Half-fill a 10- to 12-quart pan with water. Cover and bring to boiling on high heat; add pasta. Cook uncovered, stirring often, until pasta is just tender to bite, 12 to 15 minutes. Drain, and immerse at once in cold water. Drain when cool. Serve or, if made ahead, cover airtight and chill up until the next day.

Present pasta in a large bowl. Reheat in a microwave oven or in hot water as directed above. Makes enough for 20 servings.

PER SERVING: 168 calories, 5.8 g protein, 34 g carbohydrates, 0.7 g fat (0.1 g saturated), 0 mg cholesterol, 3.2 mg sodium

ROASTED VEGETABLES

16 large (about 4 lb. total) carrots, peeled and thinly sliced
4 large (about 2½ lb. total) red bell peppers, stemmed, seeded, and cut into thin strips
4 large (about 1¾ lb. total) onions, thinly sliced
1½ pounds mushrooms, rinsed and thinly sliced
⅓ cup balsamic or red wine vinegar
3 tablespoons extra-virgin olive oil or salad oil
1 cup regular-strength chicken broth

In 2 pans (10 to 12 by 15 in. each), divide carrots, peppers, onions, mushrooms, vinegar, and oil evenly; mix well. Roast uncovered in a 450° oven, stirring often with a wide spatula, until vegetables are browned and browned bits stick to pan, 60 to 70 minutes. If using 1 oven, switch pan positions every 20 minutes.

Add ½ cup chicken broth to each pan; stir to scrape browned bits free.

Roast vegetables until the liquid evaporates, stirring often, about 15 minutes more. Serve or, if made ahead, cool, cover airtight, and chill up to 2 days. Makes about 10 cups.

PER ½ CUP: 88 calories, 2.5 g protein, 15 g carbohydrates, 2.8 g fat (0.4 g saturated), 0 mg cholesterol, 35 mg sodium

CHEESES TO LAYER

5⅓ cups (or 3 containers, 15 oz. each) part-skim ricotta cheese
¾ pound jack or mozzarella cheese, shredded
1 cup (4 to 5 oz.) shredded parmesan cheese
½ cup regular-strength chicken broth

Lasagne bar presents ribbons of cooked pasta to layer with soft cheeses, browned meat, roasted vegetables, broccoli, tomato sauce, and parmesan cheese. Keep lasagne components hot (see suggestions), or you can zap individual portions in a microwave oven.

In a bowl, mix together ricotta, jack, and parmesan cheese, and broth. If made ahead, cover and chill up until next day. Use cold if warming individual servings of lasagne in a microwave oven (directions on preceding page). Or serve hot, heated by one of the following methods.

To heat in microwave oven, mix cheeses and broth in a microwave-safe bowl. Heat at half power (50 percent) for 3-minute intervals, stirring in between, until mixture is warm, 10 to 14 minutes.

To heat in the oven, mix cheeses and broth in a shallow 2- to 2½-quart pan. Cover with foil and place in a 300° oven. Stir often until cheese is warm, about 25 minutes.

With either method, the cheese mixture separates and looks curdled if it gets too hot; however, it is still good to eat.

To serve the cheese mixture warm, set on a warming tray or return, uncovered, to oven at lowest setting. Makes 7½ cups.

PER ¼ CUP: 116 calories, 9 g protein, 2.4 g carbohydrates, 7.8 g fat (2.7 g saturated), 26 mg cholesterol, 175 mg sodium

HERBED TOMATO SAUCE

4 large cans (28 oz. each) Italian-style tomatoes
1 large can (12 oz.) tomato paste
1 cup dry red wine
¼ cup minced fresh or 2 tablespoons dried basil leaves
3 cloves garlic, minced or pressed
1 tablespoon minced fresh or 1 teaspoon dried rosemary leaves
1 tablespoon minced fresh or 2 teaspoons dried oregano leaves

In a 5- to 6-quart pan, combine tomatoes and their liquid, tomato paste, red wine, basil, garlic, rosemary, and oregano. Smash tomatoes into small chunks with a slotted spoon. Bring to a boil over medium-high heat.

Simmer gently, uncovered, until the tomato sauce is reduced to 12 cups, about 45 minutes; stir occasionally. Serve, or cool, cover, and chill up to 2 days. Makes 12 cups.

PER ½ CUP: 41 calories, 1.9 g protein, 8.9 g carbohydrates, 0.5 g fat (0.1 g saturated), 0 mg cholesterol, 328 mg sodium

Warm Winter Punches

CHASE AWAY THE CHILLS *with blends of hot fruit juice and wine. Wine cuts the sweetness of the juice, adding freshness and sophistication to these adult beverages. Moderately priced wines high in fruit, with minimum oak flavor, work best.*

The beverage mixtures take only minutes to heat to simmering on the range or in a microwave oven.

HOT GINGERED PEAR-WINE CIDER

3 cups canned unsweetened pear
 nectar
2 tablespoons sugar
1 tablespoon minced crystallized
 ginger
1 tablespoon lemon juice
1 cup dry Sauvignon Blanc
 Lemon slices (optional)

In a 1½- to 2-quart pan over medium-high heat, mix pear nectar, sugar, ginger, lemon juice, and wine. Cook, uncovered, until hot, about 7 minutes. (Or heat in a 1½- to 2-quart microwave-safe container in a microwave oven at full power, 100 percent, until hot, about 7 minutes.)

Pour cider into mugs, and garnish each with a lemon slice. Makes 4 or 5 servings, 5 to 6 ounces each.

PER SERVING: 127 calories, 0.2 g protein, 27 g carbohydrates, 0 g fat, 0 mg cholesterol, 9.1 mg sodium

HOT CRANBERRY-WINE CIDER

3 cups cranberry juice cocktail
¼ cup frozen orange juice
 concentrate
1 tablespoon firmly packed brown
 sugar
⅛ teaspoon almond extract
1 cup Gamay Beaujolais, Zinfandel,
 or Merlot
 Thin orange slices (optional)

In from the cold, sip steaming mugs of ginger- and lemon-flavored pear nectar spiked with dry white wine. Drinks heat quickly on the range or in a microwave oven.

In a 1½- to 2-quart pan over medium-high heat, mix cranberry juice cocktail, orange juice concentrate, sugar, almond extract, and wine. Cook, uncovered, until hot, about 7 minutes. (Or heat in a 1½- to 2-quart microwave-safe container in a microwave oven at full power, 100 percent, until hot, about 7 minutes.)

Pour cider into mugs; garnish each with an orange slice. Makes 4 or 5 servings, 5 to 6 ounces each.

PER SERVING: 128 calories, 0.4 g protein, 26 g carbohydrates, 0.1 g fat (0 g saturated), 0 mg cholesterol, 5.5 mg sodium

More February Recipes

OTHER FEBRUARY ARTICLES *feature a hearty split pea soup from the Netherlands and a giant shortbread cookie for Valentine's Day.*

DUTCH SPLIT PEA SOUP
(*Erwtensoep*)

Hearty, simple foods of the meat and vegetable variety form the basis of the Netherlands' traditional winter cuisine. Split pea soup is one such national favorite.

This version gains flavorful substance from bacon, sausage, and vegetables. Readily available kielbasa stands in for the smoked frankfurter sausage called rookworst that is used in the Netherlands. The recipe comes from Die Port van Cleve in Amsterdam. In a city where menus lean toward the international, the hotel's restaurant is best known for offering native Dutch fare.

  1 **pound leeks**
  ½ **pound sliced bacon, chopped**
  2 **cups peeled, diced celery root, or chopped celery**
  1 **large (about ½ lb.) onion, chopped**
  ¼ **cup chopped parsley**
  1 **pound green split peas, sorted of debris and rinsed**
  1 **quart regular-strength chicken broth**
  1 **pound kielbasa (Polish) sausage, sliced ½ inch thick**
    Parsley sprigs
    Pepper

Cut off and discard tough green tops, outer leaves, and root ends from leeks. Split leeks lengthwise and rinse well; slice thinly and set aside.

In a 5- to 6-quart pan over medium-high heat, stir bacon often until brown. With a slotted spoon, transfer bacon to paper towels; set aside. Discard all but 2 tablespoons fat from pan. To pan, add leeks, celery root, onion, and chopped parsley. Stir often over medium heat until vegetables are limp, about 15 minutes.

Return bacon to pan with split peas, broth, and 1 quart water. Bring to a boil over high heat. Cover and simmer until peas are mostly dissolved, about 1½ hours; stir soup occasionally. Add kielbasa. Stir often until sausage is hot, about 10 minutes longer.

Serve soup hot; if made ahead, let cool, cover, and chill up to 3 days.

Valentine puzzle has sweet message, sweet reward. To make chocolate "ink" on buttery shortbread, press chocolate baking chips into dough before baking.

Reheat, stirring often. Ladle into bowls and garnish with parsley sprigs. Season to taste with pepper. Makes 3 quarts, 6 to 8 servings.

PER SERVING: 494 calories, 26 g protein, 46 g carbohydrates, 24 g fat (8.1 g saturated), 47 mg cholesterol, 834 mg sodium

LOVE YOU TO PIECES SHORTBREAD

Be mine? Love you? What will the valentine reveal? Sandee Cameron creates a sweet mystery with her Love You to Pieces shortbread valentine. With the help of her two young sons, she uses chocolate bits to stud an abbreviated billet-doux traced on the super-size heart. Baked whole, the warm cookie is then cut apart randomly and presented as a puzzle.

What will your puzzle valentine say when assembled?

  2 **cups all-purpose flour**
  ⅔ **cup sugar**
  ⅓ **cup cornstarch**
  1 **cup (½ lb.) butter or margarine, at room temperature**
    About ½ cup semisweet chocolate baking chips, small candy-coated chocolates, or raisins

In a food processor or with a mixer, combine flour, sugar, and cornstarch.

Add butter, in chunks. Whirl or mix until dough is well blended.

Scrape dough onto a lightly buttered 14- by 17-inch baking sheet. Using hands, pat dough out ¼ inch thick, then shape into a heart that is about 12 inches tall and 14 inches wide.

With the tip of a skewer or sharp knife, write a message on the heart, scoring lightly (it's helpful to write the message first on a heart-size piece of paper). If you don't like the results, pat smooth and try again. Press chocolate pieces into lines.

Bake cookie in a 275° oven until pale gold, about 1 hour. At once, cut cookie with a sharp knife into 6 to 10 pieces of random shapes, but leave pieces in place until cool.

With a wide spatula, gently transfer pieces to a large platter or board, disassembling the heart and message. Serve, or wrap airtight up until the next day; freeze to store longer. Invite your youngest (or other selected) guest to reassemble the puzzle and read the message. Break into chunks to eat. Makes a 1¾-pound cookie, 12 to 16 servings.—*Sandee Cameron, Burlingame, Calif.*

PER OUNCE: 129 calories, 1.1 g protein, 15 g carbohydrates, 7.5 g fat (4.6 g saturated), 18 mg cholesterol, 67 mg sodium

Chunky muffins contain dried apricots, granola cereal, whole-wheat flour.

APRICOT GRANOLA MUFFINS

- ¼ cup (⅛ lb.) butter or margarine
- ½ cup firmly packed brown sugar
- 2 large eggs
- ½ cup nonfat milk
- ¼ teaspoon almond extract
- ¾ cup all-purpose flour
- ½ cup whole-wheat flour
- 2 teaspoons baking powder
- 1 teaspoon ground cinnamon
- 1 cup granola cereal
- ½ cup dried apricots, chopped
- ½ cup slivered almonds, chopped

In a large bowl, beat butter with sugar until smoothly mixed. Beat in eggs, 1 at a time. Stir in milk and almond extract.

In another bowl, stir together all-purpose flour, whole-wheat flour, baking powder, cinnamon, granola, apricots, and almonds. Add to butter mixture and beat just until moistened.

Divide batter equally among 12 greased or paper-lined muffin cups (2½-in. size). Bake in a 325° oven until muffins are browned and spring back when lightly touched in center, 25 to 30 minutes. Serve warm or cool. If made ahead, wrap airtight when cool; hold at room temperature up until next day or freeze to store longer. Makes 12.— *Heather Green, Lava Hot Springs, Idaho.*

PER MUFFIN: 222 calories, 5.3 g protein, 30 g carbohydrates, 9.6 g fat (4 g saturated), 46 mg cholesterol, 134 mg sodium

Canned tomato, tuna, and beans unite in a hearty, 30-minute main-dish soup.

TUNA BEAN SOUP

- 1 large (about 10 oz.) onion
- ¼ pound mushrooms, rinsed
- 5 cups regular-strength chicken broth
- 2 cans (15 oz. each) pinto beans
- 2 cans (15 oz. each) kidney beans
- 1 can (28 oz.) chopped tomatoes
- 1 can (8 oz.) tomato sauce
- ½ teaspoon dried oregano leaves
- 2 cans (about 6 oz. each) water-packed albacore tuna, drained
  Minced green onions (optional)

Chop onion and slice mushrooms. Put in a 5- to 6-quart pan over medium-high heat; cover. Cook until vegetables exude juices, 5 to 8 minutes. Uncover and boil over high heat until liquid evaporates and browned bits form in pan; stir often. Add ¼ cup broth; stir to scrape browned bits free. Boil until liquid evaporates and vegetables are browned.

Rinse beans; drain. Add to pan with remaining broth, tomatoes and their liquid, tomato sauce, and oregano. Bring to a boil over high heat. Cover; simmer 15 minutes. (If made ahead, cool, cover, and chill up to 1 day. Reheat over medium heat; stir often.) Stir in tuna; ladle into bowls and top with green onions. Makes about 3½ quarts, 8 to 10 servings.—*Ellen S. Thomas, Portland.*

PER SERVING: 199 calories, 19 g protein, 25 g carbohydrates, 2.6 g fat (0.3 g saturated), 13 mg cholesterol, 1,127 mg sodium

Maple syrup and orange juice bring out sweetness in tender curried carrots.

CURRY-GLAZED CARROTS

- 1 teaspoon curry powder
- 1¼ pounds carrots, cut diagonally into ¼-inch slices
- 1 tablespoon grated orange peel
- ¾ cup orange juice
- 2 tablespoons maple syrup
- 1 teaspoon cornstarch mixed with 1 tablespoon water
- 2 tablespoons minced parsley
  Salt and pepper

In a 10- to 12-inch frying pan, stir curry powder over medium-high heat until powder smells toasted, about 2 minutes. To pan, add carrots, orange peel, orange juice, and maple syrup. Bring mixture to a boil over high heat; then reduce heat and simmer, uncovered, until carrots are just tender when pierced, about 15 minutes. Stir cornstarch mixture into carrots and cook, stirring, until sauce is boiling.

Pour carrots and sauce into a serving bowl. Sprinkle with parsley and add salt and pepper to taste. Makes 4 servings.—*Virginia Banks, Bremerton, Wash.*

PER SERVING: 113 calories, 1.9 g protein, 27 g carbohydrates, 0.4 g fat (0 g saturated), 0 mg cholesterol, 52 mg sodium

CHICKEN CAPOCOLLO

4 green onions, ends trimmed
2 teaspoons olive oil
2 cloves garlic, minced or pressed
4 boned and skinned chicken breast halves (about 1 lb. total)
4 thin slices (about 1 oz. total) capocollo (or coppa) sausage or prosciutto
¼ cup regular-strength chicken broth or dry white wine
2 tablespoons Dijon mustard
1 tablespoon lemon juice
½ teaspoon dried basil leaves

Chop onions and put in a 10- to 12-inch frying pan over medium heat with oil and garlic. Stir often until vegetables are lightly browned, about 3 minutes.

With a flat mallet, gently pound chicken breasts between sheets of plastic wrap until meat is evenly ⅓ to ½ inch thick. Lay a slice of capocollo on each breast, pressing lightly so that chicken and sausage stick together.

Pushing vegetables aside, lay chicken pieces in pan. Cook just until edges of breasts begin to brown on underside, about 4 minutes. Turn over and cook until breasts are no longer pink in center (cut to test). Transfer meat, sausage up, to a platter; keep warm.

In pan, mix broth, mustard, lemon juice, and basil. Stir on high heat until boiling rapidly, then pour over meat. Makes 4 servings.—*Maggie Morgan, Sun City, Ariz.*

PER SERVING: 176 calories, 28 g protein, 2.8 g carbohydrates, 4.9 g fat (0.9 g saturated), 70 mg cholesterol, 410 mg sodium

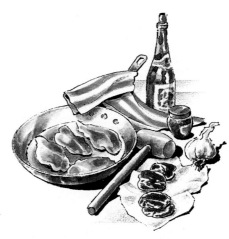

Spicy capocollo sausage and chicken breasts, pounded, pan-brown together.

MEXICAN POLENTA

2 slices (about 1¼ oz. total) bacon
1 small (about 6 oz.) onion, chopped
1 package (10 oz.) frozen corn, thawed
2 large (about 5 oz. total) fresh Anaheim or New Mexico chilies, stemmed, seeded, and minced
½ cup minced fresh cilantro (coriander)
3 to 3½ cups regular-strength chicken broth
1½ cups polenta or yellow cornmeal
About 1 cup purchased salsa (optional)

Place bacon in a shallow 1½- to 2-quart microwave-safe casserole. Cook at full power (100 percent), uncovered, until

bacon is crisp and browned, about 2 minutes. Remove bacon and drain on absorbent towels.

In casserole, mix drippings with the onion, corn, and chilies. Cook at full power, uncovered, for 3 minutes. Stir in cilantro, 3 cups broth, and polenta. Cook at full power until liquid is absorbed and mixture is thick but still creamy, 15 to 20 minutes; stir every 2 to 3 minutes. If mixture gets too stiff to stir, mix in remaining broth.

Crumble bacon over polenta. Offer salsa to add to taste. Makes 6 to 8 servings.—*Linda M. Pickenpaugh, Redding, Calif.*

PER SERVING: 175 calories, 5 g protein, 31 g carbohydrates, 3.9 g fat (1.2 g saturated), 2.9 mg cholesterol, 54 mg sodium

Microwave-cooked polenta, chilies take an occasional stir; offer with salsa.

IRISH CREAM CHOCOLATE SAUCE

1 cup unsweetened cocoa
1¼ cups sugar
½ cup Irish cream liqueur or strong coffee
⅓ cup half-and-half (light cream)
¼ cup (⅛ lb.) butter or margarine
Ice cream, pound cake, or fresh fruit and angel food cake

In a 2- to 3-quart pan, mix cocoa and sugar, then blend in liqueur and half-and-half. Add butter and stir over medium heat until sugar dissolves,

butter melts, and mixture is smooth.

If made ahead, let sauce cool; cover and chill up to 1 week. Stir over low heat until warm and smooth.

Pour warm sauce over ice cream or sliced pound cake, or put in a small bowl and serve as a dessert dip for fruit and angel food cake. Makes 1½ cups.—*Ellen Ross-Cardoso, Poulsbo, Wash.*

PER TABLESPOON: 88 calories, 0.8 g protein, 14 g carbohydrates, 3.6 g fat (2.2 g saturated), 8.9 mg cholesterol, 22 mg sodium

Smooth, rich chocolate and liqueur sauce slides over ice cream.

Chefs of the West®
Adventures with Food

INTERSTATE 5 BETWEEN *Grants Pass and Roseburg, Oregon, is a stately roller coaster of a road that takes you through forests and farms over four passes. In the valley between Stage Road Pass and Smith Hill Summit lies Wolf Creek, one of those places in which the elevation exceeds the population by a considerable amount. Travelers in a hurry know it as a place to fuel up, while seasoned travelers know it as the site of the Wolf Creek Tavern, a restaurant in a restored historic stage stop.*

From now on, Chefs of the West will know it as the home of Lennart Pugh's Wolf Creek Macaroni and Cheese. Preparation is simplicity itself, requiring just two pans and no oven. The secrets of its success are the vegetables and the cheese sauce, which will make you sing "Oh, what a beautiful Mornay!"

WOLF CREEK MACARONI & CHEESE

- 1 tablespoon butter or margarine
- 1 medium-size (about 5 oz.) onion, chopped
- ¼ cup all-purpose flour
- 1 cup milk
- 1 cup regular-strength chicken broth
- ¾ pound sharp cheddar cheese, shredded
- 1 tablespoon Dijon mustard
- 3 large (about ¾ lb. total) carrots, thinly sliced
- 4 cups broccoli flowerets
- 2 cups cauliflowerets
- 1½ cups dried elbow macaroni
  Paprika
  Salt and pepper

Melt butter in a 2- to 3-quart pan over medium-high heat; add onion and stir often until limp, about 5 minutes. Stir in flour; remove from heat and smoothly blend in milk and broth. Return to high heat and stir until boiling. Add cheese and mustard, reduce heat to low, and stir until cheese is melted. Keep the sauce warm.

Meanwhile, bring 3 quarts water to a boil in a 6- to 8-quart pan over high heat; add carrots, broccoli, cauliflower, and macaroni. Cook, uncovered, until vegetables are just tender when pierced and macaroni is just tender to bite, about 7 minutes. Drain well. Pour into a wide, shallow bowl, and mix with warm cheese sauce. Dust with paprika. Add salt and pepper to taste. Makes 10 cups; serves 8 to 10.

PER SERVING: 275 calories, 14 g protein, 24 g carbohydrates, 14 g fat (8.5 g saturated), 42 mg cholesterol, 312 mg sodium

Lennart Pugh

Wolf Creek, Oreg.

"This historic stage stop is the home of Wolf Creek Macaroni and Cheese."

"Sardine Appetizers need only one bowl, one fork, and one knife to prepare."

MANY WOULD-BE *Chefs of the West submit recipes of Byzantine intricacy, with long lists of ingredients and complex instructions. It is a rare occasion when someone is bold enough to send in a recipe that has only four ingredients and needs only one bowl, one fork, and one knife to prepare.*

Steve Stephenson sends us this example of Doric simplicity. In his Sardine Appetizers, the basic ingredients are certainly basic enough: cream cheese lightens and extends the flavor of sardines, and thin rye toast offers solid support. The surprise ingredient is Japanese pickled ginger (buy it refrigerated or canned in Oriental food stores).

This ginger comes from a plant that is closely related to the more familiar ginger that gives us the powdered spice and the fresh or preserved root. It is miyoga ginger, a plant widely grown in Japan for its shoots rather than its roots. These shoots, finely cut, are pickled and used as a garnish in many Japanese dishes; you may have seen them wrapped in rice and seaweed in sushi. This ginger's flavor is almost impossible to describe, but sharp, warm, and fragrant are adjectives that readily come to mind.

SARDINE APPETIZERS

1 package (8 oz.) neufchâtel (light cream) cheese or cream cheese
1 can (3¾ oz.) brisling sardines in olive oil, drained and mashed
About 24 pieces rye melba toast
About ¼ cup thin slices or fine slivers of red or pink pickled ginger

In a small bowl, stir together cheese and sardines. Spread on toast and top each portion with about ½ teaspoon ginger. Makes about 24; serves 8 to 10.

PER PIECE: 54 calories, 2.7 g protein, 4.5 g carbohydrates, 2.8 g fat (1.5 g saturated), 13 mg cholesterol, 122 mg sodium

San Jose

PORK SHOULDER STEAKS *make a savory main dish with a little help from the four musketeers of Mexican cuisine—chili powder, cumin, green chilies, and sour cream. Wayne Gordon uses the first two, along with vinegar, to make a coating for the steaks. The chilies form the base of a salsa, along with tomato, onion, and the omnipresent cilantro. Sour cream garnishes each portion.*

That the red and green chilies and the sour cream are the colors of the Mexican flag is probably no more than a coincidence.

PORK STEAKS WITH GREEN CHILI SALSA

4 boned pork shoulder steaks (about 6 oz. each), cut ½ inch thick
1 tablespoon chili powder
¼ teaspoon ground cumin
1 tablespoon red wine vinegar
About 4 teaspoons salad oil
Green chili salsa (recipe follows)
Sour cream
Salt

Trim and discard fat from pork; put pieces of meat between sheets of plastic wrap and pound with flat mallet until about ⅛ inch thick. If you do this step ahead, wrap meat airtight and chill up until next day.

In a small bowl, stir together chili powder, cumin, and vinegar. Remove wrap from pork; rub chili mixture evenly on all sides of meat.

Heat 1 teaspoon oil in a nonstick 10- to 12-inch frying pan over high heat; add pork without crowding and cook until edges turn white. Turn and cook until no longer pink in center (about 2½ minutes total; cut to test). Transfer to platter as cooked and keep warm. Add meat to pan as space is available; add more oil as needed. Serve pork with salsa, sour cream, and salt to taste. Makes 4 servings.

PER SERVING: 422 calories, 40 g protein, 1.2 g carbohydrates, 27 g fat (8.3 g saturated), 148 mg cholesterol, 115 mg sodium

Green chili salsa. Core and chop 1 large (about ½ lb.) firm-ripe **tomato.** Mix with ½ cup chopped **onion,** 1 can (4 oz.) **diced green chilies,** and 1 tablespoon chopped **fresh cilantro** (coriander). Makes 2 cups.

PER ¼ CUP: 12 calories, 0.5 g protein, 2.7 g carbohydrates, 0.1 g fat (0 g saturated), 0 mg cholesterol, 89 mg sodium

Lahaina, Maui, Hawaii

"The chilies and sour cream are the colors of the Mexican flag."

February Menus

HEARTS AND FLOWERS *bring romance to a valentine dinner for two. If others in the family have consented to eat earlier, start preparing this intimate meal while tending to them; the whole family gets full attention other nights.*

Two suppers round out our menus. One is a spruced-up old favorite, macaroni and cheese, made with a fanciful pasta and a light sauce plus a vegetable. It goes together in a series of quick steps. The other takes inspiration from Indian cuisine and makes use of aromatic seasonings to give complexity and polish to an all-vegetable main dish.

ROMANTIC DINNER FOR TWO

Roast Rack of Lamb
with Petite Vegetables
Heart Rolls
**Chocolate Ice Cream with
Fruit Wines or Cordials**
Merlot or Pinot Noir

As much as a day ahead, you can pan-brown the lamb rack and chill with the seasonings; you can also bake the rolls. At the same time, ready vegetables for cooking. With these tasks completed, the meal takes only one pan and about 45 minutes in the oven.

Dessert couldn't be easier: a selection of fruit-rich or late-harvest dessert wines, or fruit cordials, to pour onto scoops of chocolate ice cream.

ROAST RACK OF LAMB
WITH PETITE VEGETABLES

1 **rack of lamb (2 to 2½ lb.), rib ends trimmed (French-cut) and chine (back) bone removed or cracked**
3 **tablespoons *each* Dijon mustard and honey**
3 **cloves garlic, minced or pressed**
1½ **teaspoons minced fresh or dried rosemary leaves**
   About ½ teaspoon pepper
4 **large (about 1 lb. total) carrots**
1 **tablespoon olive oil**

Candlelight enhances romantic Valentine's dinner perfect for two: rack of lamb served with petite roasted vegetables and crusty, heart-shaped rolls.

8 **small (each about 1½ in. wide) thin-skinned potatoes, scrubbed**
8 **small (each about 1 in. wide) onions**
⅓ **pound slender green beans, ends and strings removed**
½ **cup *each* dry red wine and regular-strength chicken broth**
2 **teaspoons cornstarch mixed with 1 tablespoon water**
   About 1 cup watercress sprigs, rinsed and crisped (optional)
   Salt

Trim fat from lamb. In a 10- to 12-inch nonstick frying pan over high heat, brown meat side of rack and the 2 ends, about 4 minutes total. Transfer meat, bones down, to a plate.

Mix together mustard, honey, garlic, rosemary, and ½ teaspoon pepper. Coat rack with mustard sauce; chill at least 1 hour or up to overnight (when cool, wrap airtight).

Meanwhile, peel carrots. Cut a V-shaped gutter (about ¼ in. deep and ¼ in. wide) down the length of each carrot. Then slice carrots crosswise into ¼-inch-thick pieces. To make hearts, trim round sides of slices to a point opposite gutter. Discard scraps.

THE DETAILS

Carrot hearts. *Cut V-shaped trough down carrot side; slice. Trim to make hearts.*

Heart rolls. *Stretch and twist thawed frozen bread dough; loop into crusty hearts.*

Nosegay napkin. *Wired ribbon makes napkin holder; tuck a rose under bow.*

Fruit essences. *Offer a selection of fruity, sweet wines or cordials with dessert.*

Pour oil into a 10- by 15-inch pan; add potatoes and onions and mix well. Bake in a 400° oven for 15 minutes. Stir and add carrots and green beans. Bake, stirring often with a wide spatula, for 15 minutes more (vegetables will darken at edges).

Push vegetables to one side of pan. Set lamb, bones down, in clear space. Increase oven temperature to 500°. Cook until a meat thermometer inserted through thickest part of meat to bone reaches 150°; this should take 15 to 20 minutes. Put meat and vegetables on a platter; keep warm.

Quickly add wine and broth to pan. Over high heat, stir to release browned bits, and boil until liquid is reduced to about ¾ cup. Stirring, add cornstarch mixture, and continue to stir until boiling. Pour sauce through a fine strainer into a small bowl. Discard residue.

Cut rack into 4 double-rib pieces. On 2 warmed dinner plates, arrange lamb, vegetables, and watercress. Offer sauce, salt, and pepper to add to taste. Makes 2 servings.

PER SERVING: 877 calories, 51 g protein, 101 g carbohydrates, 31 g fat (8.7 g saturated), 140 mg cholesterol, 914 mg sodium

HEART ROLLS

> 1 loaf (1 lb.) thawed frozen white or whole-wheat bread dough
> About 2 tablespoons olive oil
> About 2 teaspoons kosher salt

Cut loaf into 4 equal pieces. On a lightly floured board, squeeze and gently pull each piece to make a 22-inch rope. Twist each rope about 8 turns, then loop to form a heart about 4 inches wide on a lightly oiled 14- by 17-inch baking sheet (or 2 pans, 10 by 15 in.); keep hearts at least 2 inches apart. Brush dough with oil; cover lightly with plastic wrap, and let rise until puffy-looking, about 20 minutes.

Sprinkle hearts with salt. Bake in a 400° oven until rolls are golden brown, about 20 minutes (if using 2 pans in 1 oven, switch pan positions halfway through baking). Serve warm, or cool and wrap airtight up to the next day. To reheat, place on baking sheet in a 400° oven until warm, about 5 minutes. Makes 4 rolls; each serves 1 or 2.

PER PIECE: 158 calories, 4.3 g protein, 25 g carbohydrates, 4.6 g fat (0.5 g saturated), 0 mg cholesterol, 698 mg sodium

Peas and whimsical pasta, with a light cheese sauce, go with smoked pork chops.

A '90s MACARONI & CHEESE SUPPER

Smoked Pork Chops with Pasta & Cheese
Mixed Green Salad
Milk   Zinfandel
Toasted Pound Cake with Berry Jam
Earl Grey Tea

Nowadays, macaroni is better known as pasta. And to make this up-to-date version of macaroni and cheese, we use whimsical wagon wheel–shaped pasta. To the cooking pasta, you add green peas—an Italian touch. Then combine the hot, drained mixture with a light cheese sauce. As pasta cooks, mix the salad.

(Continued on next page)

A comforting conclusion for the meal is also an old favorite—pound cake, home-made or purchased. Toast slices under the broiler or in a toaster, then serve warm with jam and an aromatic tea. This is also an ideal refreshment for teatime.

SMOKED PORK CHOPS WITH PASTA & CHEESE

4 smoked pork loin chops (about 1¼ lb. total; each chop about ¾ in. thick)
6 ounces dried wagon wheels, rotelle, or bow-shaped pasta
1 package (10 oz.) frozen petite peas
1 tablespoon butter or margarine
1 large (10 oz.) onion, chopped
1 tablespoon all-purpose flour
1½ cups low-fat milk
1 tablespoon Dijon mustard
¼ teaspoon pepper
1 cup (4 oz.) shredded Swiss cheese

In a 10- to 12-inch nonstick frying pan over medium-high heat, brown chops well, about 10 minutes total. Remove from pan; keep warm.

As meat browns, bring about 3 quarts water in a 5- to 6-quart pan to boiling on high heat. Add pasta and cook, uncovered, just until tender to bite, about 8 minutes. Hit package of peas against a counter to break peas apart. Stir into cooked pasta; drain and set mixture aside.

As water heats, melt butter in frying pan over medium-high heat. Add onion; stir often until limp, about 6 minutes. Stir in flour; remove the pan from heat and smoothly stir in milk, mustard, and pepper.

Return sauce to heat and stir until boiling. Add cheese and mix until melted. Remove from heat, add pasta, and mix well. Pour pasta onto platter with meat. Makes 4 servings.

PER SERVING: 651 calories, 47 g protein, 62 g carbohydrates, 23 g fat (11 g saturated), 100 mg cholesterol, 1,962 mg sodium

INDIAN DAL DINNER

Yellow Split Pea Dal
with Brown Rice &
Broccoli
Orange Slices
with Brown Sugar
Chenin Blanc or Beer

This low-fat, satisfying vegetable-based dal, made with dried split peas, has the rich flavors of an Indian curry.

YELLOW SPLIT PEA DAL WITH BROWN RICE & BROCCOLI

1 cup yellow split peas
About 5½ cups regular-strength chicken broth
2 large (10 oz. each) onions, chopped
2 large (½ lb. total) carrots, diced
2 tablespoons minced fresh ginger
2 large cloves garlic, minced or pressed

2 teaspoons *each* ground turmeric and chili powder
1 large can (28 oz.) crushed tomatoes
1 pound banana or hubbard squash, peeled and cut into ¾-inch cubes
About 6 cups hot cooked brown rice
3 cups hot cooked broccoli flowerets
½ cup fresh cilantro (coriander) leaves
About 1 cup unflavored nonfat yogurt
Lime wedges
Crushed dried hot red chilies and salt

Sort split peas to remove debris; rinse and let drain.

In a 6- to 8-quart pan, mix 1 cup broth, onions, carrots, ginger, and garlic. Stir often on high heat until liquid evaporates and vegetables start to brown, 12 to 15 minutes. Stir in ⅓ cup broth, releasing browned bits. Stir often until mixture browns again, about 4 minutes. Repeat about 3 more times until vegetables are richly browned, using about 1 cup broth total.

Add peas, turmeric, chili powder, tomatoes and juice, and remaining broth. Bring to a boil; cover and simmer 1 hour.

Add squash; cover and simmer until tender to bite, 40 to 50 minutes more, stirring often. Spoon rice and broccoli onto plates; add dal to each. Season to taste with cilantro, yogurt, lime, chilies, and salt. Makes 6 or 7 servings.

PER SERVING: 425 calories, 20 g protein, 80 g carbohydrates, 4.1 g fat (0.8 g saturated), 0.6 mg cholesterol, 300 mg sodium

MARCH

Sorbet in Cookie Tulips (page 60)

Salute our southern
neighbor with a festive dinner featuring one of Mexico's
finest traditional dishes—mole poblano, a mellow sauce rich
with chilies, chocolate, and aromatic herbs and spices.
For springtime barbecues, try the succulent skewered tidbit
combinations; you prepare them in advance, then pop
skewers on the grill when guests arrive. Our luscious May
desserts revel in tropical pleasures; chefs from some of
Hawaii's leading restaurants share fruit sorbets and treats
featuring coconut, macadamia nuts, and fresh pineapple.

Mexico's Regal Sauce

MOLE POBLANO *may belong to Puebla, but all of Mexico honors it as one of the nation's finest dishes. This rich, thick sauce of chilies and other indigenous ingredients also contains chocolate—to the uninitiated, a rash choice; to the knowing, an inspiration.*

The word mole actually has broader meaning. It comes from mulli in the language of the pre-Columbian Nahuatl Indians in Mexico and loosely translates as sauce. An example of an everyday encounter is in guacamole, Mexico's ubiquitous avocado sauce.

The Pueblans named their mole for themselves; poblano means the people of Puebla. In addition to mole poblano, the area is known for several other moles with chocolate, all characteristically thick and complex.

Moles, however, are not exclusive to Puebla. The Mexican state of Oaxaca is famous for moles of a distinctly different kind, including seven moles often called the Seven Sisters.

Mole poblano has a precise birthplace and exceptionally detailed, though contradictory, dates of origin. Usually, the inventor is a 17th-century nun, Sister Andrea de la Asunción, at the Santa Rosa Convent. The Mother Superior called upon her to create a special dish for visiting dignitaries expected on a Sunday sometime between 1657 and 1688, or later, depending on the source. Legend has it that the request came on short notice, and Sister Andrea had to scramble to come up with something new from her existing supplies of ingredients. It seems fairly obvious that she, or more likely the native women helping in the kitchen, started with mixtures they all knew well, like local chili paste blends, herbs, seeds, and vegetables. But the big leap from standard mole to mole poblano was the chocolate that Sister Andrea or one of her assistants added, which gave the mixture a uniquely mellow, sophisticated complexity. It's not surprising that a native woman would find chocolate to be a perfect ingredient in a dish for regal gentlemen: in Aztec culture, chocolate was reserved for royal males.

Turkey, a native bird, was used in the first mole poblano; chicken and other meats—and even vegetables—are commonly used now. But the mole takes no back seat to the meat. First-time tasters of mole poblano (or any kind of mole) may be daunted by foods swimming in sauce. But Mexicans view the sauce to be as important as the meat and scoop the abundance freely onto tortillas or ladle it over rice—tasty combinations, we agree.

Sister Andrea is, no doubt, still savoring her success in Heaven. But the guests bestowed upon the convent a lasting material award. They had the kitchen refurbished with magnificent tiles. This tiled kitchen was a first in the New World.

You can still visit it in the former convent, now the Museo de Artesanías, at 12 Poniente and Calle 3 Norte; it's open 10 to 5 daily except Mondays.

One wonders if it was pride in these tiles that spurred the development of Puebla's renowned ceramics.

Among moles, mole poblano is usually quite mellow, slightly sweet, and certainly regal. Each Pueblan cook personalizes the balance of flavors, and our own version captures the essence of various interpretations.

Blends of chilies bring warmth; assorted vegetables, including corn in tortillas, give volume and flavor; fruits and aromatic spices sweeten, perfume, and soften the impact of the chilies; nuts and seeds add not only nuances of taste, but also thickness and body.

Finally, all the potions are poured into one large pan and simmered to unite the flavors. Then comes the magic ingredient, chocolate, adding its elusive presence to the sauce.

Traditional moles of Puebla often include volumes of lard. To accommodate today's tastes, we opted to dry-roast rather than fry components; the results are comparable in flavor and significantly lighter in calories.

Mexican chocolate (sweetened and flavored with cinnamon) and dried chilies for mole are available where Mexican foods are sold; many chilies are found in supermarkets.

One mail-order source for a wide selection of chilies is Coyote Cafe General Store, 132 W. Water St., First Floor, Santa Fe, N.Mex. 87501; for costs, call (505) 982-2454 between 11 and 7 mountain time. You may need to order the green tomatillos at a produce market.

MOLE POBLANO

Four steps create the sauce; each element can be made a day or so ahead. A fifth step tells you how to use the sauce.

Finally, we offer a simple but traditional menu featuring mole poblano.

1 ROASTING THE CHILIES

- ½ **pound (about 16) dried mulato chilies**
- ¼ **pound (about 8) dried ancho chilies**
- 2 **ounces (about 3) dried pasilla chilies**
- 1 **dried chipotle chili (or 2 teaspoons minced canned chipotle chilies)**

Lay dried mulato, ancho, pasilla, and chipotle chilies in a single layer in 10- by 15-inch pans (add canned chipotle later). Bake in a 300° oven until chilies smell lightly toasted and are flexible, 5 to 8 minutes. While they are still warm, discard stems and shake out seeds.

Rinse chilies and put in a large bowl; add 8 cups boiling water. Let stand until soft, 20 to 30 minutes. Drain; save liquid. Smoothly purée chilies (and canned chipotle), a portion at a time, in a food processor or blender. Add a total of 2 cups reserved liquid. (In processor, use a little liquid to get mixture moving; add rest when puréed.) Rub firmly through fine strainer into a bowl; discard residue. Use, or chill airtight up to 1 day.

2 ROASTING THE VEGETABLES

- 2 **large (about 1 lb. total) onions, quartered**
- 1 **medium-size (about ½ lb.) tomato**
- ½ **pound tomatillos, husked and rinsed**
- 1 **medium-size (about 3 oz.) head garlic, cut in half horizontally**
- 2 **corn tortillas (each about 7 in.)**

In a 10- by 15-inch pan, combine onions, tomato, tomatillos, garlic (cut side down), and tortillas. Bake in a 450° oven, turning occasionally, until the vegetables and tortillas have dark brown spots or edges. Let cool. Pull off vegetable skins and discard.

(Continued on page 56)

Sunday dinner with the Moraleses in Puebla features lavish sauce—mole poblano—with chicken. Thick, mellow sauce is also ladled over rice and scooped onto tortillas. Located southeast of Mexico City, Puebla is famous for its colorful ceramics.

Chilies to roast. *Typical choices for mole base (clockwise from top left) are ancho, guajillo, pasilla, chipotle, New Mexico, mulato, chili seed.*

Vegetables to roast. *Onions, garlic, tomatoes, and tomatillos are used in moles as a background for other, more pronounced flavors.*

Smoothly purée mixture in a food processor or blender; add a total of 1 cup reserved chili-soaking liquid from step 1. (In processor, use a little liquid to get mixture moving; add rest when puréed.) Rub firmly through fine strainer into a bowl; discard residue. Use, or chill airtight up to 1 day.

3 COOKING THE SEASONINGS & THICKENERS

½ **cup sesame seed**
2 **tablespoons salad oil**
1 **small (about ½ lb.) ripe plantain (skin is black), peeled and chopped**
½ **cup** *each* **dry-roasted almonds and peanuts**

½ **cup chopped, pitted prunes**
⅓ **cup raisins**
2 **sticks cinnamon, each about 2 inches long**
1 **teaspoon** *each* **coriander seed and anise seed**

In a 10- to 12-inch frying pan over medium heat, stir sesame seed until toasted, about 4 minutes; set aside.

To pan, add oil, plantain, almonds, peanuts, prunes, raisins, cinnamon, coriander, and anise. Stir often over medium heat until mixture is richly browned, 10 to 15 minutes. Smoothly purée mixture and sesame seed in a food processor or blender. Add remaining chili-soaking liquid from step 1. (In

processor, use a little liquid to get mixture moving; add rest when puréed.) Use, or chill airtight up to 1 day.

4 ASSEMBLING THE MOLE

Roasted chilies (preceding)
Roasted vegetables (preceding)
Seasonings and thickeners (preceding)
2 **cups regular-strength chicken broth**
4 **ounces Mexican chocolate (or 4 ounces semisweet chocolate and ½ teaspoon ground cinnamon)**

In a 5- to 6-quart pan, mix chilies, vegetables, seasonings and thickeners, and broth. Bring to a simmer on medium heat; cover and simmer to blend flavors, about 2 hours, stirring often.

Seasonings and thickeners. *Chocolate (disk, above right) is the key element in moles of Puebla. Mole poblano uses fruits, nuts, tortillas, and aromatic spices and seeds; other moles use similar ingredients in different proportions, and often savory herbs like oregano, thyme, and marjoram.*

Chop chocolate; mix with sauce until melted. Use mole as suggested, following; or chill airtight up to 1 week or freeze up to 3 months. Makes 10 cups; allow 1 to 2 cups for a serving.

PER CUP: 412 calories, 13 g protein, 59 g carbohydrates, 19 g fat (4 g saturated), 0 mg cholesterol, 46 mg sodium

5 SERVING MOLE POBLANO

The Morales family in Puebla served us this easy-to-duplicate dinner (once the sauce is made) featuring mole poblano with cooked chicken. This festive dish is a favorite for family gatherings and holidays and is often served in their tree-shaded garden.

MOLE POBLANO DINNER

String Cheese   Guacamole
Warm Corn Tortillas
Mole Poblano with Poultry
Hot Rice
Refried Beans with Cheese
Green Salad   Hard Rolls
Pineapple   Watermelon

Start with string cheese and guacamole to eat with tortillas. Also, serve tortillas with the mole.

Sprinkle beans (canned or homemade) with crumbled cotija (a Mexican cheese) or grated parmesan cheese.

To present mole poblano for 6 to 8 servings, pour 6 to 8 cups warm **mole poblano** sauce over 6 to 8 warm, poached or baked skinned **chicken breast halves** (about 3 lb. total) or 1½ to 2 pounds warm, sliced cooked boned and skinned turkey breast. Scatter **toasted sesame seed, fresh cilantro** (coriander) **sprigs,** and thin **onion** slices over sauce. Offer **salt** and **lime wedges.**

OTHER WAYS WITH MOLE

Ladle the warm sauce over slices of any cut of roast, grilled, or unseasoned braised **pork.** Mole also suits grilled **beef** such as skirt steaks, flank steaks, and tenderloin.

Tidbits on Skewers

FLAVORFUL MORSELS *on a stick—peppered beef with savory-tart onion marmalade, shrimp with pancetta, and pork enriched with a maple syrup–miso marinade—make great menu starters. They can also be prepared up to a day ahead.*

PEPPERED BEEF SKEWERS WITH RED ONION–HORSERADISH MARMALADE

> 3 cloves garlic, pressed or minced
> 2 tablespoons soy sauce
> 1 tablespoon pepper
> 1 pound tender beef, such as top sirloin or loin, about ¾ to 1 inch thick and trimmed of fat
> Red onion–horseradish marmalade (recipe follows)

In a bowl, mix garlic, soy, and pepper. Cut beef into ¼-inch-thick strips about 3 inches long. Mix with seasonings. Cover and chill for 1 hour or up until the next day.

Weave slender skewers through the meat, keeping strips flat. Place on a grill 4 to 6 inches above a solid bed of hot coals (you can hold your hand at grill level for only 2 to 3 seconds). Turn to brown evenly, about 4 minutes. Serve meat, on or off skewers, with marmalade. Makes 8 appetizers or 4 main-dish servings.

PER APPETIZER SERVING: 104 calories, 11 g protein, 1.3 g carbohydrates, 6 g fat (2.3 g saturated), 34 mg cholesterol, 282 mg sodium

Red onion–horseradish marmalade. Peel and dice 1 pound **red onions.** In a 10- to 12-inch frying pan over medium-high heat, mix onions, 1 tablespoon **olive** or salad **oil,** and 2 tablespoons firmly packed **brown sugar.** Cover; stir occasionally until any juices have evaporated and onion is golden brown, about 8 minutes.

Add ⅓ cup *each* **red wine vinegar** and **white wine** and 2 teaspoons **prepared horseradish;** stir often, uncovered, until liquid evaporates, about 6 minutes. Serve warm or cool. If made ahead, let cool, cover, and chill up to 3 days. Makes about 1 cup.

PER TABLESPOON: 28 calories, 0.3 g protein, 4 g carbohydrates, 1 g fat (0.1 g saturated), 0 mg cholesterol, 2 mg sodium

GRILLED SHRIMP & PANCETTA WITH GARBANZO SALSA

> 24 large (31 to 35 per lb.; about ¾ lb. total) shrimp
> About ⅓ pound thinly sliced pancetta or ½ pound bacon
> Garbanzo salsa (recipe follows)

Peel shrimp (leave on tail section, if desired), devein, and rinse. Divide pancetta into 24 equal pieces. Tightly wrap a pancetta piece around each shrimp.

Push a slender skewer through the pancetta and shrimp just above the shrimp's tail and out through the pancetta at the fat end of the shrimp. Push another pancetta-wrapped shrimp onto the skewer in the same fashion; use 2 shrimp per skewer. If assembled ahead, cover and chill up until the next day.

Lay shrimp on a grill 2 to 4 inches above a solid bed of medium-hot coals (you can hold your hand at grill level for only 3 to 4 seconds). Turn frequently (watch for flares from drips) to brown evenly, cooking until shrimp are opaque in center (cut to test), about 5 minutes. Dunk shrimp in salsa, as desired. Makes 12; allow 2 per serving as appetizers, 4 as a main dish.

PER SKEWER: 44 calories, 5.7 g protein, 0.2 g carbohydrates, 2 g fat (0.6 g saturated), 38 mg cholesterol, 90 mg sodium

Garbanzo salsa. Drain 1 can (8 oz.) **garbanzos;** whirl smooth in a food processor or blender with 1 cup **fresh cilantro** (coriander), ⅓ cup **unflavored nonfat**

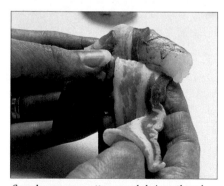

Snugly wrap pancetta around shrimp; thread two shrimp on each skewer.

yogurt, ⅓ cup chopped **green onions,** and ¼ cup **lime juice.** Add **salt** and **pepper** to taste. Makes 1 cup.

PER TABLESPOON: 14 calories, 0.8 g protein, 2.2 g carbohydrates, 0.2 g fat (0 g saturated), 0.1 mg cholesterol, 20 mg sodium

MISO- & MAPLE-MARINATED PORK WITH APPLE & ONION

Look for aka miso (red fermented soybean paste) in Japanese and Chinese food markets.

> 1 pound boned and fat-trimmed pork tenderloin or center-cut loin
> ⅓ cup aka miso
> ⅓ cup maple syrup
> ¼ cup sake, dry white wine, or water
> 2 tablespoons minced fresh ginger
> 2 medium-size (about 1 lb. total) apples such as Braeburn, Fuji, or McIntosh
> Lemon juice
> 1 large (about ½ lb.) onion, cut into wedges and separated into layers

Cut meat into ⅛-inch-thick slices 6 to 7 inches long. In a heavy plastic food bag (about 1 qt.), combine miso, syrup, sake, ginger, and pork; mix well. Seal shut and chill for at least 1 hour or up until the next day.

Core apples; cut into ½-inch wedges. Moisten wedges with lemon juice to preserve color.

Thread a thin skewer through the end of a pork slice, then a piece of onion and a piece of apple. Weave skewer through meat slice again and repeat process, dividing ingredients among 4 to 8 skewers. If made ahead, cover and chill up to 3 hours.

Lay skewers on a grill 4 to 6 inches above a solid bed of medium coals (you can hold your hand at grill level for only 4 to 5 seconds). Baste with marinade and turn often until meat is no longer pink in center (cut to test), about 10 minutes. Makes 8 appetizers or 4 main-dish servings.

PER SKEWER: 153 calories, 11 g protein, 22 g carbohydrates, 2 g fat (0.5 g saturated), 29 mg cholesterol, 438 mg sodium

Grill an assortment of skewered tidbits to make party appetizers or dinner entrées. Hot off the barbecue are peppered beef with onion–horseradish marmalade, shrimp and pancetta to go with garbanzo salsa, and marinated pork with apple and onion.

Tropical Treasures

A WARM, SANDY BEACH *seems just steps away when you're enjoying one of these tropical indulgences from Hawaii. With ingredients like sweet pineapple and coconut, aromatic mango and guava, and rich macadamia nuts, these desserts are deliciously exotic to the eye as well as to the palate.*

Consider a silken sorbet or a luscious coconut cake. What about a striking pineapple tart? They're all specialties of the Halekulani Hotel on Waikiki. If you're nuts about macadamias, don't miss the cheesecake. It's from the CanoeHouse restaurant at the Mauna Lani Bay Hotel and Bungalows on the Big Island.

Each recipe has make-ahead steps.

SORBET IN COOKIE TULIPS

The chef used a mold to shape cookies; you can form your cookies by draping each hot, pliable cookie over a food can. If you use more than one flavor sorbet, freeze the extra.

> **Guava, pineapple, and/or mango mixture (following)**
> **Cookie tulips (following)**
> **Fresh fruit (optional)**

Pour guava, pineapple, or mango mixture into an ice cream maker. Freeze as manufacturer directs. Use, or freeze airtight up to 1 week. Makes 4½ to 5 cups. Scoop into cookies; add fruit. Makes 6 servings.

Guava mixture. Mix 3 cups **guava nectar** (bottled or thawed frozen reconstituted), ⅔ cup **light corn syrup,** and ¼ cup **lime juice.**

PER ½ CUP GUAVA SORBET: 93 calories, 0 g protein, 23 g carbohydrates, 0 g fat, 0 mg cholesterol, 35 mg sodium

Pineapple mixture. In a blender or food processor, whirl 3 cups peeled and cored **fresh pineapple** chunks, ⅓ cup **light corn syrup,** and ¼ cup **lemon juice** until smooth.

PER ½ CUP PINEAPPLE SORBET: 55 calories, 0.2 g protein, 14 g carbohydrates, 0.2 g fat (0 g saturated), 0 mg cholesterol, 17 mg sodium

Mango mixture. Peel, pit, and cut ripe **mangoes** (about 4 medium-size, 2¾ lb. total) to make 3 cups chunks. In a blender

or food processor, whirl fruit with ⅔ cup **light corn syrup** and ½ cup **lemon juice** until smooth.

PER ½ CUP MANGO SORBET: 122 calories, 0.5 g protein, 31 g carbohydrates, 0.3 g fat (0.1 g saturated), 0 mg cholesterol, 36 mg sodium

Cookie tulips. In a bowl, beat ¼ cup (⅛ lb.) **butter** or margarine and ½ cup **sugar** until smooth. Mix in 7 tablespoons **all-purpose flour,** 1 teaspoon **vanilla,** and 2 large **egg whites** until smooth.

Bake 2 cookies at a time. Butter a 12-by 15-inch baking sheet. With fingertip, draw a 7-inch-wide circle on 1 corner of sheet; repeat in opposite corner. In each circle, spread 3 tablespoons batter to fill evenly.

Bake in a 350° oven until golden, 9 to 10 minutes. At once, lift cookies, 1 at a time, with wide spatula and drape each over a clean 1-pound food can; gently pinch cookie sides to form a fluted cup. Repeat to make remaining cookies. If made ahead, store airtight up to 1 day. Makes 6.

PER COOKIE: 173 calories, 2.2 g protein, 24 g carbohydrates, 7.7 g fat (4.8 g saturated), 21 mg cholesterol, 97 mg sodium

HALEKULANI COCONUT CAKE

> About 1¼ cups cake flour
> About 1 cup sugar
> 1½ teaspoons baking powder
> ¼ cup salad oil
> ¼ cup water
> 5 large eggs
> 2 teaspoons vanilla
> ¼ teaspoon cream of tartar
> 1 cup milk
> 3½ cups (11 oz.) sweetened shredded dried coconut
> 1 cup whipping cream
> Raspberry coulis (following)

For cake. Sift flour; measure 1 cup plus 2 tablespoons. Sift again with ⅓ cup sugar and baking powder into a large bowl. In another bowl, whisk oil, water, 1 egg, and 1 teaspoon vanilla; add to flour mixture and whisk until smooth.

Separate remaining 4 eggs; put yolks in a small bowl. In a clean bowl, beat egg whites and cream of tartar with a mixer until foamy. Gradually add ¼ cup sugar, beating until whites hold firm, moist peaks. Gently fold whites into flour mixture.

Spread batter in an ungreased 9-inch cheesecake pan (at least 2½ in. deep) with a removable rim. Bake in a 350° oven until cake springs back when lightly touched in center, about 30 minutes. Cool on a rack for 10 minutes. Run a knife between cake and rim; invert cake onto rack. Remove rim; slide a spatula along pan bottom and remove. Let cool; if made ahead, store airtight up to 1 day.

For pastry cream. In a 1½- to 2-quart pan, mix ⅓ cup sugar and 1½ tablespoons flour. Whisk in milk. Stir over medium-high heat until boiling, 4 to 6 minutes. Whisk about ½ cup hot mixture into yolks. Stir yolk mixture into pan; whisk over medium-low heat until slightly thicker, 30 to 90 seconds. Stir in 1½ cups coconut and 1 teaspoon vanilla. Let cool, stirring often. Cover and chill until cold, at least 2 hours or up to 1 day.

To assemble cake. With a long serrated knife, cut cake horizontally into 3 equal layers.

In a bowl, whip cream with 2 tablespoons sugar until thick enough to hold its shape; fold ¾ cup into pastry cream. Chill remainder.

Invert cake onto a platter. Slide rimless baking sheets under each of the top 2 layers and lift off. Tuck wide strips of wax paper just under bottom edge of cake. Spread layer almost to edge with half the pastry cream. Slide middle layer onto filling; spread with remaining filling. Slide last layer onto filling. Frost cake with remaining whipped cream. Pat remaining coconut into cream. Cover gently; chill 2 hours or until next day.

Ease out wax paper and discard. Pour raspberry coulis equally onto dessert plates; top with cake wedges. Makes 10 servings.

PER SERVING: 488 calories, 7 g protein, 56 g carbohydrates, 27 g fat (16 g saturated), 136 mg cholesterol, 203 mg sodium

Raspberry coulis. In a blender, whirl until smooth 1 quart (1 lb.) **fresh** or thawed frozen unsweetened **raspberries.** Rub through a fine strainer into a bowl; discard seeds. Add 1 tablespoon **sugar.** If made ahead, chill airtight up to 1 day; stir to use.

(Continued on page 62)

Waikiki sunset brings glow to tulip cookie filled with scoops of pineapple, mango, and guava sorbets and embellished with fresh fruits. To make the fluted cup, shape warm baked cookie over a can and gently pinch into shape. As cookie cools, it gets crisp and rigid.

MACADAMIA CHEESECAKE

- ¾ cup salted macadamia nuts
- ½ cup graham cracker crumbs
- 2 tablespoons butter or margarine, melted
- ½ cup sugar
- 1 small (3 oz.) and 2 large (8 oz. each) packages cream cheese
- 4 large egg yolks
- 3 tablespoons macadamia-, hazelnut-, or almond-flavor liqueur
- 1 teaspoon vanilla
  Lilikoi sauce (following, optional)
  Strawberry sauce (following, optional)
  Whipped cream, strawberries, and mint sprigs (optional)

In a blender, whirl ¼ cup nuts until ground; scrape into an 8-inch cake pan with removable rim. Add cracker crumbs, butter, and 1 tablespoon sugar; mix and press over pan bottom.

Golden passion fruit sauce swims around macadamia cheesecake.

Chop remaining nuts. In a bowl, beat smoothly with a mixer the remaining sugar, cream cheese, yolks, liqueur, and vanilla; scrape bowl as needed. Mix in chopped nuts.

Spread batter onto crust in pan. Bake in a 325° oven until cake jiggles only slightly when gently shaken, about 40 minutes. Let cool on a rack, then cover and chill until cold, at least 2 hours or up to 1 day.

Run a knife between cake and rim; remove rim. Spoon 2 tablespoons lilikoi sauce onto each dessert plate; spoon strawberry sauce in dots onto lilikoi sauce. Pull a knife tip through dots to make designs. Set cake wedges on plates; garnish with cream, berries, and mint. Makes 10 servings.

PER SERVING WITH SAUCES ONLY: 454 calories, 7.6 g protein, 39 g carbohydrates, 31 g fat (15 g saturated), 151 mg cholesterol, 280 mg sodium

Lilikoi sauce. You'll need 1¼ cups **passion fruit purée**, fresh or thawed frozen. Cut 24 passion fruit (about 2 lb. total) in half; scoop pulp and seeds into a fine strainer over a bowl. Rub firmly to remove all pulp from seeds; discard seeds. For frozen purée, call Gourmet France, Inc., at (818) 768-4300; cost is about $12 for 2 pounds, plus shipping.

In a 1- to 1½-quart pan, mix ⅓ cup **sugar** and 1 tablespoon **cornstarch;** add purée. Stir over medium-high heat until boiling, 4 to 5 minutes. Let cool; stir occasionally. If made ahead, chill airtight up to 1 day.

Strawberry sauce. In a blender, smoothly purée ½ cup **strawberries.** Rub through a fine strainer into a bowl; discard seeds. If made ahead, chill airtight up to 1 day; stir to use.

PINEAPPLE TART WITH PIÑA COLADA SAUCE

- About ½ cup sugar
- 4 large egg yolks
  About ¾ cup canned coconut milk
- 1 tablespoon rum (optional)
  All-purpose flour
- 4 frozen puff pastry shells (7 oz. total), barely thawed
- 2 medium-size pineapples (3½ lb. each with crown and peel, 1½ lb. without), peeled
  Strawberry sauce (preceding, optional)
  Mint sprigs (optional)

Pineapple–piña colada tart with berry dots serves one or two for dessert.

In a 1½- to 2-quart pan, mix ⅓ cup sugar, yolks, and ¾ cup coconut milk. Stir over medium-low heat until mixture thickly coats a metal spoon, about 10 minutes; do not boil. Stir in rum. Let cool. If made ahead, chill airtight up to 1 day. Bring to room temperature; stir. If sauce is too thick to pour, thin with a little coconut milk.

On a lightly floured board, roll each pastry shell into an 8-inch-wide round; trim edges to neaten. Set rounds slightly apart on 2 baking sheets, each 12 by 15 inches. Bake in a 400° oven until golden and crisp, 10 to 15 minutes (if using 1 oven, switch pans halfway through baking). Cool pastries on racks. If made ahead, store airtight up to 1 day.

Halve pineapples lengthwise; core. Slice crosswise ¼ inch thick. Place ½ of the pineapple on each baking sheet. Place 1 pan about 3 inches below broiler. When tinged brown, about 10 minutes, turn pineapple over and sprinkle with 1 tablespoon sugar. Broil until brown, about 6 minutes. Repeat to broil remaining fruit. If made ahead, let stand up to 2 hours.

To present, put ½ or 1 pastry (break large bubbles to flatten) on each dinner plate. Fan pineapple equally on pastries; pour coconut sauce around desserts. Spoon dots of strawberry sauce onto coconut sauce. Garnish with mint. Makes 4 to 8 servings.

PER SERVING: 308 calories, 3.7 g protein, 43 g carbohydrates, 15 g fat (4.8 g saturated), 106 mg cholesterol, 126 mg sodium

More March Recipes

OTHER MARCH articles suggest two unusual entrées: a hot main-dish scallop salad and a satisfying vegetarian entrée.

HOT SCALLOP SALAD WITH POTATO CHIPS

A surprise ingredient, potato chips, is in this first-course or main-dish salad featuring scallops glazed in hot oil and ginger. The chips provide a crisp, salty foil for the delicate shellfish. Warm juices from scallops mix with lime juice, marjoram, and green onion to make a dressing for the salad.

- 1 **pound sea scallops**
- ⅓ **cup salad oil**
- 1 **tablespoon minced fresh ginger**
- 2 **tablespoons lime juice**
- 2 **teaspoons minced fresh or 1 teaspoon dried marjoram leaves**
- 1 **teaspoon sugar**
- ¼ **teaspoon pepper**
- ⅓ **cup thinly sliced green onions**
- ½ **pound (about 8 cups, lightly packed) rinsed and crisped mixed salad leaves such as arugula, Belgian endive, butter lettuce, curly endive, escarole, radicchio, or romaine**
  About 3 ounces (4 cups, loosely filled) thick-sliced potato chips

Rinse scallops well, pat dry, and cut crosswise about ¼ inch thick.

To a 10- to 12-inch frying pan over medium-high heat, add oil and ginger. When hot, add ½ the scallops; turn often with a wide spatula until scallops are tinged with gold and no longer translucent in center (cut to test), about 4 minutes.

With a slotted spoon, transfer scallops to a small bowl. Cook remaining scallops; add to bowl. Drain accumulated juices from scallops back into frying pan; bring to a boil, then remove from heat. Stir in lime juice, marjoram, sugar, pepper, and onion.

Put leaves in a wide, shallow bowl. At once, pour hot dressing over them; mix, then push leaves to 1 side of the bowl. Mound scallops and potato chips separately beside leaves. Present salad, then mix. Makes 8 first-course, 4 main-dish servings.

PER MAIN-DISH SERVING: 392 calories, 21 g protein, 17 g carbohydrates, 27 g fat (3.7 g saturated), 37 mg cholesterol, 258 mg sodium

Crisp contrasts: thinly sliced scallops, glazed with hot oil and ginger, are paired with mixed salad leaves and crunchy potato chips. Blend scallop juices into dressing.

PINTO BEAN CAKES WITH SALSA

A smart choice for a quick low-fat supper, cumin-seasoned bean cakes are coated with cornmeal for crunch. Top with a dollop of prepared or homemade salsa.

- 1½ **tablespoons salad oil**
- 1 **small onion, finely chopped**
- ¼ **cup finely chopped red bell pepper**
- 2 **cloves garlic, minced or pressed**
- 1 **medium-size fresh jalapeño chili, seeded and finely chopped**
- 2 **cans (about 15 oz. each) pinto beans, drained and rinsed**
- ⅛ **teaspoon liquid smoke**
- ¼ **cup chopped fresh cilantro (coriander)**
- ½ **teaspoon ground cumin**
- ¼ **teaspoon pepper**
- ⅓ **cup yellow cornmeal**
  Cooking oil spray (optional)
- ½ **to 1 cup purchased or homemade tomato-based salsa**

In a 12- to 14-inch nonstick frying pan over medium heat, combine 1½ teaspoons of the oil with the onion, bell pepper, garlic, and chili. Stir often until onion is limp but not browned, about 5 minutes.

In a bowl, coarsely mash beans with a potato masher until they stick together. Stir in onion mixture, liquid smoke, cilantro, cumin, and pepper, mixing well.

Spread cornmeal on a sheet of wax paper. When bean mixture is cool to touch, divide into 8 equal portions, shaping each into a ½-inch-thick cake. Coat cakes with cornmeal.

Return the frying pan to medium-high heat. Add remaining 1 tablespoon oil. When oil is hot, add cakes and brown lightly, 8 to 10 minutes; turn cakes over once. Coat pan with cooking oil spray if cakes start to stick. Serve cakes with salsa to add to taste. Makes 4 servings.

PER SERVING: 209 calories, 9 g protein, 30 g carbohydrates, 6 g fat (1 g saturated), 0 mg cholesterol, 615 mg sodium

Eggs scrambled with peppers and onions are filling when served with hearty bulgur.

SCRAMBLED EGGS & BULGUR

2 cups regular-strength chicken broth
1 cup bulgur (cracked wheat)
1 tablespoon butter or margarine
1 medium-size (5 to 6 oz.) onion, thinly sliced
1 medium-size (about 6 oz.) red or green bell pepper, stemmed, seeded, and thinly sliced
4 large eggs
Salt and pepper
Grated parmesan cheese

In a 1- to 1½-quart pan, bring the chicken broth to a boil. Stir in bulgur. Cover tightly; let mixture stand until liquid is absorbed, 5 to 10 minutes.

In a 10- to 12-inch frying pan, stir 1 teaspoon butter, onion, and bell pepper over medium-high heat until onion is lightly browned, 5 to 8 minutes.

In a small bowl, beat eggs to blend with ¼ cup water. Add remaining butter to frying pan; turn heat to medium-low. Add eggs and cook, gently lifting cooked portion to allow uncooked portion to flow underneath, until eggs are softly set. Place ¼ of the bulgur and egg mixture on each of 4 dinner plates. Add salt, pepper, and cheese to taste. Makes 4 servings.—Helen Aunspach, Trinity Center, Calif.

PER SERVING: 254 calories, 12 g protein, 32 g carbohydrates, 9.3 g fat (3.6 g saturated), 220 mg cholesterol, 127 mg sodium

Shred red cabbage, then wilt it in hot frying pan; top with apple and nuts.

WILTED WALDORF SALAD

⅓ cup slivered almonds or chopped walnuts
6 tablespoons cider vinegar
2 tablespoons sugar
1 large (about ½ lb.) tart apple
1 tablespoon salad oil
1 large (about ½ lb.) onion, thinly sliced
1 clove garlic, pressed or minced
½ teaspoon caraway seed
4 cups (about 9 oz.) finely shredded red cabbage
Salt

In a 10- to 12-inch frying pan over medium heat, stir nuts until lightly browned, 8 to 10 minutes. Remove from pan; set aside.

In a bowl, mix ¼ cup vinegar and the sugar. Core apple and cut into ½-inch cubes; stir into vinegar mixture.

Add oil, onion, garlic, and caraway to frying pan; stir over high heat until onion is limp, 4 to 5 minutes. Add cabbage and remaining 2 tablespoons vinegar; stir until cabbage barely wilts, about 2 minutes. Pour into a shallow bowl. Top with apple mixture and nuts; mix. Add salt to taste. Makes 6 servings.—Holly Kaslewicz, Stanford, Calif.

PER SERVING: 115 calories, 2.2 g protein, 17 g carbohydrates, 5.5 g fat (0.6 g saturated), 0 mg cholesterol, 5.8 mg sodium

Pink pickled onions garnish braised pork steaks with hominy and carrots.

HOMINY & PORK CHOPS

4 shoulder pork steaks (about 2 lb. total), fat trimmed
1 cup regular-strength chicken broth
4 large (about 1 lb. total) carrots, thinly sliced
1 can (15 oz.) golden hominy, drained
Pink onions (recipe follows)
Chopped parsley
Salt and pepper

Place pork in a 10- to 12-inch frying pan; cover tightly. Cook over medium heat for 20 minutes. Uncover; cook over high heat, turning pork occasionally, until liquid evaporates and meat browns, 5 to 10 minutes. Drain off fat.

Add broth, carrots, and hominy. Cover and simmer until meat is tender when pierced, 20 to 25 minutes. Transfer pork and hominy mixture to a platter; top with pink onions and parsley. Add salt and pepper to taste. Makes 4 servings.—Frances P. Thoman, Grants Pass, Oreg.

PER SERVING: 435 calories, 32 g protein, 36 g carbohydrates, 18 g fat (5.9 g saturated), 106 mg cholesterol, 359 mg sodium

Pink onions. Thinly slice 1 medium-size (about 6 oz.) **red onion;** rinse. Mix onion with ¼ cup **white wine vinegar,** 2 tablespoons **sugar,** and ⅓ cup **water.** Chill, covered, up to 1 hour; drain.

POPCORN GRANOLA

¾ cup honey
⅓ cup (⅙ lb.) butter or margarine
1 teaspoon vanilla
3 cups unseasoned popped corn
6 cups quick-cooking rolled oats
1 cup sweetened flaked dried coconut
1 cup bran cereal
1 cup crushed shredded wheat cereal
1 cup raisins
½ cup sesame seed

In a 12- by 15-inch roasting pan, combine honey, butter, and vanilla. Place in oven and turn heat on to 350°. Meanwhile, whirl corn in a blender or food processor until finely ground. When butter is melted, after about 5 minutes, add to pan the ground corn, oats, coconut, bran cereal, wheat cereal, raisins, and sesame seed; mix well.

Bake in a 350° oven, stirring often, until richly browned, 40 to 45 minutes. Cool; serve. If made ahead, store airtight at room temperature up to 3 weeks. Makes 11 cups, 11 to 22 servings. —*Sue Hill, Palmer, Alaska.*

PER ½ CUP: 216 calories, 5 g protein, 50 g carbohydrates, 7 g fat (3.2 g saturated), 7.4 mg cholesterol, 56 mg sodium

Granola made from popcorn, oats, and cereal provides quick breakfast.

GREEN TOMATILLO CHICKEN

4 whole chicken legs with thighs attached (about 2¾ lb. total)
2 tablespoons salad oil
1 pound fresh tomatillos, husks removed, cored and chopped; or 2 cans (12 oz. each) tomatillos, drained and coarsely chopped
1 large (about ½ lb.) onion, chopped
2 large (about 1½ oz. total) fresh jalapeño chilies, stemmed and chopped
1 clove garlic, pressed or minced
½ cup fresh cilantro (coriander) leaves
Salt and pepper

Remove chicken skin. Pour oil into a 10- to 12-inch frying pan over medium-high heat. Add chicken and brown, turning as needed, 8 to 12 minutes. Add tomatillos, onion, chilies, and garlic. Cover and simmer, turning chicken occasionally, until meat is no longer pink at thighbone (cut to test), about 30 minutes. With a slotted spoon, transfer chicken to a platter; keep warm.

Boil sauce, uncovered, over high heat until most of the liquid evaporates, 6 to 8 minutes. Pour sauce over chicken. Sprinkle with cilantro. Add salt and pepper to taste. Makes 4 servings.— *Gale Noble, San Diego.*

PER SERVING: 322 calories, 38 g protein, 9.1 g carbohydrates, 14 g fat (2.6 g saturated), 143 mg cholesterol, 156 mg sodium

Green tomatillos, chilies, and cilantro season chicken legs as they braise.

BERRY YOGURT CHEESE PIE

1 quart unflavored nonfat yogurt
1 envelope (2 teaspoons) unflavored gelatin
2 cups (1 lb.) nonfat or low-fat cottage cheese
½ cup sugar
1½ teaspoons grated lime peel
2 tablespoons lime juice
Graham crust (recipe follows)
2 cups sliced strawberries

Pour yogurt into a cloth-lined strainer set over a deep bowl. Cover and chill at least 12 hours or up to next day. In a 1- to 1½-quart pan, combine gelatin and ¼ cup water; soften 5 minutes. Stir over low heat until gelatin dissolves. In a blender or food processor, whirl drained yogurt, cottage cheese, sugar, peel, juice, and gelatin mixture until smooth. Pour into crust. Cover and chill until firm, at least 4 hours or up to next day.

Top pie with berries. Makes 8 servings.—*Linda Strader, Amado, Ariz.*

PER SERVING: 332 calories, 16 g protein, 46 g carbohydrates, 9 g fat (4.7 g saturated), 26 mg cholesterol, 480 mg sodium

Graham crust. In a 9-inch pie pan, mix 1⅓ cups **graham cracker crumbs,** 3 tablespoons **sugar,** and ⅓ cup (⅙ lb.) melted **butter** or margarine. Press evenly over bottom and sides of pan. Bake in a 350° oven for 10 minutes. Cool.

Strawberries, sliced and whole, and lime leaves top yogurt cheese pie.

DICK STURZA WAS ALL SET *for a juicy beef Stroganoff: the beef was cubed, the mushrooms were sliced, and all the other necessary ingredients were at hand. Then tragedy struck. The sour cream had gone over the hill, and there was no time to replace it. He improvised brilliantly by creating this beefsteak marinara, a casserole with satisfying complexity of flavor that can be started well before the dinner hour and will require little attention until serving time.*

BEEFSTEAK MARINARA

- 1½ to 2 pounds top round beef, fat trimmed
- 2 tablespoons olive oil
- 1 large onion, chopped
- 2 teaspoons minced or pressed garlic
- ½ pound mushrooms, thinly sliced
- 1 tablespoon butter, margarine, or olive oil
- 3 tablespoons all-purpose flour
- 1 can (10½ oz.) condensed beef consommé
- ½ cup dry white or red wine
- ¼ cup tomato paste
- 2 tablespoons chopped parsley
- 1 teaspoon *each* dried basil leaves and dried oregano leaves
- 1 can (14½ oz.) stewed tomatoes
  Hot cooked spaghetti
  Salt and pepper

"All the necessary ingredients for a juicy beef Stroganoff were at hand."

Cut meat into ¾-inch cubes. Pour 1 tablespoon oil into a 10- to 12-inch frying pan over medium-high heat. When oil is hot, add meat, a portion at a time, cooking until well browned; stir often. Transfer meat with a slotted spoon to a shallow 3- to 3½-quart casserole.

Add 1 tablespoon oil to the frying pan along with onion, garlic, and mushrooms; stir often until onion is limp, about 10 minutes. With a slotted spoon, transfer mixture to casserole. Melt butter in frying pan, add flour, and stir until mixture bubbles. Smoothly blend in consommé, wine, tomato paste, parsley, basil, oregano, and tomatoes (break them up with a spoon) and their liquid; stir until boiling.

Mix sauce with ingredients in casserole. Cover tightly with foil and bake in a 350° oven until meat is very tender when pierced, about 2½ hours. Serve over hot cooked spaghetti and add salt and pepper to taste. Makes 4 to 5 cups.

PER ½ CUP: 208 calories, 23 g protein, 11 g carbohydrates, 7.9 g fat (2.3 g saturated), 52 mg cholesterol, 455 mg sodium

Camano Island, Wash.

RICK EASTES TRAVELS *to Chile routinely to arrange for shipping that country's seasonal fruits here. It's summer in Chile now, so his Berry Sorbet is seasonal, sort of. In it he uses fructose—not because this sugar is more easily digested by some people, but because he had some on the shelf the day he ran out of granulated sugar. If you've run out of fructose, you can use granulated sugar in its place.*

BERRY SORBET

- 2 cups *each* blackberries and raspberries, rinsed and drained
- ½ cup powdered fructose
- ½ cup water
- 2 tablespoons lime juice
  Additional blackberries and raspberries, rinsed and drained (optional)
  Black raspberry–flavor liqueur

In a 2- to 3-quart pan, combine the 2 cups blackberries, 2 cups raspberries, fructose, water, and lime juice. Bring to a boil over high heat, stirring often. Then reduce heat and simmer until blackberries mash readily, 3 to 4 minutes. Whirl mixture, a portion at a time, in blender or food processor until smoothly puréed. To remove seeds, rub purée through a fine strainer into a bowl.

Pour purée into a 9- to 10-inch square metal pan. Cover airtight and freeze until sorbet mixture is firm, at least 8 hours or up to 2 weeks.

Frozen sorbet has an icy texture. If you like a softer texture, break frozen sorbet into chunks and beat with a mixer until slushy; serve at once or return to freezer up to 1 hour. Top servings of sorbet with additional berries and liqueur to taste (1 to 2 tablespoons per portion). Makes about 3 cups, 4 to 6 servings.

PER ½ CUP: 94 calories, 4.4 g protein, 139 g carbohydrates, 2.5 g fat (0 g saturated), 0 mg cholesterol, 4.9 mg sodium

Visalia, Calif.

PAT PIPER OF SONOMA, *California, sends us her recipe rather assertively called Pat's Famous and Healthful Low-Cholesterol Salad Dressing. She first tried a balancing act of 1 to 1 (equal parts oil and vinegar). But overly tart results pushed her back to traditional ratios of 3 (oil) to 1 (vinegar).*

She then elected to combine predominantly monounsaturated olive oil with three significantly polyunsaturated vegetable oils, hoping to bring better nutrition by way of variety. Liking the concept of variety, she also combined two vinegars.

PAT'S SALAD DRESSING

- ¼ cup *each* extra-virgin olive oil, safflower oil, soy oil, and peanut oil
- 3 tablespoons *each* balsamic vinegar and apple cider vinegar
- 1 clove garlic, minced or pressed

"She first tried a balancing act of 1 to 1."

- 1½ tablespoons crumbled blue cheese
- 1 teaspoon soy sauce
- ½ teaspoon dry mustard
- ¼ teaspoon *each* pepper and dried basil leaves

In a small bowl or jar, whisk or shake together olive oil, safflower oil, soy oil, peanut oil, balsamic vinegar, cider vinegar, garlic, blue cheese, soy sauce, dry mustard, pepper, and basil. Makes about 1⅓ cups.

PER TABLESPOON: 95 calories, 0.1 g protein, 0.3 g carbohydrates, 11 g fat (1.5 g saturated), 0.5 mg cholesterol, 25 mg sodium

Sonoma, Calif.

March Menus

COUNTER THE LAST CHILLS *of winter with these casual, warming meals. Even if you're not Irish, a little "wearing of the green" is appropriate if you take advantage of mid-March price specials on corned beef to create a Saint Patrick's Day meal. Simple details, on facing page, add Irish humor to our feature menu.*

On a weekend morning, bake fruit focaccia for a grand brunch; use thawed frozen dough as a shortcut.

Low-fat cooking techniques enhance the wholesomeness of the soup and sandwich supper. The results are so satisfying, your family will never notice the lightened touch.

SAINT PATRICK'S DAY CELEBRATION

Corned Beef with Sweet-Hot Glaze

Two-tone Slaw in a Cabbage Bowl

Baked Yams with Flavored Vinegar

Mint-chip Ice Cream with Shamrocks

Merlot or Beer   Mineral Water

Irish Coffee

You can simmer the beef, shred the cabbage, and make the cabbage bowl up to a day ahead. Bake yams while meat reheats. Instead of butter, splash rice vinegar or a berry-flavor vinegar into split yams.

To give dessert a St. Pat's flair, decorate plates with shamrock stencils. First, cut shamrocks from paper (or buy paper shamrocks). Then rub dessert plates very lightly with butter (this keeps shamrocks in place as you work and makes the cocoa dusting adhere). Lay shamrocks on a plate and sift cocoa over plate. Carefully lift off shamrocks (use tip of sharp knife), taking care not to dislodge cocoa. Shake paper clean and repeat to decorate remaining plates.

For Irish coffee, offer whiskey (Irish or other), softly whipped cream, and sugar to add to hot coffee.

Hollowed cabbage makes dramatic bowl for slaw that goes with succulent corned beef and baked yams or sweet potatoes in this Saint Patrick's Day dinner.

CORNED BEEF WITH SWEET-HOT GLAZE

1 **piece (3½ to 4 lb.) corned beef round or center-cut brisket, fat trimmed**

1 **cup regular-strength beef broth**

¼ **cup firmly packed brown sugar**

2 **tablespoons prepared horseradish Dijon mustard**

Rinse meat well with cool water. Place in a 6- to 8-quart pan with about 3 quarts water. Bring to a boil over high heat; drain. Repeat this step until the water no longer tastes salty, 1 or 2 more times. To drained meat, add water (about 2 qt.) to cover it by about ½ inch. Bring to boiling on high heat; cover and simmer gently until meat is very tender when pierced, about 3½ hours.

Drain beef; put in a 9- by 13-inch pan. (If made ahead, cool, then chill airtight up until next day. Cover meat tightly with foil; bake in a 350° oven until hot in center, about 50 minutes; uncover.)

In pan used to simmer beef, mix broth, sugar, and horseradish. Boil over high heat until glaze is reduced to ½ cup, about 5 minutes; stir often. (If made ahead, pour into a bowl and cover; chill up until next day.)

Bake hot meat, uncovered, in a 350° oven for 20 minutes, brushing with glaze until all is used. Broil about 6 inches from heat until top browns lightly, 3 to 5 minutes. Put meat on a platter; offer mustard. Makes 10 servings, or dinner for 6 with leftovers for sandwiches.

PER SERVING: 236 calories, 16 g protein, 6.1 g carbohydrates, 16 g fat (5.4 g saturated), 83 mg cholesterol, 970 mg sodium

THE DETAILS

Cabbage bowl. *Hollow cabbage to make shell. Fill with slaw, surround with leaves.*

Lean seasonings. *Season yams with rice vinegar or berry-flavor vinegar.*

Shamrock stencils. *Dust paper shamrocks on plates with cocoa; lift off paper.*

Irish coffee. *Stubby wine glasses and glass cups show off whipped-cream floats.*

Two-tone Slaw in a Cabbage Bowl

- **1** large head (about 1¾ lb.) savoy or green cabbage, with large outer leaves attached (if available)
- **4** to 6 red savoy kale or red head cabbage leaves (optional)
- **2** cups finely shredded red cabbage
- **3** slices bacon (about 1¾ oz. total)
- **⅓** cup seasoned rice vinegar (or ⅓ cup rice vinegar and 1 tablespoon sugar)
- **½** teaspoon pepper

Carefully remove 4 to 6 large outer leaves from head cabbage. Rinse these and red savoy kale leaves; drain, wrap in towels, and enclose in a plastic bag. To crisp, chill at least 30 minutes or up until next day.

Rinse and drain head cabbage. Trim a thin slice from stem end so cabbage sits steadily upright. Slice ½ inch horizontally from cabbage top. Using a grapefruit knife, cut out center of cabbage, leaving a wall about ½ inch thick. Finely shred trimmed-out portion of cabbage; discard core.

In a bowl, mix shredded savoy with shredded red cabbage. If made ahead, wrap cabbage shell and shredded cabbage airtight and chill up until next day.

Cook bacon in an 8- to 10-inch frying pan over medium-high heat until brown and crisp, about 3 minutes. Crumble and drain on towels. Add vinegar and pepper to warm drippings in pan.

Mix bacon and warm dressing with shredded cabbage. Gently pull cabbage shell to open bowl slightly; set on a platter and surround with reserved green and red leaves. Mound salad into cabbage bowl. Makes 6 servings.

PER SERVING: 83 calories, 2.6 g protein, 8.7 g carbohydrates, 4.9 g fat (1.8 g saturated), 5.5 mg cholesterol, 81 mg sodium

---

WARMING WINTER BRUNCH

Breakfast Focaccia
Spiced Ricotta Spread
Hot Canadian Bacon
Cinnamon Tea   Coffee

The focaccia uses frozen bread dough as a time-saver; to have dough ready in the morning, put it in the refrigerator the night before to thaw. As the focaccia bakes,

For brunch, serve fruit-topped focaccia with spiced ricotta spread and Canadian bacon.

you have time to organize the rest of the breakfast elements.

The ricotta spread goes together quickly, but can be made ahead. Warm sliced Canadian bacon in a frying pan, or seal in foil and heat in oven with focaccia until meat is hot in the center.

Breakfast Focaccia

- **1** loaf (1 lb.) frozen white bread dough, thawed
- **3** large (about 1 lb. total) firm-ripe plums, or 3 cups thin apple slices
- **1½** tablespoons melted butter or margarine
- **3** tablespoons sugar mixed with 1 teaspoon ground cinnamon

(Continued on next page)

Place dough in a lightly oiled 10- by 15-inch pan. Stretch and press to fill pan evenly. (If dough is too elastic to stay in place, let rest a few minutes, then press.) Cover dough lightly with plastic wrap and let stand until puffy, about 45 minutes.

Meanwhile, pit plums and cut into ¼-inch-thick slices. Brush puffy dough with 1 tablespoon butter. Arrange plum slices, without overlapping, on dough. Brush fruit with remaining butter and sprinkle evenly with sugar-cinnamon mixture.

Bake focaccia on the bottom rack in a 350° oven until well browned on edges and bottom (lift gently with a spatula to check), about 40 minutes. Serve warm. (If made ahead, cool, wrap airtight, and hold at room temperature up until next day. Reheat, uncovered, in a 350° oven until warm to touch, 5 to 10 minutes.) Makes 6 servings.

PER SERVING: 263 calories, 6.3 g protein, 49 g carbohydrates, 5.2 g fat (2 g saturated), 8.6 mg cholesterol, 472 mg sodium

SPICED RICOTTA SPREAD

1½ cups part-skim ricotta cheese
2 tablespoons sugar
1½ tablespoons finely grated orange peel
⅛ teaspoon ground nutmeg

In a bowl, mix together cheese, sugar, 1 tablespoon peel, and nutmeg.

Spoon mixture into a small bowl and sprinkle with remaining peel. If made ahead, cover and chill up to 2 days. Makes 1½ cups.

PER TABLESPOON: 26 calories, 1.8 g protein, 1.9 g carbohydrates, 1.2 g fat (0.8 g saturated), 4.8 mg cholesterol, 19 mg sodium

---

SOUP & SANDWICH SUPPER

Spinach & Buttermilk Soup
Grilled Tuna, Cheddar & Onion Sandwiches
Carrot Sticks
Cucumber Slices
Radishes
Oatmeal Cookies
Milk   Chenin Blanc

A lean, quick soup, ideal for sipping, and sandwiches toasted in a dry pan make a light and satisfying meal. Buy or make cookies.

SPINACH & BUTTERMILK SOUP

1 package (10 oz.) frozen chopped spinach
4 cups regular-strength chicken broth
2 tablespoons grated lemon peel
2 tablespoons cornstarch
2 cups buttermilk
Salt and pepper

Combine spinach and 2 cups broth in a 3- to 4-quart pan. Bring to boil on high heat; use a spoon to break spinach apart. As soon as spinach is in chunks, pour into a blender, add 1 tablespoon lemon peel, and purée until smooth.

In pan, mix remaining 2 cups broth with cornstarch until smooth; add spinach mixture. Stir often on high heat until boiling. Mix in buttermilk and pour into bowls or mugs. Sprinkle with remaining peel and add salt and pepper to taste. Makes 4 servings.

PER SERVING: 114 calories, 8.5 g protein, 14 g carbohydrates, 2.8 g fat (1.1 g saturated), 4.9 mg cholesterol, 235 mg sodium

---

GRILLED TUNA, CHEDDAR & ONION SANDWICHES

1 large (about 10 oz.) onion, thinly sliced
1 clove garlic, minced or pressed
½ cup regular-strength chicken broth or water
2 cans (about 6 oz. each) water-packed albacore tuna, drained
½ cup minced celery
2 tablespoons reduced-calorie or regular mayonnaise
8 slices dark rye bread
¼ pound sharp cheddar cheese, thinly sliced

In a 10- to 12-inch nonstick frying pan, combine onion, garlic, and half the broth. Bring to a boil over high heat; stir often until liquid evaporates and browned bits stick in pan.

Add half the remaining broth; stir to scrape browned bits free, then boil again until liquid evaporates and browned bits form. Repeat step with remaining broth, cooking until liquid evaporates. Set onion mixture aside.

In a bowl, mix together tuna, celery, and mayonnaise. Top 4 slices bread equally with tuna mixture, onion mixture, cheese, and remaining bread.

Wipe the pan clean. Place over medium heat and add 2 sandwiches. (If you have another nonstick frying pan, toast all the sandwiches at once.) Cook until sandwiches are toasted on the bottom, about 4 minutes. Turn over and toast tops, about 4 minutes more. Makes 4 servings.

PER SERVING: 393 calories, 34 g protein, 33 g carbohydrates, 14 g fat (7.6 g saturated), 66 mg cholesterol, 826 mg sodium

APRIL

Easter buffet lunch (page 78)

Exalt in the joyful
freshness of springtime with an easygoing Easter buffet
lunch featuring succulent barbecued lamb to tuck into
pocket sandwiches. Intriguing Pacific fish offer inspiration
for a look at the innovative ways Hawaiian chefs combine
regional foods with Pacific Rim flavors. Experiment
with preserved lemons, the crucial flavoring in a quartet
of Moroccan dishes, or sample some imaginative
Southwestern recipes we discovered at last year's Scottsdale
Culinary Festival.

Hawaii's Treasures of the Deep

THE PACIFIC IS KEY to the good life in Hawaii. But only recently has the ocean been the focus for the best in Island dining. With fresh interest in regional foods and Pacific Rim flavors, Island chefs are turning away from the long-favored excesses of Continental cuisine. Now they are showcasing the array of local fish in dishes that reflect the area's own emerging cuisine.

Our primer to this new wave of cooking starts with seven Island fish most apt to be available on the Mainland. In the text are adventurous, achievable recipes from innovative Hawaiian chefs. For some suggestions on where to dine on dishes reflecting the region's changing restaurant style, see page 76.

Now through summer, these seven fish are at peak supply. Mahi mahi, swordfish, and ahi are quite familiar (they also come from non-Hawaiian waters at different times). You may need to place a special order at your fish market for hebi, ono, opah, and tombo.

Though each fish has unique qualities, all can be cooked the same way, are complemented by the same seasonings, and can be used interchangeably in recipes. This flexibility means you can use what's available at the market. Expect to pay $6 to $16 a pound.

Golden banana salsa and sautéed red bell peppers add spice to mahi mahi.

Nutrition information given with the following recipes uses ahi. For mahi mahi and swordfish, add or subtract:

PER MAHI MAHI SERVING: − 26 calories, − 5.5 g protein, same carbohydrates, − 0.3 g fat (− 0.1 g saturated), + 32 mg cholesterol, + 58 mg sodium

PER SWORDFISH SERVING: + 15 calories, − 4 g protein, same carbohydrates, + 3.5 g fat (+ 1 g saturated), − 7 mg cholesterol, + 60 mg sodium

At present, nutritional data are not available for hebi, ono, opah, or tombo; similarities to the three preceding fish suggest similar data.

Supermarkets carry many Asian items used in the recipes. For Thai Muslim curry paste, Japanese chili spice, and dried kaffir lime leaves, shop in an Asian market, or use alternatives suggested.

HAWAIIAN FISH WITH THAI BANANA SALSA

For home cooks, we've simplified the chef's multiple-sauce recipe.

- 1½ to 2 pounds Hawaiian fish (see cooking basics, page 75), cut into 6 equal portions
- ¼ cup coarsely chopped fresh cilantro (coriander)
  Thai banana salsa (following)
  Fresh cilantro sprigs
  Salt

Pat fish with chopped cilantro and sauté (see cooking basics, page 75). Set fish on 6 warm plates; spoon salsa alongside. Add cilantro sprigs and salt to taste. Makes 6 servings.—*Chef Roy Yamaguchi, Roy's Restaurant.*

PER SERVING WITH AHI: 216 calories, 27 g protein, 16 g carbohydrates, 5 g fat (0.8 g saturated), 51 mg cholesterol, 44 mg sodium

Thai banana salsa. Peel and halve lengthwise 1 large (½ lb.) firm-ripe **banana**. In a nonstick 10- to 12-inch frying pan over high heat, brown banana well in 1 teaspoon **Oriental sesame oil**, about 8 minutes.

Coarsely chop banana. Mix with ½ cup chopped **golden raisins**, 2 tablespoons chopped **fresh cilantro**, 2 tablespoons minced **fresh lemon grass** (tender part only) or 1 teaspoon grated lemon peel, and 1 teaspoon **Japanese chili spice** (*nanami togarashi*) or ¼ teaspoon cayenne and ½ teaspoon grated orange peel.

(Continued on page 74)

On Waikiki, grilled opah with papaya relish (recipe on page 75) is served at Orchids. Colorful relish includes onion, red bell pepper, cilantro, and ginger.

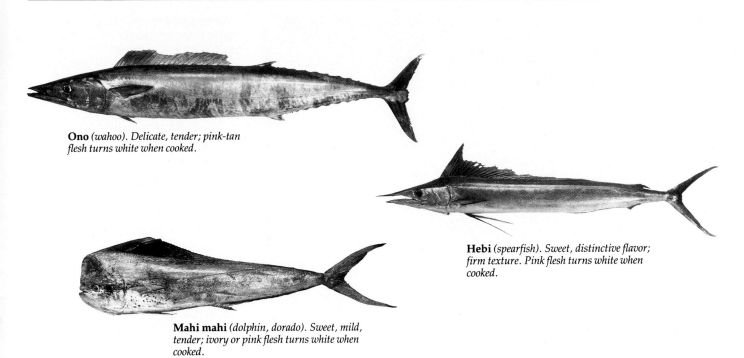

Ono *(wahoo). Delicate, tender; pink-tan flesh turns white when cooked.*

Hebi *(spearfish). Sweet, distinctive flavor; firm texture. Pink flesh turns white when cooked.*

Mahi mahi *(dolphin, dorado). Sweet, mild, tender; ivory or pink flesh turns white when cooked.*

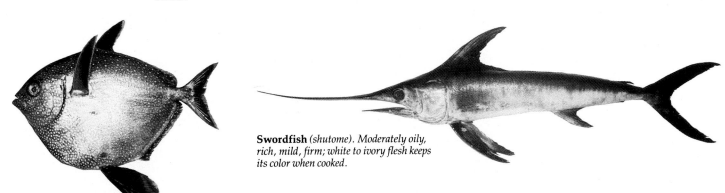

Swordfish *(shutome). Moderately oily, rich, mild, firm; white to ivory flesh keeps its color when cooked.*

Opah *(moonfish). Tender, rich, sweet; pink to red flesh turns white when cooked.*

Tombo *(albacore tuna). Mild, rich; cooking firms soft texture, turns pinkish flesh tan.*

Ahi *(yellowfin tuna). Meaty texture and flavor, raw or cooked. Red flesh cooks to light tan.*

PEPPERED HAWAIIAN FISH WITH ASIAN SLAW

1½ pounds **Hawaiian fish,** cut into 12 equal portions (see cooking basics, facing page)

2 tablespoons **peanut** or **salad oil**
    Coarsely ground pepper

8 **won ton skins,** cut into ¼-inch strips
    Asian slaw and vinaigrette (recipe follows)

2 medium-size (⅔ lb. total) firm-ripe **tomatoes,** each cut into 12 wedges

Rub fish with 1 tablespoon peanut oil instead of olive oil; sprinkle with pepper. Pour remaining oil into a 6- to 8-inch frying pan over medium-high heat. Add won ton strips; stir until strips are golden and crisp, 4 to 5 minutes. Drain on towels.

Mix slaw with half the vinaigrette. Arrange equal portions of slaw and tomatoes on 4 plates.

Sauté fish (see cooking basics, facing page); set on plates. Spoon remaining vinaigrette over fish and tomatoes. Top slaw with won ton strips. Makes 4 servings. —*Chef Alan Wong, CanoeHouse Restaurant.*

PER SERVING WITH AHI: 428 calories, 46 g protein, 30 g carbohydrates, 14 g fat (2.3 g saturated), 77 mg cholesterol, 694 mg sodium

Asian slaw and vinaigrette. In a bowl, mix 1 cup lengthwise slivers **edible-pod peas;** 1 cup shredded **carrots;** 2 cups finely cut shreds **napa** or regular **cabbage.**

In a 6- to 8-inch frying pan on medium-high heat, mix ½ cup fine slivers (2 in. long) **fresh ginger** and 1½ tablespoons **Oriental sesame oil;** stir until golden, 2 to 3 minutes. Remove from heat and stir in ¼ cup **reduced-sodium soy sauce;** 1½ tablespoons *each* **rice vinegar, mirin** (sweet sake), **sugar,** and **lime juice;** and 1 small clove **garlic** (minced).

Ahi, sautéed in peanut oil and seasoned with coarsely ground pepper, is arranged around mound of crunchy Asian slaw and garnished with tomato wedges. Spoon ginger-flavored vinaigrette over fish and tomatoes, and top slaw with crisp-fried won ton strips.

Grilled hebi sits in coconut curry sauce with finely shredded basil leaves.

GRILLED HAWAIIAN FISH IN BASIL-COCONUT CURRY SAUCE

Basil-coconut curry sauce (recipe follows)
1½ **to 2 pounds Hawaiian fish, cut into 6 equal pieces, grilled (see cooking basics, right)**
Fresh basil sprigs
Salt

Spoon sauce equally onto 6 warm plates; set fish in sauce and garnish with basil. Add salt to taste. Makes 6 servings.— *Chef Jean-Marie Josselin, A Pacific Cafe.*

PER SERVING WITH AHI: 250 calories, 28 g protein, 4.5 g carbohydrates, 12 g fat (7.8 g saturated), 51 mg cholesterol, 49 mg sodium

Basil-coconut curry sauce. In a 1½- to 2-quart pan on high heat, bring to a boil ½ cup **dry white wine;** 1½ tablespoons minced **fresh ginger;** ¼ cup minced **fresh lemon grass** (tender part only) or 2 teaspoons grated lemon peel; 1 tablespoon crumbled **dried kaffir lime leaves** or chopped fresh lemon leaves (optional); and 2 teaspoons **red curry paste** (following). Simmer, covered, for 15 minutes.

In a blender, whirl mixture with 2 teaspoons **cornstarch** and 1 cup canned **coconut milk** until smooth. Return to pan (with 1 tablespoon dried basil leaves

Cooking Basics

RECIPES ON THESE pages use grilled or sautéed fish. To retain succulence, do not overcook; remove fish from heat when it's still a little translucent in the center; fish continues to cook slightly. Most chefs prefer tombo and ahi rare.

Hawaiian fish. Select 1½ to 2 pounds of ¾-inch-thick pieces **ahi, hebi, mahi mahi, ono, opah, swordfish,** or **tombo.** (Fish may have dark-colored sections that are stronger flavored than lighter flesh.) Cut off and discard any skin. Rinse fish, pat dry, and cut into pieces as recipes direct. Rub fish all over with 1 tablespoon **olive oil.**

To grill. Place **oiled fish** on a greased grill 4 to 6 inches above a solid bed of hot coals (you can hold your hand at grill level only 2 to 3 seconds). Cook fish, turning once or twice, until done to your liking (cut to test). For rare (still the raw color in center), allow about 3 minutes total. To cook evenly (center slightly translucent), allow 5 to 6 minutes total.

To sauté. Place a 10- to 12-inch non-stick frying pan over high heat. When pan is hot, add 1 teaspoon **salad oil** and **oiled fish.** (For 2 pounds fish, cook half at a time.) Turn once or twice to brown and cook to your liking (cut to test); drippings may scorch and smoke. For rare (still the raw color in center), allow about 3 minutes total. To cook evenly (center slightly translucent), allow 5 to 6 minutes total.

if not using fresh, following). Stir sauce over high heat until boiling. If made ahead, chill airtight up to 1 day. Reheat to simmering; if needed, add coconut milk to thin. Stir in ¼ cup fine shreds **fresh basil leaves.** Use hot.

Red curry paste. Use purchased **Thai Muslim curry paste** or all of the following mixture:

Rinse 1 large **dried California** or New Mexico **chili;** stem, seed, and break into small pieces. In a 6- to 8-inch frying pan over medium heat, stir 1 clove **garlic** (minced) in 2 teaspoons **salad oil** until golden, about 2 minutes. Add chili, ½ teaspoon **ground coriander,** ¼ teaspoon **ground cumin,** and seeds of 1 **cardamom pod.** Stir just until chili browns lightly, about 45 seconds. Use hot or cold.

GRILLED HAWAIIAN FISH WITH PAPAYA RELISH

Papaya relish (recipe follows)
1½ **to 2 pounds Hawaiian fish, cut into 6 equal portions, grilled (see cooking basics, above)**
½ **cup fresh cilantro (coriander) leaves**
Salt and pepper

Arrange papaya relish and hot fish equally on 6 warm plates. Garnish plates with cilantro. Add salt and pepper to taste. Makes 6 servings.—*Chef Shawn Smith, Orchids Restaurant.*

PER SERVING WITH AHI: 192 calories, 27 g protein, 4.6 g carbohydrates, 6.8 g fat (1 g saturated), 51 mg cholesterol, 46 mg sodium

Papaya relish. In a fine strainer, rinse ¼ cup minced white **onion.** Soak onion in **ice water** for 30 minutes; drain. Mix with 1¼ cups diced ripe **papaya,** ¾ cup diced **red bell pepper,** ¼ cup chopped **fresh cilantro,** 1 tablespoon minced **fresh ginger,** 2 tablespoons **olive oil,** and 2 tablespoons **lemon juice.**

Dining in Hawaii

GONE ARE THE DAYS *when dining in Hawaii meant pretentious Continental dishes made with imported ingredients. Given the Islands' location and multicultural population, a good question to ponder is why it took so long for Pacific Rim influences to jump from neighborhood ethnic eateries to starred restaurants.*

One important change is the expanding diversity and availability of Hawaiian-grown foods, including a greater variety of produce, and fish and shellfish from small fishing and aquaculture operations.

Hawaii's chefs say today's savvier, well-traveled customers are interested in bolder flavors and regional specialties. The chefs have set aside formal rules and draw on local influences and multiethnic heritage.

Ono with Thai basil unites local fish and Pacific Rim flavors at CanoeHouse.

Fresh fish may be the premier Hawaiian specialty. On menus, you'll see the seven kinds reported here, as well as tongue twisters like opakapaka, hapu'upu'u, and onaga.

The following establishments offer particularly fine fish dishes. Prices are per person for a three-course dinner without beverages or tip. Except where noted, resort wear is appropriate. Reservations are recommended; the area code is 808.

HAWAII

The CanoeHouse Restaurant, Mauna Lani Bay Hotel and Bungalows, One Mauna Lani Drive, Kohala Coast; 885-6622 ($50). The restaurant's plantation-style structure, open to the ocean, is decorated with petroglyphs and a koa canoe. Our favorites among chef Alan Wong's dishes include ahi with Chinese sausage in a black bean sauce, seared ono on snow peas with sesame-miso dressing, and ahi tacos.

Merriman's Restaurant, Opelo Plaza shopping center, Kamuela (Waimea); 885-6822 ($30). Chef Peter Merriman aims for simple presentations to enhance fresh fish. Options include spicy coconut sauce and Chinese black bean sauce to go with the changing local catch. A champion of local producers, Merriman incorporates many of their foods, like goat cheese and produce, in the plantation house–restaurant.

KAUAI

A Pacific Cafe, 4-381 Kuhio Highway (in the Kauai Village shopping center), Kapaa; 822-0013 ($35). Chef Jean-Marie Josselin waxes poetic about produce grown in Kauai's red, rich soil and the region's seafood. He incorporates them in dishes with Japanese, Thai, Chinese, and French touches. Try wok-charred mahi mahi with a garlic-sesame crust and lime-ginger butter sauce, or grilled onaga with Thai curry sauce. Josselin's wife, Sophronia, painted the restaurant's plates and oversees a changing display of local art.

MAUI

Avalon Restaurant & Bar, 844 Front Street, Lahaina; 667-5559 ($35). Kick back beneath an umbrella and enjoy this little oasis among the boutiques. Chef Mark Ellman might conjure up deep-fried opakapaka with buttery black bean sauce. Or perhaps he'll steam the fish of the day to top with soy, ginger, and cilantro.

Prince Court Restaurant, Maui Prince Hotel, 5400 Makena Alanui, Kihei; 874-1111 ($40). Among chef Roger Dikon's creations, we admired Oriental beggar's purse, a rice paper bundle with ahi and tamarind sauce; and tuna seared in macadamia oil with cucumber, mint, and mirin salsa. Jackets are suggested at dinner.

OAHU

Orchids Restaurant, Halekulani, 2199 Kalia Road, Honolulu; 923-2311 ($45). Open-air Waikiki beach-level restaurant looks out to Diamond Head and the passing parade. Chef Shawn Smith takes inspiration from the tropics, Asia, and southern Europe. Try kiawe wood–smoked fish in ti leaves with papaya relish, and steamed onaga with shiitake mushrooms.

La Mer Restaurant, also at the Halekulani; 923-2311 ($70, or prix fixe menus at $75 and $98). When you want to splash out, go upstairs to the hotel's elegant coat-and-tie restaurant with Asian interiors. Chef George Mavrothalassitis uses his French techniques as a springboard for creative dishes featuring local products. We particularly liked onaga baked in a rock salt crust, served with a sauce including *ogo,* a local red seaweed.

Roy's Restaurant, 6600 Kalanianaole Highway, Honolulu; 396-7697 ($40). Chef Roy Yamaguchi, a major influence in Hawaiian cuisine, combines classic training and flavors from his native Japan, California, and around the Pacific Rim to create deftly seasoned dishes like seared opah with Thai salsa in a curry-lobster sauce, and grilled tuna with Maui onions and ponzu (soy sauce–citrus) vinaigrette. Savor them in the casual-chic suburban setting of Hawaii Kai; look out to Maunalua Bay and Diamond Head.

ALTHOUGH AIRY AND LIGHT IN *texture, a typical soufflé that is rich in butter and eggs sets off warning bells for anyone watching fat and cholesterol. Fortunately, a few modifications will produce delicious yet virtuous results.*

An easy place to start is by cutting back on egg yolks, keeping only a few to enrich the flavor and to maintain some of the fragile, though temporary, stability of a soufflé.

For soufflés that use butter and flour to thicken milk, you can trim calories by thickening nonfat milk with cornstarch, as in this herbed spinach and parmesan cheese main-dish soufflé.

For the original dessert omelet-soufflé, whipped yolks and whites baked floating in a butter sauce. The updated sauce uses cornstarch, not butter, to achieve similar smoothness.

Parmesan-flecked spinach soufflé is relatively low in fat. This version reduces the typical number of egg yolks and uses cornstarch, not flour, to thicken sauce.

LEAN SPINACH-MARJORAM SOUFFLÉ

- 1 cup nonfat milk
- 1½ tablespoons cornstarch
- 3 tablespoons chopped fresh or 1 tablespoon dried marjoram leaves
- 1 tablespoon instant minced onion
- ½ teaspoon pepper
- ⅛ teaspoon ground nutmeg
- ½ cup thawed and squeezed-dry frozen chopped spinach
- ¼ cup shredded parmesan cheese
- 2 large egg yolks
- 6 large egg whites
- ¼ teaspoon cream of tartar

Lightly coat interior of a 1½- to 1¾-quart soufflé or other straight-sided baking dish with oil.

In a 2- to 3-quart pan, stir milk smoothly into cornstarch. Add marjoram, onion, pepper, and nutmeg. Stir over high heat until mixture comes to a boil. Smoothly purée sauce and spinach, then whirl in a blender with 2 tablespoons of the parmesan cheese and the egg yolks.

In a large bowl, beat egg whites and cream of tartar on high speed until whites hold soft peaks. Fold spinach mixture into whites. Scrape into oiled dish. Sprinkle with remaining parmesan cheese.

With a knife tip, draw a circle on soufflé top 1 inch from edge. Bake in a 375° oven until soufflé is richly browned and center jiggles only slightly when gently shaken, about 25 minutes. Makes 4 servings.

PER SERVING: 133 calories, 12 g protein, 8.9 g carbohydrates, 5.5 g fat (2 g saturated), 111 mg cholesterol, 231 mg sodium

LEMON OMELET-SOUFFLÉ

- 11 tablespoons sugar
- 3 tablespoons lemon juice
- ½ cup orange juice
- 2 teaspoons cornstarch
- 6 large egg whites
- 2 large egg yolks
- ¾ teaspoon grated lemon peel
- ½ teaspoon vanilla
  Sweetened light sour cream or vanilla-flavored nonfat yogurt

In a 9-inch-wide ovenproof frying pan (attractive enough for serving) or in a cake pan, combine 3 tablespoons sugar, lemon and orange juices, and cornstarch; set aside.

In a large bowl, beat egg whites on high speed until foamy, then gradually beat in 6 tablespoons sugar until whites hold stiff peaks.

In another bowl, beat egg yolks until thick with remaining 2 tablespoons sugar, peel, and vanilla. Fold yolks into whites.

Over high heat, stir citrus juice mixture until boiling. Off the heat, spoon egg mixture in large dollops into the hot sauce.

Bake in a 350° oven until the omelet-soufflé is golden brown and jiggles only slightly in the center when gently shaken, 15 to 20 minutes. Spoon sauce out with soufflé; soufflé center may be slightly creamy. Offer sour cream to add to taste. Makes 6 or 7 servings.

PER SERVING REVISED OMELET-SOUFFLÉ: 104 calories, 3.4 g protein, 20 g carbohydrates, 1.3 g fat (0.4 g saturated), 53 mg cholesterol, 45 mg sodium

PER SERVING ORIGINAL OMELET-SOUFFLÉ (May 1964, page 194): 162 calories, 4.7 g protein, 18 g carbohydrates, 8.1 g fat (3.8 g saturated), 171 mg cholesterol, 93 mg sodium

Easygoing Easter Buffet

EXALTING THE JOYFUL *freshness of springtime, this handsome buffet lunch features a menu of simple, wholesome flavors appealing to all ages.*

An Easter egg salad on crisp leaves accompanies easy-to-carve butterflied leg of lamb that you stuff into pocket sandwiches. Mellow grilled and raw vegetables make up a second salad, and dessert is sweet strawberries with a choice of crisp cookies and Easter basket confections.

EASTER LUNCH

**Barbecued Butterflied Leg of Lamb
with Mint & Pocket Bread**

**Grilled Eggplant Salad
with Onion & Cucumber**

Egg Salad with Leaves

Spring Strawberries

Biscotti   Shortbread

Candy Easter Eggs

Zinfandel

Two-berry Cocktail

The only last-minute duty is barbecuing the marinated butterflied lamb. It cooks in less than an hour and yields meat of varied degrees of doneness. You can barbecue eggplant for the salad the day before, or about 30 minutes before you cook the lamb. You can also make egg salad the day before, but you might want to wait until after the Easter egg hunt and use some of the find.

Buy or make the biscotti and shortbread. Offer a white or red Zinfandel or a soft Rhône-style red wine; provide chilled raspberry-cranberry juice for children.

BARBECUED BUTTERFLIED LEG OF LAMB WITH MINT & POCKET BREAD

- 1 **leg of lamb (5 to 6 lb.), boned and trimmed of surface fat**
- ¾ **cup balsamic vinegar**
   At least ⅓ cup mint jelly
- ⅓ **cup minced fresh mint leaves**

Fresh mint sprigs (optional)
Salt and pepper
Small pocket bread (about 3½ in. wide), or regular pocket bread (about 6 in. wide) cut in half crosswise

Lay meat boned side up. Slash about halfway through thickest portions, as needed, and pull meat, patting cut edges down, to make the piece relatively even.

Place lamb in a 9- by 13-inch pan. In a 1- to 1½-quart pan over medium-high heat, stir vinegar with ⅓ cup mint jelly just until boiling. Stir in minced mint leaves and pour evenly over lamb. Cover and chill 2 hours or up to a day. Turn meat over occasionally.

On fire grate in a barbecue with a lid, ignite 50 to 60 charcoal briquets. When briquets are dotted with ash, in about 30 minutes, spread them into a single layer; scatter 10 to 12 more briquets over coals. Set grill 5 to 6 inches above coals. Lift meat onto grill; reserve marinade. Put lid on barbecue and open vents.

Turn meat as needed to brown evenly; baste often with marinade. Cook until thickest part of meat is done to your liking; for rare (140° on a thermometer) in center of thickest part, allow about 40 minutes total. Thinner sections will be well done.

Transfer lamb to a platter and let rest 5 to 10 minutes. Garnish with mint sprigs. Slice meat thin. Season to taste with mint jelly, salt, and pepper. Tuck into pocket bread or eat with knife and fork. Makes 8 or 9 servings.

PER SERVING: 264 calories, 34 g protein, 8.5 g carbohydrates, 9.4 g fat (3.3 g saturated), 108 mg cholesterol, 84 mg sodium

GRILLED EGGPLANT SALAD WITH ONION & CUCUMBER

- 2 **small (about 1 lb. each) eggplants, ends trimmed, cut into ¾-inch-thick slices**
   About 2 tablespoons salad oil
- 1 **medium-size (about 1 lb.) European cucumber, thinly sliced**
- 1 **small (about ½ lb.) red onion, thinly sliced**
- ½ **cup cider vinegar**
- 2 **tablespoons firmly packed brown sugar**
   About ½ teaspoon salt

Lightly brush eggplant slices with oil and put them on a tray.

On a barbecue with lid, place grill 5 to 6 inches over a solid bed of hot coals (you can hold your hand at grill level only 2 or 3 seconds). When grill is hot, rub it lightly with a paper towel dipped in salad oil.

Lay eggplant slices close together on grill. Cover barbecue, open vents, and cook until slices are well browned and soft when pressed, 15 to 20 minutes; turn eggplant, as needed, with a wide spatula. Return slices to the tray. If eggplant is cooked ahead, cover and chill up to a day.

In a bowl, cover cucumber and onion slices with ice water. Quickly squeeze slices to bruise lightly, then cover and chill 30 minutes to 1 hour; drain. In bowl, mix cucumber, onion, vinegar, sugar, and ½ teaspoon salt. If made ahead, cover and chill up to 4 hours. Coarsely chop eggplant and spoon onto a rimmed platter; top with cucumber and onion mixture. Add salt to taste. Makes 8 or 9 servings.

PER SERVING: 76 calories, 1.5 g protein, 12 g carbohydrates, 3.2 g fat (0.4 g saturated), 0 mg cholesterol, 127 mg sodium

EGG SALAD WITH LEAVES

- 8 **hard-cooked large eggs, shelled**
- ⅓ **cup *each* mayonnaise and unflavored nonfat yogurt**
- 3 **tablespoons minced fresh dill**
- 1 **teaspoon pepper**
   Salt
   About 2 quarts *total* rinsed and crisped Belgian endive leaves, small romaine leaves, and small butter lettuce leaves (or all of 1 kind)

In a food processor or in a bowl, finely mash eggs. Add mayonnaise, yogurt, dill, pepper, and salt to taste; mix well. Serve, or cover and chill up to a day.

Arrange leaves on a platter and put egg salad in a small bowl. Serve leaves on plates and top with salad, or scoop salad onto leaves and hold to eat. Makes 2½ cups, 8 or 9 servings.

PER TABLESPOON SALAD: 30 calories, 1.4 g protein, 0.4 g carbohydrates, 2.5 g fat (0.5 g saturated), 44 mg cholesterol, 24 mg sodium

Slices of grilled lamb to eat in pocket bread, grilled eggplant salad, and Easter egg salad to scoop onto crisp leaves make a relaxed menu. Serve sweet strawberries with a choice of cookies and Easter candies for dessert.

Southwestern Specials

CULINARY EVENTS *have come a long way from pancake breakfasts. Today, fund-raising events featuring culinary stars draw big bucks to support worthy causes. In Arizona, the 13-year-old Scottsdale Culinary Festival is a three-day feast of freewheeling Southwestern food. Among the dishes we tasted at last year's festival, three were particularly imaginative and easy for home cooks to duplicate. Those recipes—featuring tofu, crab, and lamb—begin below.*

More can be anticipated this month, as the Scottsdale League for the Arts sets in motion this year's program. Events include the Great Arizona Picnic, winemakers' black-tie progressive dinner party, wine country brunch, and dessert competition. The event benefits the Scottsdale Center for the Arts and art activities in the area. For more details, call the arts center box office at (602) 994-2787.

TOFU PEPPER TACO WITH PINEAPPLE SALSA

- 1 **pound soft tofu, rinsed and drained**
- 2 **tablespoons Oriental sesame oil**
- 2 **tablespoons soy sauce**
- 2 **teaspoons pepper**
- 2 **cloves garlic, pressed or minced**
- 8 **large leaves radicchio (about 4 oz. total), rinsed and crisped**
- 1 **cup shredded jicama**
  Salsa (recipe follows)

Cut tofu into ½-inch cubes; drain well on towels. Gently mix with sesame oil, soy sauce, pepper, and garlic. Let stand 5 to 15 minutes.

Arrange radicchio leaves on plates and fill with jicama; set aside.

Place a 10- to 12-inch nonstick frying pan on medium-high heat. Add tofu mixture and cook, turning carefully, until tofu is lightly browned, about 15

Sophisticated tofu-radicchio taco with pineapple salsa is by Michael Shortino.

minutes. Fill each radicchio cup equally with tofu. Add salsa to taste. Makes 8 first-course servings.—*Michael Shortino, Top of the Rock, Tempe.*

PER SERVING: 74 calories, 3.4 g protein, 4.3 g carbohydrates, 5 g fat (0.5 g saturated), 0 mg cholesterol, 264 mg sodium

Salsa. Mix 1 cup chopped **fresh pineapple,** ½ cup chopped **red bell pepper,** 3 tablespoons **lime juice,** ¼ cup thinly sliced **green onions,** and **fish sauce** (*nuoc mam* or *nam pla*) or salt to taste. Makes about 1½ cups.

PER TABLESPOON: 4.3 calories, 0 g protein, 1.1 g carbohydrates, 0 g fat, 0 mg cholesterol, 0.5 mg sodium

CRAB CAKES WITH PASILLA CHILI AÏOLI

- ½ **pound shelled cooked crab**
- ½ **cup reduced-calorie or regular mayonnaise**
- ½ **cup minced carrots**
- ½ **cup minced celery**
- 1½ **teaspoons lemon juice**
  Salt, pepper, and cayenne
- 2 **slices (about 2 oz. total) white bread**
  About 1 tablespoon salad oil
  Fresh cilantro (coriander) sprigs
  Pasilla chili aïoli (recipe follows)

Mix crab, mayonnaise, carrots, celery, and lemon juice. Add salt, pepper, and cayenne to taste.

Tear bread into chunks; whirl in a blender or food processor until crumbs form; mound crumbs on a plate. Drop ¼-cup portions of crab mixture into crumbs, and sprinkle crumbs over top; pat into ½-inch-thick cakes.

Place a 10- to 12-inch nonstick frying pan over medium heat. Lightly coat pan with oil and cook cakes, using a wide spatula to turn once, until browned on both sides, about 4 minutes total.

Place cakes on salad plates; keep warm. Garnish with cilantro. Add aïoli to taste. Makes 8 cakes, 4 first-course servings.—*Anton Brunbauer, Hyatt Regency Scottsdale, Scottsdale.*

PER SERVING: 216 calories, 13 g protein, 11 g carbohydrates, 13 g fat (2.7 g saturated), 67 mg cholesterol, 410 mg sodium

Pasilla chili aïoli. Remove and discard stems and seeds from 1 large (about 1 oz.) **dried pasilla** or New Mexico **chili;** rinse chili. With scissors, cut the chili in ½-inch pieces.

Drain 1 jar (4 oz.) sliced **pimientos;** pat dry.

In a 10- to 12-inch frying pan, combine 1 tablespoon **olive oil,** chili, pimientos, and 1 chopped **garlic** clove. Stir over medium heat for 2 minutes. Add 3 tablespoons **dry white wine** and 1 teaspoon **lemon juice.** Stir over high heat until most of the liquid evaporates, about 1 minute. Add ¼ cup **regular-strength chicken broth;** boil, uncovered, until liquid is reduced to ¼ cup, about 2 minutes. Let cool.

Whirl mixture in a blender or food processor with ¼ cup **reduced-calorie** or regular **mayonnaise** until smoothly puréed. Add **salt** and **pepper** to taste. Makes ½ cup.

PER TABLESPOON: 56 calories, 0.7 g protein, 3.6 g carbohydrates, 4.4 g fat (0.8 g saturated), 2.5 mg cholesterol, 47 mg sodium

RACK OF LAMB WITH SPICY PEPPER RELISH

2 lamb racks, trimmed weight
about 1½ pounds each (rib ends
trimmed and chine—back-
bones removed or cracked)
6 sprigs fresh rosemary or
1 tablespoon dried rosemary
Salt and pepper
Spicy pepper relish (recipe
follows)

Trim surface fat from lamb. Cut each rack in half. Place lamb on a grill above a solid bed of medium-hot coals (you can hold your hand at grill level only 3 to 4 seconds). Turn to brown evenly and cook to doneness desired. For rare (140° on a thermometer inserted in thickest part), allow 15 to 20 minutes total. Just before removing from grill, burn 2 sprigs rosemary or all the dried leaves on coals under lamb (takes about 1 minute).

Transfer lamb to plates. Garnish with remaining rosemary sprigs. Add salt, pepper, and relish to taste. Makes 4 servings.—*Vincent Guerithault, Vincent Guerithault on Camelback, Phoenix.*

PER SERVING: 256 calories, 30 g protein, 0 g carbohydrates, 14 g fat (5.1 g saturated), 99 mg cholesterol, 93 mg sodium

Spicy pepper relish. Stem, seed, and cut in fine strips 2 large *each* (about 2 lb. total) **red bell peppers** and **yellow bell peppers** and 8 (about 3 oz. total) **red** or green **serrano chilies.** Mix with 1 cup **sugar** and ⅔ cup **distilled white vinegar.**

In a 10- to 12-inch frying pan over medium heat, cook pepper mixture, uncovered; stir often until most of the liquid evaporates, about 30 minutes. Cool; if made ahead, chill airtight up to 1 week. Makes about 1½ cups.

PER ¼ CUP: 167 calories, 1.2 g protein, 42 g carbohydrates, 0.6 g fat (0.1 g saturated), 0 mg cholesterol, 5 mg sodium

Colorful relish of red and yellow bell peppers and hot chilies complements grilled rack of lamb, created at festival by Vincent Guerithault.

Shortcut to a Moroccan Banquet

PRESERVED LEMONS *play a crucial seasoning role in the well-spiced dishes of Morocco, in northern Africa. The lemons acquire a distinctive salty, bitter-sour flavor when mixed with salt and set in the sun to ferment for several months.*

However, there is a faster, nontraditional way that doesn't depend upon endless sunshine and patience.

Jo Kadis of The Catering Caravan in Palo Alto, California, created this simplified, speedy process in order to have an ample supply of preserved lemons for the dishes she presents at her renowned Moroccan banquets.

She cuts the lemons in quarters and freezes them briefly to hasten softening of the fruit cells. Mixed with salt, the thawed fruit takes only about a week to ferment and develop the ideal texture and flavor. Refrigerated, the lemons keep up to 6 months.

LAMB WITH ARTICHOKES & PRESERVED LEMONS

- 3 **pounds boneless lamb shoulder**
- 1 **small (about 5 oz.) onion, chopped**
- 2 **cloves garlic, pressed or minced**
- 1½ **teaspoons ground ginger**
- ½ **teaspoon ground turmeric**
- 1/32 **teaspoon powdered saffron (optional)**
- 3 **tablespoons vinegar**
- 12 **small (about 2½ in. wide, about 1¼ lb. total) artichokes**
- 8 **to 12 Moroccan preserved lemon quarters (recipe below)**
- ½ **cup calamata olives**
- 2 **tablespoons lemon juice (optional)**

Trim fat off lamb. Cut meat into 1½-inch chunks. In a 5- to 6-quart pan, combine lamb, onion, garlic, ginger, turmeric, and saffron. Cook, tightly covered, over medium heat for 30 minutes.

Meanwhile, in a bowl combine vinegar and 1 quart water. Trim off stems, tough outer leaves, and sharp tips of artichokes, leaving pale, tender interior leaves. Cut in half lengthwise; scoop out and discard hairy chokes. As artichokes are trimmed, immerse in vinegar-water.

After meat cooks 30 minutes, increase heat to high, uncover pan, and stir often until juices evaporate and meat browns, 15 to 20 minutes. Stir in 2 cups water; simmer, covered, for 1 hour.

Drain artichokes and add to lamb; simmer, covered, for 20 minutes. Add 8 preserved lemon quarters and olives; simmer, covered, until artichokes are tender when pierced, about 10 minutes longer. Add 2 tablespoons liquid from preserved lemons or lemon juice. Skim and discard fat from stew. Pour stew into a bowl and garnish with remaining lemon quarters. Makes 6 to 8 servings.

PER SERVING: 375 calories, 42 g protein, 9.3 g carbohydrates, 19 g fat (6 g saturated), 137 mg cholesterol, 1,510 mg sodium

TOMATO & PEPPER RELISH WITH MOROCCAN LEMONS

Serve with chicken, pork, beef, or fish. Or offer as an appetizer to spoon into pocket bread triangles. You can make this refreshing relish up to a day before serving.

- 2 **small (about ¾ lb. total) green bell peppers**
- 1 **can (28 oz.) tomatoes**
- 1 **clove garlic, pressed or minced**
- 2 **tablespoons olive oil**
- ¾ **teaspoon ground cumin**
- ¼ **teaspoon paprika**
- ¼ **teaspoon pepper**
- 2 **or 3 Moroccan preserved lemon quarters (recipe at left), chopped**

Place bell peppers in a 9- to 10-inch-wide pan; broil 4 inches from heat, turning as needed, until charred on all sides, 15 to 20 minutes. Cool. Remove peel, stems, and seeds. Chop peppers. Drain tomatoes, reserving juice for another use. Coarsely chop tomatoes; drain well.

In a bowl, mix bell peppers, tomatoes, garlic, oil, cumin, paprika, and pepper. Add preserved lemon to taste.

To Preserve Lemons

USE POTENT PRESERVED LEMONS to add a tart, salty, slightly bitter flavor to foods.

For refreshing contrast, simmer with richly spiced braised meats, as in the recipes on these pages.

For a piquant touch, mince lemon and add to taste to salads.

For a bright accent, sparingly sprinkle chopped lemon over fish. Because salt is an essential ingredient, the sodium content of dishes using the lemons (especially the liquid) will be quite high.

MOROCCAN PRESERVED LEMON QUARTERS

**Eureka or Meyer lemons (4 to 5 oz. each), rinsed
Kosher salt**

Quarter lemons lengthwise and put in a noncorrodible airtight container. Freeze for 8 hours. Add 1 tablespoon salt per lemon (4 quarters). Store airtight at room temperature for 6 days; shake occasionally. Use as suggested here. To store, chill up to 6 months (color darkens). Each lemon makes 4 pieces.

PER PIECE: 5.7 calories, 0.3 g protein, 3 g carbohydrates, 0.1 g fat (0 g saturated), 0 mg cholesterol, 1,104 mg sodium

Sprinkle coarse salt over frozen lemon quarters. Let cure at room temperature for 6 days, then use.

Serve, or cover and chill up to a day. Makes about 2½ cups relish, 6 to 8 servings.

PER TABLESPOON: 62 calories, 1.4 g protein, 7.1 g carbohydrates, 3.8 g fat (0.5 g saturated), 0 mg cholesterol, 439 mg sodium

SPINACH SALAD WITH MOROCCAN LEMON

   2 **pounds spinach**
1½ **cups (3 oz.) finely chopped parsley**
   1 **cup (2½ oz.) coarsely chopped cilantro (coriander)**
   1 **cup (2 oz.) chopped celery leaves**
   3 **cloves garlic, pressed or minced**
  ½ **teaspoon paprika**
  ¼ **teaspoon chili powder**
   1 **tablespoon olive oil**
   2 **Moroccan preserved lemon quarters (recipe on facing page), finely chopped**
   2 **tablespoons lemon juice**
   6 **cherry tomatoes, stemmed, cut in half**

Trim off spinach roots and remove bruised and yellowed leaves; discard. Rinse spinach leaves well, drain, and coarsely chop.

In a 5- to 6-quart pan, combine spinach, parsley, cilantro, and celery leaves. Stir over high heat just until greens are wilted, 3 to 5 minutes. Pour vegetables into a colander set over a bowl. Press spinach mixture to remove liquid; place vegetables in a serving bowl. (If made ahead, cover and chill up to a day.)

Return drained spinach liquid to pan; add garlic, paprika, and chili powder. Boil, uncovered, over high heat until reduced to about ¼ cup, 3 to 5 minutes. Add oil, preserved lemon, and lemon juice. (If made ahead, cover and chill up to a day.)

Top greens with tomatoes and pour dressing over the vegetables. Makes 4 servings.

PER SERVING: 93 calories, 6.4 g protein, 12 g carbohydrates, 4.3 g fat (0.6 g saturated), 0 mg cholesterol, 705 mg sodium

MOROCCAN CHICKEN WITH PRESERVED LEMONS

For less sodium, use ripe olives instead of calamatas.

   2 **tablespoons olive oil**
   3 **pounds chicken thighs, skinned and rinsed**
   1 **large (about ½ lb.) chopped onion**
   2 **teaspoons paprika**

Salt-cured lemons give lively, bitter tang to spiced braised lamb with artichoke hearts. Use additional preserved lemon quarters to garnish finished dish.

   1 **teaspoon ground ginger**
  ½ **teaspoon ground turmeric**
  ½ **teaspoon pepper**
  ½ **cup calamata olives (optional)**
  6 **to 10 Moroccan preserved lemon quarters (recipe on facing page)**
  ¼ **cup finely chopped fresh cilantro (coriander), optional**

Pour oil into a 10- to 12-inch frying pan over medium-high heat. Add chicken and turn pieces often to brown on all sides, about 15 minutes. Lift out chicken; set aside.

Remove all but 1 tablespoon oil from pan. Add onion; stir often over medium-high heat until tinged with brown, about 5 minutes. Stir in paprika, ginger, turmeric, and pepper. Add 1 cup water, chicken, olives, 6 preserved lemon quarters, and 1 tablespoon preserved lemon liquid.

Cover pan and simmer, turning once, until meat is no longer pink at bone (cut to test), 20 to 25 minutes. Skim and discard fat; transfer chicken and sauce to a wide bowl. Garnish chicken with remaining lemon wedges and cilantro. Makes 4 servings.

PER SERVING: 298 calories, 40 g protein, 12 g carbohydrates, 11 g fat (2.5 g saturated), 161 mg cholesterol, 2,378 mg sodium

Seafood Custards to Start a Meal

INSPIRED BY JAPANESE AND *Chinese egg classics, these delicate, savory seafood custards start a meal lightly and elegantly.*

Unlike richer custards, our lean versions use clam juice or nonfat milk instead of cream. When baked, they set into a soft, moist, silky custard.

SAVORY SEAFOOD CUSTARD

This custard may weep slightly when cut; that is not a sign of being overcooked.

4 cooked clams (recipe follows) or ¼ pound shelled cooked crab
1 bottle (8 oz.) clam juice
4 large egg whites
    About 2 teaspoons fish sauce (nam pla or nuoc mam) or soy sauce
2 teaspoons minced fresh ginger
    About 2 tablespoons finely shredded green onion

Place 1 clam in each of 4 custard cups or bowls (¾-cup size). Set the cups in a large baking pan at least 2 inches deep.

In a bowl, combine reserved ¼ cup liquid from cooked clams (or water if using crab), clam juice, ¼ cup water, egg whites, 2 teaspoons fish sauce, and ginger; beat lightly just to blend. Pour ¼ of the mixture into each cup.

Set pan on center rack of a 325° oven. Pour boiling water into pan around cups to level of custard. Bake until custard jiggles only slightly when gently shaken, 25 to 35 minutes. Lift cups from pan. Let stand at least 10 minutes. If made ahead, cool, cover, and chill up to a day. Garnish with onion. Offer warm or cold, with fish sauce to add to taste. Makes 4 servings.

PER SERVING: 39 calories, 6.5 g protein, 1.7 g carbohydrates, 0.5 g fat (0.1 g saturated), 6 mg cholesterol, 194 mg sodium

Cooked clams. Scrub and rinse 4 **clams in shells,** suitable for steaming (about 1½ in. wide). In a 1- to 1½-quart pan, bring ¼ cup **water** to a boil. Add clams; cover and simmer until they open, about 5 minutes.

Or, to cook in microwave oven, place clams in a microwave-safe 1-quart container. Cover with plastic wrap and cook at full power (100 percent), checking every 30 seconds, until clams open, 2 to 3 minutes total.

Remove the clams as they open; continue cooking until all are open. (If a

Ginger-seasoned egg white custard surrounding steamed clam has silky, soft texture. Serve warm or cool with radishes and sesame crackers as a first course.

clam doesn't open, discard it and cook another.) Use clams warm or cool. Reserve ¼ cup of the cooking liquid.

SHRIMP CUSTARD

¼ pound shelled, cooked tiny shrimp
1 cup nonfat milk
2 large eggs
4 teaspoons dry sherry
    About 2 teaspoons fish sauce (nam pla or nuoc mam) or soy sauce
2 teaspoons minced fresh ginger
1 clove garlic, minced or pressed
¼ teaspoon Oriental sesame oil (optional)
⅛ teaspoon white pepper
1 tablespoon sesame seed

In each of 4 custard cups or bowls (¾-cup size), place ¼ of the shrimp. Set cups in a large baking pan at least 2 inches deep.

In a bowl, combine milk, eggs, sherry, 2 teaspoons fish sauce, ginger, garlic, oil, and pepper; beat lightly just to blend. Pour ¼ of the mixture into each cup.

Set pan on center rack of a 325° oven. Pour boiling water into pan around cups to level of custard. Bake until custard jiggles only slightly when gently shaken, 25 to 35 minutes. Lift cups from pan. Let stand at least 10 minutes. If made ahead, let cool, then cover and chill up to a day.

Meanwhile, toast sesame seed in a 6- to 8-inch frying pan over medium-low heat, shaking pan often, until seed is golden, about 8 minutes; remove from pan and set aside. Just before serving, garnish custards with sesame seed. Offer warm or cold, with fish sauce to add to taste. Makes 4 servings.

PER SERVING: 110 calories, 12 g protein, 5.3 g carbohydrates, 4.3 g fat (1.1 g saturated), 163 mg cholesterol, 128 mg sodium

Let the Oven Do the Work

AMONG THE APPEALS *of a traditional simmered supper are the ease of putting it together, its no-fuss progress, and the delicious gravy that slow cooking produces.*

Harold Johnson of Seattle lets the oven convert a pork shoulder roast to effortless tenderness while four root vegetables develop rich flavor as they gently stew in the pork broth.

HAROLD'S PIG & ROOTS

    1 **boned pork shoulder or butt roast
       (about 3 lb.)**
       Rich pork stock (recipe follows)
    1 **tablespoon minced fresh or 1
       teaspoon rubbed dried sage leaves**
    3 **tablespoons lemon juice**
 1¼ **pounds carrots, peeled and cut
       into 2-inch pieces**
    1 **pound russet potatoes, peeled
       and quartered**
  ¾ **to 1 pound turnips, peeled
       and quartered**
  ¾ **to 1 pound parsnips or rutabagas,
       peeled and quartered**
    1 **large head (about 1¾ lb.) green
       cabbage, cored and quartered**
 1½ **tablespoons cornstarch mixed
       with ⅓ cup water**
       Salt and pepper

Have your market trim pork of fat, then bone, roll, and tie the meat, saving the bones (or do this yourself).

Place meat in a 5- to 6-quart oven-proof pan on medium-high heat. Turning often, cook until meat is well browned all over, about 10 minutes. Add stock, sage, and lemon juice; stir to scrape browned bits from pan. Cover very tightly and bake in a 325° oven for 1 hour.

Add carrots and potatoes to meat. Cover and bake until vegetables are barely tender when pierced, about 20 minutes. Add turnips and parsnips; cover and bake until all vegetables are tender when pierced, about 40 minutes longer.

When vegetables are done, place cabbage in a 10- to 12-inch frying pan with ½ inch water. Bring water to boiling over high heat, cover, and simmer until cabbage is tender when pierced, about 10 minutes.

Transfer meat and vegetables to a large platter; keep warm. Skim fat from pan juices; bring juices to a boil over high heat. Add cornstarch mixture and bring to a second boil, stirring. Pour into a small pitcher. Slice meat and serve with vegetables; add gravy and salt and pepper to taste. Makes 6 servings.

PER SERVING: 551 calories, 48 g protein, 48 g carbohydrates, 18 g fat (6.1 g saturated), 148 mg cholesterol, 274 mg sodium

Rich pork stock. Place reserved **pork bones** in a 10- by 15-inch pan with 2 large (about 1 lb. total) **onions,** chopped, and 2 large **carrots,** cut in pieces. Roast in a 450° oven, mixing occasionally, until bones are well browned, 40 to 50 minutes.

Add ½ cup **water** to pan; stir vigorously to free browned bits. Scrape mixture into a 5- to 6-quart pan. Add 1 quart **water;** 2 stalks **celery,** cut in pieces; and ½ teaspoon **dried thyme leaves.** Bring to a boil over high heat, then cover and simmer for 1½ hours.

Uncover pan and boil over high heat until liquid is reduced to 2½ cups, about 10 minutes. Pour mixture through a fine strainer into a bowl. Discard bones and vegetables. If stock is made ahead, cool, cover, and chill up to 2 days. Skim or lift off fat and discard.

Oven supper steeps succulent pork with carrots, potatoes, turnips, and parsnips. Meat and vegetable juices form a fine sauce; steamed cabbage is final addition.

Eau de Vie: The Essence of Fruit

POUR A GLASS of eau de vie and savor its taste and aroma—an ineffable mix of one part pure ripe fruit and one part pure late summer in the countryside. "It's almost Proustian," says Randall Grahm of Bonny Doon Vineyard. "Eau de vie is the essence of a fruit, and it triggers a lot of sensory memories that affect people strongly."

Grahm of course is biased: he's one of the new crop of California and Oregon winemakers coupling traditional European eau de vie production methods with high-quality Washington pears, Oregon cherries, California apricots, plums, and other fruit.

Traditionally served either at room temperature (the European preference) or chilled (the American), a glass of a good eau de vie can make a fine finish to a special meal. The name means, simply, water of life.

FROM ORCHARD TO POT STILL TO BOTTLE

Though made from fruit—pears, berries, and cherries are among the most common sources—eaux de vie bear little resemblance to sweet fruit wines or cordials. They're colorless, not at all sweet, and potent: alcohol content is about 40 percent (similar to bourbon or brandy).

Basically they are fruit brandies, and they're distilled like brandies in alembic pot stills. But unlike brandies, eaux de vie aren't aged. Rather, they're bottled directly to preserve the fresh fruit flavor. (To some palates, lack of aging imparts an unpleasantly raw quality.)

Understandably, American eau de vie makers see themselves somewhat as voices in a wilderness. When German-born Jörg Rupf first began making Pear William in his Alameda, California, distillery, "people didn't know what an eau de vie was. I'd tell them about it and just get blank looks."

Randall Grahm began experimenting with eaux de vie because he originally wanted to make marc, a French brandy produced from grape pomace (seeds, stems) in a fashion similar to eau de vie. Trendy Italian grappa, too, is produced much the same way; most eau de vie makers produce a grappa or marc along with their eaux de vie.

"Essence of fruit" is how one winemaker describes the spirit. Pear, cherry, apricot, and plum are among choices.

Below is a listing of Western eau de vie makers. All will welcome you for a visit. (California liquor laws prevent sampling, though you may be allowed an informal tour of the premises; Oregon does allow tasting.) If you can't make the trip, look for eaux de vie in well-stocked liquor stores, or call the distillery to find a source.

Oregon. Clear Creek Distillery, 1430 N.W. 23rd Ave., Portland 97210; (503) 248-9470. Pear, framboise, apple brandy, grappa.

Eve Atkins Distillery, 4420 Summit Dr., Hood River 97031; (503) 354-2550. Apple brandy, marionberry, pear.

California. Bonny Doon Vineyard, 10 Pine Flat Rd., Santa Cruz 95060; (408) 425-3625. Prunus (plum, cherry, apricot), pear (available only on-site), cherry.

Creekside Vineyards, 5055 Gordon Walk Rd., Suisun 94585; (707) 427-3840. Apple brandy, grappa.

St. George Spirits, 2900 Main St., Alameda 94501; (510) 769-1601. Pear, framboise, kirsch, quince, grappa, and marc.

Vineyard workers sample eau de vie from Bonny Doon Vineyard in Santa Cruz County. Served at room temperature or chilled, it makes a fine finish to a special meal.

Matzo Meal for Crunchy Desserts

MATZO, UNLEAVENED BREAD *with an appealing toasted flavor, is an important part of the eight-day Jewish Passover celebration and is crushed into matzo meal for use in traditional Passover dishes. But matzo meal's flavor suggests other uses as well, such as in these unusually crunchy cookies and as a topping for rhubarb cobbler.*

Although these desserts are designed to meet religious requirements, you should check with a local rabbi to be certain all ingredients are kosher. In the supermarket, you usually find matzo meal with ethnic or Passover foods.

MATZO MEAL COOKIES

- ¼ cup sweetened shredded dried coconut
- 1 cup matzo meal
- ⅓ cup firmly packed light brown sugar
- ⅓ cup (⅙ lb.) margarine or butter, cut in chunks
- 1 tablespoon water
- 1 teaspoon vanilla
  About ¼ cup jam (optional)

In a food processor or with a knife, mince coconut. In processor or bowl, whirl or rub together coconut, matzo meal, sugar, margarine, water, and vanilla until the crumbly dough sticks together when packed.

Compact dough into tablespoon-size balls. Place 2 inches apart on 2 ungreased 12- by 15-inch baking sheets. Flatten balls to about 1½ inches wide.

Bake in a 325° oven until cookies are a rich brown, 25 to 35 minutes. Transfer to racks. For jam centers, let cookies cool for about 3 minutes, then press the handle end of a wooden spoon into each cookie, making a depression about ¼ inch deep. Fill each hollow with jam (¼ to ½ teaspoon; do not overfill); let cool. Serve, or store airtight up to 4 days; freeze to store longer. Makes about 20 cookies.

PER COOKIE WITHOUT JAM: 71 calories, 0.7 g protein, 9.5 g carbohydrates, 3.4 g fat (0.8 g saturated), 0 mg cholesterol, 39 mg sodium

PASSOVER RHUBARB COBBLER

- 1¾ cups sugar
- ¼ cup quick-cooking tapioca
- 4 cups ½-inch pieces rhubarb
- 1 cup fresh or frozen unsweetened raspberries
- 2 tablespoons lemon juice
- 1 cup matzo meal
- ½ cup (¼ lb.) margarine or butter
- ⅛ teaspoon ground nutmeg
  Raspberry or lemon sorbet (optional)

In a shallow 1½- to 2-quart baking dish, mix 1¼ cups sugar and tapioca. Add rhubarb, raspberries, and lemon juice; mix gently but thoroughly. Let stand 15 minutes to 1 hour to soften tapioca; mix several times.

Meanwhile, in a food processor or a bowl, whirl or rub together with your fingers the matzo meal, the remaining ½ cup sugar, margarine, and nutmeg until fine crumbs form. Squeeze to compact into lumps, then crumble over rhubarb mixture. Bake in a 375° oven until cobbler is bubbling in center and top is golden brown, about 1 hour. Let cool 15 minutes; spoon cobbler into bowls and top with sorbet, if desired. Makes 6 to 8 servings.

PER SERVING: 373 calories, 2.4 g protein, 66 g carbohydrates, 12 g fat (1.9 g saturated), 0 mg cholesterol, 138 mg sodium

Cookies and rhubarb cobbler use matzo meal for mellow toasted flavor and crunchy texture. Matzo meal is an important ingredient in Jewish Passover dishes.

ASPARAGUS WITH CITRUS CREAM SAUCE

- 1 **medium-size (about ½ lb.) orange**
- 1 **large (about ¼ lb.) lime**
- 1 **cup regular or light sour cream or unflavored nonfat yogurt**
- ⅛ **teaspoon white pepper**
- 2 **pounds asparagus, tough ends trimmed off**
  Salt

From colored surfaces of orange and lime, grate enough of the orange peel to make 1 teaspoon and enough of the lime peel to make ½ teaspoon.

From centers of orange and lime, cut 1 or 2 thin crosswise slices apiece; wrap slices airtight and chill. Ream 3 tablespoons juice from orange, 1 tablespoon juice from lime. In a bowl, mix orange and lime peel, orange and lime juice, sour cream, and pepper. Makes 1¼ cups. Serve or, if made ahead, cover and chill up to a day.

Bring 1½ to 2 inches water to a boil in a 10- to 12-inch frying pan over high heat. Add asparagus and cook, uncovered, until stems are just tender to pierce, 5 to 7 minutes.

Drain asparagus well, then place hot spears on a warm platter; garnish with reserved orange and lime slices. Offer flavored sour cream and salt to add to taste. Makes 8 servings.—*Roxanne E. Chan, Albany, Calif.*

PER SERVING WITH SAUCE: 78 calories, 2.8 g protein, 4.3 g carbohydrates, 6.2 g fat (3.8 g saturated), 13 mg cholesterol, 16 mg sodium

Sour cream, laced with orange and lime peel, seasons tender asparagus spears.

ITALIAN-STYLE LAMB CHOPS

- 8 **lamb rib chops (about 2 lb. total), cut 1 inch thick**
- 1 **cup dry red wine**
- ¼ **cup chopped onion**
- 3 **tablespoons soy sauce**
- 2 **tablespoons lemon juice**
- 1 **tablespoon sugar**
- 2 **teaspoons *each* dried oregano leaves and dried thyme leaves**
- 3 **tablespoons finely chopped parsley (Italian, if available)**

Trim fat from chops and discard. Rinse chops and place in a heavy plastic food bag. Add wine, onion, soy sauce, lemon juice, sugar, oregano, and thyme. Seal bag; rotate to mix ingredients well. Chill at least 30 minutes or up to 6 hours; turn occasionally.

Lift out chops, draining; reserve marinade. Place chops on a lightly oiled rack on a broiler pan. Broil chops about 6 inches from heat, basting several times with marinade. Turn chops once to brown evenly, and cook until done to your taste. For medium-rare (still pink in center; cut to test), allow 8 to 10 minutes total. Transfer chops to a warm platter and sprinkle with parsley. Makes 4 servings.—*Carole Van Brocklin, Port Angeles, Wash.*

PER SERVING: 207 calories, 21 g protein, 3.9 g carbohydrates, 9.5 g fat (3.4 g saturated), 66 mg cholesterol, 451 mg sodium

Broiled lamb chops are permeated by robust marinade of red wine and herbs.

PASTA WITH SAKE CLAM SAUCE

- 2 **cans (about 6½ oz. each) chopped clams**
- ¾ **cup finely chopped onion**
- 2 **cloves garlic, minced or pressed**
- 1 **cup sake or dry vermouth**
- 2 **tablespoons canned capers, drained**
- 10 **ounces dried linguine or vermicelli**
- ¼ **cup finely chopped parsley**
  About ¼ cup freshly grated parmesan cheese (optional)
  About ⅛ teaspoon crushed dried hot red chilies

Drain clams and reserve juice. In a 10- to 12-inch frying pan, combine ½ cup of the clam juice, onion, garlic, and ¼ cup sake. Stir on high heat until about ¼ of the liquid remains. Add remaining sake, clams, and capers; simmer 3 to 4 minutes. Keep warm.

Meanwhile, bring 4 quarts water to a boil in a 6- to 8-quart pan on high heat. Add pasta; cook, uncovered, until tender to bite, about 8 minutes. Drain pasta and pour into a wide bowl; add clam mixture. Lift and mix with 2 forks until most of the liquid is absorbed, about 1 minute. Top pasta with parsley, cheese, and chilies; mix again. Makes 4 servings.—*Laura Wyckoff, Portland.*

PER SERVING: 409 calories, 22 g protein, 59 g carbohydrates, 2.1 g fat (0.3 g saturated), 32 mg cholesterol, 173 mg sodium

Linguine will be dressed with clams, sake, garlic, parmesan, and capers.

Cherry Tomato Salsa

2 cups (about ¾ lb.) red or yellow
  cherry tomatoes, stemmed,
  rinsed, and cut in halves
Herb blend (recipe follows)
2 tablespoons finely chopped
  green onion
2 tablespoons lime juice
  Salt and pepper
  About 3 cups cucumber slices
  Tortilla chips (optional)

Coarsely chop tomatoes and herb blend
in a food processor or with a knife. Stir
in onion and lime juice. Add salt and
pepper to taste. Present in a small bowl
and scoop onto cucumber slices or tortilla chips. Makes about 2 cups, 6 servings.—*Nancy Fas, Cardiff, Calif.*

PER SERVING: 22 calories, 1 g protein, 5.1 g carbohydrates, 0.2 g fat
(0 g saturated), 0 mg cholesterol, 7.3 mg sodium

Herb blend. In a bowl, combine 1 clove
garlic, ⅓ cup packed **fresh cilantro**
(coriander), and 2 stemmed and seeded
fresh jalapeño chilies.

*Flavorful cherry tomatoes make good salsa to
go with cucumbers and chips.*

Chicken with Onion Marmalade

6 boned and skinned chicken breast
  halves (4 to 5 oz. each)
3 tablespoons cream sherry
2 medium-size (about 6 oz. each)
  red onions
½ cup dry red wine
1 tablespoon red wine vinegar
1 tablespoon honey
  Parsley sprigs (optional)
  Salt and pepper

Rinse chicken and put in a heavy plastic
food bag; add 2 tablespoons sherry. Seal
bag; rotate. Chill at least 30 minutes or
up to 6 hours; turn over several times.

Meanwhile, thinly slice onions; wrap
several slices airtight and chill up to 6
hours. In a 10- to 12-inch frying pan
over medium-high heat, combine
remaining onion slices, wine, vinegar,
and honey. Stir often until liquid evaporates. (If made ahead, cover and set
aside up to 6 hours; stir often over
medium-high heat to warm.) Remove
from heat and mix in the remaining
1 tablespoon sherry.

Arrange breasts in a single layer with
marinating liquid in a 9- by 13-inch pan.
Bake, uncovered, in a 450° oven just
until meat is white in thickest part (cut
to test), 12 to 15 minutes. With a slotted
spoon, transfer chicken to a warm platter. Spoon onion mixture over chicken.
Garnish with reserved onion slices and
parsley. Add salt and pepper to taste.
Makes 6 servings.—*Mrs. L. K. Ross, Elk
Grove, Calif.*

PER SERVING: 167 calories, 27 g protein, 9.4 g carbohydrates, 1.5 g fat
(0.4 g saturated), 66 mg cholesterol, 82 mg sodium

*Bake chicken breasts, then top with honey-
sweet red onion marmalade.*

Lemon Tea Cake

½ cup (¼ lb.) butter or margarine,
  cut in chunks
1 cup sugar
2 large eggs
½ cup milk
1 teaspoon vanilla
1¼ cups all-purpose flour
½ cup chopped pecans
  Lemon sauce (recipe follows)

In a bowl, beat with a mixer to blend
butter, sugar, eggs, milk, and vanilla.
Stir in flour and pecans until flour is
evenly moistened. Pour batter into an
oiled and flour-dusted 8-inch square
pan. Bake in a 350° oven until cake is
lightly browned and springs back when
pressed in center, about 45 minutes.

Run a knife between cake and pan
rim; hold a rack on pan top. Invert to
release cake, then tip back into pan.
Pierce cake top all over with a fork and
pour hot lemon sauce over surface. Serve
hot or warm; cut from pan or serve from
a platter. Makes 8 or 9 servings.—*Yvonne
Visteen, Portland.*

PER SERVING: 331 calories, 4.2 g protein, 44 g carbohydrates, 16 g fat
(7.3 g saturated), 77 mg cholesterol, 128 mg sodium

Lemon sauce. In a 1- to 1½-quart pan
over high heat, stir 3 tablespoons grated
lemon peel, 6 tablespoons **lemon juice,**
and ¼ cup **sugar** just until sugar is dissolved. Use hot.

*Sweet-tart lemon sauce seeps into simple tea
cake; enjoy cake while it's warm.*

Chefs of the West®
Adventures with Food

THE CYNICAL MAY SNEER *at tofu as a meat substitute, but to vegetarians it is a chief source of protein. Scoffing meat eaters, who are sometimes put off by tofu's amorphous texture and lack of pronounced flavor, aroma, or color, will appreciate it more if they think of it as a blank sheet of paper on which a beautiful poem may be written.*

The Chinese and Japanese have scores of ways to deal with tofu. But Amelia Leslie reaches further afield and prepares tofu in an Indonesian fashion, with a sauce based on peanut butter. If you like spicy-hot food, you could make the dish even more Indonesian in character by adding hot chilies or a hot sauce.

"Think of it as a blank sheet of paper on which a beautiful poem may be written."

TOFU INDONESIAN-STYLE

    ¼ cup *each* smooth peanut butter, soy sauce, and water
    ½ teaspoon Oriental sesame oil
    ½ teaspoon ground ginger
    1 teaspoon rice vinegar
    1 tablespoon firmly packed brown sugar
    2 cloves garlic, minced or pressed
    1 tablespoon sesame seed
    3 green onions, ends trimmed, thinly sliced
    1 pound regular tofu, drained
      Hot cooked rice
      Major Grey chutney

In a small bowl, stir together peanut butter, soy sauce, water, sesame oil, ginger, vinegar, and sugar until smooth. Mix in garlic, sesame seed, and onions.

Spoon about ¼ of the peanut butter mixture into an 8-inch square pan. Cut tofu into 4 equal slices. Lay slices side by side in pan (trim slices to fit, if needed, tucking scraps into corners). Spoon remaining sauce over tofu. If made ahead, cover and chill up to 4 hours.

Bake, uncovered, in a 375° oven until tofu is hot in center, about 25 minutes. Transfer tofu to plates with a spatula; spoon sauce onto tofu and cooked rice. Offer chutney to add to taste. Makes 4 servings.

PER SERVING: 228 calories, 15 g protein, 11 g carbohydrates, 15 g fat (2.4 g saturated), 0 mg cholesterol, 1,115 mg sodium

Amelia Leslie

Bend, Oreg.

OMAR KHAYYÁM, WHOSE *paradise required only a book of verses, a loaf of bread, and a jug of wine, might have suffered seriously from malnutrition (along with the mysterious Thou, who sang beside him) if the loaf were the bubble bread we are all familiar with. Although this flabby loaf contains niacin, thiamine, riboflavin, and a rich assortment of mono- and di-glycerides (ethoxylated and otherwise), it is not especially rich in protein and fiber, two pillars of contemporary sound diet.*

Oats and rye provide these two elements. Oats have kept horses (and Scots) in protein for centuries. As for fiber— well, oats don't exactly ream the arteries like Roto-Rooter, but they do seem to lower cholesterol. Still, the best reason for baking James Lee's oatmeal-rye bread is that it tastes great.

OATMEAL-RYE BREAD

    1 package active dry yeast
    2½ cups warm water (about 110°)
    1 tablespoon granulated sugar
    2 cups rye flour
      About 5½ cups all-purpose or bread flour
    1 cup regular rolled oats
    ⅓ cup firmly packed brown sugar
    1 teaspoon salt
      Butter or margarine (optional)

"Paradise required only a book of verses, a loaf of bread, and a jug of wine."

The night before, sprinkle yeast over warm water in a large (at least 4-qt.) bowl and let stand for 5 minutes to soften. Then add granulated sugar and rye flour; beat to blend well. Cover bowl tightly with plastic wrap and let stand at room temperature up to a day (at least 12 hours). Stir in 5¼ cups all-purpose flour, rolled oats, brown sugar, and salt.

To knead by hand, scrape dough onto a board lightly coated with all-purpose flour. Knead, adding flour as required to prevent sticking, until dough is smooth and elastic, about 10 minutes. Place dough in a greased bowl, turn over to grease top, and cover with plastic wrap.

To knead with a dough hook, beat until dough pulls cleanly from bowl. If dough still feels sticky, beat in flour, 1 tablespoon at a time; remove dough hook and cover bowl with plastic wrap.

Let dough rise in a warm place until doubled, about 1 hour. Punch down and divide into 3 equal portions. Shape each portion into a loaf and set in a greased 4- by 8-inch loaf pan. Cover loaves lightly with plastic wrap and let rise in a warm place until about doubled in volume, about 1 hour. With a sharp knife or razor blade, slash top of each loaf in about 3 places, making cuts about ⅛ inch deep. Brush tops lightly with water.

Bake in a 350° oven; after 10 minutes, brush tops lightly with more water. Continue baking until loaves are well browned, about 40 minutes total. For a shiny finish, rub tops of hot loaves with soft butter. Invert onto racks. Serve warm or cool. If loaves are made ahead, cool and package airtight up to a day; freeze to store longer. Makes 3 loaves, each about 1½ pounds.

PER OUNCE: 56 calories, 1.5 g protein, 12 g carbohydrates, 0.2 g fat (0 g saturated), 0 mg cholesterol, 33 mg sodium

San Mateo, Calif.

MUSHROOM SOUP IS SO *readily available in cans that it seldom occurs to the cook to make it from scratch. The canned product is, in fact, so universal, reliable, and chameleon-like in flavor that it has become the base of a thousand casseroles.*

If you seek a more intense mushroom flavor, however, look no further. Eric Lie, tooting his own horn, claims to have the answer to your prayers right here.

Flour plays a part in the thickening of this soup, but the basic body and emphatic statement of mushroom flavor come from cooking some of the mushrooms with onions until they are mellow and lightly browned, then puréeing them.

The flavor is further enhanced by adding sliced mushrooms before the final heating.

CREAM OF MUSHROOM SOUP

1 **pound mushrooms, rinsed and drained**
2 **tablespoons butter or margarine**
1 **large onion, chopped**
½ **teaspoon dried thyme leaves**
¼ **cup all-purpose flour**
6 **cups or 1 large can (49½ oz.) regular-strength chicken broth**
1 **dried bay leaf**
1 **cup whipping cream**
2 **to 3 tablespoons dry sherry**
  Salt and pepper

Chop half the mushrooms; thinly slice the remaining mushrooms and set aside.

Melt butter in a 5- to 6-quart pan over medium-high heat; add chopped mushrooms, onion, and thyme. Stir often until the vegetables are lightly browned, 15 to 20 minutes. Mix flour with vegetables.

Pour into a blender or food processor; whirl, adding as much broth as needed to smoothly purée the mixture. Pour mixture back into pan; add remaining broth, sliced mushrooms, bay leaf, and cream.

Bring soup to a boil on high heat, stirring frequently. Reduce heat to low and simmer to blend flavors, about 10 minutes. Add sherry, salt, and pepper to taste. Makes about 8 cups, 6 to 8 first-course servings.

PER SERVING: 178 calories, 4.3 g protein, 9.7 g carbohydrates, 14 g fat (7.9 g saturated), 41 mg cholesterol, 84 mg sodium

Edmonds, Wash.

"Tooting his own horn . . . for a more intense mushroom flavor."

April Menus

CELEBRATE THE GLORIES of spring with meals that show off the season's finest produce. Feast on tender spears of green asparagus in a pretty make-ahead patio lunch or supper.

Sweet spring strawberries brighten breakfast on a weekend morning. For a speedy supper, try the stir-fried combination that makes a complete main dish. And for dessert, choose mangoes; they're imported from many locales and are more plentiful these days.

ASPARAGUS FEAST

Cold Cooked Asparagus
Cool Roast Turkey Breast
Watercress Sauce
Asparagus Breadsticks
Butter
Dry Sauvignon Blanc
Sparkling Water
Cream Puffs

This spring menu expands easily to any number of servings and holds up well until guests are ready to eat.

For each serving, buy 8 to 10 ounces untrimmed asparagus. Snap off and discard tough ends. For a sweeter flavor and more tender texture, peel stalks with a vegetable peeler or special asparagus peeler. Boil the spears in water to cover just until barely tender when pierced, 3 to 4 minutes; drain and immerse in ice water to preserve color. Drain cold spears and serve, or cover and chill up to a day.

Roast a boned and tied turkey breast or, if you're in a hurry, buy sliced roast turkey from a deli. For each serving, allow ¼ pound raw (or 3 oz. cooked) turkey. You might roast a larger piece of turkey to have leftovers for the next day.

The breadsticks (1 or 2 per serving) and watercress sauce (about ¼ cup per serving) can be made up to 1 day ahead. If bread is made ahead, recrisp before serving. If time does not permit making the breadsticks, buy them or crusty baguettes.

Purchase or make cream puffs for dessert.

WATERCRESS SAUCE

Look for the fish sauce in some supermarkets and Asian grocery stores.

- ¾ cup (about 1¾ oz.) packed chopped watercress
- ¾ cup unflavored nonfat yogurt
- ¾ cup reduced-calorie or regular mayonnaise
- 1 tablespoon lemon juice
- ½ teaspoon dried tarragon leaves
- 1 clove garlic
- 1 to 2 teaspoons fish sauce (nuoc mam or nam pla) or anchovy paste

In a blender or food processor, combine watercress, yogurt, mayonnaise, lemon juice, tarragon, and garlic; whirl until smoothly puréed. Add fish sauce to taste; whirl to blend. (If sauce is made ahead, cover and chill up to a day.) Makes about 1½ cups.

PER TABLESPOON: 25 calories, 0.5 g protein, 1.2 g carbohydrates, 2.1 g fat (0.5 g saturated), 2.6 mg cholesterol, 47 mg sodium

Salute the season of asparagus with this patio lunch. Cool green watercress sauce dresses both the poached spears and sliced roast turkey breast.

Asparagus centerpiece. *Stand in florist's foam (discard later) or tie around glass.*

Asparagus breadsticks. *With scissors at angle, snip 4 inches on one end of dough.*

Asparagus dish. *For fun, asparagus dish has a well designed to hold dipping sauce.*

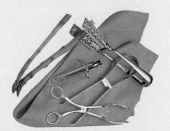

Asparagus tongs. *The genteel approach: tongs to serve spears come in many choices.*

ASPARAGUS BREADSTICKS

> 2 loaves (1 lb. each) frozen white or whole-wheat bread dough, thawed
> 1 large egg white
> ¼ cup grated parmesan cheese
> 1 teaspoon dried tarragon leaves
> 1 teaspoon dried dill weed

Set loaves on a floured board and pat each loaf into a 5- by 10-inch rectangle. Cover lightly with plastic wrap and let rise until puffy, 45 minutes to 1 hour.

Cut each loaf crosswise into 9 equal pieces. Pick up the ends of each piece, and stretch it to the length of a 12- by 15-inch greased baking sheet and set on pan; if dough snaps back, let rest a few minutes, then stretch again. Repeat to make each stick, spacing about 1½ inches apart.

With scissors at a 45° angle, snip dough to make cuts about ½ inch apart along about 4 inches of 1 end of each stick (see picture at left).

Beat egg white until slightly frothy; brush dough lightly with egg white. Mix cheese, tarragon, and dill. Sprinkle evenly over dough.

Bake in a 350° oven until breadsticks are browned, 20 to 25 minutes. (If using 1 oven, switch pan positions halfway through baking; chill remaining pans of dough until oven is free.) Transfer breadsticks to racks.

Serve warm or cool. If you make sticks ahead, let cool, package airtight, and hold up to 4 hours, or freeze. To recrisp, bake breadsticks (thawed, if frozen), uncovered, on pans in a 350° oven until warm, about 5 minutes. Makes 18.

PER STICK: 120 calories, 4.5 g protein, 22 g carbohydrates, 1.4 g fat (0.2 g saturated), 0.9 mg cholesterol, 317 mg sodium

---

CRÊPE & BERRY BREAKFAST

Cornmeal Crêpes with Berries
Poultry Breakfast Sausages
Tangerine Juice
Coffee or Milk

Brown sausages as you make these thin pancakes laced with cornmeal. Spread crêpes with apricot jam and fold into quar-

Lightly sugared sliced berries tumble over jam-filled crêpes. Serve with sausages.

ters. Guests can embellish them with yogurt or sour cream and lightly sweetened berries.

CORNMEAL CRÊPES WITH BERRIES

> 3 cups sliced strawberries
> 2 tablespoons sugar
> 1 cup milk
> 3 large eggs
> ⅔ cup all-purpose flour
> ¼ cup yellow cornmeal
> 1 teaspoon vanilla
> About 2½ teaspoons butter or margarine
> About ¼ cup apricot jam
> Vanilla low-fat yogurt or light or regular sour cream

In a bowl, mix strawberries and sugar; set aside. In a blender, whirl milk, eggs, flour, cornmeal, and vanilla until no lumps remain.

Place a flat-bottom 7- to 8-inch-wide frying or crêpe pan over medium-high heat. When pan is hot, add ¼ teaspoon butter and swirl to coat surface. Pour in

¼ cup batter all at once; quickly tilt pan so batter flows over entire surface (don't worry if there are a few holes). Cook until surface is dry and edge is lightly browned, about 1 minute. Turn with a spatula and brown other side. Turn out onto a plate; keep warm. Repeat to cook remainder, stirring batter thoroughly before cooking each crêpe (cornmeal sinks) and stacking crêpes as made.

Spread 1 side of each crêpe lightly with jam; fold in quarters. Offer crêpes with berries and yogurt to add to taste. Makes 8 to 10 crêpes, 3 or 4 servings.

PER SERVING WITH BERRIES: 334 calories, 10 g protein, 55 g carbohydrates, 8.5 g fat (3.7 g saturated), 173 mg cholesterol, 101 mg sodium

---

QUICK COUSCOUS SUPPER PLATTER

Stir-fried Spiced Pork on Couscous
Beer or Iced Tea
Mango Blossoms
Sesame Cookies

Once you prepare and cut the ingredients, it takes only minutes to cook the couscous, stir-fry the meat, and dress the cabbage. Mound the hot couscous and pork and onion on cool cabbage for a one-dish main course. The cabbage can be on a platter or individual plates.

Conclude the meal with mangoes cut to resemble blossoms. For the most effec-tive results using this cutting technique, choose the round, plump-cheeked, red-flushed mango varieties.

Select ready-to-eat mangoes, if you can; they give slightly when gently pressed, much like a ripe avocado. Keep firm mangoes at room temperature until ripe; if you chill unripe fruit, the cold tempera-ture halts the ripening process.

STIR-FRIED SPICED PORK ON COUSCOUS

- 4 cups (about 10 oz.) shredded red cabbage
- ¼ cup seasoned rice vinegar, or cider vinegar plus 1 tablespoon sugar
- 2 cups regular-strength chicken broth
- 1 cup (6 oz.) couscous
- 2 tablespoons salad oil
- 1 pound boneless pork loin or shoulder, fat trimmed, cut in ½- by 3-inch strips
- 1 large (about ½ lb.) onion, thinly sliced
- 1 tablespoon minced fresh ginger
- 2 cloves garlic, pressed or minced
  Sauce (recipe follows)
- ¼ cup chopped fresh mint or cilantro (coriander) leaves

Mix cabbage with vinegar; set aside.

In a 1½- to 2-quart pan, bring broth to a boil. Stir in the couscous, cover pan tightly, remove from heat, and let stand until couscous is tender to bite and most of the liquid is absorbed, about 5 minutes.

Meanwhile, place a wok or 10- to 12-inch frying pan over high heat. When pan is hot, add 2 teaspoons oil and half the pork; stir-fry until pork is lightly browned, about 3 minutes. Remove from pan; add 2 teaspoons oil and remaining pork to pan, and repeat stir-frying step. Add to cooked meat.

To pan, add 2 more teaspoons oil, onion, ginger, and garlic; stir-fry 2 min-utes. Return pork to pan and add sauce. Stir until sauce boils, about 2 minutes.

Place cabbage in a layer on a large platter, or divide among 4 dinner plates. Mound hot couscous on cabbage. Spoon pork and sauce over couscous. Sprinkle with mint. Makes 4 servings.

PER SERVING: 505 calories, 33 g protein, 54 g carbohydrates, 18 g fat (4.6 g saturated), 68 mg cholesterol, 639 mg sodium

Sauce. Stir together ¾ cup **regular-strength chicken broth**, ½ cup **orange juice**, 4 teaspoons **cornstarch**, 2 table-spoons **soy sauce**, 1 teaspoon **ground coriander**, ½ teaspoon **ground cumin**, and ¼ teaspoon **cayenne**.

MANGO BLOSSOMS

- 2 large (about 1 lb. each) firm-ripe mangoes
- 1 large orange (about ½ lb.), cut into wedges

Slide a sharp knife parallel to broad side of mango and against pit; cut off both sides. Place halves cut side up; cut flesh to the skin, but not through, to make ½-inch squares. Gently push up the skin to flare out mango sections; serve with orange wedges. Makes 4 servings.

PER SERVING: 121 calories, 1.1 g protein, 31 g carbohydrates, 0.5 g fat (0.1 g saturated), 0 mg cholesterol, 3.1 mg sodium

MAY

Red greens in three salads (page 96)

Salad greens tinged with
red have returned, and these crisp greens with a rosy blush
show off in May's salads and appetizers. This month three
chefs share quick yet creative ways to prepare fresh fish.
Classic tortellini in cream is lightened up and streamlined in
a new version: potsticker skins wrapped around a chicken
filling. Seasonings from Asia and the Caribbean add
fresh interest to guacamole. And we begin a new series
in which we discover why certain things happen as we cook;
this month we learn why cooked vegetables change color.

Red Greens

R**ED GREENS FOR** *salad are back. Years ago, many lettuces sported a red blush, but current fashion preferred green leaves. Now, style dictates red in greens as a way to command premium prices. So plant breeders are busy crossing red lettuces, which contain a pigment called anthocyanin, with green types to produce greens flushed rusty red to fuchsia.*

Most blush lettuces somewhat resemble and taste like their green cousins. The red color shows most prominently on outer leaves and leaf edges. Inner leaves may be primarily green with pink freckles.

The commonest red lettuces are butter (Merveille des Quatre Saisons and Perella Red) and loose-leaf (common leaf and frilly Lollo Rosso). Maroon romaine (Rouge d'Hiver) has a smoother, more tender texture than its green form. Oak leaf lettuce, with pointed notched leaves, has a slightly nutty flavor.

Other red greens include mustard, Belgian endive, salad savoy (ornamental kale), and radicchio (round heads of chioggia or less common elongated trevisano).

Use red-tinged lettuces raw in salads and appetizers. Pungent varieties (hot mustard, and bitter radicchio and Belgian endive) can be used as a flavor accent when mixed with mild greens. Sturdy radicchio, salad savoy, and Belgian endive can also be cooked.

WARM RADICCHIO CHEESE PUDDLES

- 2 **teaspoons extra-virgin olive oil**
- 2 **teaspoons lemon juice**
- 6 **large (about 4 oz. total) radicchio leaves, rinsed and dried**
- 3 **ounces teleme or jack cheese, cut into ¼-inch-thick slices**
  Freshly ground pepper

Mix oil and lemon juice; brush mixture all over radicchio leaves. Set leaves, cupped side up, in a 9- by 13-inch baking dish. Place an equal portion of the cheese in each radicchio cup. Sprinkle with pepper.

Bake in a 350° oven just until the cheese melts, 4 to 6 minutes. Serve hot or warm. Makes 6 first-course servings.

PER SERVING: 56 calories, 2.7 g protein, 1.3 g carbohydrates, 4.5 g fat (0.2 g saturated), 2.6 mg cholesterol, 77 mg sodium

RED GREENS & PEARS WITH NUT VINAIGRETTE

- 3 **quarts mixed bite-size pieces red greens (choose from Belgian endive, butter, leaf, mustard, oak leaf, radicchio, romaine, and salad savoy), rinsed and crisped**
- 2 **medium-size (about 1 lb. total) firm-ripe red or green Anjou pears, cored and thinly sliced**
  Nut vinaigrette (recipe follows)
  Salt and pepper

In a large bowl, combine greens and pears. Add dressing, and salt and pepper to taste; mix. Makes 6 to 8 servings.

PER SERVING: 109 calories, 2 g protein, 12 g carbohydrates, 6.6 g fat (0.7 g saturated), 0 mg cholesterol, 8.3 mg sodium

Nut vinaigrette. In a 6- to 8-inch frying pan, stir ⅓ cup chopped **hazelnuts** in 2 tablespoons **salad oil** over low heat until nuts are golden, 5 to 8 minutes. Cool. Add 1 teaspoon finely shredded **lemon peel,** 3 tablespoons *each* **lemon juice** and **water,** and ½ teaspoon **sugar.**

RED LETTUCE QUARTERS WITH ORANGES

- 1 **medium-size head (6 to 8 oz.) red oak leaf, leaf, or romaine lettuce**
- 2 **large (about 1½ lb. total) oranges**
- ¼ **cup reduced-fat mayonnaise**
- 1 **tablespoon sherry or cider vinegar**
- 2 **teaspoons honey**
- 2 **teaspoons canned green peppercorns, drained and chopped**

Cut lettuce lengthwise through core into quarters. Immerse in water and gently swish to remove dirt; shake gently to remove water. Wrap in towels, slip into plastic bags, and chill 30 minutes or up to a day.

Grate enough orange peel to make ½ teaspoon. Cut remaining peel and white membrane off oranges. Over a bowl, cut between membranes to remove orange sections. Squeeze membrane over bowl. Drain off all the juice and measure; you need 3 tablespoons (save extra juice for another use).

Whisk together the 3 tablespoons orange juice, orange peel, mayonnaise, vinegar, honey, and peppercorns. If made ahead, cover and chill fruit and dressing separately up to 4 hours. On each of 4 salad or dinner plates, place 1 wedge of lettuce. Top with equal portions of fruit and dressing. Makes 4 servings.

PER SERVING: 120 calories, 1.7 g protein, 21 g carbohydrates, 4.5 g fat (1.1 g saturated), 5 mg cholesterol, 85 mg sodium

RED CHEESE SPEARS

- **About ½ pound red Belgian endive (4 or 5 heads), bases trimmed**
- 5 **to 6 ounces chèvre fromage blanc or whipped cream cheese**
- 3 **tablespoons chopped salted pistachios**

Trim base of endive heads to separate large outer leaves (save extras for other uses, such as mixed salads).

In cup of each leaf place about 1 teaspoon cheese; sprinkle cheese with the nuts and arrange leaves on a tray. Makes 3 to 4 dozen appetizers.

PER PIECE: 12 calories, 0.6 g protein, 0.4 g carbohydrates, 1 g fat (0 g saturated), 0 mg cholesterol, 33 mg sodium

Show off red-tinged leaves in dramatic presentations (clockwise, from top left): baked radicchio leaf cradles warm teleme cheese for simple knife-and-fork first course; toasted hazelnut vinaigrette dresses mixed red greens and pear slices; orange segments cascade over a quartered head of red oak leaf lettuce; and spears of red Belgian endive hold tangy chèvre cheese and pistachios for a quick appetizer.

Quick Ways with Fresh Fish

WHEN TIME IS SHORT, *fish is a quick, nutritious dinner choice. We asked three California chefs for creative ways to prepare readily available Pacific halibut, tilapia, and rockfish, which broil in minutes.*

HALIBUT PICCATA

- 1 **large clove garlic, minced or pressed**
- 2½ **tablespoons olive oil**
- ½ **cup dry white wine**
- 3 **tablespoons lemon juice**
- 2 **tablespoons drained canned capers**
- 1½ **pounds Pacific halibut fillets, ¾ to 1 inch thick**
  Pepper
- ½ **cup finely shredded parmesan cheese**

In a 6- to 8-inch frying pan over medium-high heat, stir garlic in ½ tablespoon oil until limp, about 2 minutes. Add wine, lemon juice, and capers. Boil, uncovered, over high heat until reduced to ½ cup, 3 to 4 minutes; keep sauce warm.

Rinse fish, pat dry, and cut into 4 to 6 equal portions. Rub fish with remaining oil, sprinkle with pepper, and arrange in a single layer in a 12- by 17-inch broiler pan (without rack).

Broil about 3 inches from heat for 3 minutes. Turn fish over, sprinkle with cheese, and broil until opaque but still moist-looking in center of thickest part (cut to test), about 3 minutes longer. Transfer to a platter and pour sauce onto fish. Makes 4 to 6 servings.—*Charlie Palladin, Olde Port Inn Restaurant, Avila Beach, Calif.*

PER SERVING: 228 calories, 27 g protein, 1.2 g carbohydrates, 11 g fat (2.7 g saturated), 43 mg cholesterol, 289 mg sodium

Capers in clear lemon-wine sauce season Pacific halibut fillet broiled with parmesan. Keep sauce warm while fish cooks.

ASIAN-STYLE TILAPIA WITH BABY CORN RELISH

1½ pounds tilapia fillets, about ½ inch thick

    Asian sauce (recipe follows)

1⅓ pounds regular broccoli or ¾ to 1 pound broccoli rabe (rapini)

8 green onions (white part only), sliced

1 can (15 oz.) baby corn, drained

Rinse fish and place in a heavy plastic food bag with the Asian sauce; seal bag and turn to coat fillets. Chill at least 30 minutes or up to 2 hours, turning occasionally. Lift fillets from sauce; reserve sauce. Arrange fish in a single layer in a 12- by 17-inch broiler pan (without rack). Pour sauce into a 10- to 12-inch frying pan.

Trim broccoli stems or broccoli rabe, then peel if tough. Cut broccoli into 5-inch lengths about ½ inch thick.

Fill a 3- to 4-quart pan ¾ full of water and bring to a boil over high heat. Add broccoli or broccoli rabe; cook 1 minute. Lift from water with a slotted spoon and add to sauce in frying pan. Cook onions in boiling water about 30 seconds; add, with corn, to sauce.

Broil fish about 3 inches from heat for 3 minutes. Turn fish over and broil until opaque but still moist-looking in center of thickest part (cut to test), about 2 minutes longer; keep warm on a platter.

Stir sauce and vegetables over high heat until boiling; place on platter beside fish. Makes 6 servings.—*Robert Reash, Jr., John Dominis Restaurant, Newport Beach, Calif.*

PER SERVING: 209 calories, 26 g protein, 10 g carbohydrates, 7.6 g fat (0.7 g saturated), cholesterol not available, 855 mg sodium

Asian sauce. Pour 2 tablespoons **Oriental sesame oil** or salad oil into a 10- to 12-inch frying pan. Place over medium-high heat until oil just starts to smoke, about 2 minutes. All at once, add 1 tablespoon minced **fresh ginger,** 1 tablespoon minced **shallot,** ½ teaspoon **crushed dried hot red chilies,** and ½ teaspoon **ground coriander.** Stir for 30 seconds.

At once, add ½ cup **rice vinegar,** ⅓ cup **reduced-sodium soy sauce,** and 2 tablespoons **oyster sauce** (or more soy sauce). Boil, uncovered, over high heat until sauce is reduced to 1 cup, about 1 minute. Let cool.

Golden shreds of coconut blanket rockfish fillets. Serve with quickly made relish of corn, olives, and red bell pepper.

COCONUT ROCKFISH

½ cup sweetened shredded dried coconut

1 tablespoon minced or pressed garlic

¾ cup sliced green onions

2½ tablespoons olive oil

2¾ cups (1 lb.) freshly cut or frozen corn kernels

1 cup minced red bell pepper

1 can (2¼ oz.) sliced pitted black ripe olives, drained

¼ cup chopped parsley

1½ pounds rockfish fillets, about ½ inch thick, cut into 4 to 6 portions

2 tablespoons lemon juice

    Lemon wedges

    Parsley sprigs

    Salt and pepper

In a 3- to 4-quart pan over medium heat, stir coconut until golden, 3 to 5 minutes. Remove from pan; set aside.

Add garlic, onions, and 1 tablespoon oil to pan; stir often over medium heat until onions are limp, 3 to 5 minutes. Add corn, bell pepper, olives, and 2 tablespoons water; cook, covered, until corn is tender to bite, about 5 minutes. Mix in chopped parsley; keep warm.

Rinse fish and pat dry. Rub fillets with lemon juice and remaining 1½ tablespoons oil. Arrange in a single layer in a 12- by 17-inch broiler pan (without rack). Broil about 3 inches from heat for 3 minutes. Turn fish over; broil until opaque but still moist-looking in center of thickest part (cut to test), 2 to 3 minutes longer. Transfer to a warm platter.

Spoon corn relish onto platter; sprinkle coconut over fish. Garnish with lemon wedges and parsley sprigs. Season fish with lemon and salt and pepper to taste. Makes 4 to 6 servings. —*Charles Frankenfield, Ritz-Carlton, Marina del Rey, Calif.*

PER SERVING: 281 calories, 27 g protein, 21 g carbohydrates, 11 g fat (3.1 g saturated), 42 mg cholesterol, 196 mg sodium

Lightening Up Sunset Classics: Tortellini in Cream

PASTA GETS GOOD *marks in today's diet if you accessorize it trimly. You can do this easily with these speedy-to-make tortellini, shaped in round potsticker skins. The sauce is rich tasting but low in fat.*

Lightened-up Tortellini

To cut won ton skins into rounds, use a 3- to 3¼-inch cookie cutter.

> 6 **dozen (1 package, 12 to 14 oz.) potsticker (gyoza) skins, or won ton skins, trimmed to rounds**
> **Chicken-prosciutto filling (recipe follows)**
> 1 **large egg white**
> **Lean cream sauce (recipe follows)**
> **About ½ cup grated parmesan cheese**

Working with 1 skin at a time, put an equal amount of chicken filling (about 1 teaspoon) in each center.

Moisten skin edge with egg white, fold over filling, align edges, and press to seal. Bring pointed ends together, overlapping; moisten ends with white and press to seal tortellini. As shaped, set on flour-dusted baking sheets in a single layer; keep tortellini and skins covered with plastic wrap to prevent drying. Repeat until all skins are filled. If made ahead, chill up to 4 hours, or freeze on baking sheets and package airtight to store.

In two 5- to 6-quart pans, bring about 3 quarts water to a boil over high heat. Drop ½ the tortellini (unthawed, if frozen) into each pan. Cook, uncovered, until just tender to bite, 4 to 5 minutes (about 6 minutes if frozen). If tortellini stick to each other or pan bottom, stir very gently 1 or 2 times. Reduce heat, as needed, to maintain a gentle simmer.

Pour ⅓ of the sauce into a warm bowl. Gently drain tortellini; pour into bowl. Add remaining sauce. Top with cheese. Makes 6 to 8 servings.

PER SERVING: 308 calories, 29 g protein, 35 g carbohydrates, 5.3 g fat (2.4 g saturated), 48 mg cholesterol, 552 mg sodium

Drenched in a lean cream sauce, tortellini promise rich flavor with little fat. Use potsticker (gyoza) skins to enclose chicken-prosciutto filling.

Chicken-prosciutto filling. Mince ¼ pound thinly sliced **prosciutto.** Bone and skin a 1-pound **chicken breast;** cut meat into ½-inch pieces.

In a 10- to 12-inch frying pan over high heat, combine 1 large (10 oz.) **onion,** chopped, and 1 cup **regular-strength chicken broth.** Boil, uncovered, until liquid evaporates and onion starts to brown, about 12 minutes; stir often. To deglaze, add ⅓ cup **water** and stir to release browned bits. Boil until browning begins again; deglaze with ⅓ cup water and boil dry. Add chicken and prosciutto; stir until chicken is no longer pink in center (cut to test), about 3 minutes.

Coarsely grind meat mixture in a food processor or mince. Mix with 1 **large egg white,** ¼ cup grated **parmesan cheese,** 2 tablespoons **all-purpose flour,** 2 tablespoons **regular-strength chicken broth,** ¼ teaspoon **ground nutmeg,** and **salt** and **pepper** to taste. If made ahead, cover and chill up to a day.

Lean cream sauce. In a 10- to 12-inch frying pan, combine 1 large (10 oz.) **onion,** minced, and 1 cup **regular-strength chicken broth.** Boil, uncovered, on high heat until liquid evaporates and onion starts to brown, about 12 minutes; stir often.

Deglaze as directed for filling (preceding). Repeat until onion is browned. If made ahead, cover and chill up to a day. Mix into onions 1 tablespoon **cornstarch,** ¼ teaspoon **ground nutmeg,** 2 cups **extra-light** (1 percent fat) **milk,** and ½ cup **regular-strength chicken broth;** stir until boiling. Use hot.

Onward & Upward with Guacamole

MILD, BUTTERY *avocados go well with a wide variety of flavors. For a change of pace from the usual guacamole, try one of these recipes as an appetizer at your next party.*

ASIAN GUACAMOLE

Look in Asian markets for black sesame seed, pickled ginger, and wasabi powder (green horseradish). Most supermarkets sell rice vinegar.

- 1 **tablespoon black or white (regular) sesame seed**
- 1 **large (about ¾ lb.) firm-ripe avocado**
- 1 **tablespoon shredded pickled ginger**
- 3 **tablespoons seasoned rice vinegar (or 3 tablespoons cider vinegar plus 1 teaspoon sugar)**
- ½ **teaspoon wasabi powder or prepared horseradish**
  Potsticker crisps (recipe follows)

Place sesame seed in a 7- to 8-inch frying pan over medium-high heat. Shake pan often until seed begins to pop, 3 to 4 minutes. Pour from pan; let cool.

Peel and pit avocado; dice into a bowl.

Add ½ teaspoon sesame seed, ginger, vinegar, and wasabi; mix gently. Transfer to a serving bowl and sprinkle with remaining seed. Serve with potsticker crisps. Makes 4 to 6 appetizer servings.

PER SERVING: 81 calories, 1.1 g protein, 4.8 g carbohydrates, 7.2 g fat (1.1 g saturated), 0 mg cholesterol, 27 mg sodium

Potsticker crisps. One at a time, dip 12 round **potsticker skins** (*gyoza*) in water; shake off excess. Lay in a single layer on a greased 12- by 15-inch baking sheet.

Bake in a 450° oven until browned and crisp, 4 to 8 minutes, depending on thickness. Cool on racks. If made ahead, package airtight and store at room temperature up to 2 days.

PER CRISP: 39 calories, 1.8 g protein, 7.8 g carbohydrates, 0.1 g fat (0 g saturated), 0 mg cholesterol, 3.9 mg sodium

CARIBBEAN GUACAMOLE

- About ½ **pound Hawaiian or Portuguese sweet bread**
- 2 **tablespoons sweetened flaked dried coconut**
- 1 **small (about 1 lb.) firm-ripe papaya**
- 1 **large (about ¾ lb.) firm-ripe avocado**

Sweet-hot salsa pairs papaya with chili-spiked avocado.

- 2 **tablespoons lime juice**
- 1 **teaspoon sugar**
- ¼ **teaspoon crushed dried hot red chilies**

Cut bread into ¼-inch-thick slices, then cut diagonally into triangles. Arrange in a single layer in a 10- by 15-inch pan. Bake in a 300° oven until lightly browned, about 10 minutes; turn slices over halfway through baking. Cool on racks. If made ahead, wrap airtight and store at room temperature up to a day.

In a 7- to 8-inch frying pan, stir coconut over medium-high heat until golden brown, about 3 minutes. Pour from pan; set aside.

Cut papaya in half lengthwise. Discard seeds and peel, leaving halves intact. From 1 half, cut 2 lengthwise slices, each about ¼ inch thick. Dice remaining papaya; set fruit aside.

Cut avocado in half lengthwise. Discard pit and peel, leaving halves intact. From 1 half, cut 2 lengthwise slices, each about ¼ inch thick. Sprinkle slices with 1 teaspoon lime juice; set aside. Dice remaining avocado and mix with remaining lime juice, sugar, and red chilies.

On a platter, arrange avocado mixture and diced papaya side by side in separate mounds. Fan reserved avocado slices next to diced papaya, and reserved papaya next to avocado mixture. Sprinkle with coconut. Serve with toasted bread. Makes 6 to 8 appetizer servings.

PER SERVING: 157 calories, 2.8 g protein, 21 g carbohydrates, 7.3 g fat (1.1 g saturated), 0 mg cholesterol, 172 mg sodium

Guacamole with black sesame seed gets a kick from shredded pickled ginger and horseradish. Potsticker crisps bake quickly but can also be made ahead.

Why? Answers to Your Cooking Questions

COOKING IS AN EVERYDAY *application of science. When you understand why something happens, you can more readily count on a predictable outcome. You'll get better results when altering recipes or making up your own, and you can also evaluate the significance of contrary directions in similar recipes.*

This month we begin a new feature for you to shape. Share with us questions, puzzling observations, or contradictory information you've encountered about recipes and foods. We'll try to set the record straight. To do so, we'll call on the collective efforts of Sunset's food editors and the expertise of food scientists, primarily Dr. George K. York, extension food technologist in UC Davis's Department of Food Science and Technology.

If you have food questions you'd like us to answer, write to Why? Sunset Magazine, 80 Willow Rd., Menlo Park, Calif. 94025.

SO—WHY DO GREEN VEGETABLES CHANGE COLOR WHEN COOKED?

At the first blast of heat, in hot water, steam, or fat, green vegetables get brighter, but with longer cooking the green fades.

What happens? Heat forces the gases surrounding the vegetable cells to expand and escape. As a result, you can see the green pigment, chlorophyll, more clearly. It's rather like fog fading away to let light reveal the color.

Fried vegetables, as in tempura, cook so quickly the color stays quite green if vegetables are eaten hot.

Boiled or steamed (including microwaved) vegetables like green beans, peas, asparagus, broccoli, cabbage, and leafy greens are ready to eat (tender to tender-crisp) while still brightly colored. But if you want to serve vegetables cold or reheat them later, you must stop their cooking with a shock to arrest color change. Drain vegetables and at once immerse them in ice water until cool; this stabilizes the chlorophyll. When reheated, the vegetables don't fade as rapidly as when first cooked. (This is why frozen green vegetables keep their color longer when cooked.)

Vegetables that take more cooking, like artichokes, lose their bright color.

WHAT DO BAKING SODA & COPPER PENNIES DO TO GREEN VEGETABLES?

In the past, cooks often added baking soda or copper pennies to cooking water because they made green vegetables stay brightly colored.

Baking soda is alkaline (acid's opposite), and because it prevents hydrogen from replacing magnesium in chlorophyll, the pigment gets brighter. The negative: soda rapidly breaks down pectin that holds cell walls together, making vegetables mushy.

Copper coins and unlined copper pans contain free copper or zinc ions that also replace magnesium in chlorophyll, giving the green color a bluish cast. The vegetable texture is not affected, but you might be: eating too much copper sulfate can make you sick.

WHY DO GREEN VEGETABLES TURN GRAYISH YELLOW?

Heat is rough on chlorophyll, which is very unstable. One reason recipes direct you to boil vegetables uncovered is so that color-destructive gases surrounding the cells can dissipate rapidly.

If you cook vegetables in lots of boiling water, rather than just a little, heat is distributed faster, and vegetables have better color because there is less time for chlorophyll to fall apart.

Green vegetable color fades to olive, then to grayish yellow, as heat displaces the magnesium atoms in the chlorophyll, shifting its chemical structure and the color.

Acid has the same visual effect on chlorophyll as heat does. But another factor is at work. The acid's hydrogen atoms replace the magnesium in chlorophyll, turning the color to a yellowish gray-green. This is why green vegetables turn drab if they stand in a tart dressing for more than a few minutes. To minimize the color change, dress vegetables just before serving.

WHY DOES RED CABBAGE TURN BLUE WHEN COOKED?

Red cabbage and other blue-red vegetables are a war zone for two color pigments, anthocyanins (red) and betacyanins (blue). The red color needs acid (lemon juice, vinegar) to anchor it; otherwise red vegetables get the blues. For a little drama, cook red cabbage in a little water. Then add acid, such as lemon juice or vinegar, to taste and cook further, watching the unappetizing blue-purple color shift rapidly to red.

Acid changes the color of vegetables. Lemon juice (or any tart dressing) turns cooked beans to drab olive. Lemon juice helps brighten and set red pigments in cabbage; without it, blue pigments take over when cabbage is cooked.

On-the-go Breakfast Bars

POWERHOUSE COOKIE BARS *turn break-fast on the run or anytime snacks into a wholesome treat.*

These mildly sweet and slightly chewy cookie bars are made without added fat and contain egg whites (no yolks), whole-wheat flour or rolled oats, and crystallized ginger, dates, or raisins and bananas.

To store: *wrap bars airtight and hold at room temperature up to a day; freeze to keep longer, pulling out a piece at a time, as needed.*

GINGER BARS

> 1 cup whole-wheat flour
> ¼ cup sugar
> ½ teaspoon baking soda
> 3 tablespoons coarsely chopped crystallized ginger
> ¼ cup nonfat milk
> ¼ cup molasses
> 2 large egg whites

In a large bowl, stir together flour, sugar, soda, and crystallized ginger. Add milk, molasses, and egg whites; beat until smoothly blended.

Spread batter evenly in a nonstick (or lightly oiled regular) 8-inch-square pan.

Bake in a 350° oven until cake begins to pull from pan sides and springs back when lightly touched in center, 20 to 25 minutes. Serve warm or cool, cut into about 2-inch squares. Store as directed above. Makes 16 pieces.

PER PIECE: 64 calories, 1.6 g protein, 15 g carbohydrates, 0.1 g fat (0 g saturated), 0.1 mg cholesterol, 37 mg sodium

Satisfying but low fat, sweet but unsticky, wholesome cookie bars suit on-the-go breakfast. Freeze squares individually, then pull out a piece at a time, as needed.

MAPLE DATE BARS

> ¾ cup whole-wheat flour
> ½ teaspoon baking powder
> ½ teaspoon baking soda
> ½ cup chopped dates
> ½ cup maple syrup
> 2 large egg whites
> ½ teaspoon vanilla

In a large bowl, stir together flour, baking powder, soda, and dates. Add syrup, egg whites, and vanilla; beat until smoothly mixed.

Spread batter evenly in a nonstick (or lightly oiled regular) 8-inch-square pan.

Bake in a 350° oven until cake is golden brown, just begins to pull from pan sides, and springs back when lightly touched in the center, about 20 min-utes. Serve warm or cool, cut into about 2-inch squares. Store as directed above left. Makes 16 pieces.

PER PIECE: 62 calories, 1.3 g protein, 15 g carbohydrates, 0.1 g fat (0 g saturated), 0 mg cholesterol, 47 mg sodium

BANANA OAT BARS

> 1⅓ cups all-purpose flour
> 1 cup quick-cooking rolled oats
> ½ cup sugar
> 2 teaspoons baking powder
> 1 teaspoon ground cinnamon
> ½ teaspoon baking soda
> ½ cup raisins
> 1 cup mashed ripe bananas (about 2 medium-size, ¾ lb. total)
> ¼ cup nonfat milk
> 2 large egg whites
> 1 teaspoon vanilla

In large bowl, stir together flour, oats, sugar, baking powder, cinnamon, soda, and raisins. Add bananas, milk, egg whites, and vanilla; beat until smoothly mixed.

Spread batter evenly in a nonstick (or lightly oiled regular) 9- by 13-inch pan.

Bake in a 350° oven until cake is golden brown, just begins to pull from pan sides, and springs back when lightly touched in center, 35 to 40 minutes. Serve warm or cool, cut into about 2-inch squares. Store as directed above left. Makes 24 pieces.

PER PIECE: 75 calories, 1.8 g protein, 17 g carbohydrates, 0.3 g fat (0.1 g saturated), 0.1 mg cholesterol, 59 mg sodium

Apple Syrup

REFRESHINGLY TART WITH *intense fruit flavor, this apple syrup enlivens both sweet and savory foods. Try it—as we did in The Netherlands—spread on bread to go with cheese, and stirred into mashed potatoes to make a dish called hot lightning. Or serve the syrup American-style over pancakes and waffles.*

To make syrup, boil down apple juice concentrate with lemon juice.

Rose-colored syrup made from apple juice goes well spread on bread to serve with cheese. This tart, concentrated fruit syrup comes from The Netherlands.

TART APPLE SYRUP

> 2 large cans (16 oz. each) frozen apple juice concentrate
> ½ cup lemon juice

In a 4- to 5-quart pan over high heat, boil apple juice concentrate and lemon juice, uncovered, until reduced to 1 pint, 20 to 30 minutes. Use syrup hot or cool; if made ahead, chill airtight up to 3 months. Reheat syrup, if desired. Makes 1 pint.

PER TABLESPOON: 59 calories, 0.2 g protein, 15 g carbohydrates, 0.1 g fat (0 g saturated), 0 mg cholesterol, 9.6 mg sodium

HOT LIGHTNING
(Hete Bliksem)

As an alternative to the apple syrup, you can use apples and sugar.

> 2 pounds (about 3 very large) russet potatoes, peeled and cut into 2-inch chunks
> ½ cup tart apple syrup (recipe precedes); or 2 medium-size (about ¾ lb. total) Granny Smith apples, peeled, quartered, and cored
> 2 tablespoons sugar (optional)
> ¼ to ½ cup milk
> Salt and pepper
> Melted butter or margarine (optional)

In a 3- to 4-quart pan, bring 1 inch water to a boil over high heat. Add potatoes. If you're not using syrup, add apples now (or use syrup later). Cover and simmer until potatoes are very tender when pierced, 20 to 25 minutes. Drain liquid from pan.

With a potato masher or mixer, beat potatoes into fine lumps. Add ⅓ cup syrup or the sugar, and milk to make a soft mixture; mash or beat until smooth.

Spoon potato mixture into a bowl; make a well in center and pour remaining syrup into it. Season to taste with salt, pepper, and butter. Makes 4 cups, 6 servings.

PER SERVING: 195 calories, 3.2 g protein, 44 g carbohydrates, 0.8 g fat (0.2 g saturated), 1.4 mg cholesterol, 28 mg sodium

Kulfi: India's Ice Cream

ICE CREAM IN INDIA, *called kulfi, is almost a candy. Like many Indian desserts, it's based on milk and sugar concentrated by boiling. This intense liquid gives kulfi a delicate caramelized flavor and a smooth, taffylike texture. Flavorings such as cardamom, saffron, and pistachio add to the richness and make kulfi a dessert to savor in small portions.*

Indians typically buy kulfi in sweet-shops, but it's easy to make at home, and you don't need an ice cream maker to do it. Just stir the flavoring into the boiled milk and sugar, then freeze the mixture in paper cups or homemade paper cones.

CARDAMOM KULFI POPS

  1½ **quarts whole milk**
  ⅓ **cup sugar**
  ¾ **teaspoon ground cardamom**
  8 **paper cups (3-oz. size); or cooking parchment or waxed paper**
  8 **ice cream sticks (optional)**

In a 6- to 8-quart pan over high heat, stir milk, sugar, and cardamom until simmering. Boil over medium-high heat until reduced to 2 cups, 25 to 35 minutes, stirring often; slide pan partially off heat if milk threatens to boil over. Let cool; to speed cooling, set pan in ice water.

Set paper cups in a rimmed pan. Or, to make cones, cut 8 pieces of parchment or waxed paper into 7½-inch squares. Fold each piece in half to make a triangle. With long edge toward you, bring one of the 45° angles to the top of the triangle, then roll toward other angle. To close hole at bottom, starting from the top, press 1 inside sheet to the opposite side. Tape the cone in a few places to hold it together. Support each cone, pointed end down, in a cup slightly taller than the cone; set cups in a rimmed pan.

Divide milk mixture among cups or cones. Freeze until kulfi is thick but not hard, 1 to 1½ hours; then, if desired, push an ice cream stick into each container. Freeze until firm, about 2 hours longer. To eat, peel off paper. To store, seal kulfi (still in cups or cones) in a large plastic bag; freeze for up to 2 weeks. Makes 8 servings.

PER SERVING: 144 calories, 6 g protein, 17 g carbohydrates, 6.1 g fat (3.8 g saturated), 26 mg cholesterol, 90 mg sodium

Easy-to-make Indian ice cream can be made in three unusual flavors: saffron, cardamom, and pistachio.

SAFFRON KULFI POPS

Follow directions for **cardamom kulfi pops** (recipe precedes), but omit cardamom. Place ¹⁄₃₂ teaspoon **powdered saffron** or ⅛ teaspoon saffron threads in a small bowl. Add 1 tablespoon boiling **water,** stir, and let stand for 5 minutes. Break up threads with a spoon. Scrape mixture into warm reduced-milk mixture. Makes 8 servings.

PER SERVING: 143 calories, 6 g protein, 17 g carbohydrates, 6.1 g fat (3.8 g saturated), 26 mg cholesterol, 90 mg sodium

PISTACHIO KULFI POPS

Follow directions for **cardamom kulfi pops** (recipe precedes), but omit the cardamom. Coarsely chop ½ cup **shelled roasted pistachios;** stir into the cooled reduced-milk mixture. Makes 8 servings.

PER SERVING: 190 calories, 7.7 g protein, 19 g carbohydrates, 10 g fat (4.3 g saturated), 26 mg cholesterol, 90 mg sodium

MEXICAN STUFFED MUSHROOMS

Baked mushrooms, mounded high with stuffing, make hearty appetizers.

12 large (about 1½ lb. total) mushrooms, each about 2½ inches in diameter, rinsed
⅓ cup thinly sliced green onions
1 clove garlic, minced or pressed
¾ teaspoon *each* ground cumin and chili powder
1 can (8 oz.) tomato sauce
1 can (4 oz.) diced green chilies
¼ pound jalapeño jack cheese, shredded
2 cups unseasoned stuffing mix
2 teaspoons salad oil

Twist mushroom stems free, trim off dried ends, and finely chop stems.

In a 10- to 12-inch frying pan over medium heat, combine stems, onions, garlic, cumin, chili powder, and ¼ cup water. Stir often until vegetables begin to brown. Add 2 tablespoons water, scrape browned bits free, and repeat step. Add tomato sauce, chilies, and ½ of the cheese. Remove from heat and gently stir in the stuffing mix.

Rub mushrooms with oil. Set cup side up in a 9- by 13-inch pan. Mound all the filling onto caps. Sprinkle with remaining cheese. Bake in a 400° oven until cheese is lightly browned, 15 to 20 minutes. Makes 6 appetizer servings.— *Kathy Addington, Albuquerque.*

PER SERVING: 199 calories, 9.6 g protein, 23 g carbohydrates, 8.7 g fat (3.6 g saturated), 20 mg cholesterol, 731 mg sodium

GAZPACHO SHRIMP & ARTICHOKE SALAD

Boil artichokes, then make shrimp and avocado filling to serve in them.

2 tablespoons vinegar
1 teaspoon black peppercorns
4 medium-size (3- to 4-in.-wide) artichokes, rinsed
1 pound shelled cooked tiny shrimp
Cilantro dressing (recipe follows)
Salt

In a 4- to 5-quart pan, bring 2 quarts water, vinegar, and peppercorns to boiling. Meanwhile, remove coarse outer artichoke leaves, trim stems even with bases, cut off top third of each, and trim off remaining thorny leaf tips.

Boil artichokes gently, covered, until bottoms are tender when pierced, 25 to 30 minutes. Drain; use warm or chilled. Pull out tiny, thorn-tipped center leaves; with a spoon, scoop out fuzzy centers. Set artichokes upright on plates, flaring leaves slightly. Mix shrimp with dressing; spoon equally into artichokes. Season to taste with salt. Makes 4 servings.—*Janet Lauck, Fresno, Calif.*

PER SERVING: 316 calories, 29 g protein, 18 g carbohydrates, 16 g fat (2.4 g saturated), 221 mg cholesterol, 382 mg sodium

Cilantro dressing. Mix 3 tablespoons **olive oil;** ¼ cup **white wine vinegar;** 1 clove **garlic,** minced or pressed; 1 tablespoon *each* minced **green onion** and **celery;** 1 small (about 5 oz.) firm-ripe **tomato,** finely chopped; 1 small (about 5 oz.) **avocado,** peeled, pitted, and diced; and 1 tablespoon minced **fresh cilantro** (coriander).

LAMB & SPINACH POCKET SANDWICHES

Seal lamb patties around sliced eggs and olives; broil. Tuck into pocket bread.

1¼ pounds ground lean lamb
½ cup chopped onion
2 tablespoons *each* soy sauce and prepared hot mustard
½ teaspoon *each* celery seed and dill seed
2 tablespoons minced parsley
2 hard-cooked eggs, thinly sliced
1 can (2 oz.) sliced ripe olives
4 pocket bread rounds (6 in. wide)
2 cups slivered spinach leaves
About 1 cup thin cucumber slices
Sauce (recipe follows)

In a bowl, mix lamb, onion, soy, mustard, celery seed, dill seed, and parsley. Shape 8 patties, each 4 inches wide; place egg and olives equally in center of 4. Pinch remaining patties on top to seal. On a rack in a broiler pan, broil 4 inches from heat until done to your taste, about 5 minutes a side for medium. Fill bread equally with meat, spinach, cucumber, and sauce. Makes 4 servings.—*Barbara Keenan, Fort Morgan, Colo.*

PER SERVING: 682 calories, 41 g protein, 48 g carbohydrates, 30 g fat (10 g saturated), 207 mg cholesterol, 1,420 mg sodium

Sauce. Mix 1 cup **unflavored nonfat yogurt;** ¼ cup cooked, crumbled **bacon;** and 2 tablespoons **sunflower seed.**

CRISP CHINESE PORK

2 to 2¼ pounds boned pork butt or shoulder, fat-trimmed and cut into 2-inch chunks
2 cloves garlic, minced or pressed
1½ tablespoons Chinese five spice (or 1 teaspoon anise seed and ½ teaspoon *each* ground cinnamon and ground cloves)
¼ cup soy sauce
4 to 6 cups hot cooked rice
    Thinly sliced green onion
    Fresh cilantro (coriander) sprigs
    Hoisin or Chinese plum sauce

In a 4- to 5-quart pan on high heat, combine meat, garlic, five spice, soy, and 1 quart water. Bring to a boil; cover and simmer until meat is very tender when pierced, about 1½ hours. Boil, uncovered, on high heat until sizzling, about 30 minutes; stir often. Drain fat from pan.

With 2 forks, shred meat; put into a 9- by 13-inch pan. Bake in a 400° oven until pork begins to crisp, 15 to 20 minutes. Spoon over rice; add onion, cilantro, and hoisin to taste. Serves 6 to 8.—*Karin Andersen, Monarch Beach, Calif.*

PER SERVING: 313 calories, 20 g protein, 30 g carbohydrates, 12 g fat (4 g saturated), 66 mg cholesterol, 566 mg sodium

Chinese flavors season simmered and baked pork; serve on hot rice.

PASTA WITH ROASTED PEPPERS & SAUSAGE

1 pound mild Italian sausage
1 small (about 2 oz.) head garlic
1 large (about ¾ lb.) onion, sliced
2 large (about 1¼ lb. total) red or yellow bell peppers, stemmed, seeded, and sliced
¼ cup balsamic or red wine vinegar
2 tablespoons Dijon mustard
1 teaspoon dried oregano leaves
1 pound dried penne (or other tube pasta)

Place sausage, whole garlic, onion, and peppers in a 12- by 17-inch pan; pierce meat all over. Bake in a 425° oven until vegetables are limp and have dark brown edges, about 1 hour; stir often. Thinly slice sausages; keep warm.

Cut garlic in half crosswise; squeeze pulp into a bowl. Add vinegar, mustard, and oregano; stir well.

Bring 3 quarts water to a boil in a 5- to 6-quart pan over high heat. Add pasta; cook, uncovered, until just tender to bite, 8 to 10 minutes. Drain; pour into a bowl. Add sausage and garlic mixtures. Mix well. Serve hot or at room temperature. Makes 6 to 8 servings.—*Josie Ingber, Berkeley.*

PER SERVING: 453 calories, 17 g protein, 53 g carbohydrates, 19 g fat (6.5 g saturated), 43 mg cholesterol, 535 mg sodium

Roast Italian sausages and vegetables, then mix with hot cooked pasta.

BLACK FOREST BROWNIE PIE

¼ cup (⅛ lb.) butter or margarine, melted
2 ounces unsweetened chocolate, melted
⅔ cup sugar
1 large egg
¼ cup milk
½ teaspoon vanilla
½ cup all-purpose flour
½ cup chopped walnuts
    Chocolate crust (recipe follows)
    Frosting (recipe follows)
1 can (15 oz.) cherry pie filling

Combine butter, chocolate, sugar, egg, milk, and vanilla; beat well. Add flour and nuts; mix well. Spread batter into crust. Bake in a 350° oven until top looks dry and feels firm when gently touched, 18 to 20 minutes. Cool; spread top with frosting. When frosting is cool, transfer cherries from can with a slotted spoon to top dessert. Makes 8 servings.—*Gale Franko, Pullman, Wash.*

PER SERVING: 485 calories, 5.2 g protein, 63 g carbohydrates, 26 g fat (11 g saturated), 58 mg cholesterol, 233 mg sodium

Chocolate crust. Finely crush enough **chocolate wafers** (about 24) to make 1¼ cups crumbs; pour into a 9-inch pie pan. Mix with 3 tablespoons melted **butter** or margarine and press firmly over pan bottom and up side. Bake in a 350° oven until darker brown at rim, 8 to 10 minutes. Cool.

Frosting. In a 1- to 1½-quart pan over low heat, stir ½ cup (3 oz.) **semisweet chocolate baking chips** with 2 tablespoons **whipping cream** just until smooth. Use warm.

Tart cherry pie filling enhances wedges of moist, dense brownie pie.

Chefs of the West®
Adventures with Food

UNEASY SIT THE *haunches of those constrained to ride the fluttery windup planes that carry travelers beyond the hub airports to land—or rather, skip and frolic—on gopher-pocked grassy fields. Most of these nervous passengers merely bite their fingernails; the tough-minded ones struggle to get some work done, take notes, or make plans.*

Dr. Gary Fauskin prefers to devise recipes, and his French Gulch Corn Casserole is the happy result of his self-administered in-flight psychotherapy.

On a recent trip from San Jose to Redding en route to French Gulch, he warded off apprehension by considering the inadequacies of existing corn casseroles and planning improvements. This is his winning formula.

FRENCH GULCH CORN CASSEROLE

- 2 **tablespoons butter or margarine**
- ¾ **cup minced onion**
- 1 **medium-size (5 to 6 oz.) red bell pepper, stemmed, seeded, and diced**
- 2 **cans (17 oz. each) cream-style corn**
- 1 **tablespoon chopped fresh cilantro (coriander)**
- ⅓ **cup peeled, seeded, and chopped tomatoes**
- 2 **tablespoons cornstarch blended with 2 tablespoons water**
  Salt and pepper
- ½ **cup shredded sharp cheddar or jack cheese**

Melt butter in a 10- to 12-inch frying pan over medium-high heat. Add onion and bell pepper; stir often until vegetables are limp, 5 to 8 minutes. Remove from heat and mix in corn, cilantro, tomatoes, cornstarch mixture, and salt and pepper to taste.

Scrape mixture into a shallow 1½-quart casserole; sprinkle with cheese. Bake in a 350° oven until bubbling around edges, 30 to 40 minutes. Makes 6 to 8 servings.

PER SERVING: 159 calories, 4.2 g protein, 26 g carbohydrates, 5.8 fat (3.4 g saturated), 15 mg cholesterol, 418 mg sodium

Gary N. Fauskin

El Cajon, Calif.

LENTILS WERE EATEN *long before Rome was founded; it is generally thought that the pottage for which Esau sold his birthright to Jacob (Genesis 25) was a stew of lentils. Sidney Taylor offers a better deal: his recipe and keep your birthright. And we may assume that his lentil bisque is smoother. Jacob had no blender.*

"The tough-minded passenger struggles to get some work done, take notes, or make plans."

Sherried Lentil Bisque

- 11 cups regular-strength chicken broth
- 3 cups chopped celery
- 3 cups chopped carrots
- 3 large (about 1½ lb. total) onions, chopped
- 1 small (about ¼ lb.) red or green bell pepper, stemmed, seeded, and finely chopped
- 1 medium-size (about 6 oz.) zucchini, ends trimmed, finely diced
- 2 packages (12 oz. each, or 3½ cups total) lentils, sorted for debris and rinsed
- 3 tablespoons dry sherry
- 1½ tablespoons cream sherry
  Thinly sliced green onions, including tops
  Sour cream
  Salt and pepper

In an 8- to 10-quart pan, combine broth, celery, carrots, chopped onions, bell pepper, zucchini, and lentils. Bring to a boil over high heat, then cover and simmer until lentils are very soft to bite, 50 to 55 minutes.

Whirl mixture, a portion at a time, in a blender or food processor until smooth. Return to pan and stir in dry sherry and cream sherry. (If made ahead, or if there are leftovers, cover and chill up to 4 days; or freeze in 2- or 3-serving portions.) Heat until steaming and ladle into bowls. Add green onion, sour cream, and salt and pepper to taste. Makes 6 quarts; allow 2 cups for a serving.

PER SERVING: 268 calories, 19 g protein, 43 g carbohydrates, 2.2 g fat (0.5 g saturated), 0 mg cholesterol, 93 mg sodium

Tacoma

NEARLY 50 YEARS AGO *during the food shortages of World War II, Sunset Magazine deplored the use of canned baby food (always, apparently, in good supply) as a substitute for scarcer products. Now, after half a century, we turn to baby food once again, this time to recommend it as a principal ingredient in Maureen W. Valentine's Oriental Plum-glazed Chicken.*

Why baby-food plums? They're already puréed, saving preparation time, and they're available all year.

Oriental Plum-glazed Chicken

- ¼ cup canned puréed plums for babies
- 3 tablespoons dry white wine
- 2 tablespoons soy sauce
- 2 tablespoons firmly packed brown sugar
- 2 tablespoons lemon juice
- 2 tablespoons finely chopped green onion, including tops
- ½ teaspoon Chinese five spice or ground allspice
- 6 chicken legs, thighs attached (about 4 lb. total), skin and fat pulled off
  Fresh cilantro (coriander) sprigs

Mix together plums, wine, soy, sugar, lemon juice, onion, and five spice.

Rinse chicken and pat dry. Arrange legs in a 10- by 15-inch pan. Brush with plum sauce. Bake, uncovered, in a 375° oven for 25 minutes. Turn chicken pieces over, brush with remaining plum sauce, and continue to bake until meat at thigh bone is no longer pink (cut to test), 20 to 25 minutes longer. Baste with pan juices during last 10 minutes of baking.

Lift chicken onto a platter and garnish with cilantro. Skim fat from pan juices; add ¼ cup water to pan and stir over high heat just until boiling. Serve juices with chicken. Makes 6 servings.

PER SERVING: 241 calories, 35 g protein, 7.3 g carbohydrates, 6.6 g fat (1.7 g saturated), 138 mg cholesterol, 495 mg sodium

Seattle

THE POTATO HAS HAD *a roller-coaster history. From South America, its culture spread rapidly in the years following the discovery of the New World. Spain and Italy grew the potato first on the Continent, and it was firmly established in England by 1629, when John Parkinson, in his A Garden of Pleasant Flowers, pronounced the Virginian potato, as he called it, almost as good as the Spanish potato (we call the latter sweet potato). He recommended cooking this sweet vegetable with wine, sugar, and spices.*

For sheer comfort, few dishes can equal a steaming baked, buttered potato. The addition of a meat or cheese topping makes the baked potato a substantial entrée. From Moscow, Idaho, home of the baking potato, A. J. Marineau sends us a recipe for such a dish.

"From the New World, potato culture spread rapidly."

Moscow Idaho Bakers

- 4 large (about ½ lb. each) russet potatoes, scrubbed
- 1 tablespoon butter or margarine
- ½ cup chopped onion
- ½ cup milk
- 5 teaspoons cornstarch
- ¼ cup buttermilk
- ½ cup dry marsala or madeira
- 1 cup (¼ lb.) shredded jack cheese
- 6 to 8 ounces cooked ham, cut into julienne strips (1 to 1½ cups)
- 1 tablespoon Dijon mustard
- 1 tablespoon prepared horseradish
  Chopped parsley
  Salt and pepper

Pierce potatoes in several places with a fork. Set potatoes on oven rack and bake at 400° until potatoes give readily when squeezed, about 1 hour.

Meanwhile, melt butter in a 1½- to 2-quart pan over medium-high heat. Add onion and stir often until limp, about 5 minutes. Mix milk with cornstarch and stir into pan along with buttermilk and marsala. Stir over medium-high heat until boiling. Add cheese and stir until melted. Stir in ham, mustard, and horseradish; if sauce is ready before potatoes, set aside. To use, stir over medium-high heat until hot.

Split potatoes in half lengthwise; fluff centers with a fork. Set 2 halves on each plate and spoon sauce onto potatoes. Sprinkle with parsley; season to taste with salt and pepper. Makes 4 servings.

PER SERVING: 486 calories, 23 g protein, 52 g carbohydrates, 17 g fat (3.8 g saturated), 63 mg cholesterol, 987 mg sodium

Moscow, Idaho

May Menus

COOKS FIND MAY *a distracting month. As longer days unfold and the weather grows warmer and gentler, the desire to present meals in keeping with the season competes with a valid desire to get out of the kitchen. We see no reason not to grant both wishes.*

First, take a new look at pizza. Cut preparation time with a ready-to-use purchased crust; top with Thai flavors. Then cook two meals at once: you can start the breakfast tart or supper soup a day ahead, while preparing another meal.

THAI PIZZA LUNCH

Individual Thai Pizzas
**Carved Kiwi Fruit &
Blood Oranges**
Pineapple Wedges   Litchis
Asian Beer   Sparkling Water
Thai Iced Tea

Tropical touches give these fast pizzas and the fruits a Southeast Asian look.

The pizzas start with single-serving cooked bread bases. Heat the bread with a piquant Asian peanut sauce, crunchy bean sprouts, and shredded jack cheese; then top with shrimp and green onion. The result is visually appealing and a refreshing play upon the contrasts of hot and cold, crisp and melting, spicy and sharp.

In Thailand, fruit is often presented simply but in a decorative fashion achieved by cutting and carving. You can borrow this technique to make a centerpiece dessert. Halve kiwi fruit and blood (or regular) oranges (½ piece of each fruit per person) with zigzag cuts. Also, cut a pineapple (about 2½ lb. for 4 to 6 portions) lengthwise through crown into 4 to 6 wedges. Cut fruit into bite-size sections but leave attached to peel. Arrange fruit on a platter for self-service; if you like, include canned, drained litchis. Scoop kiwi fruit and oranges from their skins with a spoon; cut pineapple from skin with knife and fork.

Prepare quick lunchtime pizzas using purchased crusts, shrimp, and Thai seasonings. For dessert, cut kiwi fruit, oranges, and pineapple Thai-style, with zigzag notches.

Enjoy pizzas with beer or sparkling water. With the fruit, offer strong iced tea (use 1 tablespoon tea leaves per cup water); flavor with sweetened condensed milk, as the Thais do. As the dense milk slowly settles into the tea, it makes fascinating patterns and adds a surprisingly exotic flavor.

As much as a day ahead, you can make the peanut sauce, prepare most of the ingredients for the pizzas, and brew the tea. Up to 5 hours ahead, cut fruit decoratively, but wrap airtight and keep cool until time to serve.

THE DETAILS

Pizza starters. *Build small pizzas on bread shells, pocket bread, or English muffins.*

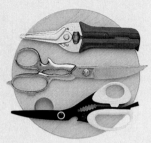

Cut and snip. *For pizza wedges, snip with kitchen scissors.*

Carved fruit. *Zigzag-cut kiwi fruit, blood oranges. Cut pineapple into wedges.*

Thai iced tea. *Sweetened condensed milk sinks slowly into tea. Offer with dessert.*

INDIVIDUAL THAI PIZZAS

6 small (about 5½ in. wide and 4½ oz. each) baked Italian bread shells, pocket bread rounds (about 5 in. wide), or English muffins
Thai peanut sauce (recipe follows)
1 cup (about 6 oz.) bean sprouts, rinsed and drained
6 ounces jack cheese, shredded (1½ cups)
⅓ pound shelled cooked tiny shrimp, rinsed and drained
¼ cup finely chopped green onion
Crushed dried hot red chilies

Place bread shells (or pocket bread rounds), cup sides up, on 2 baking sheets, each 12 by 15 inches (or split muffins and lay cut sides up). Spread sauce equally over cups in bread (or coat muffins to rims). Scatter bean sprouts equally on crusts, then sprinkle with cheese.

Bake in a 350° oven until cheese has melted and begins to brown, 12 to 15 minutes (if using 1 oven, switch pan positions after 7 minutes). Place pizzas on dinner plates; top equally with shrimp and onion. Add chilies to taste; eat with knife and fork, or cut into wedges to pick up and eat. Makes 6 servings.

PER SERVING: 684 calories, 33 g protein, 82 g carbohydrates, 25 g fat (2.6 g saturated), 75 mg cholesterol, 1,347 mg sodium

Thai peanut sauce. In a bowl, stir to mix well ⅔ cup **smooth peanut butter**, 3 tablespoons **hoisin sauce** (or 2 tablespoons water, 2 teaspoons *each* soy sauce, cider vinegar, and sugar), 2 tablespoons **seasoned rice vinegar** (or 2 tablespoons rice vinegar and 1 teaspoon sugar), and 1 teaspoon **Oriental sesame oil.**

BERRY TART BREAKFAST

**Strawberry Ricotta Tart
Crisp Bacon
Orange Juice
Coffee or Cocoa**

Elegant enough to linger over, this breakfast is also fast enough for a weekday start. The night before, make the toasted oatmeal

Glossy strawberries tumble over ricotta-topped oatmeal pastry. Serve with orange juice and crisp bacon.

tart shell and ricotta filling, and clean the strawberries. In the morning, spread cheese into the pastry and top with fruit while bacon cooks crisply brown and you make coffee or cocoa.

On other occasions, when a berry dessert is in order, keep this tart in mind.

STRAWBERRY RICOTTA TART

2 cartons (each 8 oz.), or about 2 cups part-skim ricotta cheese
½ cup powdered sugar
1 teaspoon vanilla
Oatmeal crust (recipe follows)
About 6 cups strawberry halves

(Continued on next page)

In a bowl or food processor, beat or whirl cheese, sugar, and vanilla until well blended. If made ahead, cover and chill up to a day; drain off any liquid that accumulates in bowl.

Spread cheese mixture evenly over crust. Remove pan rim. Set tart on a serving plate and arrange 3 cups berries on cheese. Cut tart into wedges; offer remaining berries to add to taste. Makes 6 servings.

PER SERVING: 387 calories, 13 g protein, 46 g carbohydrates, 18 g fat (10 g saturated), 53 mg cholesterol, 208 mg sodium

Oatmeal crust. In a food processor or with a mixer, whirl or beat ⅓ cup (⅙ lb.) **butter** or margarine, 3 tablespoons **sugar,** and 1 tablespoon **water** until creamy. Whirl or beat in ¾ cup **all-purpose flour** and ⅓ cup **regular rolled oats.** With floured fingers, pat dough evenly over bottom of a lightly oiled and flour-dusted 9-inch cake pan with removable rim. Bake in a 325° oven until rich golden brown, about 40 minutes. Let cool; if made ahead, wrap pastry airtight and hold up to a day.

SPRING SOUP SUPPER

Split Pea & Lamb Soup
Whole-grain Bread
Feta Cheese
Grapefruit with a Twist

Does cooking two meals at once seem too demanding for a busy night? Not if the second meal is a simmering soup that takes little attention on a back corner of the range. And, to the tastes of many, the soup will be even better given a day for flavors to mellow.

Buy a hearty loaf of bread to go with the soup. Eat cheese with the bread or break chunks into soup.

While the soup heats for supper, you've ample time to segment fresh grapefruit for the light and refreshing dessert. You can also make the syrup while the soup simmers, either the day before or while the soup reheats.

SPLIT PEA & LAMB SOUP

> 1 **package (12 oz., about 2 cups) green or yellow split peas**
> 4 **cups thinly sliced celery**
> 1 **large (about ½ lb.) onion, chopped**
> ½ **pound boned lamb shoulder or neck, cut into ½-inch chunks**
> 2 **cloves garlic, chopped**
> 1 **large dried bay leaf**
> **About 7 cups regular-strength chicken broth**

Sort peas, discarding any debris. Rinse peas, drain, and set aside.

In a 5- to 6-quart pan over high heat, combine celery, onion, lamb, garlic, bay leaf, and ½ cup water. Cover and simmer rapidly for 10 minutes. Uncover, turn heat to high, and stir often until browned bits stick in pan. Deglaze by adding ⅓ cup water and stirring to scrape browned bits free. Stir often until liquid evaporates and browned bits form again. Repeat deglazing step several more times until vegetables are a rich brown, about 30 minutes total.

To pan, add split peas and 7 cups broth; bring to a boil on high heat. Cover and simmer until peas mash easily, about 1 hour.

Discard bay leaf. (You can chill soup at this step, and continue the next day.) Transfer 3 cups soup (but no meat) to a blender or food processor. Whirl until smoothly puréed. Return to pan. For thinner soup, add more broth. Stir on high heat until hot. Makes 4 to 6 servings.

PER SERVING: 357 calories, 24 g protein, 42 g carbohydrates, 11 g fat (4.1 g saturated), 27 mg cholesterol, 165 mg sodium

GRAPEFRUIT WITH A TWIST

The aromatic flavor of gin, which comes from juniper berries, complements the bitter-tart taste of grapefruit. Use orange juice as a nonalcoholic option.

> ⅓ **cup sugar**
> 4 **to 6 thin strips lemon peel (yellow part only), each 1 to 2 inches long**
> 2 **or 3 large (2 to 3 lb. total) ruby or yellow grapefruit**
> **Citrus leaves, rinsed and patted dry (optional)**
> **Gin or orange juice**
> **Lemon wedges**

In a 3- to 4-cup pan, combine sugar and ⅔ cup water. Boil, uncovered, over high heat until reduced to ½ cup. Gently twist lemon peel and drop into syrup; let cool. If made ahead, cover and chill up to 3 days.

With a sharp knife, cut peel and all white membrane from grapefruit. Over a bowl, cut between membranes to release fruit segments; squeeze juice from membrane into bowl. Discard membrane. If made ahead, cover and let stand up to 3 hours.

Spoon fruit, juice, and syrup equally into 4 to 6 dessert bowls. Garnish with leaves. To each portion add to taste about 1 tablespoon gin or orange juice, and juice from lemon wedges. Makes 4 to 6 servings.

PER SERVING: 100 calories, 0.4 g protein, 17 g carbohydrates, 0.1 g fat (0 g saturated), 0 mg cholesterol, 0.3 mg sodium

JUNE

Scoop-and-eat appetizers (page 117)

Entertaining shifts into an easy, laid-back mode as parties move outdoors to the patio, the pool, and the garden. Our summer parties take a relaxed approach with foods that hold up well on hot days and have many make-ahead steps. Start off with a scoop-and-eat appetizer buffet, made up to a day ahead and ready in the refrigerator. You'll find a varied selection of salads, all prepared well before company arrives, meats that cook quickly on the grill, and an open-face dessert tart piled high with the season's plump, fresh blueberries.

113

THE GERSHWINS' SONG *pegged summer perfectly as a time "when the livin' is easy." But summer is also a time when the entertaining is easy. As warm weather adds the patio, the pool, and the garden to your stages for home entertaining, it invites a laid-back approach.*

Our poolside barbecue for a crowd is appealing; most of the dishes are ready, waiting, and temperature resistant. As the meat grills, let guests nibble appetizers; choose two or three of the make-ahead

appetizers on page 117. An ice-filled tub becomes the beverage bar: tuck individual bottles or cans of fruit juices, soft drinks, mineral water, and beer in ice; as a cooling wine, try White Zinfandel or White Grenache.

Use the roasted vegetable salads on pages 118–119, or create your own using the chart as a guide. For each person, you'll want to allow 2 cups total of the salads; they can all wait at least a day before serving.

Break bread into chunks and pour olive oil into tiny bowls for dunking; the oil holds up better than butter in warm weather.

Dessert for the adults is fruit in wine (multiply recipe to match the number of adults). Have fruit or frozen fruit juice bars for children.

to lay flat—so they cook quickly on the grill. Long metal skewers threaded through the meat serve two purposes: they make the meat easy to handle, and they secure colorful vegetables tucked into the meat for flavor.

To prepare barbecue. Ignite 50 to 60 charcoal briquets on fire grate in a barbecue with a lid. When coals are covered with gray ash, about 30 minutes, bank half on each side of grate; place a drip pan in center. To maintain temperature, add 6 briquets to each side now and every 30 minutes of cooking time that follows. Place grill 5 to 6 inches above drip pan.

Shell holds olive oil for bread. Salads are roasted vegetables, alone or in combination.

POOLSIDE BARBECUE FOR 24

Appetizer Buffet (see page 117)
Beverage Bar
Butterflied Beef Cross-Rib with Cilantro-Jalapeño Cream
Roasted Potato & Carrot Salad (for salads, see pages 118–119)
Broccoli & Roasted Garlic Salad
Roasted Fennel, Potato & Green Bean Salad
Roasted Pepper & Black Bean Salad
Roasted Eggplant Salad
Roasted Tomatoes
Crusty Loaves & Rolls
Extra-virgin Olive Oil
Fruit & Wine Splashes (page 120)

ROASTS FOR FAST GRILLING

Choose either boned beef cross-rib or a pork loin roast (see page 116) for this menu. They are butterflied—cut open

BUTTERFLIED BEEF CROSS-RIB WITH CILANTRO-JALAPEÑO CREAM

 1 boned beef cross-rib roast
   (5 to 5½ lb.), surface fat trimmed
 ½ cup orange juice
 ½ cup lime juice
 1½ teaspoons ground cumin
 ½ cup minced fresh cilantro
   (coriander)
 2 large (about ¾ lb. each) red and
   yellow bell peppers, stemmed,
   seeded, and thinly sliced
   lengthwise (or 2 bell peppers
   of same color)
   Fresh cilantro sprigs
   Cilantro-jalapeño cream (recipe
   follows)
   Salt and pepper

Rinse beef and pat dry; if roast is tied, snip off strings. With a sharp knife, cut lengthwise down center of roast about ⅔ of the way through meat. Pull cut open to spread out meat. Holding knife

(Continued on page 116)

Jump right in at your own pace. While slowpokes nibble at the appetizer table, grilled beef and a selection of wilt-resistant salads hold well. Beverages stay cool in a large, ice-filled tub. A smooth-running party takes planning; for tips to ensure success, see page 121.

Butterflied beef is unevenly thick, yielding rare to well-done pieces.

at about a 45° angle from center of meat, cut lengthwise about ⅔ through the 2 thick sections. Pull cuts open and pat meat to make as evenly thick as possible. At even intervals, make 6 crosswise cuts about ⅔ through roast.

Combine orange juice, lime juice, cumin, and minced cilantro; reserve ¼ cup. Pour remainder into a deep bowl or 2-gallon heavy plastic food bag. Add meat, turn to coat, then cover (or seal) and chill, turning occasionally, for 2 hours or up to a day. Cover and chill reserved marinade.

Lift meat from marinade; drain briefly; discard meat marinade. Lay meat flat, cut side up. In crosswise slashes, fit the bell pepper strips, distributing evenly.

Thread 3 long (at least 18 in.), sturdy metal skewers parallel to each other lengthwise through meat, securing peppers as you go.

Lay meat, pepper side up, on prepared grill over drip pan. Put lid on barbecue, open vents, and cook beef,

brushing occasionally with reserved marinade, until a thermometer inserted into thickest part (not touching skewers) registers 135° to 140° for medium-rare, 40 to 45 minutes; thinner parts will be well done; do not turn meat over.

Transfer to carving board; garnish with cilantro sprigs. Remove skewers to slice meat; offer cilantro-jalapeño cream and salt and pepper to add to taste. Makes 20 to 24 servings.

Per Serving: 242 calories, 26 g protein, 5.9 g carbohydrates, 12 g fat (4.9 g saturated), 75 mg cholesterol, 73 mg sodium

Cilantro-jalapeño cream. In a small bowl, mix 1 cup minced **fresh cilantro;** 1 cup **light sour cream** (or regular sour cream or reduced-calorie mayonnaise); 2 stemmed, seeded, and minced **fresh jalapeño chilies;** and 2 tablespoons **lime juice.** If made ahead, cover the mixture and chill up to a day. Makes about 1⅓ cups.

Per Tablespoon: 20 calories, 0.8 g protein, 1 g carbohydrates, 1.5 g fat (0.8 g saturated), 3.8 mg cholesterol, 0.5 mg sodium

Butterflied Pork with Apricot-Sesame Glaze

- ¾ **cup apricot jam**
- ¼ **cup seasoned rice vinegar (or ¼ cup rice vinegar and 2 teaspoons sugar)**
- 3 **tablespoons Oriental sesame oil**
- 1 **boned center-cut pork loin roast (5 lb.), surface fat trimmed**
- 12 **to 18 green onions, ends trimmed**
- 1 **tablespoon sesame seed Salt and pepper**

Mix together jam, vinegar, and oil; set aside.

Rinse pork and pat dry. Lay fattiest side down. With a sharp knife, cut lengthwise ⅔ of the way through meat down center of roast. Pull cut open to spread out meat. Holding knife at about a 45° angle from center of meat, cut lengthwise about ⅔ through the 2 thick sections. Pull cuts open and pat meat to make as evenly thick as possible.

At equal intervals, cut 6 crosswise slashes about ⅔ of the way through

meat. Lay 1 or 2 green onions in each slash. Thread 3 long (at least 18 in.) sturdy metal skewers parallel to each other lengthwise through the roast, securing onions as you go.

Lay meat, onions down, on prepared grill over drip pan. Put lid on barbecue and open vents. Cook until edges of roast just begin to brown and juices begin to drip, 10 to 12 minutes.

Brush meat with about ⅓ of the apricot mixture. Supporting roast with skewers, turn it over and brush top with another ⅓ of the apricot mixture. Replace lid and cook until meat is browned and a thermometer inserted into the thickest part (not touching skewers) registers 155° for meat that is white throughout, 20 to 25 minutes longer; turn once or twice.

About 5 minutes before meat is done, brush with remaining glaze and sprinkle with sesame seed.

Transfer meat to a carving board. Remove skewers and tuck remaining green onions into slashes. Season with salt and pepper. Makes 20 to 24 servings.

Per Serving: 325 calories, 28 g protein, 22 g carbohydrates, 14 g fat (3.8 g saturated), 85 mg cholesterol, 74 mg sodium

Green onions straddle barbecued butterflied pork loin roast.

FOR RELAXED ENTERTAINING, *flavorful mixtures to scoop up and eat are among the most easily managed appetizers. They can be ready on call and require no last-minute assembly or individual touches. Each of these five appetizers is so simple to make, you can whip it up in minutes. All of them can wait up to a day in the refrigerator. If served chilled, they stay fresh at least 3 hours.*

All can be served from bowls, but the carrot hummus (a wholesome and colorful variation on traditional hummus) and the two cheeses are firm enough to swirl into mounds and present on handsome platters, surrounded by their accompaniments. Look for tahini (ground sesame paste) for hummus with fancy foods in the supermarket.

DILLED EGG SALAD

> 10 hard-cooked large eggs, shelled and mashed
> ½ cup unflavored nonfat yogurt, light sour cream, or sour cream
> 2 tablespoons lemon juice
> 2 tablespoons chopped fresh dill or 2 teaspoons dried dill weed
> 2 teaspoons prepared horseradish
> ½ teaspoon Worcestershire
> Salt
> Fresh dill sprigs
> Toasted pocket bread

In a bowl, stir together eggs, yogurt, lemon juice, dill, horseradish, Worcestershire, and salt to taste. Serve, or chill airtight up to a day. Mound in a bowl and garnish with dill sprigs. Scoop onto toasted pocket bread. Makes about 2½ cups, 20 servings.

PER TABLESPOON: 21 calories, 1.7 g protein, 0.4 g carbohydrates, 1.3 g fat (0.4 g saturated), 53 mg cholesterol, 19 mg sodium

CARROT HUMMUS

> 1¼ pounds (5 large) carrots, peeled and cut into 1-inch pieces
> 2 cans (15½ oz. each) garbanzos, drained
> ⅔ cup tahini (sesame seed paste)
> 3 cloves garlic
> ⅔ cup lemon juice
> Salt
> Baby carrot (optional)
> Toasted pocket bread or crackers

In a 2- to 3-quart pan, combine carrots and 3 cups water. Cover; bring to a boil.

Simmer until carrots mash easily, 15 to 20 minutes; stir occasionally. Drain.

In a food processor, whirl carrots, garbanzos, tahini, garlic, and lemon juice until smoothly puréed (or rub through a food mill). Add salt to taste. Serve, or cover and chill up to a day. Mound into a bowl; top with baby carrot. Scoop onto pocket bread. Makes 5 cups, 20 servings.

PER ¼ CUP: 114 calories, 3.9 g protein, 15 g carbohydrates, 4.9 g fat (0.7 g saturated), 0 mg cholesterol, 151 mg sodium

TROPICAL SALSA

Scoop onto taro or plantain chips, or blue or yellow corn tortilla chips; you'll need at least 4 cups.

> 2 medium-size (about 2¼ lb. total) firm-ripe papayas
> 1 medium-size (about ¾ lb.) ripe mango
> 1 large (about 10 oz.) firm-ripe avocado
> 2 small fresh serrano chilies (or 1 jalapeño), stemmed, seeded, and finely chopped
> ½ teaspoon grated lime peel
> ¼ cup lime juice
> ¼ cup chopped fresh cilantro (coriander)
> Salt

Peel and seed papayas. Peel and pit mango. Peel and pit avocado. Cut all fruit into about ¼-inch dice. Mix gently in bowl with chilies, lime peel, lime juice, cilantro, and salt to taste. Serve or, if made ahead, cover and chill up to a day. To eat, scoop onto chips. Makes 5 cups, 20 servings.

PER ¼ CUP: 84 calories, 1.1 g protein, 13 g carbohydrates, 3.9 g fat (0.3 g saturated), 0 mg cholesterol, 65 mg sodium

RED BELL CHEESE

> 1 jar (about 7 oz., or ¾ cup) roasted red bell peppers or pimientos, patted dry
> 3 packages (about 4 oz. each) herb-seasoned cheese such as boursin or rondelé
> About 1 pound Belgian endive
> 2 tablespoons minced parsley

In a food processor or blender, smoothly purée peppers. Whirl or stir in the cheese. Mound cheese on a platter. Serve, or cover and chill up to 2 days.

Rinse endive; trim off discolored leaves and stem ends. If prepared ahead, wrap in towels, enclose in a plastic bag,

Party appetizers include toasted pocket bread for scooping tropical salsa, egg salad, and carrot hummus.

and chill up to 2 days. Cut stem ends to release leaves, separating endive; arrange leaves, pointed ends out, on a platter beside cheese. Sprinkle cheese with parsley. Makes 1¾ cups cheese, 10 servings.

PER TABLESPOON: 42 calories, 1.5 g protein, 1.6 g carbohydrates, 3.5 g fat (0 g saturated), 12 mg cholesterol, 48 mg sodium

GREEN HERB CHEESE & TOMATOES

> ½ cup packed fresh basil leaves
> ⅓ cup packed fresh dill
> 4 packages (about 4 oz. each) black pepper–flavored cheese such as boursin or rondelé
> ¾ cup (4 oz.) drained oil-packed dried tomatoes, chopped
> Additional dried tomatoes, drained if oil-packed
> Additional fresh basil leaves
> Cracker bread

In a food processor or blender, whirl basil and dill with cheese to purée smoothly; push cheese frequently from container side down into blades. Stir chopped tomatoes into cheese mixture. Serve, or chill airtight up to a day.

Shape cheese into a mound on a platter. Surround with additional tomatoes and garnish with remaining basil. Spread cheese onto cracker bread; add tomato pieces. Makes about 2 cups cheese, 10 to 12 servings.

PER TABLESPOON: 59 calories, 1.7 g protein, 1.8 g carbohydrates, 5.2 g fat (0.2 g saturated), 14 mg cholesterol, 139 mg sodium

WITHERING HEAT *intensifies the flavors and natural sweetness of the vegetables used in these durable salads. You can roast the vegetables ahead; cover and chill up to a day. But for best flavor, let them come to room temperature before serving. From the refrigerator, they'll hold 3 hours without noticeable loss of quality. Use the chart on the facing page as a guide for creating new salads.*

BROCCOLI & ROASTED GARLIC SALAD

About 1¼ pounds (about 9 cups)
broccoli flowerets, rinsed
2 tablespoons soy sauce
1 teaspoon Oriental sesame oil
1 batch roasted garlic (see chart)

In a 5- to 6-quart pan, bring 3 to 4 quarts water to a boil over high heat. Add broccoli and cook, uncovered, until tender to bite, about 5 minutes. Drain; at once immerse broccoli in ice water until cold. Drain again. If made ahead, chill broccoli airtight up to a day.

In a shallow bowl, mix soy sauce and sesame oil with broccoli and cloves of garlic. Makes about 6 cups.

PER CUP: 123 calories, 6.3 g protein, 22 g carbohydrates, 2.7 g fat (0.3 g saturated), 0 mg cholesterol, 372 mg sodium

Cold boiled broccoli tangles with golden cloves of mild-flavored roasted garlic.

Red bell peppers mingle with black beans in a cilantro dressing.

ROASTED PEPPER & BLACK BEAN SALAD

3 cans (15 oz. each) black beans,
drained and rinsed well
Cilantro dressing (recipe follows)
1 batch roasted red bell peppers
(see chart)
Fresh cilantro (coriander) sprigs
Salt and pepper

Mix beans with cilantro dressing and roasted peppers and their juices. Pour into a bowl; garnish with cilantro sprigs. Season to taste with salt and pepper. Makes about 6 cups.

PER CUP: 248 calories, 8.4 g protein, 31 g carbohydrates, 11 g fat (1.5 g saturated), 0 mg cholesterol, 349 mg sodium

Cilantro dressing. Mix ½ cup **seasoned rice vinegar,** ¼ cup **extra-virgin olive oil,** 1 tablespoon **honey,** ½ teaspoon **chili oil,** ¼ cup minced **fresh cilantro,** and 2 tablespoons chopped **green onion.**

ROASTED EGGPLANT SALAD

1 batch roasted eggplants (see chart)
1 batch roasted red bell peppers
(see chart)
1 batch roasted garlic (see chart)
3 tablespoons balsamic vinegar
(or 3 tablespoons wine vinegar
and 2 teaspoons sugar)
2 tablespoons chopped parsley
Salt and pepper

Combine eggplants, peppers, garlic, and vinegar in a shallow bowl. Sprinkle with parsley. Add salt and pepper to taste. Makes about 4 cups.

PER CUP: 215 calories, 6.6 g protein, 43 g carbohydrates, 4 g fat (0.5 g saturated), 0 mg cholesterol, 21 mg sodium

ROASTED POTATO & CARROT SALAD

2 batches roasted thin-skinned
potatoes (see chart)
2 batches roasted carrots (see chart)
Citrus dressing (recipe follows)
Fresh basil sprigs
Salt and pepper

In a shallow bowl, combine potatoes, carrots, and citrus dressing. Garnish with basil and add salt and pepper to taste. Makes about 8 cups.

PER CUP: 196 calories, 3.5 g protein, 36 g carbohydrates, 5.1 g fat (0.6 g saturated), 0 mg cholesterol, 83 mg sodium

Citrus dressing. In a small bowl, blend 2 teaspoons grated **orange peel,** ½ cup **orange juice,** 2 tablespoons **white wine vinegar** or distilled white vinegar, 2 tablespoons chopped **fresh basil leaves,** 1 tablespoon **honey,** 2 teaspoons **Dijon mustard,** 1 teaspoon **ground cumin,** 2 cloves **garlic** (minced or pressed), and 1 **fresh jalapeño chili,** stemmed, seeded, and minced.

ROASTED FENNEL, POTATO & GREEN BEAN SALAD

1 batch roasted fennel (see chart)
1 batch roasted russet potatoes
(see chart)
1 batch roasted green beans
(see chart)
Sherry dressing (recipe follows)
Salt and pepper

Green fig leaves frame roasted eggplant, bell pepper, and garlic salad.

In a bowl, mix fennel, potatoes, and beans with dressing. Season to taste with salt and pepper. Makes 5 cups.

PER CUP: 223 calories, 5.9 g protein, 36 g carbohydrates, 6.2 g fat (0.8 g saturated), 0 mg cholesterol, 140 mg sodium

Sherry dressing. In a 6- to 8-inch frying pan over medium heat, stir 1 teaspoon *each* **mustard seed, cumin seed,** and **fennel seed** until fragrant, 2 to 5 minutes. Off heat, add ⅓ cup **sherry vinegar,** ⅓ cup **Gewürztraminer** or orange juice, and 1 tablespoon grated **lemon peel.** Use, or cover and chill up to a day.

TOMATO & WHITE BEAN SALAD

> 3 **cans (15 oz. each) white cannellini beans**
> 2 **tablespoons** *each* **chopped fresh thyme and basil leaves, or 2 teaspoons** *each* **of the dried herbs**
> 1 **batch roasted tomatoes (see chart)**
> 1 **batch roasted red onion (see chart)**
>   **Fresh thyme sprigs (optional)**
>   **Salt and pepper**

In a 2- to 3-quart pan, bring beans and liquid with thyme (or both dried herbs) to a boil on high heat; simmer about 3 minutes, stirring often. Pour beans into a fine strainer; drain and reserve liquid. Put beans in a bowl; tap herbs from strainer into the beans.

Coarsely chop 8 tomato pieces and stir into bean mixture with fresh basil and onion. Arrange remaining tomatoes on salad; garnish with thyme sprigs. Add reserved liquid to moisten, if desired. Season with salt and pepper. Makes about 4½ cups.

PER CUP: 246 calories, 13 g protein, 45 g carbohydrates, 3.6 g fat (0.5 g saturated), 0 mg cholesterol, 679 mg sodium

Roasting Vegetables, Alone or with Flavor Partners

Vegetable	Pan Size	Roasting
Thin-skinned Potatoes. 1 pound small (about 1½ in. wide). Scrub and cut into 1-in. chunks.	8- to 10-in. square; 10 by 15 in. for 2 batches or 2 vegetables.	Mix with 2 teaspoons olive oil. Bake in a 475° oven until richly browned, 35 to 45 min.; turn occasionally.
Russet Potatoes. 2 large (1½ lb. total). Peel and cut into 1-in. chunks.	8- to 10-in. square; 10 by 15 in. for 2 batches or 2 vegetables.	As directed for thin-skinned potatoes (above); allow 1 to 1¼ hours.
Carrots. 4 large (1 lb. total). Peel; cut into 1-inch chunks.	8- to 10-in. square; 10 by 15 in. for 2 batches or 2 vegetables.	As directed for thin-skinned potatoes (above).
Garlic. 3 large heads (about ¾ lb. total). Peel cloves.	8- to 10-in. square; 10 by 15 in. for 2 batches or 2 vegetables.	As directed for thin-skinned potatoes (above); cook until tinged with brown, 20 to 30 min.
Fennel. 2 large heads (about 3 in. wide). Rinse; trim off base, bruises, stems. Cut head into 1-in. chunks.	10-in. square or 9 by 13 in.; 10 by 15 in. for 2 batches or 2 vegetables.	As directed for thin-skinned potatoes (above); cook until tinged with brown, about 1 hour.
Green Beans. 1 pound slender. Snap ends; pull off strings; rinse.	10 by 15 in. for each batch of beans.	As directed for thin-skinned potatoes (above); cook until ends are browned, about 40 min.
Red Onion. 1 large (about ¾ lb.). Peel; cut into ¾-in.-thick chunks.	8- to 10-in. square; 10 by 15 in. for 2 batches or 2 vegetables.	Mix with ½ teaspoon olive oil and 2 tablespoons balsamic or wine vinegar. Roast as directed for thin-skinned potatoes (above); cook until edges are dark brown, 40 to 50 min.
Roma-type Tomatoes. 12 to 14 medium-size (about 1¾ lb. total). Rinse; cut in half lengthwise.	9 by 13 in.; 10 by 15 in. for 2 batches. Do not combine with other vegetables.	Rub lightly with olive oil (about 1¾ teaspoons total); set cut side up in pan. Sprinkle lightly with salt. Bake in a 475° oven until edges are dark brown, about 1 hour and 10 min.
Red Bell Peppers. 2 medium-size (about 1 lb. total). Rinse; cut in half lengthwise.	10-in. square or 9 by 13 in. Do not combine with other vegetables.	Broil cut side down 4 to 6 inches from heat until skins are charred, about 8 min. Let cool, draped with foil. Pull off and discard skins, stems, seeds; save juice. Cut into strips or chunks.
Oriental Eggplants. 1 pound (5 or 6) slender. Trim off stems. Cut eggplants in half lengthwise. Turn cut side down; cut each piece lengthwise into thirds.	10 by 15 in. Do not combine with other vegetables.	Rub skin very lightly with olive oil (about 1 teaspoon total). Lay skin side down in oiled pan. Bake in a 475° oven until richly browned and soft when pressed, 20 to 30 min.

TALL, COOL GLASSES *of refreshing beverages are a summer signature. Many of the cooling liquids can do duty in desserts as well. Here we explore two adult coolers, a playful collection of wines aromatic with the ripening array of summer fruits, and a fruit and wine dessert that is easily multiplied.*

Chilled, slightly sweet to sweet wines are suited to summer meals if the sweetness is balanced by acid to counteract any cloying blandness. A listing of wines for summer meals follows; all are good cool or with ice.

You can pour many of these wines over fruit (following). Serve the dessert as made, nest the serving container steadily in ice in a larger bowl to keep cool longer, or let the dessert sit for several hours to blend flavors.

SUNRISE

½ **cup orange juice**
⅓ **cup lemon-flavor vodka**
    About 1 tablespoon lime juice
    Ice cubes
    Lime wedges

In a 10- to 12-ounce glass, combine orange juice and vodka. Add lime juice to taste. Add ice and lime wedges. Makes 1 serving.

PER SERVING: 229 calories, 0.9 g protein, 14 g carbohydrates, 0.1 g fat (0 g saturated), 0 mg cholesterol, 4.4 mg sodium

CHILI SCOTCH

1½ **cups sparkling water**
½ **cup Scotch or whiskey**
    Chipotle water (recipe follows)
    Ice
    Thin lemon slices
    Fresh small red chilies

In 2 glasses, each 12 ounces, combine sparkling water and Scotch equally. Add chipotle water to taste. Add ice; garnish with lemon and red chili on a swizzle stick. Makes 2 servings.

PER SERVING: 139 calories, 0 g protein, 0.1 g carbohydrates, 0 g fat, 0 mg cholesterol, 0.6 mg sodium

Chipotle water. Rinse 2 **dried chipotle chilies.** In a 1- to 1½-quart pan, combine chilies and 1 cup **water.** Cover and simmer for 15 minutes. Let cool. Remove chilies; save for other uses. Use water, or cover and chill up to a day. Makes about ⅓ cup, enough for 2 or 3 servings.

WINES FOR LAZY SIPPING

Be sure to read labels carefully; many of these wines have both dry and sweet (some late-harvest) versions, often by the same maker.

You can detect sweetness in wines with 0.5 to 1 percent residual sugar (of comparable sweetness, 0.5° to 1° brix, 5 to 10 grams sugar per liter), but if residual sugar is 2 percent or more, many find the wines a bit sweet for meals, though pleasing with dessert. Others enjoy wines that are this sweet or sweeter with food; it's a matter of taste. Our listings, when applicable, range from driest to sweetest.

Chenin Blanc. The gentle flavor of this wine makes it easy to like and serve with almost any light summer foods.

Chappellet, Napa Valley (touched by wood aging); Martin Brothers, Paso Robles; Folie à Deux, Napa Valley; Dry Creek, California; Hacienda, Clarksburg; Grand Cru, Clarksburg; Simi, Mendocino; Guenoc, Lake County; Hogue, Washington.

Johannisberg Riesling. The best of these wines (also called White Riesling or just Riesling) have an almost floral perfume. Their range of sweetness is considerable. Serve with foods that have natural sweetness, including cold cracked crab.

Trefethen, Napa Valley; Firestone, Santa Ynez Valley Dry; Freemark Abbey, Napa Valley; Smith-Madrone, Napa Valley; Jekel, Arroyo Seco/Monterey; Greenwood Ridge, Anderson Valley; Hogue, Washington.

Gewürztraminer. Of all white wine types that regularly find their way to dinner tables, this is the most aromatic. Mild Gewürztraminers remind many of carnations. Rich examples suggest litchis. The most intense are, as their name promises in German, outright spicy.

All call for foods of some character: smoked chicken or turkey, barbecued pork, smoked or spiced sausages, and spicy Asian cuisines like Thai.

Bouchaine, Carneros; Davis Bynum, Russian River; Gundlach-Bundschu, Sonoma Valley; Thomas Fogarty, Monterey (Ventana Vineyard); Navarro, Anderson Valley; Handley, Anderson

Valley; Husch, Anderson Valley; De Loach, Russian River Valley; Buena Vista, Carneros; Grand Cru, Alexander Valley.

White Zinfandel & kin. Black grapes can be used to make white or pale pink wines, Zinfandel being the most famous. The best White Zinfandels capture the variety's blackberry-like flavors to perfection. They, and similar rosés, are extremely versatile with foods. Styles range from light, crisp, and nearly dry to almost dessert-sweet.

William Wheeler, Sonoma County; De Loach Vineyards, Russian River Valley; Grand Cru, California; Seghesio, Sonoma County; J. Pedroncelli, Sonoma County; Sutter Home, California; Gallo White Grenache, California.

Gamay or Gamay Beaujolais. A handful of reds benefit from chilling. Nearly all are based on Napa Gamay or Gamay Beaujolais, or a blend of the two.

Charles F. Shaw Napa Valley Gamay Beaujolais; Fetzer Mendocino Gamay; J. Lohr Monterey Gamay; Louis M. Martini North Coast Gamay Beaujolais; Preston Dry Creek Valley Gamay.

FRUIT & WINE SPLASHES

1 **cup (5 to 6 oz.) bite-size pieces fruit (choices follow)**
1 **bottle (750 ml.) wine (choices follow)**
    Ice cubes

In a large bowl, combine fruit and wine. Serve, or let stand up to 3 hours. Ladle into glasses. Add ice to cool. If desired, offer spoons to eat fruit. Makes 6 to 8 servings.

PER SERVING WITH PEACHES AND WHITE WINE: 73 calories, 0.2 g protein, 3.1 g carbohydrates, 0 g fat, 0 mg cholesterol, 4.7 mg sodium

Fruit: whole blueberries, blackberries, boysenberries, loganberries, olallieberries, raspberries, grapes; sliced firm-ripe nectarines; sliced strawberries; peeled, sliced firm-ripe peaches; sliced firm-ripe plums.

Wine: Gamay Beaujolais; Chenin Blanc; Gewürztraminer; Johannisberg Riesling; Muscat wines such as Benzinger Muscat Canelli, Robert Mondavi Moscato Canelli, Quady Orange Muscat, sparkling Ballatore; White Zinfandel.

Summer Entertaining: Party Planner Tips

DINING OUTDOORS *is one of summer's most appealing aspects in nearly all parts of the West. The party meals and recipes in this special section have built-in logistics that keep events running smoothly. As you plan your own summer parties, use these tips to ensure success. Most important, organize for food safety. Next, keep foods looking fresh, and hold them at their most appetizing temperatures. Finally, have a cleanup plan.*

PLAY IT SAFE

The same temperatures that keep you comfortable provide the ideal environment for bacterial growth in foods, which can cause at least discomfort and at worst serious illness. Simple steps will help you avoid trouble.

Most bacteria that might be present on food surfaces (fruits and vegetables, as well as meats) are destroyed at 160°. But even cooked foods can be recontaminated, enabling bacteria to flourish again; this might happen if you stir raw foods, then use the same spoon, unwashed, to stir cooling cooked foods.

The simplest precaution is to assume that bacteria are always present. Thoroughly rinse fruits and vegetables in cool water, and drain on a clean surface (such as a tray lined with a clean towel). To peel or trim, use a clean knife. Clean, dry fruits and vegetables aren't likely to harbor harmful bacteria but can pick them up from surfaces, hands, and utensils.

High-acid foods, such as salads with tart dressings and fruit in wine, resist bacterial growth.

Remember that it is the combination of time and temperature that permits bacteria to multiply to dangerous levels. Some food scientists prefer a built-in safety factor and insist that perishable foods be held for no more than 2 hours at 40° to 120°. But 3 hours at warm temperatures (mid-70s to 80s) is a safe period *if foods are well chilled and come directly from the refrigerator or out of ice.*

Three hours is ample time for guests to assemble and dine at leisure on food you have ready and waiting when the party starts.

Make-ahead dinner, designed for a warm evening, lets hosts relax. Chilled pork tenderloins and other cold dishes stay fresh over ice; for instructions, see page 122.

KEEP FOODS FRESH

Not only do you want foods to be safe to eat, but you want them to stay fresh-looking and appealing, too.

The easiest tactic: provide shade. Hot, direct sunlight heats up and dries out foods quickly. Make use of umbrellas, roof overhangs, a building's shadow, or greenery (trees, shrubs, vines). But avoid placing food where debris can drop on it.

Some foods—roasted vegetables, sliced tomatoes and cucumbers—are naturally long-lasting. Large pieces of food stay fresh longer than small ones; opt for chunks of meat or cheese and whole loaves of bread or rolls.

Some foods should be kept on ice: leafy greens and other foods that go limp when hot, creamy dressings and sauces, sliced meats, cold beverages, and other things that simply taste best cool. You can easily improvise an ice-chilled server by resting a rimmed food container on the lip of a larger, deeper unit filled with crushed ice.

Or set the food container into another, larger container (a handsome pan, even an ice chest) and surround the food container with ice. Be sure it is firmly positioned on the bottom of the other container—not on ice—or it is apt to tip as ice melts.

HAVE A PLACE FOR ALL THINGS

To avoid clutter and chaos, be sure to place baskets or bags for litter in several locations. Also have baskets or pans in which to deposit used utensils, plates, and glasses. Cleanup is easier, and the entertaining area stays clear for other activities.

Unexpected flavor *combinations give a fanciful lilt to this twilight menu for 8 to 10. All the foods can be made in advance and, if served chilled or kept cold as directed, will stay fresh and appetizing up to 3 hours, even when the evening is hot. The meat is barbecued or roasted pork tenderloins; allow 3 to 3½ pounds total. Cook them until they reach 155° in the center, then let cool, cover, and chill up to a day.*

To serve, slice meat thin and mound in a deep bowl. Nest the bowl in a larger one filled with ice to keep the meat cool. (Before adding ice, be sure that the larger bowl supports the one for the meat; otherwise, the meat bowl may tilt as ice thaws and be swamped with water.) Use the same arrangement to keep the yogurt dressing for the pasta salad cool.

TWILIGHT DINNER FOR 8 TO 10

Appetizer Buffet (see page 117)
Chilled Pork Tenderloins
Dilled Pasta Salad
Red Cabbage & Poached Peach Salad
Cucumber & Green Onion Salad
Rye Bread Loaves   Butter
Coarse-ground Mustard
Blueberry Tart
Dry Gewürztraminer
Gamay Beaujolais

Summer dinner party is illuminated by setting sun and glowing fire. Self-service menu allows guests to socialize, eating as they wish.

DILLED PASTA SALAD

1 pound dried orecchiette (ear-shape) pasta or small shell pasta
2 tablespoons olive oil
3 tablespoons chopped fresh dill or 2 teaspoons dried dill weed
⅓ cup lemon juice
Yogurt-dill dressing (recipe follows)

In a 6- to 8-quart pan on high heat, bring about 4 quarts water to boiling. Add pasta and cook, uncovered, just until tender to bite, 10 to 15 minutes. Drain, cover with cold water, and drain again.

Meanwhile, in a wide bowl, stir together oil, dill, and lemon juice. Add pasta and mix gently. Serve, or cover and chill up to 6 hours. Serve from refrigerated to room temperature; mix occasionally to keep surface moist. To each portion, add yogurt-dill dressing to taste. Makes 8 to 10 servings.

PER SERVING WITHOUT DRESSING: 198 calories, 5.9 g protein, 35 g carbohydrates, 3.8 g fat (0.7 g saturated), 0 mg cholesterol, 5.3 mg sodium

Yogurt-dill dressing. In a small bowl, stir together 1½ cups **unflavored non-fat yogurt,** 2 tablespoons chopped **fresh dill** or 1½ teaspoons dried dill weed, and 1½ teaspoons **caraway seed.**

Use, or cover and chill up to a day. Nest bowl in a larger bowl filled with ice to keep dressing cool up to 3 hours. Garnish with **fresh dill sprigs.** Makes about 1½ cups.

PER TABLESPOON: 9.6 calories, 0.8 g protein, 1.1 g carbohydrates, 0.2 g fat (0.1 g saturated), 0.9 mg cholesterol, 10 mg sodium

RED CABBAGE & POACHED PEACH SALAD

1 tablespoon finely shredded orange peel
2 tablespoons lemon juice
½ cup sugar
½ cup red wine vinegar
1 cup cranberry juice cocktail
2 cups dry red wine (or 2 more cups cranberry juice cocktail)
4 or 5 medium-size (1⅔ to 2 lb. total) firm-ripe peaches
1 large (at least 3 lb.) red cabbage
1 large (about ½ lb.) onion
1 tablespoon salad oil
Salt

In a 5- to 6-quart pan, combine peel, lemon juice, sugar, vinegar, cranberry juice, and wine. Boil, uncovered, over high heat until reduced to 3 cups. Peel, pit, and halve peaches; add to pan. Cover and simmer until peaches are tender when pierced, about 10 minutes; turn fruit over occasionally. Pour into a bowl.

Gently ease 8 to 10 large leaves from cabbage; rinse leaves, drain, and wrap in towels. Enclose in a plastic bag; chill up to a day. Shred remaining cabbage; discard core.

Mince onion. Rinse and dry pan, set over medium heat, and add onion and oil. Stir often until onion is limp, about 10 minutes. Add shredded cabbage and ½ cup peach poaching liquid. Stir often on high heat until cabbage is limp and liquid evaporates, about 10 minutes. Pour into a bowl; let cool. Cover and chill up to a day.

Drain liquid from peaches into pan. Boil, uncovered, on high heat until reduced to about ¾ cup, 15 to 20 minutes. Pour over peaches. Cover and chill up to a day.

Drain about ⅔ of the peach liquid into cooked cabbage; mix. Arrange leaves on a platter; mound cabbage mixture in them. Serve peaches with cabbage or from bowl. Serve from refrigerated to room temperature. Add salt to taste. Makes 8 to 10 servings.

PER SERVING: 164 calories, 2.2 g protein, 30 g carbohydrates, 1.7 g fat (0.2 g saturated), 0 mg cholesterol, 16 mg sodium

CUCUMBER & GREEN ONION SALAD

> 3 **European cucumbers (about 3 lb. total), thinly sliced**
> **About 1 tablespoon salt**
> ½ **cup thinly sliced green onion (tops included)**
> 1 **tablespoon sugar**
> ⅓ **cup seasoned rice vinegar (or ⅓ cup rice vinegar and 1 tablespoon sugar)**

In a bowl, lightly crush cucumbers and 1 tablespoon salt with your hands. Let stand 20 to 30 minutes. In a colander, squeeze cucumbers gently and let drain. Rinse with cool water, squeeze gently, and drain again. If prepared ahead, cover and chill up to a day.

In a bowl, mix cucumbers with sliced onion, sugar, and vinegar. Serve in the bowl, or transfer with a slotted spoon to a platter. Serve from refrigerated to room temperature. Season with salt to taste. Makes 6 cups, 8 to 10 servings.

PER SERVING: 24 calories, 0.8 g protein, 5.4 g carbohydrates, 0.2 g fat (0 g saturated), 0 mg cholesterol, 224 mg sodium

BLUEBERRY TART

> 3 **cups blueberries, rinsed and drained**
> **Press-in pastry crust (directions follow)**
> ½ **cup grape jelly**
> 3 **tablespoons berry-flavor liqueur or grape juice**
> **Mint sprigs (optional)**

Pour berries into pastry. In a 1½- to 2-cup pan, stir jelly and liqueur over medium heat until jelly melts. Spoon evenly over berries. Chill until jelly sets, about 30 minutes. Serve or, if made ahead, cover and chill up to a day. Garnish with mint. Serve from refrigerated to room temperature. Makes 8 to 10 servings.

PER SERVING: 212 calories, 1.7 g protein, 30 g carbohydrates, 9.5 g fat (5.8 g saturated), 25 mg cholesterol, 99 mg sodium

Press-in pastry crust. Combine 1 cup **all-purpose flour**, ½ cup (¼ lb.) **butter** or margarine, and ½ cup **powdered sugar.** Whirl in a food processor or rub with your fingers until dough holds together. Press dough over bottom and 1 inch up sides of a 9-inch tart pan with removable rim. Bake in a 350° oven until golden brown, 25 to 35 minutes. If made ahead, let pastry stand up to 4 hours, or cover and chill up to a day.

Plump blueberries shimmer in press-in pastry crust beneath a jelly-and-liqueur glaze. Fruit tart can be made up to a day ahead, then refrigerated until serving time.

Lean Terrine

PALE PINK SALMON *wraps tiers of sole and vegetables in this refreshing terrine. Serve chilled with a creamy herb sauce for an eye-pleasing, make-ahead dish for up to a dozen guests.*

SALMON, SOLE & VEGETABLE TERRINE

- 2 **medium-size (¼ lb. each) zucchini, ends trimmed**
- 2 **large (¼ lb. each) carrots, peeled, ends trimmed**
- 2 **medium-size (5 to 6 oz. each) thin-skinned potatoes, peeled**
- 1 **pound salmon fillets, skinned**
- ½ **pound sole fillets, skinned**
- ½ **cup *each* regular-strength chicken broth and bottled clam juice**
- 1 **envelope (2 teaspoons) unflavored gelatin**
  Fresh fennel or dill sprigs (optional)
  Herb pesto (recipe follows)
  Salt and white pepper

Slice zucchini and carrots lengthwise into thin strips. Cut potatoes in half lengthwise, then crosswise to make thin half-rounds. In a 10- to 12-inch frying pan over high heat, bring about ½ inch water to a boil. In separate batches, simmer each vegetable, uncovered, until just barely tender to bite; allow about 4 minutes for zucchini, 8 to 10 minutes for carrots, and about 15 minutes for potatoes. As vegetables are cooked, lift them out with a slotted spoon. Immerse zucchini in ice water until cold; lift out and drain on towels. Transfer remaining vegetables from pan to towels.

Cut salmon and sole lengthwise into long, ¼-inch-thick slices.

In a 2- to 3-quart pan, combine broth, clam juice, ⅓ cup water, and gelatin. Let stand about 5 minutes to soften gelatin. Bring to a boil over high heat, stirring until gelatin dissolves; set aside. If mixture thickens before you are ready to use it, warm and stir until it becomes liquid again.

Line a 4- by 8-inch loaf pan smoothly with foil, allowing foil to overlap pan rim; lightly oil foil. Cover pan bottom and sides with a single layer of salmon, fitting pieces together (trim as needed

Slice of terrine shows off colorful layers of sole and vegetables enclosed in salmon wrapping. Baked terrine is served cold with herb pesto.

to fill corners and at pan rim; do not overlap slices). Pour ¼ cup gelatin mixture over salmon in pan, then top with neat layers of ⅓ the potatoes, ⅓ the carrots, and ⅓ the zucchini. Cover with ¼ cup gelatin mixture. Top with a neat layer of ½ the sole. Repeat potato, carrot, and zucchini layers, cover with gelatin, and top again with sole. Repeat until all these ingredients are in pan, then cover with remaining salmon. Cover with oiled foil and press firmly against pan.

Set loaf in a larger pan (at least 2 in. deep). Pour 1 inch boiling water into large pan. Bake in a 350° oven until terrine is firm in center when pressed, 35 to 40 minutes. Cool on a rack; chill at least 8 hours or up to a day.

Uncover; slide a knife between foil and pan sides. Invert a platter on top of terrine. Holding containers together, invert; lift off pan and carefully pull away foil.

Garnish terrine with fennel sprigs. With a sharp knife, cut terrine into ¾-inch-thick slices and transfer to plates on a wide spatula. Accompany with herb pesto and salt and pepper to add to taste. Makes 10 to 12 first-course servings.—*Chef Carmine Gazineo, The Donatello, San Francisco.*

PER PLAIN SERVING: 101 calories, 12 g protein, 6 g carbohydrates, 2.8 g fat (0.4 g saturated), 30 mg cholesterol, 64 mg sodium

Herb pesto. Mix ½ cup **mayonnaise,** 2 tablespoons **whipping cream,** 1 tablespoon **cognac** (optional), 2 teaspoons minced **fresh chives** or green onion, and 1 teaspoon *each* minced **fresh rosemary** (or ¼ teaspoon dried rosemary), **fresh sage** (or ¼ teaspoon dried rubbed sage), **parsley,** and **fresh fennel leaves** or dill (optional). Makes about ⅔ cup.

PER TABLESPOON: 73 calories, 0.2 g protein, 0.3 g carbohydrates, 8 g fat (1.6 g saturated), 8.2 mg cholesterol, 53 mg sodium

Gardening Chefs Share Their Favorite Recipes

RESTAURANT TRENDS *come and go in the West, but emphasis on fresh regional ingredients endures. Finicky chefs seek out the finest produce; some even grow their own. Three chefs acclaimed for their use of fresh, seasonal vegetables and herbs share these recipes featuring their garden bounty.*

MUDD'S HONEY MUSTARD VINAIGRETTE

Allow 1 to 2 tablespoons dressing for 1 cup salad greens.

2 tablespoons *each* **honey and sherry vinegar**
1 tablespoon *each* **Dijon mustard, coarse-grain mustard, and dried thyme leaves**
2 teaspoons **lemon juice**
¼ cup **olive oil**
6 tablespoons **salad oil**

In a food processor or blender, whirl to mix honey, sherry vinegar, Dijon and coarse mustards, thyme, and lemon juice. With motor running, add olive oil and salad oil. Makes about ¾ cup.— *Chef Ron Ottobre, Mudd's Restaurant, San Ramon, Calif.*

PER TABLESPOON: 115 calories, 0.1 g protein, 3.6 g carbohydrates, 12 g fat (1.5 g saturated), 0 mg cholesterol, 51 mg sodium

BERINGER'S MOZZARELLA & TOMATO SALAD

1 cup **Chardonnay**
6 ounces **chanterelle mushrooms,** rinsed well and soiled edges trimmed, sliced thin
1 tablespoon **olive oil**
1 clove **garlic,** minced
2 **shallots,** minced
6 ounces **fresh goat or cow mozzarella cheese**
32 ripe **'Currant' tomatoes** or very small cherry tomatoes, stemmed and rinsed
Basil oil (directions follow)
Tiny fresh **basil leaves**
Salt and freshly ground **pepper**

In an 8- to 10-inch frying pan, boil wine on high heat, uncovered, until reduced to 2 tablespoons. Pour out and save.

To pan add mushrooms, olive oil, garlic, and shallots. Stir often over medium-high heat until juices evaporate and mushrooms are lightly browned, about 10 minutes. Off the heat, add wine. Use, or let stand up to 4 hours.

A sprig of fragrant basil and tiny 'Currant' tomatoes complement chanterelle mushrooms and sliced fresh mozzarella.

Thinly slice cheese and arrange in centers of 8 plates; surround with tomatoes and mushrooms. Drizzle each salad with 2 to 3 teaspoons basil oil; garnish with basil leaves. Season with salt and pepper. Makes 8 servings.— *Chef Jerry Comfort, Beringer Vineyards, St. Helena, Calif.*

PER SERVING: 250 calories, 4.6 g protein, 4 g carbohydrates, 25 g fat (2.9 g saturated), 15 mg cholesterol, 19 mg sodium

Basil oil. Immerse ⅓ cup firmly packed **fresh basil leaves** in 2 quarts boiling **water.** Drain at once and immerse leaves in ice water to cover. Drain well on towels.

In a blender or food processor, smoothly purée basil, then add ⅔ cup **extra-virgin olive oil** and whirl about 2 seconds. Line a strainer with 2 layers of cheesecloth and place over a small bowl. Pour oil through cloth. Discard purée. Use oil, or cover airtight and hold at room temperature up to 2 days. Makes about ½ cup.

THE HERBFARM'S SQUASH BLOSSOM FRITTERS

3 large (about ¾ lb. each) **tomatoes**—1 red, 1 yellow, 1 green—peeled if desired
Squash blossom fritters (directions follow)
Basil oil (recipe precedes)
Fresh **basil leaves**
Salt

Cut each tomato into 12 equal wedges. Trim out center part with seeds (reserve centers for other uses).

Alternating colors, arrange tomato wedges on 6 salad plates. Set a squash fritter on each plate. Drizzle each salad with about 1 tablespoon basil oil; garnish with basil leaves. Add salt to taste. Makes 6 servings.—*Chef Jerry Traunfeld, The Herbfarm, Fall City, Wash.*

PER SERVING: 474 calories, 6.7 g protein, 20 g carbohydrates, 43 g fat (6.2 g saturated), 40 mg cholesterol, 299 mg sodium

Squash blossom fritters. In a blender or food processor, smoothly combine 1 **large egg yolk,** ¾ cup **milk,** ½ cup **all-purpose flour,** 1 tablespoon **cornstarch,** ½ teaspoon **baking powder,** and ¼ teaspoon **salt.**

Gently rinse 6 **squash blossoms** (each 2½ to 3 in. long). Pull pistils from centers. Divide 3 ounces (⅓ cup) **fresh goat cheese** into 6 portions; put a portion into each blossom. Press blossom against cheese.

In a deep 2- to 3-quart pan, heat 1 inch **salad oil** to 360°. Holding blossoms shut, dip 1 at a time in batter to coat all over, let drain briefly, then add to hot oil. Repeat to fill pan without crowding. Cook until golden brown, about 2 minutes; turn once. Drain on towels; keep warm. Repeat to cook all blossoms; use hot.

Tricolor trio of 'Champion', 'Evergreen', and 'Taxi' tomatoes adorns squash blossom fritter. Goat cheese hides inside.

A Bumper Crop of Summer Squash

A MIDSUMMER ABUNDANCE *of summer squash in your garden can stretch your culinary creativity as you look for new ways to use the surplus. We propose these three quick-fix ideas as ways to add variety when your squash supply seems endless, or when you just want to make the most of bargain-priced squash at the market.*

In the first recipe, raw zucchini is shredded, mixed with olive oil and vinegar, and topped with almonds and parmesan for a refreshing salad. For the second salad, you roast zucchini, then marinate it with balsamic vinegar, herbs, and chilies. Last is a stir-fry of crookneck squash accented by green onions and feta cheese.

Keep in mind that green and yellow zucchini work the same in these recipes, offering even more variety.

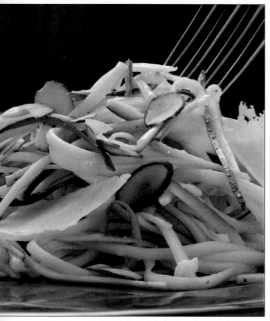

Long, tangled strands of crisp, shredded zucchini make a refreshing salad.

SHREDDED ZUCCHINI SALAD

- ¼ **cup sliced almonds**
- 1¼ **pounds zucchini (about 3 large), ends trimmed**
- 3 **tablespoons cider vinegar**
- 2 **tablespoons extra-virgin olive oil**
  Salt and pepper
- 2 **ounces thinly shaved parmesan cheese**

Place almonds in a 7- to 8-inch pan over medium-high heat. Stir or shake often until almonds are golden brown, about 3 minutes. Pour from pan and let cool.

Finely shred zucchini into long, thin strands (an Oriental shredder works well). Drain in a colander 20 to 30 minutes; gently squeeze to remove excess liquid. Place strands in a bowl; fluff with a fork. Add vinegar, oil, and salt and pepper to taste; mix well. If made ahead, cover and chill up to 1 hour. Mound portions equally onto plates. Sprinkle with almonds and cheese. Makes 4 to 6 servings.

PER SERVING: 114 calories, 5.2 g protein, 4.1 g carbohydrates, 9.1 g fat (2.4 g saturated), 6.4 mg cholesterol, 155 mg sodium

ZUCCHINI WITH MINT & BASIL

- 1½ **pounds small (about 6, each about 5 in. long) zucchini**
- 2 **teaspoons olive oil**
- 2 **cloves garlic, minced or pressed**
- 3 **tablespoons balsamic or red wine vinegar**
- 2 **tablespoons minced fresh or 2 teaspoons crumbled dried mint leaves**
- 2 **tablespoons minced fresh or 2 teaspoons crumbled dried basil leaves**
- ½ **teaspoon crushed dried hot red chilies**
- 4 **large butter lettuce leaves, rinsed and crisped**
  Mint or basil sprigs (optional)
  Salt

Trim zucchini ends. Cut squash lengthwise into ¼-inch slices. Lay slices in a single layer on a lightly greased or nonstick 12- by 15-inch baking sheet.

Mix oil and garlic. Brush evenly over zucchini slices. Bake slices in a 450° oven until browned and soft when pressed, about 30 minutes. Cool 5 minutes.

With a spatula, gently transfer squash to a bowl and add vinegar, mint, basil, and chilies. Mix gently. Let stand at room temperature up to 1 hour or, if made ahead, cool completely, then cover and chill up to a day.

Place a lettuce leaf on each of 4 plates. Divide zucchini evenly among plates, piling it on lettuce. Garnish with mint leaves; add salt to taste. Makes 4 servings.

PER SERVING: 51 calories, 2.3 g protein, 6.5 g carbohydrates, 2.5 g fat (0.3 g saturated), 0 mg cholesterol, 6 mg sodium

MEDITERRANEAN SQUASH STIR-FRY

- 1 **large (about 10 oz.) onion, chopped**
- ½ **pound mushrooms, thinly sliced**
- 1 **tablespoon minced fresh or 1 teaspoon crumbled dried thyme leaves**
- 2 **tablespoons lemon juice**
- 1⅓ **pounds (about 3 medium-size) yellow crookneck squash or yellow zucchini, ends trimmed, cut crosswise into ¼-inch-thick slices**
- ½ **pound (about 2 medium-size) firm-ripe Roma-type tomatoes, cut crosswise into ¼-inch slices**
- ⅓ **cup oil-cured black olives, pitted and coarsely chopped**
- ½ **cup thinly sliced green onions**
- 3 **ounces (about ½ cup) feta cheese, crumbled**

Combine chopped onion, mushrooms, and thyme in a 10- to 12-inch frying pan over medium heat. Cover tightly and cook until vegetables are juicy, about 20 minutes. Uncover pan; stir often over high heat until liquid evaporates and browned bits form in pan. Add ¼ cup water, stir to release browned bits, and boil until liquid evaporates and browned bits again form in pan.

Add another ¼ cup water, lemon juice, and squash. Cover pan and simmer until squash is barely tender when pierced, 3 to 4 minutes.

Uncover pan and stir over high heat until liquid evaporates. Remove from heat and gently stir in tomatoes and olives. Transfer mixture to serving dish. Sprinkle with green onions and cheese. Makes 4 to 6 servings.

PER SERVING: 120 calories, 5.0 g protein, 13 g carbohydrates, 6.5 g fat (2.5 g saturated), 13 mg cholesterol, 428 mg sodium

Oil-free Salad Dressings

ASIAN SEASONINGS *that are thick and virtually oil-free often make ideal bases for light salad dressings. In preserved ginger, hoisin sauce, and plum jam (a subtle variation on Asian plum sauce), the "cling" needed to coat vegetables derives from sugar or a little cooked starch. This ends up being much less caloric than the oil used in a traditional vinaigrette.*

Try the seasonings in salads tailored to complement their flavors.

RED & ORANGE GINGER SALAD

1 **pound (about 3 medium-size) thin-skinned potatoes, peeled**
1 **pound (about 4 medium-size) beets, scrubbed and rinsed**
¾ **pound (about 2 medium-size) firm-ripe nectarines, pitted**
Ginger dressing (recipe follows)
Nasturtium flowers (optional)
Salt

Place potatoes in a 3- to 4-quart pan with water to cover. Bring to a boil over high heat. Cover and simmer until just tender when pierced, about 15 minutes. With a slotted spoon, transfer potatoes to a colander; let cool.

Add beets to pan; return to a boil over high heat, then cover and simmer until tender when pierced, about 20 minutes. Drain beets and let cool; trim ends and peel.

Cut potatoes, beets, and nectarines into ½-inch chunks. Arrange in a wide bowl or on plates. Pour dressing on top; decorate with nasturtiums. Add salt to taste. Makes 6 servings.

PER SERVING: 121 calories, 2.6 g protein, 28 g carbohydrates, 0.4 g fat (0 g saturated), 0 mg cholesterol, 50 mg sodium

Ginger dressing. In a blender, whirl until smooth ¼ cup coarsely chopped **preserved ginger in syrup** (including about 1 teaspoon of the syrup), ¼ cup **distilled white vinegar,** 2 tablespoons **water,** and ⅛ teaspoon **cayenne.**

GREEN & WHITE SESAME SALAD

3 **tablespoons sesame seed**
⅔ **pound slender green beans, ends trimmed**
1 **pound slender asparagus, tough ends trimmed**
¾ **pound jicama, peeled and cut into long matchsticks**
⅓ **cup seasoned rice vinegar (or distilled white vinegar plus 1 teaspoon sugar)**
1 **tablespoon *each* sugar, hoisin sauce, and Dijon mustard**

Place sesame seed in a 10- to 12-inch frying pan over medium-high heat and shake the pan often until seed is golden, 2 to 4 minutes. Pour seed out of pan and set aside.

Fill pan with ½ inch water and bring to a boil over high heat; add beans and asparagus, cover, and simmer until vegetables are just tender-crisp to bite, about 2 minutes; drain. Immerse in cold water; drain when cool.

On a platter or on plates, arrange beans, asparagus, and jicama. In a bowl, stir vinegar, sugar, hoisin, mustard, and sesame seed; drizzle dressing over vegetables. Makes 6 servings.

PER SERVING: 101 calories, 4.6 g protein, 16 g carbohydrates, 2.7 g fat (0.4 g saturated), 0 mg cholesterol, 170 mg sodium

PEKING SPINACH SALAD

12 **won ton skins (each about 3 in. square)**
1½ **quarts (about ¾ lb.) lightly packed spinach leaves, rinsed and crisped**
¼ **pound mushrooms, rinsed, and sliced thin if large**
¾ **cup shredded carrots**
¾ **cup lightly packed, coarsely chopped fresh cilantro (coriander) sprigs**
2 **medium-size (about ⅓ lb. total) firm-ripe red-skinned plums, pitted and sliced thin**
Plum dressing (recipe follows)

Quarter won ton skins and lay them flat on a greased 12- by 15-inch baking sheet; spray or brush with water. Bake in a 500° oven until golden, about 3 minutes; watch carefully.

Salad trio includes ginger-flavored potatoes, nectarines, and beets; cool asparagus, jicama, and beans with sesame-hoisin dressing; and spinach with crisp won tons and plum dressing.

Place spinach in a large bowl and arrange won tons, mushrooms, carrots, cilantro, and plums on top. At the table, mix gently with dressing. Makes 8 servings.

PER SERVING: 92 calories, 3.2 g protein, 21 g carbohydrates, 0.4 g fat (0 g saturated), 0 mg cholesterol, 172 mg sodium

Plum dressing. In a bowl, whisk ⅓ cup **plum jam,** 1 tablespoon **soy sauce,** 3 tablespoons **lemon juice,** and ½ teaspoon **ground cinnamon.**

Tortilla Sundaes

CRISP DISKS OF *cinnamon sugar–dusted pastries, known as buñuelos in Mexico, become the base for this sundae dessert bar. The elements can be assembled ahead, ready to serve.*

But instead of making dough and shaping it, start with purchased flour tortillas. Fried crisp, they are as flaky as homemade ones. Offer scoops of vanilla ice cream, cottage cheese (much like the cheese used in Mexico), fruit, and caramel sauce as toppings; guests build their desserts to taste.

Cajeta, a caramel sauce made with goat's milk, is available in Mexican grocery stores.

Guests build sundaes using buñuelos as a base. Toppings include ice cream, cottage cheese, orange and mango slices, and warm caramel sauce.

BUÑUELO SUNDAE DESSERT BAR

    2 tablespoons sugar
    ¼ teaspoon ground cinnamon
       About 3 cups salad oil
   10 flour tortillas (about 6 in. wide)
    1 to 2 quarts vanilla ice cream
    4 large (about 3 lb. total) oranges
    2 large (about 2 lb. total) firm-ripe
       mangoes, peeled and sliced,
       or 1 can (27 oz.) mango halves,
       drained and sliced
       About 1 cup (8-oz. carton) small-
       curd cottage cheese (optional)
       About 1 cup (12 oz.) purchased
       caramel ice cream topping or
       cajeta

Mix sugar and cinnamon; set aside. Pour 1 inch oil into a deep 3- to 4-quart pan. Over medium heat, bring oil to 370°. Cook tortillas, 1 at a time, until golden brown, about 1½ minutes; turn once. Transfer to paper towels to drain. While tortillas are still warm, sprinkle each with about ½ teaspoon of the sugar mixture. When they are cool, stack on a platter.

If tortillas are cooked ahead, store airtight at room temperature up to a day or freeze up to a week. Thaw unwrapped. To recrisp tortillas, arrange in single layers on baking sheets (about 12 by 15 in.). Bake in a 350° oven until hot, 4 to 6 minutes.

Up to a day or at least 1 hour ahead, scoop ice cream into balls and place in a single layer in a pan. Freeze until firm, then transfer to a chilled bowl, cover, and freeze until served.

Cut peel and white membrane off oranges. Cut between membranes to remove segments. In a large bowl, mix oranges and mangoes. If done ahead, cover and chill up to 8 hours. Spoon cottage cheese into a bowl; cover and chill until served.

In a small microwave-safe bowl, warm caramel topping in a microwave oven at full power (100 percent) until hot, about 1½ minutes. Or set jar (lid off) in about 1 quart water in a 2- to 2½-quart pan; simmer until hot, about 5 minutes. Pour into a bowl. Present tortillas, ice cream, fruit, cottage cheese, and caramel topping. Makes 10 servings.

PER 1 TORTILLA, ⅓ CUP ICE CREAM, ⅓ CUP FRUIT, AND 2 TABLESPOONS CARAMEL: 446 calories, 5.8 g protein, 81 g carbohydrates, 13 g fat (4.2 g saturated), 24 mg cholesterol, 187 mg sodium

ANCIENT GREEKS, *when they wished to thank the gods for favors received (or to ask for favors), sacrificed animals and roasted them on altars. The gods, it was thought, fed on the smoke. The garlic-laden aroma from J. Beck McDowell's Orange & Ginger–glazed Smoked Turkey would have delighted Zeus and his crowd.*

ORANGE & GINGER–GLAZED SMOKED TURKEY

- 1 **turkey, 12 to 14 pounds**
- 1 large (about ½ lb.) **onion, quartered**
- 1 quart **hickory chips**
- 2 medium-size (3 to 4 oz. each) heads **garlic**
- 1 can (6 oz.) thawed frozen **orange juice concentrate**
- ½ cup (about 2½ oz.) minced fresh **ginger**
- 1 tablespoon **salad oil**
  Giblet sauce (recipe follows)

Remove and save turkey giblets and neck. Pull off and discard all lumps of fat. Rinse bird inside and out; pat dry. Fold wings akimbo.

Place 2 onion quarters in neck cavity; bring skin over opening and secure to back with a metal skewer. Place remaining onion pieces in body cavity.

Place chips in a bowl with water to make them float; set aside.

Break garlic heads into cloves; cut cloves in half. With a fork, mix juice concentrate, ginger, and oil.

Ignite about 50 charcoal briquets on fire grate in a barbecue with lid. When coals are dotted with gray ash, about 30 minutes, push equally to each side of fire grate. Set a foil or metal pan on grate between coals. Position grill 4 to 6 inches above grate; lightly grease grill.

Place turkey, breast up, on grill directly above drip pan. Drop a handful of soaked wood chips and about half the garlic onto hot coals. Cover barbecue and open dampers. Every 35 to 40 minutes, add 4 or 5 (8 to 10 total) briquets to each side of the fire grate and add more wood chips and garlic to maintain an even supply of smoke. During last 45 minutes, brush bird generously and frequently with orange juice mixture, using it all.

Cook until a meat thermometer inserted at breastbone in thickest part reaches 160°, 2 to 2½ hours.

Transfer turkey to a platter; let stand 20 minutes before carving.

While turkey is resting, lift drip pan from barbecue and pour drippings into a glass measure. Skim and discard fat; add drippings to giblet sauce, following. Offer sauce to spoon over individual portions of turkey. Makes 16 to 18 servings.

PER SERVING WITHOUT SAUCE: 277 calories, 46 g protein, 6 g carbohydrates, 6.5 g fat (2 g saturated), 142 mg cholesterol, 154 mg sodium

Giblet sauce. As soon as turkey is on the barbecue, put reserved turkey **giblets** (except liver) and **neck** in a 3- to 4-quart pan. Add 1 large (about ¼ lb.) **carrot,** cut into chunks; 1 medium-size (about 5 oz.) **onion,** quartered; 2 **chicken bouillon cubes;** 4 **whole black peppercorns;** and 3 cups **water.** Bring to a boil over high heat; cover, reduce heat, and simmer until giblets are tender when pierced, about 1¼ hours.

Add **liver** the last 5 minutes of cooking.

Pour broth through a fine strainer into a bowl; set giblets aside and discard vegetables. Chill broth until turkey is done. Skim and discard fat from broth. Measure broth; you need 1½ cups. Add water, or boil to reduce to this amount. If desired, chop giblets and pull meat in shreds from neck.

While turkey is resting to carve, in the 3- to 4-quart pan, smoothly blend ¼

"The gods, it was thought, fed on the smoke."

cup *each* **cornstarch** and **dry sherry** or water and broth. Stir over high heat until boiling. Stir in chopped giblets and skimmed **drippings from turkey.** Add **salt** to taste. Makes about 3 cups.

PER ¼ CUP: 70 calories, 7.2 g protein, 3.5 g carbohydrates, 2.1 g fat (0.6 g saturated), 58 mg cholesterol, 36 mg sodium

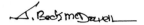

Spokane

OUR KNOWLEDGE OF THE *Aztecs does not tell us if their diet included fast food, but they were a fast-moving people who established an empire within a century, then lost it within two years to invading Spaniards.*

Cardie Molina's Aztec Fast Food is not, as you might think, something rolled up in a tortilla and consumed on the run. It is something entirely new, in our experience. We view it as a union of gado gado, the Indonesian spicy peanut sauce used to season vegetables, and a taco in which the tortilla has been replaced by another corn product, hominy.

AZTEC FAST FOOD

- 1 large can (29 oz.) **hominy**
- ⅓ cup smooth **peanut butter**
- ½ teaspoon **garlic salt**
  Cayenne
- 2 cups finely shredded **cabbage**
- 1 medium-size (about ½ lb.) firm-ripe **avocado,** pitted, peeled, and sliced
  About 1 cup thin slices red **radish**
  Lemon wedges
  Salt

Drain hominy and pour ⅓ cup of the liquid into a 2- to 3-quart pan. Add peanut butter and garlic salt; stir until smooth. Add hominy and cayenne to taste (a bit hot). Stir often, uncovered, over medium heat until hominy is hot. Divide cabbage equally among 4 wide salad bowls. Spoon hominy mixture onto cabbage and top with avocado and radishes. Season to taste with lemon and salt. Makes 4 servings.

PER SERVING: 355 calories, 11 g protein, 39 g carbohydrates, 19 g fat (3.1 g saturated), 0 mg cholesterol, 778 mg sodium

C Molina

Los Angeles

Sunset's Kitchen Cabinet®

Favorite recipes from our readers.

Strands of aromatic basil top grilled chicken breasts with peanut sauce.

GRILLED PEANUT CHICKEN

Asian-inspired chicken gets a delicate smoky flavor on the grill from smoldering wood chips.

- 2 cups hickory or other wood chips for smoking (optional)
- ⅓ cup smooth peanut butter
- 2 tablespoons Worcestershire
- 2 tablespoons soy sauce
- ¼ to ½ teaspoon cayenne
- 4 chicken breast halves (about 2¼ lb. total), skinned
- 2 tablespoons sliced green onion
- ¼ cup thin shreds fresh basil leaves

Place wood chips in a bowl with water to cover; let stand at least 30 minutes.

In a large bowl, whisk until smoothly blended the peanut butter, ⅓ cup warm water, Worcestershire, soy, and cayenne to taste. Turn chicken in the sauce to coat pieces evenly.

Drain wood chips and scatter over a solid bed of medium-low coals (you can hold your hand at grill level only 5 to 6 seconds) in a barbecue with a lid. Lightly oil grill. Lift chicken from sauce and place on grill.

Cover barbecue and close dampers about ¾ shut. Cook chicken, turning and basting every 5 minutes with sauce, until no longer pink at bone (cut to test), 25 to 30 minutes.

Place chicken on a platter and sprinkle onion and basil on the meat. Makes 4 servings.—*Shannon Young, Forest Grove, Oreg.*

PER SERVING: 353 calories, 45 g protein, 6.6 g carbohydrates, 16 g fat (3.2 g saturated), 103 mg cholesterol, 787 mg sodium

---

Plump, round biscuits use whole-wheat flour; serve warm from the oven.

SOFT SESAME BISCUITS

These tender, buttery little breads are a cross between drop biscuits and muffins.

- 1 cup whole-wheat flour
- 1 cup all-purpose flour
- 2 tablespoons sugar
- 1 teaspoon baking soda
- ¼ teaspoon salt
- 2 tablespoons sesame seed
- ⅓ cup (⅙ lb.) butter or margarine
- 1 cup buttermilk

In a large bowl, stir to mix whole-wheat and all-purpose flours, sugar, soda, salt, and 1 tablespoon of the sesame seed. With a pastry blender or your fingers, cut or rub in butter until it's the size of small peas. Add buttermilk and stir with a fork until ingredients are evenly moistened.

With oiled hands, shape dough into 12 equal balls. Space evenly on an oiled 12- by 15-inch baking sheet. Pat each ball to flatten to about 1 inch. Sprinkle biscuits evenly with the remaining sesame seed.

Bake biscuits in a 450° oven until deep golden brown, 12 to 14 minutes. Serve warm. Makes 12.—*Chris Petersen, Moscow, Idaho.*

PER BISCUIT: 145 calories, 3.4 g protein, 19 g carbohydrates, 6.6 g fat (3.4 g saturated), 14 mg cholesterol, 187 mg sodium

---

Zucchini shreds combine with dried noodles from Oriental soup mix in a salad.

ORIENTAL ZUCCHINI SALAD

- ⅓ cup sliced almonds
- ¼ cup rice vinegar or cider vinegar
- ¼ cup thinly sliced green onions
- 3 tablespoons soy sauce
- 1 tablespoon Oriental sesame oil or salad oil
- 2 tablespoons sugar
- 5 medium-size (about 1½ lb. total) zucchini
- 1 package (3 oz.) instant Oriental noodle soup mix; save seasoning packet for other uses

In a 6- to 8-inch frying pan over medium heat, stir almonds often until pale gold, 3 to 4 minutes. Set aside.

In a wide, shallow salad bowl, combine vinegar, onions, soy sauce, sesame oil, and sugar.

With a shredder (regular or Oriental), make thin lengthwise strands of zucchini. Break noodles into small chunks.

Add zucchini, noodles, and almonds to bowl with dressing; mix and serve at once. (On standing, the salad ingredients get limp and soggy.) Makes 6 servings.—*Simone Jacobson, Tucson.*

PER SERVING: 150 calories, 4.3 g protein, 18 g carbohydrates, 7.8 g fat (0.6 g saturated), 0 mg cholesterol, 607 mg sodium

---

Grapefruit, Raspberry & Avocado Salad

½ pound watercress
5 large (⅓ lb. total) butter lettuce leaves
1 tablespoon walnut or salad oil
⅓ cup raspberry or red wine vinegar
2 teaspoons ground coriander
2 large (2⅓ lb. total) grapefruits
1 large (⅔ lb.) firm-ripe avocado
⅔ cup raspberries, rinsed and drained dry
Salt and pepper

Discard tough stems from watercress and lettuce. Rinse greens, drain, wrap in towels, enclose in a plastic bag, and chill at least 30 minutes or up to a day.

In a small bowl, mix together a dressing of oil, vinegar, and coriander.

Put greens in a wide, shallow bowl. With a sharp knife, cut peel and white membrane from grapefruits. Hold fruit over greens and cut between inner membranes to free segments; arrange fruit on greens. Pit avocado, peel, and slice. Arrange with grapefruit. Scatter raspberries onto salad, and spoon dressing over salad. Add salt and pepper to taste. Makes 6 to 8 servings.— *Carmela M. Meely, Walnut Creek, Calif.*

PER SERVING: 94 calories, 2 g protein, 9.8 g carbohydrates, 6.2 g fat (0.8 g saturated), 0 mg cholesterol, 16 mg sodium

Colorful fruits make bright topping for crisp lettuce and watercress.

North Beach Bruschetta

⅔ cup part-skim ricotta cheese
¼ cup shredded carrot
¼ cup dried currants
2 tablespoons chopped green onion
At least 1 tablespoon Dijon mustard
½ teaspoon dried basil leaves
½ pound (½ or 1 whole loaf) crusty bread such as Italian ciabatta or French bread
½ to ¾ pound very thinly sliced pastrami
⅓ cup shredded mozzarella cheese
Parsley sprigs

In a bowl, combine ricotta, carrot, currants, onion, 1 tablespoon mustard, and basil. Cut bread in half horizontally. Set crust-side down; if needed, trim from cut side to make pieces about 1 inch thick. Trim crust so bread sits steadily. Cut each piece in half crosswise.

Spread cut sides of bread with the ricotta mixture. Loosely pleat pastrami onto cheese, covering bread; then sprinkle meat with mozzarella. Place bread on a 12- by 15-inch baking sheet. Bake in a 400° oven until mozzarella melts, 7 to 10 minutes. Garnish with parsley and accompany with mustard. Makes 4 servings.—*Roxanne E. Chan, Albany, Calif.*

PER SERVING: 329 calories, 23 g protein, 43 g carbohydrates, 6.9 g fat (3.8 g saturated), 45 mg cholesterol, 1,258 mg sodium

On baked sandwich, pastrami and mozzarella conceal ricotta base.

Homemade Peach Custard Ice Cream

Adding hot milk mixture to eggs will destroy any salmonella.

3 large eggs
2 tablespoons all-purpose flour
1½ cups sugar
2 cups milk
2 cups coarsely chopped peeled peaches
2 tablespoons lemon juice
1½ cups whipping cream
1 teaspoon vanilla

In a large bowl, beat eggs to blend. In a 3- to 4-quart pan, whisk flour, 1 cup of the sugar, and milk until smooth. Stir often over medium-high heat until boiling, about 8 minutes. Whisking rapidly, pour hot sauce into eggs.

In a blender, smoothly purée peaches with lemon juice and remaining ½ cup sugar. Stir into cooked mixture and chill, covered, until cold, 1½ to 2 hours or up to a day. Stir in cream and vanilla.

Freeze peach mixture in a regular or self-refrigerated ice cream maker (at least 1½-qt. capacity) according to manufacturer's directions. Serve when softly frozen, or package airtight and store in freezer up to 2 weeks; let soften at room temperature about 10 minutes before scooping. Makes 1½ quarts.—*Jeanne Bowers, Fresno, Calif.*

PER ½ CUP: 246 calories, 3.9 g protein, 32 g carbohydrates, 12 g fat (7 g saturated), 92 mg cholesterol, 47 mg sodium

Juicy summer peaches, puréed, flavor this smooth homemade ice cream.

June Menus

TWILIGHT STRETCHING *into June eve-nings makes supper outdoors an attractive choice, even for weeknights if the menu has plenty of impromptu options. The country outing for family and friends came together quickly by making use of this month's plentiful produce, cooked ribs from a market delicatessen, and a bake-and-carry cobbler.*

Efficient kitchen tools—the blender or food processor and the microwave oven— whip out a fine brunch in minutes. For a simple dinner, nachos with canned beans take on a company flair.

SUPPER IN THE COUNTRY

**Golden Tomato-Papaya
Gazpacho with Basil**

**Edible-pod Peas, Orange
Bell Peppers & Red Radishes**

Pork Spareribs

Crusty Bread

Merlot   Apple Juice

Ice Water

**Apricot-Blueberry Cobbler
with Biscuit Topping**

You can make the gazpacho and cobbler the day before your picnic. Just before leaving, pack the vegetables on ice in a leakproof container. Along the way, pick up the cooked and seasoned spareribs at a gourmet shop, deli, or meat market; allow ½ to ¾ pound for each person.

GOLDEN TOMATO-PAPAYA GAZPACHO WITH BASIL

    2 pounds ripe yellow tomatoes
       (regular or cherry)
    1 large (about 1¼ lb.) ripe papaya,
       peeled, seeded, and diced
    1 cup diced cucumber
    ¼ cup minced white onion
    2 tablespoons white wine vinegar
    2 cups regular-strength chicken
       broth
    2 tablespoons minced fresh basil
       leaves
    ⅛ teaspoon liquid hot pepper sauce
       Salt
       Fresh basil sprigs

Impromptu supper in the country offers foods that travel well—market spareribs, crusty bread, golden gazpacho to sip, vegetables to munch, and warm fruit cobbler.

Stem small tomatoes or core large ones; rinse and drain. Dice tomatoes; put into a large bowl. Stir in papaya, cucumber, onion, vinegar, broth, basil, and liquid pepper. Add salt to taste. Cover and chill until cold, 1 hour or up to a day.

Serve, or transport in a chilled thermos; to enjoy cold, serve within 2 hours. Garnish with basil sprigs. Makes 10 to 12 servings.

PER SERVING: 34 calories, 1.3 g protein, 7.1 g carbohydrates, 0.5 g fat (0.1 g saturated), 0 mg cholesterol, 17 mg sodium

APRICOT-BLUEBERRY COBBLER WITH BISCUIT TOPPING

    1 cup and about 2 tablespoons sugar
    ¼ cup quick-cooking tapioca
    2 quarts sliced, pitted firm-ripe
       apricots (about 3 lb. total)
    1⅓ cups blueberries, rinsed and
       drained
    2 tablespoons lemon juice
       Biscuit topping (recipe follows)
    1 large egg white

Insulation news. Wrap yesterday's paper around foil-sealed hot ribs; tie with twine.

Swimming vegetables. Pack with ice in a leakproof container to keep them crisp.

Dressed-up cobbler. Wrap a large napkin or dish towel around baking dish; tie ends.

Freshen up. Jar holds water- and lemon-moistened paper cloths, or buy moist wipes.

In a shallow 3-quart baking dish, combine 1 cup sugar and tapioca. Add apricots, blueberries, and lemon juice; mix gently. Let stand at least 15 minutes or up to 1 hour to soften tapioca; stir fruit mixture gently several times.

On a floured board, roll or pat biscuit dough into a ½-inch-thick cake. Cut into rounds with a 2½-inch-diameter cutter. Reroll scraps, and cut. Place biscuits slightly apart on fruit. Beat egg white slightly, then brush lightly on biscuits; sprinkle with about 2 tablespoons sugar.

Bake in a 400° oven until fruit is bubbly in center, 40 to 50 minutes. Serve warm or cool. If made ahead, cover and store at room temperature up to 1 day. Makes 10 to 12 servings.

PER SERVING: 290 calories, 3.9 g protein, 52 g carbohydrates, 8.5 g fat (4.9 g saturated), 22 mg cholesterol, 234 mg sodium

Biscuit topping. In a food processor or bowl, mix 1½ cups **all-purpose flour**, 3 tablespoons **sugar**, 1½ teaspoons **baking powder**, and ½ teaspoon **salt**. Add ½ cup (¼ lb.) **butter** or margarine; whirl or rub with your fingers until mixture is coarse crumbs. Pour in ⅓ cup **milk**; whirl or stir just until evenly moistened. Gather dough into a ball.

PETITE BRUNCH

Mango-Peach Yogurt Shake
Toasted Croissants
Double Raspberry Microwave Jam
Café au Lait

Heat purchased croissants, uncovered, in a 200° oven to warm and crisp, about 15 minutes. Enhance jam with fresh raspberries, then whirl mangoes and peaches into a thick yogurt shake.

For café au lait, blend equal parts hot, strong coffee and hot milk (if desired, froth hot milk with a whisk).

MANGO-PEACH YOGURT SHAKE

1 medium-size (about ¾ lb.) firm-ripe **mango**, peeled and sliced
1 medium-size (about ½ lb.) firm-ripe **peach**, peeled and sliced
2 cups unflavored nonfat **yogurt**

Spoon fresh raspberries in jam onto crisp croissants; sip filling mango-peach yogurt shakes and hot coffee.

2 tablespoons thawed frozen **orange juice concentrate**
1 teaspoon **vanilla**
1½ cups crushed **ice**
Fresh **mint** sprigs

In a blender or food processor, whirl until smooth the mango, peach, yogurt, orange juice concentrate, vanilla, and ice. Pour into 4 tall or stemmed glasses; garnish with mint. Makes about 5 cups, 4 servings.

PER SERVING: 138 calories, 7.3 g protein, 27 g carbohydrates, 0.4 g fat (0.2 g saturated), 2.3 mg cholesterol, 88 mg sodium

(Continued on next page)

DOUBLE RASPBERRY MICROWAVE JAM

In a 2- to 3-cup microwave-safe bowl, heat ½ cup **raspberry jam made with fruit concentrate** (or sugar), uncovered, in a microwave oven on full power (100 percent) until warm, about 1 minute; stir every 30 seconds. Add ½ cup rinsed and drained **raspberries;** stir to crush a few of the berries. Serve hot, warm, or cool. Makes about 1 cup.

PER TABLESPOON: 23 calories, 0 g protein, 5.7 g carbohydrates, 0 g fat, 0 mg cholesterol, 0 mg sodium

---

BORDER NACHOS DINNER

Black Bean & Fresh Corn Nachos with Tomato Salsa

Jicama & Avocado Salad with Orange Vinaigrette

Coffee Ice Cream with Chocolate-Cinnamon Sauce

Iced Beer

Sparkling Water

A festive nacho platter combines canned black beans, kernels of fresh corn, jalapeño cheese, and a red or yellow tomato salsa; garnish with avocado just before serving. You can season the beans as early as a day ahead.

For dessert, stir a little ground cinnamon into chocolate sauce for ice cream.

BLACK BEAN & FRESH CORN NACHOS WITH TOMATO SALSA

> **Black beans (directions follow)**
>
> 2 **cups fresh-cut corn kernels (from 2 medium-size ears yellow or white corn, or 1 ear of each)**
>
> 1 **cup (4 oz.) shredded jalapeño jack cheese**
>
> 1 **bag (about 14 oz.) blue or yellow corn tortilla chips, or 12 (7-in.-size) warm flour tortillas**
>
> **Thin avocado slices or fresh cilantro (coriander) leaves (optional)**
>
> **Tomato salsa (recipe follows)**

Spoon black beans onto a large, ovenproof platter; spread level into about a 10-inch-long oval. Top beans with corn, then cover with cheese. Bake, uncovered, in a 400° oven until hot in center, about 10 minutes.

Remove from oven and tuck some tortilla chips beside beans; serve with remaining chips. (Or place rolled flour tortillas beside beans.) Garnish with avocado. Spoon onto plates and top with some salsa. Scoop onto chips or roll into tortillas; add more salsa to taste. Makes 5 or 6 servings.

PER SERVING: 693 calories, 21 g protein, 75 g carbohydrates, 37 g fat (8.4 g saturated), 37 mg cholesterol, 1,179 mg sodium

Black beans. Coarsely chop ½ pound **bacon,** 1 medium-size (5 to 6 oz.) **onion,** and 1 clove **garlic.** In a 10- to 12-inch frying pan over medium heat, stir bacon, onion, and garlic until bacon is crisp, 8 to 10 minutes. Drain and discard fat.

Drain 2 cans (15 oz. each) **black beans,** reserving ½ cup liquid. Add beans, reserved liquid, and 1 tablespoon **distilled white vinegar** to pan. Coarsely

mash beans with spoon; if made ahead, cover and chill up to 1 day.

Tomato salsa. Core and dice 3 medium-size (about 1¼ lb. total) ripe **yellow** or red **tomatoes.** Stem, seed, and mince 1 **fresh hot chili.**

Mix tomato and chili with ½ cup minced **yellow** or red **bell pepper,** 1 tablespoon **lime juice,** 2 teaspoons minced **fresh cilantro,** and **salt** to taste. Serve, or cover and let stand up to 6 hours. Makes about 3 cups.

PER ½ CUP: 21 calories, 0.8 g protein, 4.8 g carbohydrates, 0.3 g fat (0 g saturated), 0 mg cholesterol, 8.4 mg sodium

JICAMA & AVOCADO SALAD WITH ORANGE VINAIGRETTE

Save a few avocado slices to decorate nachos.

> 6 **cups thin slivers rinsed and crisped romaine lettuce**
>
> 1 **cup thin slivers jicama**
>
> 1 **medium-size (about ½ lb.) firm-ripe avocado, peeled, pitted, and sliced**
>
> 1 **teaspoon Dijon mustard**
>
> 1 **teaspoon grated orange peel**
>
> ¼ **cup orange juice**
>
> 2 **tablespoons salad oil**
>
> **Salt and pepper**

Arrange lettuce in a bowl; top with jicama and avocado slices.

In a small bowl, mix mustard, orange peel, orange juice, and salad oil. Pour over salad; mix gently and add salt and pepper to taste. Makes 6 servings.

PER SERVING: 108 calories, 1.8 g protein, 6.4 g carbohydrates, 9 g fat (1.3 g saturated), 0 mg cholesterol, 34 mg sodium

JULY

Peppered Salmon (page 136)

Salmon on the grill takes a
fresh twist this month. First marinated in spicy brine, then
topped with a honey glaze and peppercorns, the fish is
slowly cooked in a covered barbecue until it takes on a lightly
smoked, peppery flavor. Enjoy this handsome delicacy
hot or cold, as appetizer or main dish. Menus that will travel
include a tapas picnic, an elegant soup-and-sandwich
supper, and a beach brunch. Other ideas to brighten summer
menus include a selection of salad-salsas, make-your-own
low-fat sausages, and an ice cream toffee torte.

Peppered Salmon

SMOKED SALMON HAS *earned its place as a delicacy. But what happens if you take it yet another step and create peppered salmon? The result is even more flavorful and reflects characteristics of pastrami (lightly smoked, peppered corned beef), the food that inspired this salmon evolution.*

In the spirit of lighter eating, peppered salmon is a delicious alternative to that spicy meat. Enjoy peppered salmon hot or cold, as an appetizer or a main dish, accompanied with the usual accessories: sour cream (or light sour cream to keep fat down), chopped onions, lemons or limes, and crisp toast.

Slow smoking in a covered barbecue is easy to control. Use vents to regulate heat and an oven thermometer to guide you.

Offer salmon warm, cool, or chilled with condiments as an appetizer or entrée.

PEPPERED SALMON

1 **cup firmly packed brown sugar**
6 **tablespoons salt**
1 **tablespoon minced fresh ginger**
2 **or 3 dried bay leaves**
1 **teaspoon crushed whole allspice**
1 **salmon fillet with skin, 3 to 3½ pounds and 1 to 1½ inches thick**
  About ½ cup mixed whole peppercorns (pink, green, white, black; for mildest flavor, use mainly pink and green peppercorns)
  About ½ cup apple or hickory wood chips
1 **tablespoon honey**
2 **or 3 thin red onion slices**
  Fresh dill sprigs
  Condiments (suggestions follow)

In a 1- to 1½-quart pan, bring 1½ cups water, sugar, salt, ginger, bay leaves, and allspice to boiling over high heat; stir until sugar dissolves completely. Let cool slightly.

Rinse salmon fillet, pat dry, and lay flat with skin down in a rimmed pan about 12 by 15 inches. Pour sugar-salt mixture over salmon. Cover pan tightly and chill fish at least 4 or up to 24 hours. Occasionally spoon brine over the fish.

Mound 16 charcoal briquets on the fire grate of a barbecue with a lid. Ignite briquets.

Meanwhile, pour enough hot water over peppercorns to float them; soak at least 15 minutes. Also pour enough warm water over wood chips to make them float; let soak at least 15 minutes.

Pour brine off fish; rinse fish with cool water and pat dry. Set skin side down on a large sheet of foil; cut foil along outline of fish.

Rub honey over top of fish; drain peppercorns and scatter evenly over fish, patting to set them lightly in place.

When coals are dotted with gray ash, 25 to 30 minutes, push half to each side of fire grate. Drain wood chips and scatter 2 tablespoons on each mound of coals. Set grill 4 to 6 inches above the fire grate; lightly oil the grill.

Place salmon on foil in center of grill (no coals should be beneath fish). Set an oven thermometer on the center of the fish. Put lid on barbecue and adjust vents to make ¼-inch openings. After 30 minutes, add 3 briquets to each mound of coals; repeat every 30 minutes of cooking.

Check thermometer often to be sure temperature stays about 160°. If temperature drops, open vents slightly; if

Inspired by the spicy flavorings of pastrami, peppered salmon takes on a savory air. Bathed in a seasoned brine, then glazed with honey and topped with a peppercorn crust, the fillet cooks slowly in a covered barbecue. Foil beneath fish keeps skin from sticking to the grill.

temperature goes up, close 1 or 2 of the vents. Add wood chips as needed to produce a faint, steady stream of smoke. Moisture that accumulates on fish will evaporate. Cook salmon until it is 140° in center of thickest part, about 1½ hours.

Using foil and wide spatulas, slide fillet onto a baking sheet without sides, then transfer fish from sheet to a platter. Serve salmon warm, cool, or chilled.

If making ahead, cover airtight and chill up to 3 days.

Garnish with onion and dill. Cut fish across grain into ¾-inch-wide slices; lift off skin. Serve with condiments. Makes 12 to 14 main-dish servings.

PER SERVING WITHOUT CONDIMENTS: 153 calories, 18 g protein, 5.6 g carbohydrates, 5.9 g fat (0.9 g saturated), 51 mg cholesterol, 513 mg sodium

Condiments. Present in small bowls: ¼ cup drained **canned capers,** 1 cup minced **red onion** mixed with 1 tablespoon **lime** or lemon **juice,** 1 cup **sour cream, thin toast,** and **lime** or lemon **wedges.**

Spain in a Bag

FOR A WHIMSICAL approach to an evening picnic, consider elevating the bag lunch to the bag supper. Here we have designed two menus that will travel lightly and in style. Each person carries his or her own meal using improvised bag coolers that fit easily into bicycle baskets or knapsacks.

To create bag coolers that are effective for 2 or 3 hours, seal individual servings of food and beverages (like splits of wine) in zip-lock plastic freezer bags, then slip each bag into another one along with a handful of ice cubes; seal the outer bag. Be sure to check rules concerning bottles, cans, alcohol, and even food before you set out for a public facility, such as a park, stadium, or beach.

TRAVELING TAPAS

Pistachios
Spanish-style Olives
Celery Stalks
Hard-cooked Quail Eggs
Roasted Pepper Gazpacho
Grilled Shrimp with
Prosciutto & Basil
Crusty Rolls
Miniature Marzipan Tortes
Dry Sherry
Lemonade

Tapas are best described as lots of little nibbles to savor at your own speed. Put them in a bag for a picnic. Sherry is the traditional companion, and one-portion bottles from liquor stores work well.

You can make the soup and tortes and cook the shrimp the day before. If you are short on time, omit shrimp and bring cold sliced cooked ham or Spanish ham; also, buy pastries.

For each person, allow about ½ cup pistachios, ¼ cup olives, 2 or 3 celery stalks, 1 or 2 quail eggs, 1 roll, and 2 or 3 tortes (tuck celery and eggs in with shrimp to keep cool); pack items separately in small plastic bags and distribute among individual packs.

Also include plastic tumblers (1 each for soup, sherry, and lemonade), 1 or 2 small paper plates, napkins, individually packed moistened towels, and a fork and spoon. Cushion the pieces with brightly colored tissue.

ROASTED PEPPER GAZPACHO

    3 medium-size (about 1¼ lb. total) red bell peppers
 1½ cups regular-strength chicken broth
    ¼ cup lime juice
    3 green onions (ends trimmed), finely chopped
    3 medium-size (about ½ lb. total) Roma-type tomatoes, cored and diced
    2 small (about ⅓ lb. each) bell peppers, yellow and green (or 2 of 1 color), stemmed, seeded, and diced
        Salt and pepper

Cut red peppers in half lengthwise and lay cut side down in a foil-lined 10- by 15-inch baking pan. Broil 4 to 6 inches from heat until skins are charred, about 10 minutes. Cover with foil and let stand until peppers are cool. Pull off and discard skins, seeds, and stems.

In a food processor or blender, smoothly purée peppers with broth and lime juice. Transfer to bowl and stir in onions, tomatoes, yellow and green bell peppers, and salt and pepper to taste.

Cover soup and chill until cold, at least 2 hours or up to a day. Transport in a thermos (6-cup, or 2 smaller thermoses); serve within 4 hours. Shake and pour into cups; sip and eat with a spoon. Makes about 6 cups, 4 servings.

PER SERVING: 72 calories, 3 g protein, 14 g carbohydrates, 1.5 g fat (0.3 g saturated), 0 mg cholesterol, 32 mg sodium

Festive gift bags make effective carriers for picnic supper with Spanish flavors.
Tapa-style meal offers variety of nibbles to savor at a relaxed pace.

GRILLED SHRIMP WITH PROSCIUTTO & BASIL

½ cup dry white wine
¼ cup balsamic vinegar
2 tablespoons extra-virgin olive oil or salad oil
2 cloves garlic, minced or pressed
16 to 20 colossal shrimp (10 to 15 per lb.), shelled except for tails, and deveined
8 to 10 thin slices (about 7 oz.) prosciutto
16 to 20 large basil leaves, rinsed and drained

In a bowl, mix wine, vinegar, oil, and garlic; set aside 3 tablespoons of the mixture. Add shrimp to bowl and mix; cover and chill at least 15 minutes or up to 4 hours.

Cut prosciutto slices in half lengthwise. Lay 1 basil leaf against a shrimp; spiral meat around shrimp (not tail) and basil. Repeat to wrap all shrimp. Thread long metal skewer through the middle of 3 or 4 shrimp; run another skewer through shrimp parallel to first (to prevent spinning). Repeat to skewer the remaining shrimp; discard marinade.

Lay shrimp on a barbecue grill over a solid bed of hot coals (you can hold your hand at grill level only 2 or 3 seconds). Cook just until shrimp are opaque but still moist-looking in thickest part (cut to test), 6 to 8 minutes; turn for even browning.

Push shrimp off skewers into a clean bowl; add reserved seasoning mixture and stir gently. Serve warm or, to transport, cover and chill until cold, at least 2 hours or up to a day. Carry in an improvised bag cooler (see preceding); serve within 3 hours. Makes 4 servings.

PER SERVING: 295 calories, 36 g protein, 2.8 g carbohydrates, 14 g fat (2.9 g saturated), 216 mg cholesterol, 1,268 mg sodium

MINIATURE MARZIPAN TORTES

3½ ounces (⅓ cup packed) almond paste or marzipan, crumbled
⅓ cup sugar
1 large egg
1 tablespoon orange-flavor liqueur or ½ teaspoon vanilla
2 tablespoons melted butter or margarine
½ cup all-purpose flour
1 teaspoon baking powder
About 1 tablespoon raspberry jam
¼ cup sliced almonds

In a bowl or food processor, beat or whirl almond paste, sugar, and egg until blended. Beat or whirl in liqueur and butter.

Mix flour and baking powder. Mix or whirl into batter. Spoon half the batter equally into 10 paper-lined small muffin cups (2 in. wide). Add about ¼ teaspoon jam to each cup, then top with remaining batter; gently spread batter to cover jam. Sprinkle with almonds.

Bake in a 350° oven until tortes are browned and firm to touch, 20 to 25 minutes. Remove from pan and cool on a rack. Serve or, if baking ahead, wrap airtight and store up to a day. To transport, seal in individual plastic bags. Makes 10.

PER SERVING: 144 calories, 2.9 g protein, 18 g carbohydrates, 6.8 g fat (1.9 g saturated), 27 mg cholesterol, 74 mg sodium

---

SUMMER SUPPER

Chilled Cucumber-Cilantro Soup
Roast Beef, Asiago & Chard Rolls
Yellow Cherry Tomatoes
Breadsticks
Fudge Brownies
Strawberries
Champagne Splits
Orange Juice

This is an elegant, refreshing soup-and-sandwich meal. Pack as directed for the tapas party (preceding), with cups and plates. You will not need forks or spoons.

Soup, beef rolls, and beverages need to be packed for cool traveling.

CHILLED CUCUMBER-CILANTRO SOUP

1 cucumber (about 1 lb.)
1¼ cups regular-strength chicken broth
¾ cup firmly packed rinsed and drained cilantro (coriander)
½ cup nonfat or low-fat milk
¼ cup lemon juice
Salt

Peel cucumber; cut in chunks into a food processor or blender. Whirl with broth, cilantro, milk, and lemon juice

until smoothly puréed. Season with salt to taste. Cover and chill until cold, at least 2 hours or up to a day.

Transport soup in a thermos (6-cup, or 2 smaller thermoses). Serve within 4 hours. Shake and pour into cups for sipping. Makes about 4 cups, 4 servings.

PER SERVING: 37 calories, 2.4 g protein, 6 g carbohydrates, 0.7 g fat (0.2 g saturated), 0.6 mg cholesterol, 42 mg sodium

ROAST BEEF, ASIAGO & CHARD ROLLS

To shave cheese in thin slices, you need a spade-shaped cutter with a blade in the center.

4 Swiss chard leaves, each about 8 inches wide, rinsed and drained
⅔ pound thinly sliced, fat-trimmed cold roast beef
2 tablespoons prepared horseradish
About ¼ pound asiago or parmesan cheese, shaved into paper-thin slices

Trim off chard stems; reserve for other uses. Bring about 1 inch water to a boil in a 10- to 12-inch frying pan over high heat. Immerse leaves in water, 1 at a time, just until wilted, about 10 seconds. Lift out with a slotted spoon and immerse in ice water until cold. Spread leaves out flat and pat dry. If making ahead, wrap airtight and chill up to a day; pat dry before using.

Cut each leaf in half lengthwise. Lay a section flat; leaving ½-inch borders, top with ⅛ of the meat. Spread meat with ⅛ of the horseradish and top with ⅛ of the cheese. Fold leaf over meat on 2 long sides, then roll compactly to enclose meat. Repeat to make each roll. Serve or, if assembling ahead, wrap rolls airtight and chill up to 6 hours.

To transport, seal 2 rolls in each of 4 small plastic bags. Carry in improvised bag coolers (see preceding); serve within 3 hours. Makes 4 servings.

PER SERVING: 269 calories, 33 g protein, 4.5 g carbohydrates, 13 g fat (6.5 g saturated), 81 mg cholesterol, 673 mg sodium

Beach Brunch, Vancouver-style

A MORNING STROLL *through colorful Granville Island Public Market in Vancouver, British Columbia, yielded inspiration and ingredients for this picnic brunch. We cooked it overlooking Burrard Inlet at North Vancouver's Ambleside Beach.*

Whether you cook outdoors or in your kitchen, the meal comes together easily in less than an hour. The process is worthy of an audience; guests can provoke their appetites by scrubbing the shellfish and cutting the vegetables.

North Vancouver's Ambleside Beach provides setting for picnic brunch.

For outdoor cooking, build a small fire with a brisk blaze—the equivalent of high heat on a range. Regardless of locale, you need a frying pan (12 to 14 in.); a pan with lid (5 to 6 qt.); a wide spatula; big spoons (plain and slotted); a bowl for mixing eggs, another to hold vegetables; a big bowl or bucket to hold fresh water for rinsing and scrubbing; knives for cutting melons, vegetables, bread; and bags for residue.

BEACH BRUNCH FOR 10

Cantaloupe Halves with Blueberries
Steamed Mussels
Ambleside Beach Flat Omelet
Whole-grain Bakery Loaves
Butter
Dry Sauvignon Blanc

STEAMED MUSSELS

If mussels aren't available, use 1 gallon small clams.

- 1 **small (about ¼ lb.) onion, chopped**
- ½ **cup chopped parsley**
- 1 **cup water or dry white wine**
- 1 **gallon small (about 4 lb., each 2 to 3 in. long) mussels, scrubbed**

In a 5- to 6-quart pan, combine onion, parsley, and wine. Cover and bring to boiling on high heat; cook about 5 minutes.

Discard mussels that are not tightly closed. Add remaining mussels to pan; cover, and cook until mussels open, about 10 minutes. Remove from heat; serve with a slotted spoon. Makes 10 servings.

PER SERVING: 51 calories, 6.5 g protein, 3.1 g carbohydrates, 1.2 g fat (0.2 g saturated), 15 mg cholesterol, 152 mg sodium

AMBLESIDE BEACH FLAT OMELET

- 6 **tablespoons butter or margarine**
- 1 **small (about ¼ lb.) onion, chopped**
- 1 **small (about ¼ lb.) yellow bell pepper, stemmed, seeded, and thinly sliced**
- 2 **small (about ¼ lb. each) red bell peppers, stemmed, seeded, and thinly sliced**
- 1 **pound mushrooms, rinsed with stem ends trimmed, thinly sliced**
- ½ **teaspoon fresh or dried thyme leaves**
- 20 **large eggs**
- ½ **cup water**
  About 1 cup fresh basil leaves (optional)
  Salt

In a 12- to 14-inch frying pan over high heat, melt 4 tablespoons butter; add onion, bell peppers, mushrooms, and thyme. Cook, stirring often, until juices evaporate and vegetables begin to brown, about 15 minutes. With a slotted spoon, transfer vegetables to a bowl.

Break eggs into another bowl, add water, and beat to blend. To the empty frying pan, add remaining 2 tablespoons butter. When melted, pour in eggs. Steadily, with a wide spatula, scrape cooked eggs from pan bottom so uncooked eggs can flow down to heat. (Do not stir.) Cook until eggs are set but still creamy looking on top, 10 to 15 minutes (they will be hot enough to be free of salmonella).

Scatter basil and spoon vegetables on eggs. Remove from heat and serve. Salt to taste. Makes 10 servings.

PER SERVING: 233 calories, 14 g protein, 6.1 g carbohydrates, 17 g fat (7.4 g saturated), 444 mg cholesterol, 199 mg sodium

Fire-weathered beach rocks form ring to support mussels and omelet as they cook over a brisk flame; sautéed vegetables and basil are added to omelet just before serving. Meal can also be prepared and cooked at home in the kitchen.

Salad-Salsas

COLORFUL AND CRUNCHY, *these fruit and vegetable relishes resemble salsas, yet they're also refreshingly akin to salads. Hence their hybrid name. Serve salad-salsas to accent grilled meats, or present them in more generous portions as salads.*

RED & YELLOW PEPPER SALAD-SALSA

- 1 **large (½ lb.) red bell pepper, stemmed, seeded, and diced**
- 1 **large (½ lb.) yellow bell pepper, stemmed, seeded, and diced**
- ⅔ **cup minced jicama**
- 2 **tablespoons minced fresh cilantro (coriander)**
- 1½ **tablespoons seasoned rice vinegar (or 1½ tablespoons rice vinegar plus ½ teaspoon sugar)**
- ½ **to ¾ teaspoon hot chili oil or ½ teaspoon cayenne**

In a bowl, mix red bell pepper, yellow bell pepper, jicama, cilantro, rice vinegar, and chili oil to taste. Makes about 2¾ cups.

PER ¼ CUP: 15 calories, 0.4 g protein, 2.8 g carbohydrates, 0.3 g fat (0 g saturated), 0 mg cholesterol, 1.9 mg sodium

NECTARINE, PLUM & BASIL SALAD-SALSA

- 2 **large (about ¾ lb. total) firm-ripe nectarines, pitted and diced**
- 2 **large (about 6 oz. total) firm-ripe plums, pitted and diced**
- ¼ **cup firmly packed fresh basil leaves, minced**
- 1½ **tablespoons balsamic vinegar or red wine vinegar**
- 1 **tablespoon honey**

In a bowl, mix nectarines, plums, basil, balsamic vinegar, and honey. Makes about 2¾ cups.

PER ¼ CUP: 28 calories, 0.4 g protein, 7.1 g carbohydrates, 0.2 g fat (0 g saturated), 0 mg cholesterol, 0.2 mg sodium

MELON & CUCUMBER SALAD-SALSA

- 1 **small (about 1½ lb.) cantaloupe, peeled, seeded, and diced**
- 1 **small (about 1 lb.) firm-ripe papaya, peeled, seeded, and diced**
- 1 **medium-size (about 10 oz.) cucumber, peeled, seeded, and diced**
- ⅓ **cup minced fresh mint**
- 3 **tablespoons lime juice**
- 1 **tablespoon honey**

In a bowl, mix cantaloupe, papaya, cucumber, mint, lime juice, and honey. Makes about 4 cups.

PER ¼ CUP: 22 calories, 0.4 g protein, 5.4 g carbohydrates, 0.1 g fat (0 g saturated), 0 mg cholesterol, 3.3 mg sodium

SQUASH SALAD-SALSA PROVENÇAL

- 2 **large (about ½ lb. total) zucchini, ends trimmed, diced**
- 2 **large (about ½ lb. total) yellow crookneck squash, ends trimmed, diced**
- 2 **large (about ½ lb. total) Roma-type tomatoes, cored, seeded, and finely chopped**
- ¼ **cup drained oil-packed dried tomatoes, finely chopped**
- ¼ **cup oil-cured ripe black olives, pitted and minced**
- 3 **green onions, ends trimmed, minced**
- 3 **tablespoons cider vinegar**
- 1½ **teaspoons minced fresh or ½ teaspoon dried oregano leaves**

In a bowl, mix zucchini, crookneck squash, fresh and dried tomatoes, olives, green onions, vinegar, and oregano. Makes about 4½ cups.

PER ¼ CUP: 24 calories, 0.5 g protein, 2.1 g carbohydrates, 1.8 g fat (0.3 g saturated), 0 mg cholesterol, 139 mg sodium

Brightly cupped pepper-jicama salsa accompanies grilled steak as a refreshing kick. Chopped fruit-and-vegetable relishes can also be served as salads.

LIGHTENING UP: Low-fat Sausages

JUICY, LEAN SAUSAGES *are a reality at last. Usually, sausages are about half fat. Here, we add none; these get only 18 percent of their calories from fat. Instead, we add dried apples and fat-free braised vegetables to soak up meat juices; a little flour holds juices in sausages.*

APPLE-CURRY SAUSAGES

  1 pound skinned, boned, and fat-trimmed turkey or chicken thigh (or a combination), in chunks
  1 piece (5 ft.) sausage casing
  1 large (about ½ lb.) onion, finely chopped
  3 cloves garlic, minced or pressed
 ½ teaspoon curry powder
 ½ teaspoon pepper
 ½ teaspoon fennel seed
 ½ teaspoon salt (optional)
  3 tablespoons all-purpose flour
  1 large egg white
  1 cup dried apple slices, coarsely chopped
  1 tablespoon minced fresh ginger

In a food processor or food chopper, coarsely chop ½ the turkey; set aside. Finely chop the remaining turkey; cover and chill the meat.

In a bowl, cover sausage casing with cold water; soak at least 10 minutes. Drain; slip 1 end of casing over smooth faucet tip; run cool water through casing to rinse well. Cover casing with water and keep cool.

In a 10- to 12-inch frying pan over high heat, combine onion, garlic, curry, pepper, fennel seed, salt, and ¼ cup water. Stir often until browned bits stick in pan. Deglaze by adding ¼ cup water; stir to scrape browned bits free. Stir often until liquid evaporates and browned bits form again. Repeat deglazing step several times until onions are a rich brown, about 30 minutes total. Cover and chill.

In a bowl, smoothly blend 2 tablespoons water with flour, then add turkey, onion mixture, egg white, apple, and ginger. Mix well.

Drain casing; with fingers, gently strip away water.

To fill casing, use sausage-stuffing attachment on food chopper or a plas-

Dried apples and curry-seasoned vegetables flavor these plump, low-fat poultry sausages. Serve grilled in toasted buns with mustard.

tic-lined pastry bag fitted with a plain metal tip at least ½ inch wide; add meat to chopper or fill bag.

Push casing onto tip of sausage stuffer; or push onto wooden spoon handle, then butt handle against tip of pastry bag and push casing onto tip. Remove handle. Allow 3 to 4 inches of casing to hang free.

Force meat through chopper, or twist pastry bag with even pressure, to loosely fill about 36 inches of casing; tightly filled sausages burst when cooked. Twist filled casing at 6-inch intervals (tie with cotton string, if desired); twist or tie casing at each end of sausage links. Cut sausages apart.

If air bubbles form, prick with a pin to deflate. If casing tears, force meat away from tear with your fingers and tie off casing at that point. Prick sausages all over with a pin.

In a 6- to 8-quart pan over high heat, bring 5 quarts water to a boil. Remove from heat and at once add sausages. Cover and let stand until sausages feel firm when pressed, 25 to 30 minutes. Drain. Immerse in ice water until cold; drain. Use or, if making ahead, cover and chill up to 4 days; freeze to store longer, thawing in refrigerator.

Prick sausages in several places with a fork. Broil about 8 inches from heat, or grill over medium coals (you can hold your hand at grill level only 4 or 5 seconds) until browned and hot in center, about 5 minutes. Makes 6 sausages, about 1½ pounds.

PER SAUSAGE: 164 calories, 17 g protein, 17 g carbohydrates, 3.3 g fat (1.1 g saturated), 57 mg cholesterol, 85 mg sodium

More July Recipes

OTHER JULY ARTICLES *featured an irresistible ice cream torte and, to provide balance, two low-calorie yogurt salad dressings.*

ICE CREAM TOFFEE TORTE

Ice cream lovers will find this frozen torte hard to resist. Layers of coffee ice cream, toffee candy bits, and chocolate sauce fill a buttery crust.

- ½ **gallon (2 qt.) coffee ice cream, softened slightly**
  Toffee cookie crust (recipe follows)
  Chocolate sauce (recipe follows)
- 6 **chocolate-covered hard toffee candy bars (1.4 oz. each), coarsely chopped**
  About 2 cups whipped cream (optional)

Spoon ⅓ of the ice cream onto crust; spread with ½ cup chocolate sauce and sprinkle with ¼ cup candy. Repeat; top with remaining ice cream.

Cover and freeze until firm, at least 6 hours or up to 5 days. Cover and chill remaining sauce up to 5 days; to warm, stir over low heat.

To complete dessert, unwrap torte and remove pan rim. Garnish with puffs of whipped cream and remaining candy. Let stand at room temperature to soften slightly, about 15 minutes. Cut into wedges, using a sharp knife dipped often in hot water. Add remaining chocolate sauce to taste. Makes 12 to 14 servings.

PER SERVING: 415 calories, 5.9 g protein, 46 g carbohydrates, 24 g fat (9.4 g saturated), 52 mg cholesterol, 177 mg sodium

Toffee cookie crust. In a bowl, beat ½ cup (¼ lb.) **butter** or margarine (at room temperature) with ½ cup firmly packed **brown sugar** and 1 teaspoon **vanilla.** Blend in 1 cup **all-purpose flour** and ½ cup *each* **semisweet chocolate baking chips** and chopped **almonds.** Press mixture into a 9-inch-square pan.

Bake in a 350° oven until golden brown, 20 to 25 minutes. Cool, then break into small pieces. Whirl chunks in a food processor or blender until fine crumbs form. Firmly press crumbs

For a birthday or other special occasion, offer festive make-ahead torte. Layers of coffee ice cream, bits of toffee candy, and chocolate sauce fill a buttery toffee cookie crust.

evenly over bottom and about 1 inch up sides of a 9-inch cheesecake pan with removable rim.

Chocolate sauce. In a 1- to 1½-quart pan, stir 1½ cups (9 oz.) **semisweet chocolate baking chips** with 1 cup **whipping cream** over low heat just until smooth. If desired, stir in 2 tablespoons **coffee-flavor liqueur.** Serve warm. Makes about 2 cups.

PER TABLESPOON: 67 calories, 0.7 g protein, 5.6 g carbohydrates, 4.6 g fat (1.4 g saturated), 8.4 mg cholesterol, 2.5 mg sodium

OREGANO YOGURT DRESSING

Nonfat yogurt gives you a tart, flavorful start for dressings with rich illusions. Mix the creamy, clinging dressings with salad greens, spoon over vegetables, or offer as dips.

- 1 **cup unflavored nonfat yogurt**
- 3 **tablespoons balsamic vinegar**
- ¼ **teaspoon crumbled dried oregano leaves**
- 1 **teaspoon Dijon mustard**
- 2 **to 3 teaspoons sugar**

In a bowl, mix yogurt, vinegar, oregano, and mustard. Add sugar to taste. Use, or cover and chill up to 4 days. Makes 1¼ cups.

PER TABLESPOON: 8.6 calories, 0.6 g protein, 1.4 g carbohydrates, 0 g fat, 0.2 mg cholesterol, 16 mg sodium

THAI YOGURT DRESSING

Rice vinegar and fish sauce add Asian flavors to yogurt in this version.

- 1 **cup unflavored nonfat yogurt**
- ¼ **cup rice vinegar**
- 2 **teaspoons sugar**
- 2 **teaspoons fish sauce (nam pla or nuoc mam)**

In a bowl, mix yogurt, vinegar, sugar, and sauce. Use, or cover and chill up to 4 days. Makes 1¼ cups.

PER TABLESPOON: 9.6 calories, 0.7 g protein, 1.5 g carbohydrates, 0.1 g fat (0 g saturated), 0.2 mg cholesterol, 8.6 mg sodium

Chefs of the West®
Adventures with Food

YOU CAN EAT NO HIGHER *on the hog than pork tenderloin. (Let's leave boar's head out of the discussion as not only archaic, but also too seasonal.) The tenderloin is what would otherwise be the tenderest portion of pork loin chops; it's also, as pork merchants remind us, the other white meat.*

Bud Starr sends us a recipe that goes back to his college days in Kansas. He worked as a fry cook in a restaurant whose house specialty was breaded pork tenderloin sandwiches. The following version shows what Kansas imagination can do with rather pedestrian ingredients.

BUD'S BEST BREADED PORK TENDERS

About 1½ pounds pork
tenderloin, fat trimmed
About 18 saltine crackers
(2 in. square)
½ teaspoon dried rubbed sage
(optional)
1 large egg
2 tablespoons water
About 2 tablespoons salad oil
8 to 10 large butter lettuce leaves,
rinsed and crisped
4 or 5 English muffins, split and
toasted
Apple butter, apple sauce, or
tomato-based chili sauce
Salt

Cut meat crosswise into 8 to 10 equal pieces. Place pieces between sheets of plastic wrap and pound with a flat mallet until evenly ⅛ to ¼ inch thick (if making ahead, roll pounded meat in plastic, seal in a plastic bag, and chill up to a day).

Crush crackers to fine crumbs in a food processor or blender; you should have ¾ to 1 cup. Put in a shallow pan; mix in sage.

In a shallow bowl, beat egg and water to blend. Dip meat, a slice at a time, into egg mixture, drain briefly, and turn in crumbs, pressing lightly onto meat.

Pour 2 teaspoons oil into a 10- to 12-inch frying pan over medium-high heat. When oil is hot, add pork to fill pan; brown slices and cook until meat is no longer pink in center (cut to test), about

6 minutes. Lift out and keep warm; repeat until all meat is cooked, adding oil as needed to prevent sticking.

Lay a lettuce leaf on each toasted muffin half; set meat on leaves. Serve open-faced with apple butter and salt to taste. Makes 8 to 10 sandwiches, 4 or 5 servings.

PER SANDWICH: 392 calories, 35 g protein, 34 g carbohydrates, 12 g fat (2.4 g saturated), 131 mg cholesterol, 483 mg sodium

Leonard "Bud" Starr

Tacoma

HICK CHIC—A LIFE-STYLE *much in evidence in the West—has been defined as wearing a down vest, driving a pickup truck, and owning a personal computer. People who are into (if that is the idiom) hick chic live in the country, but not too far from the city. This bucolic frame of mind has opened the door for a cuisine with rustic American roots but sophisticated details. Bill Solice's Fresh Corn Pancakes are a fine example.*

FRESH CORN PANCAKES

3 large ears corn, or 2 cups
(10-oz. package) frozen corn
kernels
1 large egg
⅓ cup diced red bell pepper
⅓ cup milk
2 tablespoons melted butter or
margarine
3 tablespoons cornmeal
⅓ cup all-purpose flour
1½ teaspoons *each* sugar and baking
powder
⅛ teaspoon ground nutmeg
Salad oil
Sour cream and jalapeño jelly
(optional)
Salt

Cut corn kernels and scrape milk from cobs; you should have about 2 cups. Put kernels in a bowl and add egg, bell pepper, milk, and butter; mix well.

Stir together cornmeal, flour, sugar, baking powder, and nutmeg. Mix dry ingredients with corn mixture.

Place a griddle or 12-inch frying pan over medium-high heat. When griddle is hot, brush lightly with salad oil, then drop batter onto griddle in ¼-cup portions about 4 inches apart. With a spoon, spread batter to form 4-inch-wide rounds. Cook pancakes until dry-looking on top and browned on the bottom; turn with a wide spatula. Remove from griddle when brown on second side. Slightly overlap cakes on a platter and keep warm; repeat to cook remaining batter.

Offer pancakes with sour cream, jelly, and salt to add to taste. Makes 9 pancakes, 3 or 4 servings.

PER PANCAKE: 108 calories, 3.2 g protein, 16 g carbohydrates, 4 g fat (2.1 g saturated), 32 mg cholesterol, 93 mg sodium

Bill Solice

San Bruno, Calif.

"He worked as a fry cook in a restaurant whose specialty was pork tenderloin sandwiches."

Supper for two is quickly cooked vegetable frittata served from the pan.

SUMMERTIME FRITTATA

About ½ pound thin-skinned
   potatoes, scrubbed and diced
½ pound mushrooms, rinsed and
   thinly sliced
2 teaspoons salad oil
3 or 4 green onions, ends trimmed,
   thinly sliced
4 large eggs
⅓ cup shredded cheddar cheese
   Salt and pepper

In a 10- to 12-inch frying pan with oven-proof handle, combine potatoes, mushrooms, oil, and ¼ cup water. Cover and cook over medium-high heat until potatoes are tender to pierce, about 12 minutes; stir occasionally. Uncover and let liquid boil away.

Set aside 2 tablespoons onions; beat remainder with eggs, cheese, and ¼ cup water to blend. Pour over cooked vegetables. Cook on low heat until eggs begin to set at pan rim, about 4 minutes.

Broil 6 inches from heat until frittata feels set when lightly touched, 2 to 3 minutes. Sprinkle with reserved onions. Serve hot or at room temperature; spoon from pan. Add salt and pepper to taste. Makes 2 servings.—*Megan Ross, Vancouver, Wash.*

PER SERVING: 392 calories, 22 g protein, 29 g carbohydrates, 21 g fat (7.7 g saturated), 445 mg cholesterol, 259 mg sodium

Cook wild rice, asparagus, and mushrooms to make a warm salad.

WARM WILD RICE & ASPARAGUS SALAD

1 cup wild rice, rinsed and drained
1 pound mushrooms, rinsed and
   thinly sliced
1 large (10 oz.) onion, chopped
   About 2½ cups regular-strength
   chicken broth
1 pound asparagus; discard tough
   ends and thinly slice spears
3 tablespoons balsamic vinegar
1 tablespoon olive oil
   Salt and pepper

In a 3- to 3½-quart pan on high heat, bring 4 cups water and rice to boiling; cover and simmer until rice is tender to bite, about 50 minutes. Drain; let cool.

In a 10- to 12-inch frying pan over high heat, combine mushrooms, onion, and ¾ cup broth. Boil on high heat, uncovered, until liquid evaporates and vegetables start to brown, about 12 minutes; stir often. Add ⅓ cup broth and stir to release browned bits. Boil until liquid evaporates and the mixture begins to brown again, 2 to 4 minutes; stir often. Repeat step until vegetables are browned, 3 or 4 more times.

Stir ⅓ cup broth into vegetables; add asparagus and stir often until asparagus is tender-crisp to bite, about 2 minutes. In a bowl, mix vegetables, rice, vinegar, and oil; add salt and pepper to taste. Makes 8 servings.—*Ruth Blakely, Bishop, Calif.*

PER SERVING: 129 calories, 6 g protein, 22 g carbohydrates, 2.6 g fat (0.4 g saturated), 0 mg cholesterol, 19 mg sodium

Cold chicken teams up with tomatoes, pasta, olives, and cheese for dinner.

COOL CHICKEN PLATTER WITH MUSTARD SAUCE

4 boned, skinned chicken breast
   halves (about 1 lb. total)
8 cups rinsed and crisped red leaf
   lettuce, in bite-size pieces
4 cups cold, cooked small pasta
   such as penne or rotelle
8 medium-size (about 1¼ lb. total)
   Roma-type tomatoes
5 ounces (⅔ cup) unripened goat
   cheese, crumbled
   About ½ cup calamata olives
   Sauce (recipe follows)
   Salt and pepper

In a 4- to 5-quart pan, bring 2 quarts water to a boil. Add chicken, cover, and remove from heat. Let stand until chicken is white in thickest part (cut to test), about 20 minutes; drain and let stand until cool.

On 4 dinner plates equally arrange lettuce; top with pasta. Thinly slice chicken and tomatoes; arrange on lettuce with cheese and olives. Spoon sauce over salads; add salt and pepper to taste. Makes 4 servings.—*Patti Devlin, Lafayette, Calif.*

PER SERVING: 622 calories, 40 g protein, 45 g carbohydrates, 32 g fat (3.1 g saturated), 66 mg cholesterol, 1,265 mg sodium

Sauce. Mix ½ cup **white wine vinegar** with ¼ cup **olive oil,** 2 tablespoons **Dijon mustard,** and 1 tablespoon **dried tarragon leaves.**

PEPPERED POTATO & TWO-BEAN SALAD

5 large (about 2 lb. total) red thin-skinned potatoes, scrubbed
1 can (14½ oz.) black beans, rinsed and drained
½ cup chopped red onion
  Dressing (recipe follows)
½ pound spinach leaves, rinsed and crisped
1 medium-size (6 oz.) red bell pepper, stemmed, seeded, and chopped
4 cups (about 1 lb.) cold, cooked green beans
  Salt

In a 5- to 6-quart pan, cover potatoes with water and bring to boiling on high heat; simmer until tender when pierced, 30 to 35 minutes. Drain, let cool, and cut in ¾-inch chunks into a bowl. Add black beans, onion, and dressing; mix. Line a platter with a few spinach leaves; sliver remainder. Mound cut spinach on platter and top with potato salad and red pepper; surround with green beans. Salt to taste. Makes 8 servings.—*Sally Vog, Springfield, Oreg.*

PER SERVING: 173 calories, 7.9 g protein, 35 g carbohydrates, 0.8 g fat (0.1 g saturated), 0.6 mg cholesterol, 140 mg sodium

Dressing. Combine 1 cup **unflavored nonfat yogurt** (or use half reduced-calorie mayonnaise); 3 tablespoons *each* minced **fresh cilantro** (coriander) and minced **fresh basil leaves;** and 2 tablespoons **lemon juice.**

Green beans, onion, red bell pepper, and herbs bring inspiration to potato salad.

STIR-FRIED BEEF WITH BEAN SPROUTS

¾ pound lean, fat-trimmed tender beef, thinly sliced
  Sauce (recipe follows)
  About 2 tablespoons salad oil
1 small (about ¼ lb.) onion, cut into thin wedges
1 small (about ¼ lb.) green bell pepper, stemmed, seeded, and thinly sliced
½ pound bean sprouts, rinsed
1 cup cherry tomatoes, rinsed, stemmed, and halved
  About 3 cups hot cooked rice
  Soy sauce

Mix beef and sauce; let stand 5 to 30 minutes. Place a 12-inch frying pan or wok over high heat; add 2 teaspoons oil, onion, and bell pepper. Stir-fry until slightly limp, about 4 minutes. Pour from pan. Add 2 teaspoons oil to pan. Lift ½ the beef from sauce and stir-fry until rare, about 2 minutes. Add to vegetables. Stir-fry remaining beef with 2 teaspoons oil. Add to cooked meat. Pour sauce into pan; stir until boiling. Add sprouts, cooked ingredients, and tomatoes; stir until hot. Serve with rice and soy to taste. Makes 4 servings.—*Lola W. Malone, Spokane.*

PER SERVING: 469 calories, 25 g protein, 56 g carbohydrates, 14 g fat (3.5 g saturated), 53 mg cholesterol, 829 mg sodium

Sauce. Mix 3 tablespoons *each* **soy sauce** and **dry sherry,** 2 tablespoons minced **fresh ginger,** and 2 teaspoons **sugar.**

Speedy beef stir-fry includes cherry tomatoes, bean sprouts, and bell pepper.

BLUEBERRY-APPLE DEEP-DISH PIE

⅔ cup sugar
3 tablespoons quick-cooking tapioca
3 cups peeled, sliced apples
2 cups blueberries, rinsed
1 tablespoon lemon juice
  Cream cheese pastry (recipe follows)
  About 2 teaspoons milk

In a shallow 2-quart casserole, mix sugar, tapioca, apples, blueberries, and lemon juice.

On a floured board, roll pastry slightly larger than casserole top; set pastry on fruit. Fold pastry under and flush with rim; flute against rim. Cut slits for vents and brush with milk. Bake in a 400° oven until richly browned, about 40 minutes. Serve hot or cool. Makes 8 servings.—*Carmela M. Meely, Walnut Creek, Calif.*

PER SERVING: 278 calories, 2.4 g protein, 40 g carbohydrates, 13 g fat (7.7 g saturated), 35 mg cholesterol, 123 mg sodium

Cream cheese pastry. In a food processor or with a mixer, mix 6 tablespoons **butter** or margarine, in chunks, and 1 small package (3 oz.) **cream cheese.** Add ¾ cup **all-purpose flour;** mix until incorporated. Chill airtight at least 2 hours or up to a day.

Crimson-blue juices of blueberries with apples ooze up through tender crust.

July Menus

STEP INTO THE GARDEN *this month to savor the warmth of the season and what it brings to the table. Gather ripe produce and flowers—perhaps from your own garden or a local farm—to brighten meals and decor.*

For an alfresco lunch or dinner, prepare a cool, make-ahead chicken salad. Greenery and blossoms twine through foods and tableware, enhancing the freshness of the open-air setting.

At breakfast, a big bowl of peaches and blueberries is a colorful, but fleeting, centerpiece to accompany hearty pancakes served with more of the berries.

SUMMER SALAD ON THE PORCH

Cool Asian Chicken Salad
Fruit Compote
Chili-Mint Lemonade

Relax! Because the foods are served cool, they can all be prepared ahead.

Combine ripe fig and apricot halves with raspberries to make a simple fruit compote. You might like to moisten fruit with raspberry or apricot syrup, or a liqueur flavored by berries, citrus, or nuts.

COOL ASIAN CHICKEN SALAD

2 **stalks fresh lemon grass, ends and coarse leaves trimmed; or 2 strips lemon peel (yellow part only, each about 3 in. long)**

6 **quarter-size slices peeled fresh ginger**

1 **pound Chinese pea pods, ends and strings removed**

4 **boned, skinned chicken breast halves (about 1¼ lb. total)**
Asian dressing (recipe follows)
Romaine lettuce leaves, rinsed and crisped
Rice triangles (recipe follows)

½ **cup roasted peanuts, coarsely chopped**

Chinese pea pods, poached chicken, and rice cakes make an exotic-looking, simple-to-prepare salad entrée for four. Serve from a large tray and add dressing to taste.

In a 4- to 5-quart pan over high heat, bring about 1½ inches water, lemon grass, and ginger to a boil. Add Chinese peas; cook just until brighter green, 1 to 1½ minutes. Quickly skim peas from water with a slotted spoon and at once immerse them in ice water.

Add chicken to boiling water, cover, and remove from heat. Let stand until breasts are white in center. Cut to test at 20 minutes; if pink, return to water until white, about 5 minutes longer. Immerse chicken in ice water with peas.

THE DETAILS

Nasturtium napery. *Flower and knotted, pleated paper cord enclose napkin.*

Leafy lemonade. *Mint sprigs decorate cool, spiced drink of lemons and chili-mint syrup.*

Herbal decor. *Set herb packs in a pot for an instant centerpiece; you can plant them later.*

Posy trays. *Tuck nontoxic garden greenery and edible flowers into flat baskets or mats.*

Pour cooking liquid through a strainer; save seasonings for dressing.

When chicken is cold, in about 30 minutes, drain off ice water. Cut chicken into 1-inch diagonal slices. Line a platter with lettuce; top with chicken, peas, and rice. If making ahead, chill airtight up to 3 hours. Add dressing and peanuts. Makes 4 servings.

PER SERVING: 566 calories, 44 g protein, 56 g carbohydrates, 18 g fat (2.7 g saturated), 82 mg cholesterol, 618 mg sodium

Asian dressing. Mince reserved **lemon grass** (see salad, preceding) and **ginger.** Mix with ½ cup **rice vinegar,** 2 tablespoons *each* **soy sauce** and **salad oil,** and 2 teaspoons **sugar.**

Rice triangles. In a 2- to 3-quart pan over high heat, bring 1 cup **medium-** or short-**grain white** (pearl) **rice** and 1¾ cups **water** to a boil. Cover and simmer until liquid is absorbed, about 20 minutes.

Firmly pack hot rice in an even layer in an 8-inch-square pan; cool. (If making ahead, cover and let stand up to 4 hours.) Run a knife between rice and pan rim. Invert pan, easing rice from pan bottom onto a counter. Cut into 2-inch triangles; rinse knife often with water.

CHILI-MINT LEMONADE

For spiciest flavor, use all the chilies.

- ¾ **cup sugar**
- 1½ **cups coarsely chopped fresh mint**
- 4 **to 8 small dried hot red chilies**
- 1 **cup lemon juice**
  Fresh mint sprigs
  Ice cubes

In a 3- to 4-quart pan over high heat, boil 2 cups water, sugar, chopped mint, and chilies, uncovered, until reduced to 1 cup, 12 to 14 minutes; stir occasionally. Let cool; pour mint- and chili-flavored mixture through a strainer into a pitcher, pressing to extract liquid. Discard mint; rinse chilies and add to pitcher along with lemon juice and 1 quart water.

Cover and chill the lemonade until cold, at least 1 hour or up to 1 week. Serve in pitcher or a tall decorative bottle, adding mint sprigs. Pour into ice-filled glasses and garnish each portion with more mint sprigs. Makes 6 cups, 4 to 6 servings.

PER CUP: 111 calories, 0.5 g protein, 29 g carbohydrates, 0.4 g fat (0 g saturated), 0 mg cholesterol, 9.1 mg sodium

Juicy blueberries and peaches nestle around hearty pancakes made with more blueberries.

BLUEBERRY PANCAKE FEAST

Whole-grain Blueberry Pancakes
Maple Syrup   Milk

Weekend-morning pancakes, made with whole-wheat flour, rolled oats, and cornmeal, have old-fashioned appeal. Serve pancakes as they're cooked, or place in a single layer on racks in a warm oven until all are made. Top stacks with fruit and sweeten with maple syrup.

(Continued on next page)

WHOLE-GRAIN BLUEBERRY PANCAKES

    3 cups blueberries
    2 large (1¼ lb. total) firm-ripe
      peaches
    1 tablespoon lemon juice
    ¾ cup all-purpose flour
    ¾ cup whole-wheat flour
    ½ cup regular rolled oats
    ⅓ cup cornmeal
    1 tablespoon sugar
    1 tablespoon baking powder
    ½ teaspoon salt (optional)
    3 large eggs, separated
    1¾ cups milk
      About 3 tablespoons salad oil

Rinse and drain blueberries. Peel peaches, if desired, then slice; mix the slices with lemon juice.

Mix all-purpose and whole-wheat flours, oats, cornmeal, sugar, baking powder, and salt. In a deep bowl, beat egg whites until stiff, moist peaks form. In a larger bowl, whisk yolks, milk, 3 tablespoons oil, and flour mixture until batter is smooth. Stir in 1½ cups blueberries. Gently fold in egg whites.

Place 2 regular or nonstick griddles or 10- to 12-inch frying pans over medium heat. When hot, lightly oil if needed. For each cake, scoop ⅓ cup batter from bottom of bowl onto griddle; spread slightly. Cook until tops are bubbly and almost dry; turn and cook until brown on bottoms. Serve with berries and peaches. Makes 18 pancakes, 6 servings.

PER PANCAKE: 128 calories, 3.9 g protein, 19 g carbohydrates, 4.3 g fat (1.1 g saturated), 39 mg cholesterol, 95 mg sodium

AUGUST

Watermelon-Strawberry Cake (page 155)

Juicy watermelons
display their versatility this month in recipes ranging
from appetizers to dessert. We visit four great midsummer
parties and share expertise and tips on what makes
a memorable event. Raspberry lovers are in for a treat:
old-fashioned recipes that feature the berries in a
juicy cobbler, a superthick milkshake, a special soda, and a
lavish brownie. Other articles include new ideas for grilled
poultry and meat, vegetable crackle chips for low-calorie
snacking, and an East-West version of linguine.

151

The Wonderful World of Watermelons

THIS GREAT SUMMER *fruit is a vegetable? Its closest relatives are cucumbers and squash—a fact to be ignored as you enjoy the sweet fruit flavor and tender-crisp texture of summer's prime watermelon offerings.*

Displayed here are the seven basic market melons of the West. They are divided into classes (such as Crimson Sweet or Red Seedless) based on surface appearance (dark to light green; solid color, striped, or mottled), size (weight), shape (long or round), flesh color (red or yellow), and seeds (with or without). Each of the basic groups includes a number of varieties, but because melons vary in taste due as much to ripeness as to genes, varietal names aren't as helpful for melon selection as deciding how much you need, what color you want, and if you can deal with seeds.

In extensive tastings at Sunset, this claim proved true. We found that a melon was a melon, and some were better than others—some of the time.

The only sure way to buy a ripe melon is to buy it cut. But clues on the underside (where melon lies) help; the area is paler and should have creamy tones, not an unripe green color.

Keep uncut melons up to a week in a cool place, away from bright sun. Once a melon is cut, keep portions covered and well chilled until ready to eat—up to several days.

(Continued on page 154)

Ice-box
Variety: Minnie-Lee;
5 to 15 pounds.

Red Seedless
Variety: Nova;
10 to 25 pounds.

Yellow Seedless
Variety: Honey Heart;
10 to 25 pounds.

Allsweet
Variety: Allsweet;
18 to 40 pounds.

Peacock/Calsweet
Variety: Picnic;
15 to 25 pounds.

Jubilee
Variety: Royal Jubilee;
20 to 45 pounds.

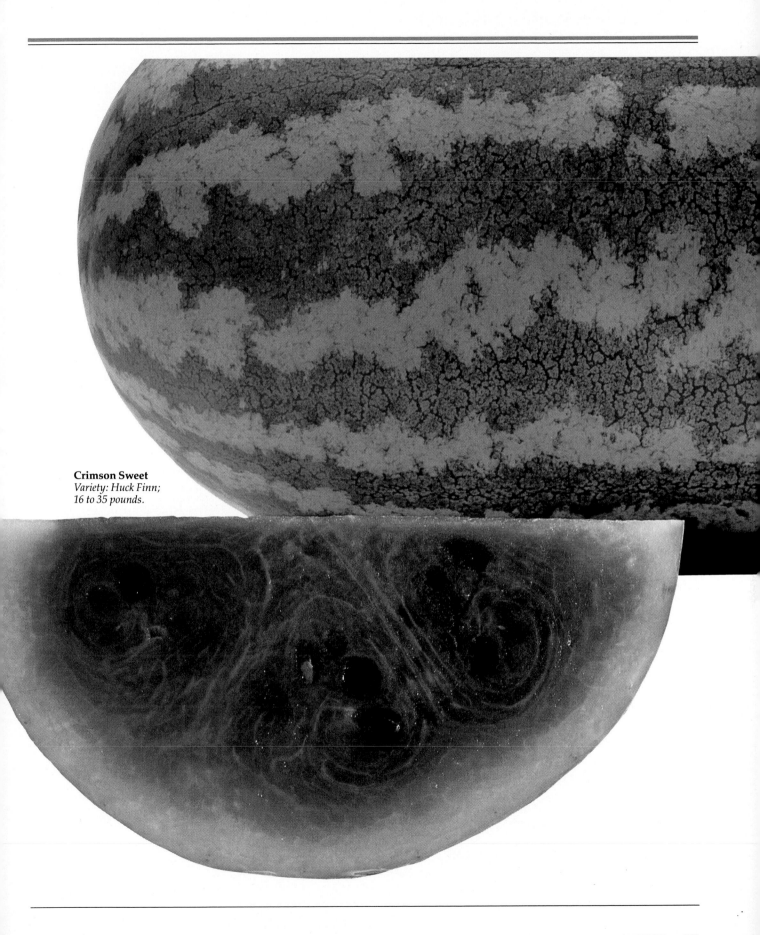

Crimson Sweet
*Variety: Huck Finn;
16 to 35 pounds.*

Slices of kiwi fruit garnish watermelon wedge; top with mint dressing.

MINTED WATERMELON WEDGED WITH KIWI FRUIT

4 **watermelon (seedless or regular) wedges, each about 3 inches wide, cut from a round 8- to 9-inch-long melon**

4 **large (about ¼ lb. each) kiwi fruit, peeled and each cut into 5 or 6 equally thick rounds**
   Mint dressing (recipe follows)

With a sharp, short-blade knife, cut between melon flesh and rind, leaving flesh in place. From apex of flesh, make 5 or 6 equidistant cuts to rind. Insert a kiwi slice into each vertical cut. Spoon mint dressing over wedges. Makes 4 servings.

PER SERVING: 117 calories, 2 g protein, 27 g carbohydrates, 1.2 g fat (0 g saturated), 0 mg cholesterol, 10 mg sodium

Mint dressing. Combine ⅓ cup **seasoned rice vinegar** (or ⅓ cup rice vinegar and 2 teaspoons sugar) and 3 tablespoons minced **fresh mint leaves.** Serve; if dressing stands, mint darkens, but it tastes fine.

WATERMELON ICICLES

8 **wooden ice cream sticks**
8 **triangle-shape pieces seedless or seeded, rind-trimmed watermelon, each about 1 inch thick and 3 inches wide at base**

Push an ice cream stick from wide end almost all the way through each melon triangle. Lay pieces flat in a metal pan; cover with plastic wrap, and freeze until solid, about 4 hours. Serve, or transfer to a freezer container and freeze up to 1 month. Makes 8.

PER PIECE: 38 calories, 0.7 g protein, 8.6 g carbohydrates, 0.5 g fat (0 g saturated), 0 mg cholesterol, 2.4 mg sodium

Frozen watermelon triangle on a stick makes a great summer snack.

Black beans represent watermelon seeds in this refreshing, whimsical salad.

WATERMELON SEED SALAD

1 **piece (5 to 6 lb.) seedless or regular watermelon**
1 **can (14½ oz.) black beans, drained and rinsed**
2 **cups very thinly sliced cucumber**
½ **cup slivered mild onion**
⅓ **cup cider vinegar**
3 **tablespoons chopped fresh basil leaves**
2 **tablespoons sugar**
   Fresh basil sprigs (optional)
   Salt and pepper

Scoop enough melon into balls (or cut rind-trimmed melon into cubes) to make 6 cups; if necessary, pick out and discard as many seeds as possible. Save remaining melon to eat later. If you cut melon ahead, cover and chill pieces up to 6 hours.

In a wide, shallow bowl, gently mix watermelon balls, beans, cucumber, onion, vinegar, basil, and sugar; garnish with basil sprigs. Season to taste with salt and pepper. Makes 6 servings.

PER SERVING: 118 calories, 3.9 g protein, 25 g carbohydrates, 1.1 g fat (0 g saturated), 0 mg cholesterol, 115 mg sodium

WATERMELON APPETIZER WITH ASIAN DIPPING SAUCE

1 small (6 to 8 lb.) or 1 cross-cut
  piece (4 to 5 in. long) watermelon
**Asian dipping sauce (recipe
  follows)**
**About 1 tablespoon crushed dried
  hot red chilies**

Cut small melon in half; trim a slice
from each rounded end so it will sit
steadily. Slice melon crosswise into
about 1-inch-thick rounds. Restack slices
and cut down through them to make
wedges about 2 inches wide at rind end.
(If using half melons, reshape wedges
on melon ends.) Place dipping sauce
and chilies each in a small bowl next to
melon. To eat, dip melon into sauce,
then chilies, as desired. Makes 16 servings.

PER SERVING: 39 calories, 0.7 g protein, 8.6 g carbohydrates, 0.5 g fat
(0 g saturated), 0 mg cholesterol, 10 mg sodium

Asian dipping sauce. Mix together ⅓
cup *each* **lime juice** and **seasoned rice
vinegar** (or ⅓ cup rice vinegar and 2
teaspoons sugar), 1 tablespoon minced
pickled ginger, 1 tablespoon **sugar,** and
1 tablespoon **fish sauce** (*nuoc mam* or
nam pla) or soy sauce.

WATERMELON- STRAWBERRY CAKE

*For a neat cake shape, use midsections of
melons.*

2 seedless or regular watermelons
  (8 to 10 lb. each and the same
  diameter), 1 with yellow flesh and
  1 with red flesh
2 narrow, unfinished, untreated
  wood strips (without cracks or
  warp, each ½ in. thick, 1 to 2 in.
  wide, and at least 1 ft. long)
12 to 16 slender skewers (5 to 6 in.
  long)
12 to 16 large strawberries, rinsed
  and drained

Crosswise, cut 4- to 5-inch-long center
section from each melon. Reserve extra
for other uses. Cut rind off center sections, trimming to make neat cylinders.

For uniform slices, spread a clean,
damp dish towel flat. Set 1 melon, flat

*Slices of yellow- and red-fleshed watermelon are paired with summer's ripe
strawberries in this colorful dessert. Recruit a friend to help you cut the melons.*

end down, on cloth. Lay wood strips,
½-inch sides up, on towel against opposite sides of melon. Hold melon; slide a
long, sharp, rigid-bladed knife along
strips; use 2 pairs of hands—1 to hold
melon, 1 to hold knife and tip.

Remove slice; repeat until you have 4
perfect slices (some will break) of 1
melon and 5 slices of the other. Save
extra to eat.

For uniform rounds, make a cardboard round (or use a pan bottom) just
slightly smaller than the smallest melon
slice. Enclose cardboard smoothly with
plastic wrap. Set cardboard on a melon

slice; with a short, sharp knife held vertically, neatly trim melon sides.

On a platter, stack alternating colors
of melon slices. At 6 to 8 equal intervals,
push pairs of skewers, slightly apart,
from top of cake to base. On extended
end of each pair of skewers, impale a
strawberry. Garnish with remaining
berries. Cut into wedges, slicing
between skewered strawberries. Makes
6 to 8 servings.

PER SERVING: 77 calories, 1.5 g protein, 17 g carbohydrates, 1 g fat
(0 g saturated), 0 mg cholesterol, 4.7 mg sodium

Memorable Summer Parties

W E'RE GIVING *a really great party. Would you like to come? You'll have a good time."*

Over the years, numerous letters and calls from Sunset readers with invitations such as this have come our way. We've accepted many of them, and most often, the promise of a good time proved to be bona fide.

As we evaluated a batch of these events for this report, it became clear that the most memorable parties were those that overflowed with a free-spirited quality that warmly welcomed each person—family, friend, or newcomer—often in wonderfully wacky ways.

Great parties are frequently repeated and swell to awesome scale. The spark might start with the host, but as it grows, others chip in as part of the fun—to contribute entertainment, food, decorations, and labor.

Here's how four of these events around the West work, with planning tips that ensure their success.

DOWN-ON-THE-FARM POTLUCK

"Through the years, this has been a relaxed, friendly event—400 relative strangers have a memorable time at our potluck," wrote Susan and Jeff Phillips. Since 1978, the Phillipses have put on this daylong grand outdoor party every other year at their Seabold Farm on Bainbridge Island, Washington.

Activities appeal to guests of varied ages and interests. Here are party tips:

• Invite 20 friends for a sleep-over work party the day before the event.

• Welcome guests with a sign-in wall; invite artistic effort.

• Offer ongoing amusements like music and volleyball.

• Post a schedule of activities: slug races, tug-of-war, whistling contest.

• Stage a cook-off between teams to barbecue the meat (beef ribs, spit-roasted lamb and pig).

• Ask guests to contribute specific dishes for the potluck.

Guest graffiti on the barn wall collects greetings, sketches (judged as art).

Fire-engine red and fitted with a grill, antique tub holds ribs for a crowd.

Gathering for the annual group photo at farm potluck is a compulsory predinner event to capture old and new friends on film. Relaxed daylong outdoor party on Bainbridge Island includes a sign-in wall, volleyball, music, races and contests, and a barbecue cookoff.

(Continued on next page)

...Memorable Summer Parties

THE MAGILL CLAN CAMP-OUT

The first Magill came to the United States in the 1840s from Ireland; the family here now numbers more than 200. About 20 years ago, the family gathered for the first time to celebrate the 80th birthday of their patriarch's grandson Vern. The now-annual reunion draws 50 to 100 people.

Strategic planning for the gathering of the clan includes these tips:

• Delegate duties at a planning meeting four months ahead.

• Scout campground; make reservation for four days.

• Send invitations two months ahead, a reminder card later.

• Organize activities for kids such as a T-shirt painting contest.

• Bring special pan to cook 50-egg omelet on trailer-towed cooker. Ask everyone to bring condiments for eggs.

• Draw family together with reading of Uncle Nick's letter.

• To defray costs of event, raffle off a family-made heirloom.

Team of cooks makes 50-egg omelet in oversize pan on custom-built barbecue.

Magill clan settles in to hear a rendition of Uncle Nick's "poetic" letter, produced by Nick (now 96) each year for this annual family camping reunion. Sites for the event vary yearly, but are always in the West; this one was in Oregon.

BASKETBALL & BARBECUE

"Our first party was in 1983. It sorta celebrated the end of the adult basketball league Phil was playing in—and also our first year in business," wrote Marti and Phil Caires of San Ramon, California. More than 300 guests cram into this suburban backyard for an afternoon-long amateur basketball tournament. A big barbecue and dance follow.

Activities keep everyone busy; here's the game plan:

• Arrange for supervised activities for kids (they make up a third of the guests): pony rides, face painting, storytelling, video games.

• Organize teenage entertainment: a band plays for the games; another group performs a skit.

• Keep menu simple—barbecued spareribs, chicken, burgers, salads. Precook 100 pounds of ribs; grill to reheat, brown. Guests help cook and assemble rest of the meal as a party activity.

• Provide music for dancing in the evening.

(Continued on next page)

High school band guests rouse team support with fight songs.

Backyard basketball round-robin games take most of the afternoon to eliminate two-man teams, seven in all, for championship finale.

Bring-Your-Own-Dinghy

BYOD has become the cry when five large boats cruise together through Northwest waters. Margaret and Bill Lewis and Betty and Ted Rowe told us how they found it difficult to get everyone aboard one boat to socialize. They solved the problem by moving into several dinghies and tying individu-ally on to the stern line of the largest anchored boat.

Here's the plan for setting up this sociable gathering afloat:

• On land, prepare food that needs minimum cooking afloat. Place in stackable plastic serving containers for easy transport and storage.

• Two host boats deliver invitations by dinghy; tie-up directions are included.

• Decorate dinghies, hats, and food.

• Set up line between anchored craft and small boats, or "raft" several boats for tie-up.

• Load appetizer and bar dinghies. These food and drink dinghies are rowed among guests.

No need to walk on water to dine afloat. To visit, or pass food and drink, dinghy sailors untie, row down the line, then tie on again. Most foods are prepared at home and carried in waterproof stackable containers. Invitations include tie-up directions.

Raspberry Heaven

BEAR LAKE, UTAH, *is tucked way up in the corner of the state. We first found ourselves there a few years ago. We were dropping down U.S. Highway 89 over the Wasatch Range from Logan. As we descended, we could see the lake shimmering beneath one of those expansive blue skies you seem to encounter only in the intermountain West. It was a hot July afternoon, and as the lake drew closer all we wanted to do was take a swim. Then we got ambushed by something we like even more than a dive into a cool lake on a hot day.*

Raspberries.

Everywhere we looked we saw raspberries. Raspberries sprouted row by row in neatly tended fields; raspberries glistened red and juicy in roadside stands; raspberries had been cooked into jam and frozen into shakes. We had discovered raspberry heaven.

Now, as we soon learned, Bear Lake raspberries are anything but a secret to the people of Utah. Growers have been planting berries here for decades and have garnered a reputation for producing fruit of unsurpassed flavor and sweetness. Grower Ted Hildt's grandfather, Theodore, founded Hildt's Bear Lake Raspberry Farm in the 1920s. Ted says the intense raspberriness of the local crop is a by-product of Utah's harsh, cold winters. "The cold means we don't get a good yield, but we do get a good flavor."

When raspberry season starts in late July (it lasts only until late August), Utah supermarkets and restaurants trumpet the arrival of the fruit, and Utahans by the hundreds make the pilgrimage to Bear Lake to load up on berries fresh from the fields or to down a raspberry milk shake at LaBeau's. (That shake was the first thing we sampled on our arrival and, as far as we're concerned, is the best drink we have ever had.)

Here, then, we honor the raspberries of Bear Lake (and of the rest of the West). We've chosen four old-fashioned recipes that show off the berry to best advantage—a cobbler, a special soda, a rich raspberry brownie, and, yes, a raspberry shake. We had no luck prying shake secrets from LaBeau's, which jealously guards its special recipe, but we feel our version is as good as you'll get short of making your own trip to Bear Lake.

If you visit, one berry good time is during Raspberry Days, August 6 through 8, in Bear Lake's metropolis, Garden City. For festival information, call (801) 946-3364. Festivities include a parade, concerts, a 10K run, and lots of people with red smears on their smiling faces.

AUNT MARTHA'S RASPBERRY COBBLER

- ¾ **cup sugar**
- 1 **tablespoon cornstarch**
- ¾ **teaspoon ground cinnamon**
- ½ **cup water**
- 6½ **cups raspberries, rinsed and drained dry**
- ¼ **teaspoon baking soda**
- 1 **teaspoon baking powder**
- 1 **cup all-purpose flour**
- ¼ **cup (⅛ lb.) butter or margarine**
- ½ **cup milk**

In a shallow 2-quart casserole, mix ½ cup sugar, cornstarch, cinnamon, water, and 6 cups raspberries.

Mix soda, baking powder, and flour.

In a bowl, beat butter and remaining ¼ cup sugar until creamy. Add milk and flour mixture; stir until moistened.

Drop batter in 8 equal spoonfuls, slightly apart, onto the raspberries. Bake in a 400° oven until batter is a deep golden brown and berries are bubbling, 35 to 40 minutes. Top with remaining berries. Spoon into bowls. Makes 8 servings.

PER SERVING: 245 calories, 3.1 g protein, 44 g carbohydrates, 7.2 g fat (4.1 g saturated), 18 mg cholesterol, 148 mg sodium

Bear Lake berry-land lies northeast of Logan, near Utah-Idaho border.

(Continued on next page)

Raspberry fun starts with superthick, supersize berry shakes at Bear Lake fest—or at home in your own kitchen. A generous topping of juicy whole raspberries finishes off the old-fashioned milkshakes.

BEAR LAKE RASPBERRY SHAKE

¼ cup milk
1¼ to 1½ cups raspberries, rinsed and drained
1 pint vanilla ice cream

In a blender or food processor, whirl milk, 1 cup berries, and ice cream until smooth; scrape sides several times. Pour into 1 very large (28 oz.) or 2 large (14 oz. each) glasses. Top with remaining berries. Makes 3¼ cups, 1 very large or 2 medium-size servings.

PER MEDIUM-SIZE SERVING: 325 calories, 6.5 g protein, 42 g carbohydrates, 16 g fat (9.6 g saturated), 64 mg cholesterol, 131 mg sodium

RASPBERRY SHRUB SODA

½ cup raspberry vinegar
½ cup sugar
4 to 5 cups club soda or sparkling water
1¼ cups raspberries, rinsed and drained
1½ cups raspberry sorbet or sherbet, in scoops
Mint sprigs

Stir together vinegar and sugar until sugar dissolves. Pour club soda into 4 tall (12- to 14-oz.-size) glasses.

Fresh berries crown dense, rich brownie cake; more raspberries sank into cake as it baked. Cut dessert into wedges to serve.

Create raspberry heaven with frothy shrub sodas and bubbling cobbler.

Divide vinegar mixture and 1 cup raspberries equally among glasses; stir to mix. Add sorbet; garnish with remaining berries and mint. Makes 4 servings.

PER SERVING: 202 calories, 0.7 g protein, 52 g carbohydrates, 0.3 g fat (0 g saturated), 0 mg cholesterol, 59 mg sodium

CHOCOLATE-RASPBERRY BROWNIE CAKE

½ cup (¼ lb.) butter or margarine
3 ounces unsweetened chocolate
1⅓ cups granulated sugar
½ cup chopped pecans or walnuts
2 large eggs
1 teaspoon vanilla
⅔ cup all-purpose flour
2½ cups raspberries, rinsed and drained dry
Powdered sugar

In a 2- to 3-quart pan over low heat, stir butter and chocolate just until melted, about 5 minutes. Remove from heat and mix in granulated sugar, pecans, eggs, and vanilla. Add flour and stir to mix ingredients well.

Spread batter in a buttered, floured 9-inch cake pan with a removable rim. Next to rim, distribute 1 cup berries in a band about 2 inches wide; gently press fruit into batter.

Bake in a 350° oven until top, at outside edge, cracks and feels firm to touch, 45 to 50 minutes. Let brownie cool in pan on a rack. If made ahead, chill airtight up to a day.

Remove rim and set brownie on a plate; dust with powdered sugar, and mound remaining 1½ cups berries in the center. Cut into wedges. Makes 12 servings.

PER SERVING: 271 calories, 3.2 g protein, 33 g carbohydrates, 15 g fat (7.4 g saturated), 56 mg cholesterol, 89 mg sodium

Spicy Rubdowns

MASSAGE PUNGENT SPICES *or season-ings into meat or poultry to flavor them for grilling. To increase succulence of meat, cure it briefly with a mixture of sugar and salt. However, this raises the sodium content considerably.*

ONION-CILANTRO TURKEY

> 1½ **pounds turkey breast tenderloins**
> **Salt cure (optional; recipe follows)**
> **Onion mixture (recipe follows)**
> **Fresh cilantro (coriander) sprigs and whole green onions**
> **Lime wedges**

Rinse turkey tenderloins and pat dry. If desired, rub salt cure over turkey; place in a bowl, cover, and chill 2 to 3 hours. Rinse turkey well with cool water and pat dry.

If turkey pieces are large, cut into serving-size portions. Place meat between sheets of plastic wrap; pound gently and evenly with a flat mallet to make ½ inch thick. If working ahead, cover and chill up to a day. Rub onion mixture over turkey pieces.

Place turkey on a grill 4 to 6 inches above a solid bed of hot coals (you can hold your hand at grill level only 2 to 3 seconds).

Grilled turkey, lightly cured, makes a low-fat entrée. Rub onion-cilantro seasoning mixture onto pounded turkey tenderloins before cooking.

Cook, turning to brown evenly, until meat is white in center of thickest part (cut to test), 7 to 9 minutes.

Serve turkey garnished with cilantro sprigs and green onions. Offer lime wedges to squeeze over portions. Makes 5 or 6 servings.

PER SERVING WITH SALT CURE: 133 calories, 28 g protein, 1.7 g carbohydrates, 0.7 g fat (0.2 g saturated), 70 mg cholesterol, 606 mg sodium

Salt cure. Mix together 1 tablespoon **salt** and 1½ teaspoons **sugar.**

Onion mixture. Combine ¼ cup minced **green onion;** 2 tablespoons minced **fresh cilantro;** 3 cloves **garlic,** pressed or minced; 1 tablespoon minced **fresh ginger;** 1 teaspoon **coarsely ground pepper;** and 1 teaspoon grated **lime peel.**

CHILI RIBS

> **Salt cure (optional; recipe precedes)**
> 2 **racks (3½ to 4 lb. total) pork loin back ribs (baby back ribs), fat trimmed**
> **Spice mixture (recipe follows)**

If desired, rub salt cure over ribs; place in a 14- by 17-inch roasting pan. Cover and chill 2 to 3 hours. Rinse meat well with cool water and pat dry; rub with spice mixture. If seasoning ahead, cover and chill up to a day.

Place ribs on grill 4 to 6 inches above a solid bed of medium coals (you can hold your hand at grill level only 4 to 5 seconds). Cook, turning to brown evenly, until meat between bones at thickest section is no longer pink (cut to test), about 20 minutes total. Makes 4 or 5 servings.

PER SERVING WITH SALT CURE: 512 calories, 37 g protein, 3.6 g carbohydrates, 38 g fat (15 g saturated), 150 mg cholesterol, 817 mg sodium

Spice mixture. Mix 2 tablespoons **chili powder,** 1 tablespoon **ground cumin,** 2 teaspoons **ground California** or New Mexico **chilies,** 1 teaspoon **dried thyme leaves,** and ¼ teaspoon **ground allspice.**

Vegetable Crackle Chips

CRISP VEGETABLE *chips that are dried make a great snack alternative to fat-laden fried munchies.*

True, dried chips aren't as snappy, but their taste and texture grow on you.

You start by blanching thin slices of carrot, parsnip, potato, yam, or zucchini in water acidified with vinegar or citrus juice to enhance and preserve flavor (which fades otherwise) and color (if they tend to darken). Blanching also softens vegetable fibers so the chips won't be hard.

You then dry the vegetable slices for several hours in a dehydrator with a heat control or an oven. Of the two, a dehydrator is easier to use. Trays are arranged so fan-blown hot air can circulate.

Despite a few drawbacks, the oven works well, too. However, air does not circulate as well, rack space is limited, and chips don't dry as evenly. Chips also taste toastier if the oven heat is higher. (In convection ovens, slices blow off racks.)

VEGETABLE CRACKLE CHIPS

**Vegetable (choices follow)
Salt (optional)**

Prepare vegetable, peeling if directed. Cut into uniformly thick 1/16-inch slices; for even slices, use a hand or power slicer such as a mandolin, a blade mounted in a slicing board (like Japanese slicers that fit over a box), or a food processor (follow manufacturer's directions). It's very difficult to cut slices of even thickness with a knife; unevenly thick slices dry unevenly.

In a 5- to 6-quart pan, combine 3 cups water and acid specified for vegetable. Bring to a boil on high heat. All at once, dump in half the slices and push underwater with a spoon. Cook as directed for vegetable. Quickly lift out of pan with a slotted spoon. Repeat to blanch remaining vegetables.

Arrange vegetable slices in a single layer (edges can touch) on dehydrator racks, or on wire cooling racks set in large pans (10 by 15 to 12 by 17 in.); if first batch of oven-dried slices sticks, lightly oil racks before using again. Sprinkle vegetables with salt.

Set dehydrator at 140° or on high and put filled racks in place. Set oven temperature at 150° (or 200°, if that is the minimum setting) and position racks equidistant in oven.

After 30 minutes, turn slices over once. Let dry until chips are crisp, firm, and very dry. To test, let a slice cool (it's more flexible warm). Slices will not be as crisp as potato chips, but they should not bend easily; if they do, dry longer. Slices dry at different rates (more so in the oven); to avoid scorching, check often and remove crisp chips. Let cool briefly; at once seal airtight (chips quickly absorb moisture from air and soften). Hold at room temperature up to 2 weeks; freeze to store longer.

VEGETABLE CHOICES

Carrots. Peel 6 large (about 1½ lb. total) **carrots.** Use 1 cup **white wine vinegar** or ½ cup lemon juice in blanching water (preceding). Immerse carrot slices in water until they look slightly less opaque, about 2 minutes. Drain and dry (preceding) 3 to 4 hours in a dehydrator, 3½ to 4 hours in an oven. Makes 1½ ounces, about 2 cups.

PER ¼ CUP: 33 calories, 0.8 g protein, 7.8 g carbohydrates, 0.1 g fat (0 g saturated), 0 mg cholesterol, 163 mg sodium

Parsnips. Peel 6 large (about 1½ lb. total) **parsnips;** follow steps for carrots (preceding), but blanch slices 1 minute longer. Makes 4 ounces, about 4 cups.

PER ¼ CUP: 27 calories, 0.4 g protein, 6.6 g carbohydrates, 0.1 g fat (0 g saturated), 0 mg cholesterol, 72 mg sodium

Potatoes. Scrub 2 medium-size (about 1 lb. total) **potatoes** (russet or thin-skinned). Use 1 cup **cider vinegar,** white wine vinegar, or malt vinegar in blanching water (preceding). Immerse slices in water until they look slightly less opaque, about 5 minutes. Drain and dry (preceding) 3 to 4 hours in dehydrator or oven. Makes 3 ounces, about 4 cups.

PER ¼ CUP: 21 calories, 0.5 g protein, 4.6 g carbohydrates, 0 g fat, 0 mg cholesterol, 70 mg sodium

Yams. Peel 2 medium-size (about 1 lb. total) **yams** or sweet potatoes. Use 1 cup **balsamic vinegar** (or white wine, red wine, or cider vinegar) in blanching water (preceding). Immerse slices in water until they look slightly less opaque, about 5 minutes. Drain and

Chips (clockwise from lower left): yam, russet and new potatoes, carrot, zucchini.

dry (preceding) 5 to 6 hours in a dehydrator, 3 to 4 hours in an oven. Makes 2 ounces, about 3 cups.

PER ¼ CUP: 39 calories, 0.5 g protein, 9 g carbohydrates, 0.1 g fat (0 g saturated), 0 mg cholesterol, 94 mg sodium

Zucchini. Trim ends from 4 large (about 1½ lb. total) **zucchini.** Use 1 cup **tarragon-flavor white wine vinegar** or ½ cup lime juice in blanching water (preceding). Immerse slices in water until they look slightly less opaque, about 1 minute. Drain and dry (preceding) 2 to 3 hours in dehydrator or oven. Makes 1 ounce, about 2½ cups.

PER ¼ CUP: 6.3 calories, 0.5 g protein, 1.4 g carbohydrates, 0.1 g fat (0 g saturated), 0 mg cholesterol, 111 mg sodium

Chinese Linguine

CHINESE LINGUINE? *Italian tofu? East and West merge in this bold pairing of Chinese and Italian ingredients. Chef Hui Pui-Wing of San Francisco's Harbor Village Restaurant takes a classic tofu dish from Sichuan, ma po tofu, and spoons it over Italian pasta for a delicious effect.*

For a quick supper, serve the spicy pasta with stir-fried sweet-sour cabbage salad; accompany with cold beer.

To achieve the most authentic flavor, you'll need to shop at a Chinese market for the Sichuan bean sauce (yellow bean sauce with chili) and the aromatic Sichuan peppercorns. If they're unavailable, use the supermarket alternatives.

MA PO LINGUINE

- ½ **pound soft tofu**
  Ma po marinade (recipe follows)
- 1 **tablespoon salad oil**
- 2 **large cloves garlic, pressed or minced**
- ½ **pound ground lean beef**
  About ½ pound fresh linguine
- 1 **tablespoon oyster sauce or soy sauce**
- 1 **teaspoon Oriental sesame oil**
- 1 **tablespoon cornstarch mixed with 3 tablespoons water**
  Chopped fresh cilantro (coriander)
  Salt

Rinse tofu with cool water; let drain. Cut tofu into ½-inch cubes; mix in a bowl with marinade.

Set a 10- to 12-inch frying pan over high heat. When pan is hot, add oil, garlic, and beef. Stir until beef is crumbled and lightly browned, about 3 minutes. Drain off and discard fat. Add tofu and marinade. Simmer, covered, over low heat until the tofu is hot, 7 to 10 minutes.

Meanwhile, in a covered 4- to 5-quart pan, bring about 3 quarts water to a boil on high heat. Add linguine; cook, uncovered, until just barely tender to bite, 2 to 3 minutes. Drain. Pour into a warm bowl and mix with oyster sauce and sesame oil.

East and West merge as hot-spiced Sichuan tofu and beef saturate bed of hot, skinny Italian pasta. Serve the spicy entrée with stir-fried sweet-sour cabbage salad for a quick supper.

Add cornstarch mixture to tofu. Stir until sauce boils; spoon over noodles. Sprinkle with cilantro, and add salt to taste. Makes 2 or 3 servings.

PER SERVING: 558 calories, 27 g protein, 53 g carbohydrates, 26 g fat (5.9 g saturated), 101 mg cholesterol, 622 mg sodium

Ma po marinade. Mix 1 cup **water;** ½ cup thinly sliced **green onions;** 2 tablespoons **tomato paste;** 2 to 3 teaspoons **Sichuan bean sauce** (use maximum amount for hottest flavor), or 2 teaspoons soy sauce plus ¼ to ½ teaspoon crushed dried hot red chilies; 1 teaspoon **Oriental sesame oil;** 1 teaspoon **sugar;** and ¼ teaspoon finely crushed **Sichuan peppercorns** or freshly ground black pepper.

WILTED CABBAGE SALAD

- 1 **tablespoon salad oil**
- 1 **tablespoon minced fresh ginger**
- 5 **cups (about ¾ lb.) 1-inch squares cabbage**
- ¾ **cup thinly sliced red onion**
- ¼ **cup rice vinegar**
- 1½ **tablespoons sugar**
  Salt

Pour oil into a wok or 10- to 12-inch frying pan over high heat. Add ginger, cabbage, and onion; stir-fry just until cabbage barely wilts, 1 to 2 minutes. Stir vinegar and sugar into cabbage. Serve hot or cool, adding salt to taste. Makes 2 or 3 servings.

PER SERVING: 109 calories, 1.9 g protein, 16 g carbohydrates, 4.9 g fat (0.6 g saturated), 0 mg cholesterol, 25 mg sodium

Why? Answers to Your Cooking Questions

ALONG WITH SUMMER *comes an abundance of fresh produce—and questions like the ones below. Answers follow.*

If you run across a food mystery you'd like solved, send your question to Why? Sunset Magazine, 80 Willow Rd., Menlo Park, Calif. 94025. With the help of Dr. George K. York, extension food technologist at UC Davis, Sunset food editors will find the solution.

WHY DO MARKET FRUITS STAY HARD? WHAT CAN I DO TO RIPEN THEM?

Very often, fresh fruits for the market are picked underripe so that they'll be less subject to damage in transit. These rock-hard fruits rarely meet our anticipation of juicy texture and toothsome flavor without being given some special attention at home.

Even though sun-ripened perfection may not be achievable with market fruit, you can greatly improve fruit's quality by ripening it until texture begins to soften and sugar and fragrance increase.

Merely enclosing fruit at room temperature accelerates the ripening process for many kinds. Use a loosely closed paper bag, a vented plastic bag, or a ripening bowl (a vented covered bowl, often in rigid plastic shaped like a big fruit). Loosely wrap fruit in paper towels first to absorb any condensation and keep fruit from spoiling.

Enclosing fruits captures ethylene gas that they produce as they ripen; the gas hastens ripening. Some venting is important; spoilage starts where moisture gathers from condensation.

Enclosed ripening works on apricots, avocados, mangoes, melons (except watermelons), papayas, peaches, pears (except Asian ones), plums, and tomatoes. However, if tomatoes have been cooled to 40° or lower, their ability to ripen in flavor is halted. They may change in looks, but they won't have the flavor or texture of ripe fruit (this is one of the main reasons store tomatoes rarely taste like vine-ripened ones).

Certain ripe fruits—apples, bananas, melons—give off a lot of ethylene. If you enclose one of these with other fruits, you can speed their ripening.

WHY DOES BLANCHING LOOSEN SKIN ON SOME FRUITS, NOT OTHERS?

Blanching—dipping briefly in boiling water—is used to loosen skin on tomatoes and freestone peaches so they will peel easily. But this process doesn't work on similar fruits, such as apricots, nectarines, cling peaches, and plums.

The reason has to do with the amount of pectin in the fruit. The pectin acts like glue between skin and fruit. (Green fruit has more pectin than ripe fruit.)

For tomatoes and freestone peaches, which are low in pectin, the heat of blanching is sufficient to break apart pectin so the skin can be pulled off easily.

Apricots, nectarines, cling peaches, and plums have more pectin; by the time the heat has broken down the pectin, the fruit is soft. (Commercial processors often use lye to remove skins.)

To blanch tomatoes or freestone peaches, immerse them in boiling water to cover. Ripe fruit may need only 10 to 15 seconds, firmer fruit 30 to 90 seconds. To test, make a little nick in the skin and pull; remove from water as soon as skin comes away easily. If fruit is heated for 30 seconds or longer, immerse it in ice water to stop cooking. Pull skin from fruit.

WHY DO RED RADISHES SOMETIMES TURN WHITE?

Even when used in small amounts, acids like vinegar or lemon juice keep enough red pigment in vegetables to prevent the color from drifting toward blue-purple. Some red may leach out, but in vegetables with an abundance of red

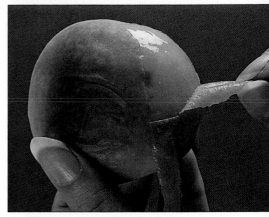

Blanched peach peels easily; heat softens skin-holding pectin.

Red pigment in radishes bleeds in acid solution but is stable in water.

pigment, such as beets or red cabbage, ample color remains.

Radishes have a much smaller concentration of red pigment (and only on the surface). If left standing in a mildly acidic solution, as in salad dressings or mayonnaise, radishes fade, and the mixture becomes pink.

The problem is easily solved: add red radishes to salads just before serving.

More August Recipes

OTHER AUGUST ARTICLES *suggest grilled chili-fish sandwiches, served on sesame buns, and a spiced fruit compote of figs, nectarines, and raspberries.*

GRILLED CHILI-FISH SANDWICHES

Bearing the sear marks of a hot grill, fish chunks, fresh chilies, sliced onion, and buns come together to make hearty sandwiches. They're anointed with mayonnaise flavored with orange.

- 6 **tablespoons reduced-calorie or regular mayonnaise**
- 1½ **teaspoons grated orange peel**
- 1 **tablespoon orange juice**
- 1 **tablespoon lemon juice**
- 6 **sesame hamburger buns (¾ to 1 lb. total), split**

Fish on a sesame bun? Add chilies and onions to get fish burgers.

- 6 **medium-size (1½ to 2 oz. each) fresh poblano (ancho or pasilla) or Anaheim (California or New Mexico) chilies, stemmed and seeded**
- 1½ **to 2 pounds firm-texture, skinned and boned fish such as mahi mahi or swordfish, about 1 inch thick, cut into 6 equal portions**
- 1 **large (½ lb.) mild onion, cut crosswise into 6 slices**
- ⅓ **cup salad oil**

Mix mayonnaise, orange peel, orange juice, and lemon juice. If mixing ahead, chill airtight up to 3 days.

Brush cut sides of buns, chilies, fish, and onion lightly with oil. Place chilies on a grill 4 to 6 inches above a solid bed of medium-hot coals (you can hold your hand at grill level only 3 to 4 seconds). Cook, turning often, until skins are blackened, about 10 minutes. Remove from grill.

Place fish and onion on grill; turn often until fish is opaque but still moist-looking in center of thickest part (cut to test), 8 to 10 minutes. Meanwhile, pull skin, stems, and seeds from chilies. Also, split buns and put cut side down on grill until toasted, about 1 minute. Spread toasted sides with mayonnaise mixture and fill with chilies, fish, and onions. Makes 6 servings.

PER SERVING: 447 calories, 27 g protein, 38 g carbohydrates, 20 g fat (3.5 g saturated), 91 mg cholesterol, 472 mg sodium

SPICED FRUIT COMPOTE

Double-season figs come and go quickly in early and late summer. Enjoy their fragile sweetness fresh, or in this delicate compote. An aromatic syrup saturates tender figs as well as nectarines and raspberries.

Ripe figs, nectarines, and raspberries soak in spiced wine syrup.

- 6 **large (about ½ lb. total) ripe figs, stems trimmed**
- 2 **medium-size (¾ lb. total) firm-ripe nectarines**
- 1 **cup raspberries**
- 2 **cups dry red wine**
- ⅓ **cup sugar**
- 2 **tablespoons lemon juice**
- 1 **cinnamon stick, 3½ inches long**
- ⅛ **teaspoon almond extract**

Rinse and drain figs, nectarines, and raspberries.

In a 2- to 3-quart pan over high heat, boil wine, sugar, lemon juice, and cinnamon, uncovered, until reduced to 1 cup, about 10 minutes. Add almond extract.

Meanwhile, cut figs in half, and pit and slice nectarines; combine in a bowl with berries. Pour hot syrup over fruit. Let stand at least 10 minutes or up to 2 hours, spooning syrup over fruit a few times. Makes 4 servings.

PER SERVING: 208 calories, 1.7 g protein, 43 g carbohydrates, 0.7 g fat (0 g saturated), 0 mg cholesterol, 8.3 mg sodium

CARROT SALAD, *a perennial favorite on the picnic and school lunch circuit, takes on a new boldness in Friar Bob's Carrot Salad, which is seasoned with orange juice, grated orange peel, onion, and even pickles to heighten flavors.*

Served on a bed of shredded spinach leaves with cottage cheese or yogurt and golden orange segments, this salad makes a surprisingly satisfying lunch, and one that will save you calories for dessert later in the day.

FRIAR BOB'S CARROT SALAD

- 4 or 5 large (1 to 1¼ lb. total) carrots
- ½ cup finely chopped red onion
- ½ cup finely chopped sweet gherkin pickles (about 5)
- 2 teaspoons grated orange peel
- ¾ cup orange juice
  Salt and pepper
  About 8 cups rinsed and crisped spinach leaves, cut into fine shreds
- 2 cups low-fat cottage cheese or unflavored nonfat yogurt
  Ground nutmeg
- 2 large (about 1 lb. total) oranges, white peel and membrane cut off and fruit segments cut from center membrane

Peel and thinly shred carrots; you should have about 4 cups. In a large bowl, combine carrots, onion, pickles, orange peel, and orange juice. Mix well and season to taste with salt and pepper. If salad is made ahead, cover and chill up to 2 hours.

Arrange spinach on dinner plates. Stir carrot salad; transfer with a slotted spoon onto spinach. Mound cottage cheese beside carrot salad. Pour liquid from carrots over salads, sprinkle with nutmeg, and garnish with orange segments. Add salt and pepper to taste. Makes 4 to 6 servings.

PER SERVING: 167 calories, 12 g protein, 29 g carbohydrates, 1.3 g fat (0.5 g saturated), 3 mg cholesterol, 512 mg sodium

Robert D Nolte

Oceanside, Calif.

MOST BURRITO PARLORS *offer a choice of beef, bean, or cheese. From Tigard, Oregon, Richard Bruno sends a recipe for a burrito based on ground lamb, a favorite meat in Greece and the Middle East.*

Other ingredients widely used in this area include olive oil, cinnamon, cloves, nutmeg, and yogurt, but tomato sauce, hot pepper seasoning, and tortillas bring more than a touch of Mexico. The results: an international burrito destined to make history.

LAMB BURRITOS

- 1 pound ground lean lamb
- ½ cup regular-strength chicken broth
- 1 large (½ lb.) onion, chopped
- 2 cloves garlic, minced or pressed
- 1 large (½ lb.) red bell pepper, stemmed, seeded, and chopped
- 1 can (8 oz.) tomato sauce
- ½ teaspoon *each* sugar and ground cinnamon
- ⅛ teaspoon *each* ground cloves and ground nutmeg
- 1 tablespoon lemon juice
- 2 tablespoons chopped parsley
- ⅛ teaspoon liquid hot pepper seasoning
- 8 flour tortillas (about 8-in. diameter)
  Salt
  Unflavored nonfat yogurt

Crumble lamb into a 10- to 12-inch frying pan over medium heat; stir often until well browned. With a slotted spoon, transfer lamb from pan. Discard drippings and wipe pan clean.

To pan add broth, onion, garlic, and bell pepper. Stir occasionally on high heat until pan is almost dry, then stir often until dark brown bits stick in pan. Stir bits free with 2 to 3 tablespoons water. Repeat until brown bits form, then deglaze pan again with 2 to 3 tablespoons water. Repeat this step until onions have a deep, rich brown color, about 15 minutes total.

Return lamb to pan along with tomato sauce, 1 cup water, sugar, cinnamon, cloves, nutmeg, lemon juice, parsley, and hot pepper seasoning. Stir to free browned bits. Bring to a boil over high heat, then reduce heat and simmer, uncovered, until mixture is reduced to 3 cups, 15 to 20 minutes.

Meanwhile, lightly brush tortillas with water, stack them on foil, and seal. Place in a 350° oven until hot, about 15 minutes.

Spoon lamb mixture onto tortillas. Add salt and yogurt to taste. Roll tortilla to enclose filling, and hold to eat. Makes 8 servings.

PER SERVING: 304 calories, 14 g protein, 30 g carbohydrates, 14 g fat (5.8 g saturated), 41 mg cholesterol, 422 mg sodium

Tigard, Oreg.

"Carrot salad is a perennial favorite on the picnic and school lunch circuit."

Golden bread gets color from ripe mango, subtle texture from coconut.

MANGO BREAD

- 1 **cup puréed mango (about 1 ripe, 1-lb.-size mango)**
- ¾ **teaspoon baking soda mixed with 2 teaspoons water**
- 1 **cup sugar**
- 2 **large eggs**
- ½ **cup sweetened flaked dried coconut, minced**
- ¼ **cup salad oil**
- 2½ **cups all-purpose flour**
- 1½ **teaspoons baking powder**

In a large bowl, stir together mango purée and baking soda mixture. Let stand 5 minutes.

To mango mixture add sugar, eggs, coconut, and oil; beat to blend. Stir flour with baking powder and add to mango mixture. Beat until the batter is very well blended. Pour into an oiled 5- by 9-inch loaf pan.

Bake in a 350° oven until loaf is richly browned and has pulled slightly from pan sides, and top springs back when firmly pressed, 50 to 55 minutes. Let stand 10 minutes, then invert bread from pan onto a rack. Serve warm or cool. If making ahead, let cool, wrap airtight, and store at room temperature up to a day. Freeze to store longer. Makes 1 loaf, about 2¾ pounds.—*Rosella Balken, Vista, Calif.*

PER OUNCE: 66 calories, 1.1 g protein, 12 g carbohydrates, 1.8 g fat (0.5 g saturated), 9.7 mg cholesterol, 34 mg sodium

Lamb marinated in rosemary-berry sauce is also basted with it on grill.

BARBECUED LAMB WITH BLACKBERRY SAUCE

- ½ **cup blackberry jam**
- ⅓ **cup balsamic or red wine vinegar**
- 1 **tablespoon Dijon mustard**
- 1 **tablespoon minced fresh or 1 teaspoon crumbled dried rosemary leaves**
- 1½ **pounds boned and fat-trimmed lean lamb (leg or loin), cut into 1-inch cubes**
  Salt

In a bowl, mix jam, vinegar, mustard, and rosemary. Pour ⅓ of the mixture into a small container; cover and chill up to a day.

Add lamb cubes to bowl with remaining jam mixture. Stir well, cover, and chill at least 1 hour or up to a day.

Thread lamb equally on 4 to 6 metal skewers (12- to 14-in. size); discard marinade. Lay lamb on a lightly oiled grill 4 to 6 inches above medium-hot coals (you can hold your hand at grill level only 3 to 4 seconds). Cook, turning and basting with reserved jam mixture, until lamb is medium-rare (pink in center; cut to test), about 8 minutes total. Push from skewers onto plates. Add salt to taste. Makes 4 servings.—*Mary Anne League, Sutherlin, Oreg.*

PER SERVING: 362 calories, 37 g protein, 29 g carbohydrates, 10 g fat (3.5 g saturated), 114 mg cholesterol, 205 mg sodium

Zucchini shells cradle savory blend of zucchini, rice, green onions, and cheese.

STUFFED ZUCCHINI

- 4 **medium-size zucchini, each 4 to 5 inches long, ends trimmed**
- 1 **tablespoon butter or margarine**
- 6 **green onions, finely chopped**
- 1 **cup cooked brown rice**
- ½ **cup shredded Swiss cheese**
- 1 **large egg**
- ¼ **cup seasoned dry bread crumbs**

Cut zucchini in half lengthwise. With a small knife or spoon, scoop out zucchini centers, making ¼-inch-thick shells. Finely chop zucchini centers.

In an 8- to 10-inch frying pan over medium-high heat, combine chopped zucchini with 2 teaspoons butter and onions. Stir often until zucchini is lightly browned, about 10 minutes.

Stir together zucchini mixture, rice, cheese, and egg. Mound filling equally into zucchini shells in a 9- by 13-inch pan. Cover tightly with foil and bake in a 400° oven until zucchini shells are tender when pierced, about 20 minutes.

Rinse and dry frying pan; over medium heat, melt remaining butter and mix with crumbs. Uncover zucchini; sprinkle evenly with crumbs. Broil 4 to 6 inches from heat until crumbs brown, 1 to 2 minutes. Makes 4 to 8 servings.—*Dodie Nelson, Anchorage, Alaska.*

PER SERVING: 105 calories, 5.1 g protein, 12 g carbohydrates, 4.4 g fat (2.4 g saturated), 37 mg cholesterol, 146 mg sodium

PASTA WITH FRESH TOMATO SAUCE

- 3 pounds Roma-type tomatoes, cored and coarsely chopped
- 2 large (about 1 lb. total) yellow bell peppers, stemmed, seeded, and chopped
- 1 cup (about ½ oz.) lightly packed slivered fresh basil leaves, or ¼ cup dried basil
- 2 cloves garlic, minced or pressed
- ¾ pound fresh or dried linguine Fresh basil sprigs (optional) About ½ cup parmesan cheese Salt

In a 3- to 4-quart pan over medium heat, combine ⅔ of the tomatoes, ⅔ of the peppers, ½ of the slivered basil, and all the garlic. Stir often until tomatoes begin to fall apart, about 20 minutes. Use hot, or let stand until room temperature; cover when cool to hold up to 6 hours. Stir in remaining tomatoes, peppers, and slivered basil.

Bring 3 quarts water to boiling in a 5- to 6-quart pan over high heat. Add pasta and cook, uncovered, just until tender to bite, about 8 minutes. Drain pasta well. To serve hot, pour into a wide bowl. To serve cold, immerse pasta in cool water until cold, then drain well and pour into the wide bowl.

Spoon hot sauce onto hot pasta, cool sauce onto cool pasta; mix to serve. Garnish with basil sprigs. Add parmesan and salt to taste. Makes 4 to 6 servings.—*Joanne Benvenist, Culver City, Calif.*

PER SERVING: 264 calories, 13 g protein, 47 g carbohydrates, 4.2 g fat (1.4 g saturated), 72 mg cholesterol, 161 mg sodium

Tomatoes, bell peppers are foundation for pasta dish to serve hot or tepid.

PINEAPPLE CHICKEN WITH HERB DRESSING

- 1 large (about 4 lb.) pineapple
- 2 large (about 1¼ lb. total) firm-ripe avocados
- 8 cups coarsely chopped, rinsed and crisped iceberg lettuce
- 4 cups finely shredded, rinsed and crisped napa cabbage
- 3 cups bite-size pieces cooked, boned, and skinned chicken Herb dressing (recipe follows) Salt

Cut top and rind from pineapple. Slice fruit into ½-inch-thick rounds; cut slices in half crosswise. Save about ¼ cup of the juice exuded while cutting.

Peel and pit avocados, and cut them lengthwise into ½-inch slices. Moisten slices with pineapple juice.

Mix together lettuce and cabbage; spread out on a large platter or divide among individual plates. Arrange pineapple, avocado, and chicken decoratively on greens. Add dressing and salt to taste. Makes 6 servings.—*Julia A. Hess, Redmond, Wash.*

PER SERVING: 392 calories, 24 g protein, 31 g carbohydrates, 22 g fat (3.8 g saturated), 62 mg cholesterol, 257 mg sodium

Herb dressing. Mix ½ cup **lemon juice,** 2 tablespoons **salad oil,** 1 tablespoon **soy sauce,** 3 drops **liquid hot pepper seasoning,** and 1 tablespoon *each* minced **fresh rosemary, thyme,** and **sage leaves.**

Sweet-tart pineapple, smooth avocado, tender chicken await herb dressing.

PLUM OR PEACH FROZEN YOGURT

- 1¼ pounds (about 5 large) soft-ripe plums or (about 4 medium-size) ripe peaches
- 4 containers (8 oz. each) nonfat or low-fat vanilla-flavor yogurt (with peaches, use peach-flavor yogurt)
- ½ cup sugar
- 1 teaspoon vanilla
- ½ teaspoon almond extract

Peel plums and cut into chunks (or peel peaches, pit, and cut into chunks). In a blender or food processor, purée fruit. In a bowl, mix fruit with yogurt, sugar, vanilla, and almond extract.

Cover and chill mixture until cold, at least 2 hours or up to a day. Pour mixture into a 1-quart or larger ice cream freezer container (regular or self-refrigerated). Freeze according to manufacturer's directions or until dasher is hard to turn. Serve softly frozen yogurt or, if making ahead, store airtight in freezer up to 1 week. Makes about 1½ quarts.—*Marsha Konegni, Golden, Colo.*

PER ½ CUP: 125 calories, 4.3 g protein, 27 g carbohydrates, 0.3 g fat (0 g saturated), 2.2 mg cholesterol, 53 mg sodium

Homemade frozen yogurt starts with fruit-flavor yogurt and ripe plums.

August Menus

AUGUST SIZZLES. *Cool off with meals that put the thermometer in its place. Turn a family dinner or weekend lunch into a party by serving it by the pool or in a shady part of the garden. Rely on simple foods, simple flavors, and prime seasonal produce. One easy touch: serve fruit juice and enhance its taste by chilling with frozen chunks of fruit or more fruit juice frozen into cubes.*

The hot climate of the Caribbean and popular jerk seasonings from that region provide inspiration for the second meal, prepared on the grill.

COOL POOL PARTY

**Shrimp Pasta Salad
with Pesto Dressing**
Cheese Pocket Bread Crackers
Cucumber Spears
Fruit Coolers
Fruit Ice Cubes
Super Cookies

The salad, dressing, and pocket bread crackers can all be made several hours ahead. Bake cookies in rounds 4 to 5 inches wide, or buy oversize cookies.

To make fresh fruit coolers, *use any juice or purée of summer fruits diluted with sparkling water and sweetened to taste. Fruits to purée: apricots, berries (any kind), grapes, mangoes, melons (cantaloupe to watermelon), nectarines, papayas, peaches, plums, and pineapple. Add lemon juice to purées of grapes, peaches, and nectarines to keep from darkening. Chill with fruit ice cubes.*

To make fruit ice cubes, *freeze fruit juice or purées in cubes, or freeze fruit such as melon (in small cubes) or berries. Set fruit on a pan, slightly apart. Freeze solid; transfer to a container and freeze up to a week.*

Pasta salad with shrimp has a crisp lettuce base, tomatoes on top; there's pesto dressing to add. Crisp toast is made from pocket bread. Frozen fruit chunks cool beverages.

Safe plastic. *Plastic ware, bright and playful, reduces breakage hazards at poolside.*

Fruit coolers. *Freeze berries, melon chunks; nibble, or add to fruit juice in place of ice.*

Simple icer. *Nest a bowl in larger one filled with ice as a way to keep salads, soups cold.*

Super cookies. *Boldly oversize cookies make an amusing dessert. Buy or bake.*

SHRIMP PASTA SALAD WITH PESTO DRESSING

> 6 **cups regular-strength chicken broth**
> 1 **cup (½ lb.) rice-shaped (orzo) pasta**
> 1 **pound shelled cooked tiny shrimp**
> 1 **cup chopped green onions**
> 1 **tablespoon grated lemon peel**
> ½ **cup lemon juice**
> 1 **small (about 1 lb.) iceberg lettuce, rinsed and crisped**
> 3 **cups tiny cherry tomatoes, rinsed and stemmed**
> **Pesto dressing (recipe follows)**
> **Cheese pocket bread crackers (recipe follows)**

In a 4- to 5-quart pan over high heat, bring broth to a boil. Add pasta and cook, uncovered, just until tender to bite, about 5 minutes. Drain, reserving liquid for other uses. Let pasta cool. Mix pasta, shrimp, green onions, lemon peel, and lemon juice; if assembling ahead, cover and chill pasta mixture up to 4 hours.

Shred the lettuce and place in a wide, shallow bowl. Mound pasta mixture on lettuce; surround with cherry tomatoes.

To keep salad cool while serving, nest in a larger bowl filled with ice. Add pesto dressing to taste. Accompany with pocket bread crackers. Makes 5 or 6 servings.

PER SERVING: 280 calories, 25 g protein, 37 g carbohydrates, 3.4 g fat (0.7 g saturated), 148 mg cholesterol, 244 mg sodium

Pesto dressing. In a blender or food processor, purée ½ cup *each* chopped **fresh basil leaves** and chopped **fresh cilantro** (coriander) **leaves,** 1 cup **unflavored nonfat yogurt,** and 1 tablespoon **white wine vinegar.** If making ahead, cover and chill up to 4 hours. Makes 1¼ cups.

PER TABLESPOON: 7.7 calories, 0.7 g protein, 1.2 g carbohydrates, 0 g fat, 0.2 mg cholesterol, 8.9 mg sodium

Cheese pocket bread crackers. Separate 6 **pocket bread rounds** (about 6 in. wide) into halves to make 12 rounds. Lay cut side up on 2 baking sheets, each 12 by 15 inches. Brush bread lightly with **olive oil** (about 2 tablespoons total); sprinkle with shredded **parmesan cheese** (about ½ cup total).

Hamburgers and corn on the cob get tropical pungency from quick-to-make jerk sauce.

Bake in a 375° oven until crisp and golden brown, 7 to 10 minutes; alternate pans after 4 minutes and rotate positions to brown evenly. Remove pieces as they are browned. Serve, or let cool and store airtight up to a day. Makes 12.

PER PIECE: 122 calories, 4.1 g protein, 18 g carbohydrates, 3.5 g fat (0.9 g saturated), 2.6 mg cholesterol, 244 mg sodium

---

CARIBBEAN JERK SUPPER

Hamburgers & Corn with Jerk Sauce
Orange Honeydew Melon
Ice Cream Bars with Thick Chocolate
Iced Tea   Beer

Jerk sauces are aromatic spice blends used in savory ways in the Caribbean. This version gets under the husk of grilling corn and goes onto beef patties, too.

(Continued on next page)

HAMBURGERS & CORN WITH JERK SAUCE

4 **large (about 12-in.-long) ears corn**
Jerk sauce (recipe follows)
1 **to 1½ pounds ground lean beef**
4 **hamburger buns**
Rinsed and crisped lettuce leaves
Mayonnaise and salt

Pull husks down from corn, but leave attached to cob. Remove and discard silk. Rinse corn and pat dry. Smear about 1 tablespoon jerk sauce over each ear. Lay husks back around corn; tie with cotton string.

Shape beef into 4 equal patties, each ¾ inch thick. If convenient, cover and chill corn and beef up to 2 hours.

Place corn on a grill 4 to 6 inches above a solid bed of hot coals (you can hold your hand at grill level only 2 to 3 seconds). Turn corn as needed to keep husks from burning; grill until kernels are very hot, 15 to 20 minutes.

Place beef patties on grill, timing to remove with corn. Allow about 8 minutes for rare, 10 minutes for medium, 15 minutes for well done.

Serve beef on buns with lettuce; add jerk sauce, mayonnaise, and salt to taste. Husk corn and season to taste with more jerk sauce and salt. Makes 4 servings.

PER SERVING WITH 1 TABLESPOON JERK SAUCE: 612 calories, 33 g protein, 82 g carbohydrates, 21 g fat (6.9 g saturated), 72 mg cholesterol, 487 mg sodium

Jerk sauce. In a blender or food processor, mince 1 cup chopped **green onions;** ¼ cup **lime juice;** 2 tablespoons *each* **dark molasses, soy sauce,** and chopped **fresh ginger;** 2 cloves **garlic;** 2 **fresh jalapeño chilies,** stemmed and seeded; ½ teaspoon **ground cinnamon;** and ¼ teaspoon *each* **ground allspice** and **ground nutmeg.** Makes ¾ cup.

PER TABLESPOON: 16 calories, 0.4 g protein, 3.7 g carbohydrates, 0 g fat, 0 mg cholesterol, 177 mg sodium

Make-your-own Gazpacho Extravaganza (page 176)

Enjoy the leisurely
days of late summer with a casual outdoor party; our
festive make-your-own gazpacho buffet salutes one
of Spain's great dishes. College football fans throughout
the West share favorite recipes to make ahead for fabulous
feasts. For Rosh Hashanah, the Jewish New Year, we
suggest a lightened-up cake and cookies prepared
with honey. To perk up summer meals, you'll also find
soups using fresh fava beans, easy fish suppers, quick
broccoli dishes, and salsas to can or freeze.

Spain's Great Summer Soup

BARCELONA'S SUMMER *Olympics and Seville's Expo '92 have turned the world's attention to Spain this year, making it a fitting time to pay tribute to one of Spain's great dishes: gazpacho.*

Creating a buffet menu around gazpacho is an appealing way to entertain for some very practical reasons: it's a meal of choice (guests create servings to suit their own preferences at their own rate of speed), the elements are inherently handsome, and you can organize them well in advance.

In most people's minds, gazpacho is red because it's based on tomatoes. But this was not always so. In Andalusia, where gazpacho was born, the basic form was bread pounded with olive oil and seasoned with garlic, almonds, and vinegar—sometimes with a garnish of fruit-like tart grapes; it's the kind of dish you learn to like by growing up with it.

When tomatoes were taken back to Spain by the explorers, they were the first of a parade of New World ingredients, including avocados, to diversify this soup. Today's gazpacho is quite international. In Mexico, bread isn't basic; peppers (from bells to chilies) are often included, as is tomato juice or broth for a light, refreshing base. Sour cream might be added for smoothness.

Certainly, many such gazpachos have made their way into the repertoire of the Western kitchen. What's really best? We think you ought to decide, and a gazpacho buffet provides the test arena.

Madrid market offers New World tomatoes for the evolved gazpacho.

GAZPACHO BUFFET FOR 12

Make-your-own Gazpacho Extravaganza
Whole-grain & Crusty Breads
Sangría   Mineral Water
Flan   Almond Macaroons

Make the broth base several days ahead; prepare condiments in the morning. You can purchase a wine-based sangría, or make one using a favorite recipe.

For dessert, caramel-coated flan is more flavorful if made the day before.

Wide soup bowls work best for the gazpacho.

MAKE-YOUR-OWN GAZPACHO EXTRAVAGANZA

Andalusian broth (recipe follows)
6 **cups chilled tomato juice or Bloody Mary mix**
Garden buffet (choices follow)
Salted roasted almonds (1½ to 2 cups)
Garlic croutons (recipe follows)
Sherry vinegar (at least 1½ cups)
Extra-virgin olive oil (at least 1 cup)
Liquid hot pepper seasoning
Salt and pepper
3 **cups light sour cream or unflavored yogurt**
Lemon or lime wedges (at least 4 whole fruit)

Pour broth and tomato juice into separate serving containers such as tureens, handsome bowls, or pitchers. To keep liquids cold, set containers in larger, shallow ones and pile ice cubes around them. Or add ice cubes to individual servings.

Arrange containers and elements of the garden buffet, almonds, and croutons beside the broth. Put vinegar, olive oil, and liquid hot pepper seasoning in small bottles or cruets and place with foods. Have salt and pepper in small dishes, grinding mills, or shakers.

Invite each person to prepare gazpacho by the bowl to taste: ladle broth or juice (or a blend) into bowl; add a dollop of sour cream. If desired, stir sour cream into liquid to make a creamy base. Then add choices from garden buffet, almonds, croutons, vinegar or juice from lemon or lime wedges, oil, hot pepper seasoning, salt, and pepper. Makes 12 to 14 servings.

PER SERVING WITH 2 CUPS BROTH; ¼ CUP *EACH* TOMATOES, BELL PEPPERS, CUCUMBER, ONION, AVOCADO, AND GRAPES; ¼ CUP LIGHT SOUR CREAM, AND 2 TABLESPOONS ALMONDS: 404 calories, 15 g protein, 34 g carbohydrates, 26 g fat (6.6 g saturated), 20 mg cholesterol, 499 mg sodium

Andalusian broth. In a 10- to 12-quart pan, combine 6 quarts **regular-strength chicken broth,** 2 quarts **water,** 3 pounds **beef** or veal **bones** (or 2 lb. bony shank slices), 2 pounds **bony chicken parts** (backs, necks, wing tips), 2 large (about 1 lb. total) chopped **onions,** pared peel (colored part only) of 3 **lemons,** and ½ cup **sherry vinegar.** Bring to a boil over high heat. Cover and simmer for 2 hours. Pour broth through a colander into a large bowl; discard residue. Rinse pan; line colander with clean, damp cheesecloth and pour broth through it into pan. Cover and chill until fat on surface is hard, 8 hours or up to 3 days. Discard fat. You need 6 quarts; if short, add water to make this amount. Use cold.

Garden buffet. You need 4 to 4½ quarts total of at least 4 of the following choices: 6 to 8 cups diced ripe **tomatoes** (red or yellow), 4 to 6 cups diced **bell peppers** (1 or several colors), 2 to 3 cups thinly sliced **cucumber,** 1 to 2 cups paper-thin **red onion** slices (moistened with **lemon juice**), 2 to 3 cups thin **avocado** slices (moistened with lemon juice), and 3 to 4 cups **seedless grapes.** If preparing ahead, cover and chill up to 3 hours.

Garlic croutons. Cut a 1-pound loaf of **sourdough bread** into ¼-inch cubes. Mix ¼ to ½ cup **olive oil** with 4 cloves minced **garlic;** mix with bread. Spread cubes in 2 pans, each 10 by 15 inches. Bake in a 300° oven until golden and crunchy, about 35 minutes; stir often. Serve warm or cool; when cool, store airtight up to 3 days. Makes 12 cups.

PER ½ CUP: 67 calories, 1.7 g protein, 9.2 g carbohydrates, 2.6 g fat (0.3 g saturated), 0 mg cholesterol, 104 mg sodium

Colorful buffet for custom-made gazpacho: guests start with bowls of chilled broth, then add an array of garden vegetables, seasonings, and croutons. Serve with wine-based sangría and crusty breads.

Sunset's All-West Tailgate Recipes

THE TAILGATE PICNIC *has become as vital a part of Western college football as the forward pass. As pregame pep rallies for hearty appetites, tailgate feasts know no bounds. Stroll around the stadium grounds on game day and you'll see fans tackling everything from humble deli ribs to lavish grilled beef tenderloin to secret-blend chili.*

All-star tailgate menus have one thing in common: plenty of good food that travels well. We share play-by-play strategies for seven campus-inspired offerings—from beef to brownies—that team up well in movable feasts.

CAL BEAR BEEF TENDERLOIN

⅓ cup hoisin sauce or oyster sauce

3 tablespoons seasoned rice vinegar (or 3 tablespoons vinegar and 2 teaspoons sugar)

3 tablespoons minced fresh ginger

1 fat-trimmed center-cut beef tenderloin, 2½ to 2¾ pounds

10 to 16 hard-crust rolls

Dijon mustard and mayonnaise (optional)

Mix hoisin, vinegar, and ginger. Rub some of the mixture over beef; set meat on a rack in a 9- by 13-inch pan. If starting ahead, cover and chill meat and remaining hoisin mixture up to 4 hours.

Ignite 60 charcoal briquets on fire grate of a barbecue with a lid. When coals are dotted with gray ash, push half to each side of grate. Put a drip pan between coals. Place grill 4 to 6 inches above coals.

When coals are medium-hot (you can hold your hand at grill level for only 3 to 4 seconds), set beef over drip pan (not coals). Cover barbecue and open vents. Baste meat occasionally with remaining hoisin mixture. Cook beef until it is 125° in center for rare, about 30 minutes.

Serve beef hot or cold; if making ahead, cool, wrap airtight, and chill up to a day. Transport in an insulated container. Slice meat and make into sandwiches on rolls with mustard and mayonnaise. Makes 10 to 16 sandwiches.

PER SANDWICH: 279 calories, 20 g protein, 32 g carbohydrates, 7 g fat (2.3 g saturated), 46 mg cholesterol, 515 mg sodium

Tailgate feast stars Cal Bear Beef Tenderloin, Arizona Wildcat Salsa, and vegetables to munch. Beef can be served hot or cold; slice meat and tuck into hard-crust rolls.

New Mexico Lobo Chile Mole

New Mexicans insist that chile be spelled with an e, as in Spanish.

    2 pounds boned and fat-trimmed
       beef chuck, cut into ½-inch cubes
    3 large (about 1½ lb. total) onions,
       chopped
    4 cloves garlic, minced or pressed
    1 tablespoon cumin seed
    2 teaspoons dried oregano leaves
    1 teaspoon ground allspice
    2 cans (1 lb. 12 oz. size) chopped
       tomatoes
   2½ cups regular-strength beef broth
    1 can (6 oz.) tomato paste
    3 tablespoons unsweetened cocoa
    3 tablespoons chili powder
       Shredded cheddar cheese
       (optional)

In a 5- to 6-quart pan, combine meat, onions, garlic, cumin seed, oregano, allspice, and ½ cup water. Cover and bring to a boil on high heat. Reduce heat and simmer 30 minutes. Uncover and boil on high heat, stirring often, until liquid evaporates and browned bits stick to pan. Add ½ cup water, stir browned bits free, and boil until bits stick again.

Add tomatoes and their liquid, and broth; stir to free browned bits. Stir in tomato paste, cocoa, and chili powder. Cover and bring to a boil over high heat, then reduce heat and simmer until meat is tender when pierced, about 30 minutes.

Serve hot. If making ahead, cool, cover, and chill up to 2 days; reheat. To transport, carry hot chile in a large thermos or in a leakproof covered bowl in an insulated container. Serve with cheese. Makes 8 servings.—*Adapted from Key Cuisine: A Centennial Collection, Albuquerque Alumnae Association of Kappa Kappa Gamma Fraternity, University of New Mexico, Albuquerque.*

PER SERVING: 284 calories, 27 g protein, 24 g carbohydrates, 10 g fat (3.5 g saturated), 74 mg cholesterol, 614 mg sodium

UW Alumni Cook-off Smoked Salmon

    1 boned salmon fillet with skin,
       about 2½ pounds
    2 tablespoons melted butter or
       margarine

Decorated for a party, chile mole makes a festive tailgate dish. Transport hot chile in a large thermos or in a large leakproof covered bowl inside an insulated container.

    1 package (about 1½ oz.) fajita
       seasoning mix (or 3 bouillon
       cubes, 1 teaspoon chili powder,
       and ½ teaspoon *each* dried
       oregano leaves and sugar)
    1 small (4 to 5 oz.) onion, very
       thinly sliced
    1 lemon, thinly sliced
   ½ cup minced parsley

Mound 16 charcoal briquets on fire grate of a barbecue with a lid. Ignite the coals.

Rinse salmon, pat dry, and set skin side down on a larger piece of foil. Trim foil to fit outline of fish.

Stir together butter and fajita mix (or mash bouillon cubes in butter and add seasonings); spread evenly over fillet. Cover fillet with onion and lemon slices; sprinkle with half the parsley. Cover and chill remaining parsley.

When coals are dotted with gray ash, in 25 to 30 minutes, push half to each side of fire grate. Set grill 4 to 6 inches above fire grate. Place salmon on foil in center of grill (not over coals).

Cover barbecue and open vents. After 30 minutes, add 3 briquets to each mound of coals. Cover barbecue and cook until the thickest part of salmon

flakes when prodded with a fork, about 35 minutes longer. Supporting with foil, set salmon on a large platter. Serve hot or cool; if cooking ahead, cool, cover, and chill up to a day.

To transport, wrap cold salmon airtight and keep it cold in an insulated container up to 4 hours. To serve, sprinkle fish with remaining parsley; lift fish from skin with a small spatula or a fork. Makes 8 servings.—*Jeff Wood, University of Washington Alumni Association, Dallas Chapter.*

PER SERVING: 240 calories, 29 g protein, 3.6 g carbohydrates, 12 g fat (3.2 g saturated), 86 mg cholesterol, 389 mg sodium

Arizona Wildcat Salsa

   1¼ pounds ripe Roma-type tomatoes,
        rinsed and cored
    ¼ pound tomatillos, husked, rinsed,
        and cored
    ½ cup firmly packed minced fresh
        cilantro (coriander)
    ¼ cup lime juice
    1 fresh jalapeño chili, stemmed,
       seeded, and minced
       Salt and tortilla chips

(Continued on next page)

Football coffee cake is baked in 9- by 13-inch pan, trimmed and laced with icing.

Finely chop tomatoes and tomatillos. Mix in a bowl with cilantro, lime juice, chili, and salt to taste. Serve, or cover and chill up to a day. Transport in an insulated container. Scoop onto tortilla chips to eat. Makes about 3½ cups.

PER ¼ CUP: 11 calories, 0.5 g protein, 2.4 g carbohydrates, 0.2 g fat (0 g saturated), 0 mg cholesterol, 4.3 mg sodium

IDAHO STATE POTATO SALAD

- 3½ **to 4 pounds (7 to 8 large) thin-skinned potatoes, peeled and cut into 1-inch cubes**
- ⅓ **cup lemon juice**
- 1 **cup finely chopped celery**
- ¾ **cup *each* light sour cream and reduced-calorie mayonnaise**
- 2 **tablespoons minced fresh dill**
- 1½ **tablespoons prepared horseradish**
- 4 **or 5 ounces smoked trout, skinned, boned, and broken into flakes**
  Fresh dill sprigs
  Salt

In a 5- to 6-quart pan over high heat, bring potatoes and 2 quarts water to a boil. Cover and simmer until potatoes are tender when pierced, about 15 minutes. Drain well; mix potatoes with lemon juice and let cool.

In a bowl, mix celery, sour cream, mayonnaise, minced dill, and horseradish. Add potatoes and trout; mix. Serve or, if assembling ahead, cover and chill up to a day. Top with dill sprigs. To transport, cover and carry in an insulated container. Add salt to taste. Makes 8 to 10 servings.

PER SERVING: 206 calories, 5.7 g protein, 29 g carbohydrates, 7.6 g fat (2.4 g saturated), 16 mg cholesterol, 166 mg sodium

MONTANA GRIZZLY COWBOY COFFEE CAKE

- 1¼ **cups all-purpose flour**
- 1 **teaspoon baking powder**
- ¼ **teaspoon *each* baking soda and ground cinnamon**
- ⅛ **teaspoon ground nutmeg**
- ⅓ **cup (⅙ lb.) butter or margarine, in small pieces**
- 1 **cup firmly packed brown sugar**
- 1 **large egg**
- ½ **cup light or regular sour cream**
  Purchased white icing for piping (optional)

Mix together flour, baking powder, soda, cinnamon, and nutmeg. In a large bowl, beat butter and sugar until fluffy. Beat in egg and sour cream. Stir in flour mixture until evenly moistened.

Spread batter in a buttered 9- by 13-inch pan. Bake in a 375° oven until golden brown and top springs back when lightly pressed in center, about 20 minutes. Let cool; if baking ahead, wrap cake airtight and hold at room temperature up to a day.

Invert cake from pan, then turn top side up. If desired, with a sharp knife trim edges to make a football shape. Save scraps to serve with cake. Pipe icing onto cake to make lacings in center and stitch lines at ends. Let stand until icing is dry to touch. To transport, wrap airtight. Makes 6 servings.— *Adapted from The Grizzly Gourmet, University of Montana Athletic Department, Missoula.*

PER SERVING: 373 calories, 5.2 g protein, 57 g carbohydrates, 14 g fat (8.3 g saturated), 71 mg cholesterol, 236 mg sodium

TEXAS LONGHORN TOUCHDOWN BROWNIES

- 1¼ **cups (⅝ lb.) butter or margarine**
- ¾ **cup unsweetened cocoa**
- 2 **cups sugar**
- 6 **large eggs**
- 1 **tablespoon vanilla**
- 2 **cups all-purpose flour**
- 2 **cups pecan halves**
- ¾ **pound semisweet chocolate, cut into ½-inch chunks**

In a 3- to 4-quart pan over low heat, stir butter with cocoa until melted. Off the heat, beat in sugar; beat well. Add eggs and vanilla; beat well. Add flour, pecans, and chocolate; mix well. Spread batter in buttered 9- by 13-inch pan. Bake in a 325° oven until top feels dry in center, about 35 minutes. Cool in pan. If baking ahead, wrap airtight when cool and hold up to a day. Cut into 12 to 16 pieces.

PER PIECE: 520 calories, 6.7 g protein, 54 g carbohydrates, 34 g fat (15 g saturated), 119 mg cholesterol, 174 mg sodium

Texas Longhorn fans take the cake—and eat it—at kickoff party.

Jewish New Year Treats

H ONEY SYMBOLIZES *hope for a sweeter year ahead at Rosh Hashanah, the Jewish New Year. Honey might be presented simply as a dip for apple slices. Or it might be used in pastries. Lorraine Shapiro of Los Angeles, who has made a specialty of creating Jewish traditional dishes with a lighter touch, shares two fine examples of her efforts—a moist, tender honey and coffee–flavor chiffon cake, and honey and orange–glazed bar cookies. To meet Jewish dietary rules, do not use butter in these recipes. Sift all-purpose flour before measuring.*

HONEY CHIFFON CAKE

- 2 cups sifted all-purpose flour
- 1 tablespoon baking powder
- ¼ teaspoon baking soda
- 1½ teaspoons ground cinnamon
- ¼ teaspoon *each* ground allspice, ground ginger, and ground nutmeg
- ¼ teaspoon salt
- 7 large eggs, separated
- ¾ cup granulated sugar
- ⅔ cup honey
- ½ cup salad oil
- ⅔ cup strong, cool coffee
   About 2 tablespoons powdered sugar (optional)

In a small bowl, mix flour, baking powder, baking soda, cinnamon, allspice, ginger, nutmeg, and salt.

In a deep bowl, whip egg whites at high speed until foamy. Beating, gradually add 6 tablespoons granulated sugar, and whip until whites hold short, distinct peaks; set aside.

In another bowl, whip egg yolks, honey, and remaining granulated sugar at high speed (no need to wash beater) until mixture is thick and lighter in color; scrape bowl often. Beat in oil and coffee. Add flour mixture; beat to blend well. Stir about ¼ of the whites into batter. Gently but thoroughly fold in remaining whites.

Scrape batter into an ungreased 10-inch-wide tube pan with removable rim; smooth batter. Bake in a 325° oven until cake springs back when pressed in its center and sides begin to pull from pan, about 55 to 60 minutes.

Cool cake in pan, bottom up; support pan by setting tube over neck of a sturdy bottle (or, if rim has metal legs, on the legs). When cool, turn upright and run a thin-bladed knife between cake and pan and tube. Lift tube and cake from rim. Slide knife between cake and pan bottom. Invert cake onto a plate. Lift off tube; if desired, turn cake wide end up. Dust with powdered sugar. Serve, or wrap airtight and keep up to a day. Freeze to store longer; thaw wrapped. Slice thinly. Makes a 2¼-pound cake, 12 to 16 servings.

PER SERVING: 226 calories, 4.2 g protein, 32 g carbohydrates, 9.1 g fat (1.6 g saturated), 93 mg cholesterol, 155 mg sodium

HONEY-SESAME BARS

- 1⅓ cups sesame seed
- 1 cup sifted all-purpose flour
- ½ cup whole-wheat flour
- ½ cup sugar
- 1½ teaspoons baking powder
- ¼ teaspoon salt
- 2 large eggs
- ½ cup sugar
- ⅓ cup honey
- ¾ cup salad oil
- 1½ teaspoons grated orange peel
   Honey glaze (recipe follows)

In an 8- to 10-inch frying pan over medium heat, shake sesame seed often until toasted, 5 to 7 minutes. Pour into a large bowl and mix with all-purpose flour, whole-wheat flour, sugar, baking powder, and salt.

In another bowl, beat to blend eggs, sugar, honey, oil, and peel. Mix well with dry ingredients. Spread the batter in an oiled 9- by 13-inch pan.

Bake in a 375° oven until richly browned and center springs back when lightly touched, 18 to 20 minutes. Remove from oven and, with a slender skewer, pierce through cake to pan at

Jewish New Year treats feature honey baked in chiffon cake and in cookies.

½-inch intervals, then pour honey glaze evenly over cake. Let stand at least 10 minutes. Serve or, when cool, cover and hold at room temperature up to a day. Cut into 24 pieces. Makes 12 servings.

PER PIECE: 219 calories, 2.8 g protein, 25 g carbohydrates, 13 g fat (1.8 g saturated), 18 mg cholesterol, 73 mg sodium

Honey glaze. In a bowl, beat to blend ½ cup **honey**, 3 tablespoons melted **margarine** or butter, and 1½ teaspoons grated **orange peel**.

A Chef's Jelly Joke

A JOKE IN GOOD TASTE *aptly describes this sleight-of-hand dish. It's a simple crab salad surrounded by a colorless, soft aspic. But because the aspic is made of juice drained from ripe tomatoes, the first bite surprises. The tomato flavor is intense. Succeeding bites appeal because the taste is quite refreshing.*

Although this dish is a specialty featured by Alain Rondelli, chef at Ernie's Restaurant in San Francisco, it is easy to make. You need ripe tomatoes, plentiful now, and a head start of at least 12 hours. When you purée the tomatoes and drain them through a cloth without pressure, the flavorful liquid that comes through is clear, not red.

Chef Alain Rondelli serves crab salad surrounded by colorless tomato aspic.

CRAB CAKES WITH TOMATO WATER JELLY

- 8 **slender (about ½-in.-wide) asparagus spears, tough ends removed**
- 1 **pound shelled, cooked crab or tiny shrimp (rinse shrimp with cool water and drain)**
- ⅓ **cup light or regular mayonnaise**
- 1½ **tablespoons prepared horseradish**
  Tomato water jelly (recipe follows)
  Tomato wedges and cilantro (optional)

If desired, peel asparagus stems with a vegetable peeler. In a 10- to 12-inch frying pan over high heat, bring about 1 inch water to a boil. Cook asparagus, uncovered, until barely tender when pierced, about 2 minutes. Drain at once and immerse in ice water until cool; drain.

Cut off and reserve asparagus tips; wrap airtight and chill. Cut stalks into ½-inch lengths.

In a bowl, gently mix crab, mayonnaise, and horseradish. Smoothly line 4 ramekins or custard cups (1-cup size) with plastic wrap; leave 2 to 3 inches extending over rims.

Divide half the crab equally among the ramekins; press level with back of a spoon. Divide asparagus stems equally among ramekins; top with equal portions of remaining crab, pressing to make compact and level. Fold wrap over crab to keep airtight. Chill at least 1 hour or up to a day.

Fold back wrap and invert crab onto 4 rimmed plates; peel off wrap. Spoon tomato jelly evenly around portions. Garnish with asparagus tips, tomato wedges, and cilantro. Makes 4 servings.

PER SERVING: 188 calories, 26 g protein, 4 g carbohydrates, 7.5 g fat (1.6 g saturated), 120 mg cholesterol, 707 mg sodium

Tomato water jelly. Rinse, core, and cut into chunks 1¾ pounds **ripe tomatoes.** In a food processor or blender, smoothly purée tomatoes and ½ teaspoon **salt.** Line a colander with 2 layers of cheesecloth, overlapping rim. Set colander in a large bowl. Pour purée into cloth; enclose nested containers in plastic wrap. Chill at least 12 hours or up to 2 days. Gather cloth edges; twist gently to squeeze out any remaining clear liquid. Stop when liquid takes on any red color. Measure liquid. You need 2 cups.

Juice from puréed tomatoes drains clear from cheesecloth bag into bowl.

Soft aspic is chilled until syrupy, then spooned around crab salad.

If short, add water; if you have too much, save extra to drink. Save purée to make pasta sauce.

In a 1- to 1½-quart pan, combine 1 envelope (2 teaspoons) **unflavored gelatin,** ½ cup of the tomato liquid, and ¼ cup **water;** let stand about 5 minutes to soften gelatin. Stir over medium-high heat until gelatin melts, then whisk into remaining tomato liquid. Cover and chill until syrupy (it does not get firm), at least 4 hours or up to a day.

Fresh Favas Make Great Soups

FRESH FAVA BEANS *begin their sporadic appearances in Western markets in early spring and are usually quite plentiful by June and on through September.*

The long, fat pods hold large, flat beans in cushioned cups. Favas look like lima beans but are bigger and more delicate in flavor. The opaque membrane on each bean is edible, but it toughens as the bean matures.

These two recipes for first-course soups take full advantage of the bean's delicate flavor and color.

One caution: a few people (usually of Mediterranean descent) lack a specific enzyme and have an allergic reaction to fava beans and their pollen, so check your family history before you try favas.

TOMATO FAVA SOUP

- 2 tablespoons olive oil
- 1 large onion, chopped
- 1½ pounds (about 6 medium-size) ripe tomatoes, cored and quartered
- 2 tablespoons minced fresh or 1 teaspoon dried savory leaves
- ¾ teaspoon sugar
- ¼ teaspoon pepper
- 4 cups regular-strength chicken broth
  Blanched fava beans (directions follow)

In a 3- to 4-quart pan over medium-high heat, stir oil and onion often until onion begins to brown, about 10 minutes.

Add tomatoes, savory, sugar, and pepper. Bring to a boil; reduce heat and simmer until tomatoes are very soft when pressed, about 15 minutes.

In a blender or food processor, whirl mixture until coarsely puréed. Return to pan and add broth. If making ahead, cover and chill up to a day. Stir over high heat until hot. Ladle soup into bowls; sprinkle blanched fava beans equally into each serving. Makes 5 or 6 servings.

PER SERVING: 118 calories, 4.8 g protein, 12 g carbohydrates, 6 g fat (1 g saturated), 0 mg cholesterol, 63 mg sodium

Blanched fava beans. In a 2- to 3-quart pan, bring 4 cups **water** to a boil over high heat. Add 2 cups shelled **fava beans** (about 2 lb. in the pod) and simmer, uncovered, until beans are just tender when pierced, 3 to 5 minutes; drain and let cool. With your fingers, slip membrane off beans and discard. Use beans or, if making ahead, cover and chill up to a day.

GARLIC FAVA SOUP

- 1 tablespoon olive oil
- 2 large heads (about 7 oz. total) garlic
- 2 pounds chicken backs and necks
- 8 cups regular-strength chicken broth
- ¾ cup dry white wine
- ½ cup orange juice
  Fava bean purée (recipe follows)
  Gruyère croutons (recipe follows)

Pour oil over garlic in an 8- to 9-inch-wide pan. Bake in a 400° oven until heads are very soft when squeezed, 40 to 45 minutes. Let cool.

Meanwhile, rinse chicken. In a 5- to 6-quart pan over medium-high heat, brown chicken well, about 20 minutes; stir often. Add chicken broth, wine, and orange juice. Boil over high heat, uncovered, until reduced to 5 cups, 45 to 55 minutes. With a slotted spoon, discard chicken parts. Spoon off and discard the fat.

Cut garlic heads in half crosswise and squeeze garlic from peel into pan. Whisk until garlic is smoothly mixed with broth. If making ahead, cover and chill up to a day; reheat to continue.

Ladle the soup into bowls and mound fava purée equally into each. Accompany with the Gruyère croutons. Makes 4 servings.

PER SERVING: 213 calories, 12 g protein, 24 g carbohydrates, 8.1 g fat (1.7 g saturated), 12 mg cholesterol, 147 mg sodium

Fava bean purée. In a 2- to 3-quart pan, bring 4 cups **water** to a boil over high heat. Add 1½ cups shelled **fava beans** (about 1½ lb. in the pod) and cook, uncovered, until beans are just tender when pierced, 3 to 5 minutes. Drain and let cool. With your fingers, slip membrane off beans and discard. If making ahead, cover beans and chill up to a day.

Put beans and ½ cup hot **garlic broth** (preceding) in a blender; whirl until smoothly puréed. Use warm. (Green color dulls quickly.)

Gruyère croutons. Cut ½ of a ½-pound **baguette** crosswise into 12 diagonal slices. Arrange slices, side by side, in a 10- by 15-inch pan. Brush slices with 2 tablespoons **olive oil,** then sprinkle evenly with 1 cup shredded **gruyère** or Swiss **cheese.** Bake in a 375° oven until golden, 8 to 10 minutes. Serve hot.

PER CROUTON: 86 calories, 3.7 g protein, 5.3 g carbohydrates, 5.6 g fat (2.2 g saturated), 11 mg cholesterol, 87 mg sodium

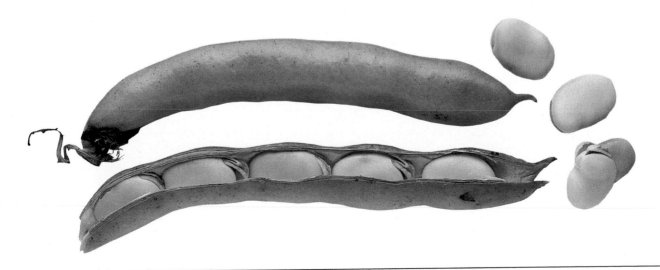

Quick & Easy Fish Suppers

MORE FAMILY MEALS *that are easy to make and are baked using everyday fish: that's a priority Western cooks often underline as needing more attention. These two dishes fit the bill. Each pairs boned, skinned fillets with a vegetable; the first combines baby salmon with squash, the second rockfish and potatoes. They bake with little attention—and you don't have to turn over the fragile fish.*

In both recipes, you start the vegetable, then add the fast-cooking fillets later. A peaceful break between steps gives you time to set the table and make a salad or prepare another vegetable to round out a simple menu.

Rockfish fillet and small thin-skinned potatoes share mustard-honey glaze.

BABY SALMON FILLETS WITH SQUASH, BROWN SUGAR & LIME

> 1½ **pounds banana or Hubbard squash, cut into 4 equal pieces**
> 1½ **cups regular-strength chicken broth**
> 2 **teaspoons salad oil**
> 4 **baby salmon fillets (each about 5 oz.), rinsed**
> ¼ **cup firmly packed brown sugar**
> ¼ **cup lime juice**
> **Lime wedges (optional)**
> **Salt and pepper**

If squash has seeds, scoop out and discard. Lay squash, skin up, in a 10- by 15-inch or 11- by 14-inch pan and add broth. Bake, uncovered, in a 350° oven until tender when pierced, 45 minutes to 1 hour. Remove from oven; turn heat up to 450°.

Turn squash over and move to one end of pan. Lift opposite end of pan and lightly oil the exposed bottom. Lay fillets, side by side (they can overlap slightly), in oiled section. Mix brown sugar and lime juice; spoon about ½ the mixture over squash and fish. Return to oven and bake until salmon is opaque but still moist-looking in center of thickest part (cut to test), about 8 minutes. After fish has baked 5 minutes, spoon remaining lime mixture over fish and squash.

Transfer fish and squash to dinner plates; garnish with limes. Stir to blend pan juices, then pour into a small pitcher. To individual portions, add juices, salt, and pepper to taste. Makes 4 servings.

PER SERVING: 331 calories, 31 g protein, 24 g carbohydrates, 12 g fat (1.9 g saturated), 78 mg cholesterol, 97 mg sodium

ROCKFISH & TINY POTATOES WITH MUSTARD-HONEY GLAZE

Accompany with a vegetable, such as green beans or broccoli.

> 1 **tablespoon olive or salad oil**
> 16 **small (1- to 1½-in. diameter) thin-skinned potatoes, scrubbed**
> ¼ **cup Dijon mustard**
> 2 **tablespoons honey**
> 4 **rockfish fillets (each about 5 oz.), rinsed**
> **Salt and pepper**

In a 10- to 15-inch pan, combine oil and potatoes; roll potatoes around until coated with oil. Bake in a 425° oven until potatoes give readily when pressed, about 25 minutes.

Meanwhile, combine mustard and honey. Brush fish with about ½ the mixture.

When potatoes are tender, push to one end of pan and brush with remaining mustard-honey mixture. Lay fish, in a single layer, in pan. Bake until fish is opaque but still moist-looking in center of thickest part (cut to test), 8 to 10 minutes.

Transfer potatoes and fish to dinner plates. Stir pan juices and pour into a small pitcher. To each portion, add juices, salt, and pepper to taste. Makes 4 servings.

PER SERVING: 488 calories, 33 g protein, 72 g carbohydrates, 7.2 g fat (1.0 g saturated), 50 mg cholesterol, 562 mg sodium

Baby salmon fillets bake with squash in sweet-tart lime sauce.

Making Salsa to Can or Freeze

AKE ADVANTAGE OF *late summer's bounty of ripe tomatoes and chilies to preserve a supply of zesty salsa, red or green. Can or freeze to enjoy in the coming months.*

Use the minimum amount of hot jalapeños to create salsa dulce, or the maximum for salsa picante. Larger, dark green poblano (ancho) chilies or similar-tasting pasilla chilies contribute mild heat and mellow flavor.

BUMPER CROP RED CHILI SALSA

⅓ to ⅔ **pound (6 to 12) fresh jalapeño chilies**

About 1 **pound (7 medium-size) fresh green poblano (ancho), pasilla, or Anaheim (California or New Mexico) chilies**

12 **cups (about 5 lb.) coarsely chopped ripe tomatoes**

2 **cups coarsely chopped onions**

1 **cup chopped fresh cilantro (coriander)**

1¼ **cups lemon juice**

2 **tablespoons minced garlic**

2 **teaspoons dried oregano leaves**

1 to 3 **teaspoons salt (optional)**

Place jalapeño and poblano chilies in a single layer and slightly apart in a 12-by 15-inch pan (in sequence if more than 1 panful). Broil 3 to 4 inches below heat until skins blister all over, about 15 minutes total; turn as needed. Let cool. Wearing gloves, pull off and discard skins and stems. Rinse out seeds. Drain and coarsely chop chilies.

In a 6- to 8-quart pan, combine chilies, tomatoes and their juice, onions, cilantro, lemon juice, garlic, and oregano. With pan uncovered, bring to simmering over high heat. Reduce heat and simmer for 10 minutes; stir occasionally. Add salt to taste.

To can or freeze, use following directions. Or let salsa cool and serve.

Cooled salsa, or canned or frozen salsa that has been opened or thawed for use, can be chilled airtight up to 10 days. Makes about 14 cups.

PER TABLESPOON: 3.9 calories, 0.1 g protein, 0.9 g carbohydrates, 0 g fat, 0 mg cholesterol, 1.4 mg sodium

To can salsa. As salsa is being prepared, place a canning rack (or other rack that fits) in bottom of an 18- to 22-quart pan. Fill pan ⅔ full of water. Cover

Red tomatoes or tart green tomatillos determine color of salsas; chilies imbue heat. Use jalapeños for hotter salsas, poblano (ancho) chilies for milder, more mellow flavor.

and bring to simmering over high heat, about 20 minutes.

Wash, rinse, and drain 7 or 8 pint-size canning jars (rims free of nicks and cracks). Heat 7 or 8 jar rings and new lids as manufacturer directs.

Ladle hot salsa into jars within ½ inch of top (serve or freeze any extra salsa). Wipe rims clean. Set hot lids and bands on jars and screw on tightly; don't force.

Using tongs, lower jars onto rack in pan. With pan uncovered, bring water to 185°, then keep temperature at 180° to 190° for 20 minutes. Lift out jars and set on a towel to cool completely. Press centers of lids; if they stay down, jars are sealed. Store sealed jars in a cool, dark place up to 2 years; chill any unsealed jars up to 10 days—or transfer to freezer containers and freeze to store longer.

To freeze salsa. Ladle cool salsa into small serving-size freezer containers, filling within ½ inch of top; close and freeze up to 6 months.

BUMPER CROP GREEN CHILI SALSA

Follow directions for **bumper crop red chili salsa** (preceding), omitting tomatoes and using 10 cups (about 4½ lb.) coarsely chopped husked **fresh tomatillos.** Increase **poblano chilies** to 2½ pounds. Omit lemon juice and use 1¼ cups **lime juice** and 1 cup **water.** Makes about 15 cups.

PER TABLESPOON: 4.6 calories, 0.2 g protein, 0.9 g carbohydrates, 0 g fat, 0 mg cholesterol, 0.5 mg sodium

More September Recipes

OTHER SEPTEMBER articles offer ideas for using new varieties of broccoli, chewy granola cookies from Britain, and an unusual watermelon dessert.

PIQUANT BROCCOLI SALAD

For both head and sprouting kinds of broccoli, cut off and discard tough ends and coarse leaves; peel stems if skin is tough. If broccoli shoots or stems are ½ inch thick or less, cut into 1½- to 2-inch lengths; cut thicker stems diagonally into ¼-inch-thick lengths.

    4 cups trimmed broccoli (directions precede)
      Pimiento dressing (recipe follows)
    2 tablespoons salt-cured olives such as niçoise or calamata (optional, or salt to taste)

In a 5- to 6-quart pan on high heat, bring 3 quarts water to a boil. Add broccoli; cook, uncovered, just until tender-crisp to bite, 2 to 3 minutes. Drain; immerse in ice water. Drain when cool. If making ahead, cover and chill up to a day. Mix broccoli, dressing, and olives. Makes 4 servings.

PER SERVING: 42 calories, 2.9 g protein, 6.3 g carbohydrates, 0.4 g fat (0 g saturated), 0 mg cholesterol, 65 mg sodium

Pimiento dressing. Mix ¼ cup **dry white wine** with 1 teaspoon **Dijon mustard.** Add 2 tablespoons chopped **green onion;** 1 tablespoon **white wine vinegar;** 1 clove **garlic,** pressed or minced; and 1 jar (2¼ oz.) **diced pimientos,** drained.

BROCCOLI-BELL PEPPER SAUTÉ WITH TOASTED PINE NUTS

To vary the appearance of broccoli dishes, try one of the new purple or chartreuse varieties now available.

Flapjacks, British-style, are soft, chewy granola cookies.

    3 tablespoons pine nuts
    4 cups trimmed broccoli (directions precede)
    1 tablespoon olive oil
    1 small (about 4-oz.) red bell pepper, stemmed, seeded, and cut into thin slivers
      Salt

In a 10- to 12-inch frying pan over medium-low heat, stir nuts until golden, 6 to 8 minutes. Pour nuts into a small bowl to cool.

To pan on medium-high heat, add broccoli pieces and ¼ cup water. Cover; stir occasionally until the broccoli is tender-crisp to bite, 2 to 3 minutes. Pour into a serving bowl.

Add oil and bell pepper to pan. Stir often until pepper is lightly browned, about 3 minutes. Pour pepper slices over broccoli; sprinkle with pine nuts. Add salt to taste. Makes 4 servings.

PER SERVING: 96 calories, 4.4 g protein, 7.1 g carbohydrates, 7.1 g fat (1.0 g saturated), 0 mg cholesterol, 24 mg sodium

BRITISH FLAPJACKS

For an American, English in England can be a sticky wicket. There, a fool or a sweet may be dessert. For elevenses, a British

---

Substituting in a Pinch

HALFWAY INTO MIXING the cake batter, you find you're missing an ingredient! Sooner or later most cooks run into a problem like this, and with the following list of baking alternatives, you just might save a trip to the store.

Baking powder
1 teaspoon double-acting baking powder = ¼ teaspoon baking soda plus ½ teaspoon cream of tartar.*

Butter
1 cup (½ lb.) butter = 1 cup (½ lb.) margarine (do not use light or whipped margarine) or solid shortening, or ⅞ cup lard.

Buttermilk
1 cup buttermilk = 1 tablespoon lemon juice or white vinegar plus enough milk to make 1 cup (let sit 5 minutes), or 1 cup unflavored yogurt.

Cake flour
1 cup unsifted cake flour = 1 cup unsifted all-purpose flour minus 2 tablespoons (minus ¼ cup, total, if recipe calls for sifted cake flour).*

Milk
1 cup milk = ½ cup canned evaporated milk plus ½ cup water, or ⅓ cup instant nonfat dried milk stirred into 1 cup water.

Self-rising flour
1 cup unsifted self-rising flour = 1 cup unsifted all-purpose flour, 1½ teaspoons baking powder, and ¼ teaspoon salt.*

Sour cream
1 cup sour cream = 1 cup unflavored yogurt.

Unsweetened chocolate
1 ounce unsweetened chocolate = 3 tablespoons unsweetened cocoa plus 1 tablespoon melted butter, margarine, or shortening.

Whipping cream
1 cup whipping cream = ¾ cup milk plus ⅓ cup melted butter or margarine. Use for baking, not whipping.

*Lightly spoon into a measuring cup or spoon; scrape top level.

way to describe late-morning tea, you might be served flapjacks, but don't expect hot pancakes. Flapjacks are these soft, chewy granola cookies.

- ¾ **cup (⅜ lb.) butter or margarine, melted**
- ¾ **cup sugar**
- ¼ **cup honey**
- 1 **large egg**
- 4 **cups regular rolled oats**
- 1 **cup coarsely chopped hazelnuts**
- ½ **cup raisins**

In a bowl, mix together butter, sugar, honey, egg, oats, nuts, and raisins. Pat mixture firmly into a buttered and flour-dusted 9-inch-square pan.

Bake in a 300° oven until deep golden, 50 to 55 minutes. Cut into 16 pieces, then let cool in pan. Redo cuts and remove from pan with a spatula. Serve, or store airtight up to 5 days; freeze to store longer. Makes 16.

PER PIECE: 272 calories, 4.8 g protein, 32 g carbohydrates, 15 g fat (6.1 g saturated), 37 mg cholesterol, 96 mg sodium

WATERMELON WITH HOT RASPBERRY VINAIGRETTE

Red on red, sweet with tart, hot on cold create a sensuous interplay of color, taste, and temperature in this marvelously light dessert. It takes just minutes to produce: heat sweetened balsamic vinegar, toss in raspberries, then splash onto ice-cold watermelon wedges.

- 4 **chilled watermelon wedges, with or without seeds, each about 3 inches thick at base and 8 to 10 inches wide**
  Hot raspberry vinaigrette (recipe follows)

Set wedges on plates. Spoon berry mixture over melon. Makes 4 servings.

PER SERVING: 117 calories, 1.7 g protein, 27 g carbohydrates, 1.2 g fat (0 g saturated), 0 mg cholesterol, 4.8 mg sodium

Hot raspberry vinaigrette. In a 1- to 1½-quart pan over high heat, bring ⅓ cup **balsamic vinegar** and 2 tablespoons **sugar** to a boil. Stir in 1 cup rinsed and drained **raspberries.** Use hot.

Warmed raspberries in a vinaigrette sauce spooned over chilled watermelon wedges create intriguing contrasts in this light, fresh fruit dessert.

Combine chicken with tarragon dressing, hazelnuts, and onions.

TARRAGON HAZELNUT CHICKEN SALAD

1 cup hazelnuts
  Tarragon dressing (recipe follows)
3 cups bite-size pieces skinned, cooked chicken
½ cup thinly sliced green onions
  Salt
  Large lettuce leaves, rinsed and crisped

Place nuts in a 9-inch pie or cake pan. Bake in a 350° oven until golden under skin, about 10 minutes. Pour nuts into a towel; rub off loose skins. Discard skins. Coarsely chop the nuts.

In a large bowl, mix tarragon dressing, chicken, onions, ⅔ cup hazelnuts, and salt to taste. Spoon salad onto lettuce-lined plates. Sprinkle with the remaining hazelnuts. Makes 4 or 5 servings.—*Emily Bader, Bothell, Wash.*

PER SERVING: 367 calories, 29 g protein, 10 g carbohydrates, 24 g fat (3.6 g saturated), 79 mg cholesterol, 157 mg sodium

Tarragon dressing. Mix together ½ cup **unflavored nonfat yogurt;** ¼ cup **reduced-calorie** or regular **mayonnaise;** 2 tablespoons **frozen orange juice concentrate,** thawed; 2 tablespoons **white wine vinegar;** 1 tablespoon minced **fresh** or 1 teaspoon dried **tarragon leaves;** and ½ teaspoon **ground white pepper.**

Grilled steak, coated with garlic and cilantro, goes with relish, garnishes.

THAI GARLIC BEEF

6 cloves garlic, pressed or minced
⅓ cup finely chopped fresh cilantro (coriander)
2 tablespoons lime juice
1 tablespoon coarsely ground pepper
1 piece boneless beef top sirloin (about 1½ lb.), 1 inch thick, fat trimmed
  Tomato and lime wedges
  Cilantro sprigs
  Thai relish (recipe follows)
  Salt

Mix garlic, chopped cilantro, lime juice, and pepper. Rub seasoning mixture over beef.

Place beef on a grill 4 to 6 inches above a solid bed of hot coals (you can hold hand at grill level only 2 to 3 seconds). Cook, turning to brown evenly, until meat is medium-rare (still pink in thickest part; cut to test), 12 to 15 minutes total. Transfer to a platter. Garnish with tomato and lime wedges, and cilantro sprigs. Slice beef thinly and serve with relish. Add salt to taste. Makes 6 servings.—*J. Hill, Sacramento.*

PER SERVING: 191 calories, 27 g protein, 5.8 g carbohydrates, 6.3 g fat (2.4 g saturated), 76 mg cholesterol, 61 mg sodium

Thai relish. Mix 1 cup *each* finely diced **cucumber** and **papaya,** ¼ cup thinly sliced **green onions,** 2 tablespoons **lime juice,** ¼ teaspoon **crushed dried hot red chilies,** and 2 cloves **garlic,** pressed or minced.

Hungarian paprika and bacon season diced potatoes as they simmer.

PAPRIKA POTATOES

4 strips (about ¼ lb. total) bacon, cut into ¼-inch-wide strips
1 pound (about 3 medium-size) thin-skinned potatoes, scrubbed
1 medium-size (about 6 oz.) onion, chopped
1 tablespoon sweet Hungarian or regular paprika
  Light or regular sour cream
  Chopped parsley
  Salt and pepper

In a 10- to 12-inch frying pan, cook bacon over medium heat until crisp, about 8 minutes; stir occasionally. Meanwhile, cut potatoes into ½-inch cubes. With a slotted spoon, remove bacon from pan; set aside. Discard all but 1 tablespoon fat. Add onion to pan; stir often until limp, about 10 minutes. Stir in paprika.

Stir in potatoes and 1 cup water. Cover and simmer over low heat until potatoes are tender when pierced, about 15 minutes; stir occasionally, and add a little water if pan gets dry. Top each portion with a dollop of sour cream, parsley, and bacon. Add salt and pepper to taste. Makes 4 servings.—*Ann Bartos Rushton, Denver.*

PER SERVING: 182 calories, 5.3 g protein, 25 g carbohydrates, 6.9 g fat (2.2 g saturated), 9 mg cholesterol, 153 mg sodium

SWEET PEPPER STIR-FRY

For a colorful dish, combine red, yellow, and green bell peppers.

- 3 medium-size (about 6 oz. each) bell peppers
- 1 tablespoon salad oil
- 1 tablespoon minced fresh ginger
- 1 clove garlic, pressed or minced
- 1 small (about ¼ lb.) onion, cut into thin slivers
- 1 cup (about 3 oz.) bean sprouts, rinsed
- 1 teaspoon Oriental sesame oil
  Soy sauce or salt

Stem and seed peppers. Cut peppers in thin slivers 2 to 3 inches long.

Place a wok or 10- to 12-inch frying pan over high heat. When pan is hot, add oil, ginger, garlic, and onion slivers; stir-fry for 1 minute. Add bell pepper strips; stir-fry until peppers are tender-crisp, about 3 minutes. Add bean sprouts and stir-fry until they barely wilt, about 1 minute.

Mix sesame oil into stir-fry mixture. Spoon onto plates; add soy or salt to taste. Makes 4 or 5 servings.—*Mickey Strang, McKinleyville, Calif.*

PER SERVING: 62 calories, 1.6 g protein, 8.7 g carbohydrates, 2.9 g fat (0.4 g saturated), 0 mg cholesterol, 3.6 mg sodium

Stir-fry a trio of colorful bell peppers with bean sprouts and onion slivers.

CURRIED TOMATO SALMON

- 1 tablespoon olive oil
- 1 small (about ¼ lb.) onion, chopped
- 2 cloves garlic, minced
- 1 tablespoon curry powder
- 2 teaspoons fresh or 1 teaspoon dried thyme leaves
- 2 large (about 1 lb. total) firm-ripe tomatoes, cored, seeded, and chopped
- 2 salmon steaks (4 to 6 oz. each), rinsed
  Salt and pepper
  Thyme sprigs (optional)

In a 10- to 12-inch frying pan, combine oil, onion, and garlic. Stir often over medium-high heat until the onion is tinged with brown, about 5 minutes.

Reduce heat to low. Stir in curry powder and thyme leaves; stir about 1 minute. Add tomatoes; simmer, uncovered, stirring occasionally, until tomatoes begin to fall apart and most of the liquid evaporates, about 5 minutes.

Lay salmon in pan, spoon sauce over fish, cover, and simmer just until fish is still moist-looking but opaque in thickest part (cut to test), about 10 minutes. Lift salmon onto dinner plates; spoon sauce over fish. Add salt and pepper to taste. Garnish with thyme sprigs. Makes 2 servings.—*Vicky Hay, Phoenix.*

PER SERVING: 283 calories, 23 g protein, 18 g carbohydrates, 14 g fat (2.0 g saturated), 55 mg cholesterol, 67 mg sodium

Salmon poached in curried tomato sauce makes quick dinner for two.

MEXICAN CHOCOLATE ICE CREAM

Look for the cinnamon-scented sweet Mexican chocolate rounds in Hispanic markets and in the fancy foods section of some supermarkets.

- 2 cakes (3½ oz. each) Mexican chocolate (or 7 oz. semisweet chocolate and 1 teaspoon ground cinnamon)
- ¾ cup sugar
- 1 quart milk or half-and-half (light cream)
- 2 large eggs, beaten to blend
- 2 teaspoons vanilla

Chop chocolate and place (with cinnamon, if used) in a 2- to 3-quart pan over lowest heat; when chocolate begins to soften, stir until smoothly melted. Add sugar, milk, and eggs. Stir often over medium-low heat until mixture coats the back of a metal spoon in an even, velvety layer, 20 to 30 minutes. Stir in the vanilla.

Cool, cover, and chill until cold, at least 3 hours or up to a day.

Pour cold milk mixture into an ice cream freezer, at least 1½-quart size. Freeze according to manufacturer's directions until firm. Serve, or cover airtight and freeze up to 2 weeks. Makes about 5 cups, 8 to 10 servings.—*Marilyn Swartz, Los Angeles.*

PER SERVING: 236 calories, 5.3 g protein, 31 g carbohydrates, 11 g fat (6.3 g saturated), 56 mg cholesterol, 61 mg sodium

Round cakes of spiced Mexican chocolate flavor ice cream for cones.

Chefs of the West®
Adventures with Food

WHAT WE SEE WHEN *we eat a scallop is a disk of tender flesh. In life it had two perfectly matched, beautifully ridged shells that it could clap together like castanets, enabling it to skip about on the sea bottom, unlike its homebound bivalve cousins the mussel and oyster. The scallop shell served as a vessel to carry the sea-born Venus to her first home on Cyprus. It also served as the badge of the pilgrims traveling to the shrine of St. James at Compostela.*

It is no wonder, then, that such a storied creature is costly. Still, it comes to market unencumbered by shell, bone, or other inedible baggage, and no one would question its delicacy of flavor. Here's how James Kircher prepares it.

"Scallops skip about on the sea bottom."

SAUTÉED SCALLOPS

- **2 pounds large scallops**
- **1 tablespoon butter or margarine**
- **2 tablespoons *each* minced onion and celery**
- **1 tablespoon chopped parsley**
- **1 clove garlic, minced or pressed**
- **1 teaspoon dried summer savory leaves**
- **½ teaspoon *each* dried thyme leaves and white pepper**
- **2 tablespoons lemon juice**
- **2 tablespoons dry white wine**

Thoroughly rinse scallops, pat dry, and cut into thin slices; set aside.

In a 10- to 12-inch frying pan over medium-high heat, combine butter, onion, celery, parsley, garlic, savory, thyme, and pepper. Stir often until onion is limp, about 5 minutes. Stir in scallops and lemon juice; turn heat to high and turn scallops often with a wide spatula just until they begin to turn opaque, 3 to 5 minutes. With a slotted spoon, transfer the scallops to a bowl.

Add wine to pan; also, as liquid accumulates with scallops, drain it into pan. Boil, uncovered, on high heat until reduced to about ¼ cup. Stir scallops back into pan to warm, then spoon at once onto dinner plates. Makes 6 to 8 servings.

PER SERVING: 119 calories, 19 g protein, 3.6 g carbohydrates, 2.3 g fat (1 g saturated), 41 mg cholesterol, 200 mg sodium

Burley, Idaho

It seems like only *yesterday that we knew only one salsa, the familiar blend of tomatoes, onions, and chilies that, along with a bowl of tortilla chips, precedes your Mexican meal and stays on the table to spice up dishes that follow. No more. Now almost any fruit or vegetable can serve as the base for a salsa, which performs the same function as a chutney, but in a fresher, lighter way. Many chefs now use salsas in place of more conventional gravies or rich oil- or fat-based sauces.*

Like chutneys, these nouveau salsas combine fruit, vegetables, sugar, and spices. Papaya, being sweet, requires no sugar; lime juice supplies fruit acid and enhances the tropical fruit flavor. Jalapeños furnish the heat, as in the Mexican classic. Sandy Szwarc uses this salsa specifically with grilled swordfish but acknowledges that it goes well with other grilled fish or meats, especially pork. Any left over can accompany brie cheese stuffed into tortillas to make exotic quesadillas.

Papaya Salsa

- 1 large (about 1 lb.) firm-ripe papaya, peeled, halved, seeded, and cut into ¼-inch dice
- ¼ cup chopped fresh cilantro (coriander)
- 3 green onions, ends trimmed, chopped
- 1 fresh jalapeño chili, stemmed, seeded, and minced
- 2 tablespoons lime juice
  Salt

In a bowl, gently mix together the diced papaya, cilantro, green onions, chili, and lime juice. Season salsa to taste with salt. Serve, or cover and chill up to a day. Makes about 2 cups.

PER ¼ CUP: 18 calories, 0.4 g protein, 4.6 g carbohydrates, 0.1 g fat (0 g saturated), 0 mg cholesterol, 2.9 mg sodium

Sandy Szwarc

NANCY CUTRIGHT'S *Chicken & Broccoli takes its inspiration and basic technique from the Chinese art of stir-frying, but with one difference. The ancient Chinese tradition, growing out of limited supplies of animal protein, often uses meat sparingly as a seasoning element in a complex dish to be served with many other dishes. Here, the protein-rich Western tradition makes chicken the main ingredient, enhanced by other elements—a principal one is a plentiful amount of broccoli. This, with rice, is a hearty one-dish meal.*

Chicken & Broccoli

- ¼ cup slivered almonds
- 6 to 8 boned and skinned chicken breast halves (1¼ to 1½ lb. total)
- 3 tablespoons reduced-sodium soy sauce
- 1 tablespoon Oriental sesame oil
- 2 teaspoons liquid hot pepper seasoning
- 4 cups broccoli flowerets
- ¼ cup thinly sliced green onions, including tops
- ½ cup thinly sliced celery
- 1 medium-size (5 to 6 oz.) red or green bell pepper, stemmed, seeded, and diced
- ½ cup sliced, peeled fresh or canned water chestnuts
- 1 tablespoon salad oil
  Cooking sauce (recipe follows)
  Hot cooked rice

Spread almonds in a shallow pan (such as a 9-in. pie pan). Bake in a 350° oven until golden brown, 3 to 5 minutes; shake occasionally. Set aside.

Cut chicken into bite-size pieces. In a bowl, stir together soy sauce, sesame oil, and hot pepper seasoning; add chicken.

Combine broccoli, onions, celery, bell pepper, and water chestnuts.

Place a 12-inch frying pan or wok over high heat. When pan is hot, add salad oil. Add chicken, about ½ at a time; stir-fry until chicken is no longer pink in center (cut to test), 3 to 4 minutes. With a slotted spoon, transfer the meat to another bowl.

To pan, add any liquid left from seasoning chicken, vegetables, and 2 tablespoons water. Stir and cook until broccoli is just tender to bite, about 3 minutes; add 1 to 2 more tablespoons water if needed to keep vegetables steaming. Add cooking sauce and chicken (with any juices). Stir until mixture boils. Serve on rice and sprinkle portions with the toasted almonds. Makes 6 to 8 servings.

PER SERVING: 188 calories, 20 g protein, 11 g carbohydrates, 6.8 g fat (0.9 g saturated), 41 mg cholesterol, 483 mg sodium

Cooking sauce. Stir together 1 teaspoon **sugar,** 4 teaspoons **cornstarch,** 2 teaspoons minced **fresh ginger,** 2 tablespoons *each* **reduced-sodium soy sauce** and **dry sherry,** and ⅔ cup **regular-strength chicken broth.**

Nancy Cutright

San Jose, Calif.

September Menus

SEPTEMBER AND SCHOOL *mark the return to more rigid schedules. But, as usual, summer makes a heated protest to its passing and spurs a flood of prime-value produce. No-fuss meals, cool foods, and freshly harvested ingredients make sensible menu companions.*

Make-ahead steps figure significantly in the patio dinner, the chilled main-dish soup, and the salmon supper.

PATIO BARBECUE

Mesquite-grilled Stuffed London Broil & New Potatoes
Mixed Tomato Salad with Arugula & Sage
Steam Beer　Sparkling Water
Apple Pie

As potatoes simmer prior to grilling, slit a pocket in the steak and fill with seasonings. While these foods cook on the barbecue, finish the salad. Or take advantage of the many make-ahead steps.

To follow old-fashioned steak, potatoes, and tomatoes, what could be more fitting than apple pie?

MESQUITE-GRILLED STUFFED LONDON BROIL & NEW POTATOES

- 1 piece (2½ to 2¾ lb.) first-cut top round beef (sometimes called London broil), about 2 inches thick
- ¼ cup minced parsley
- 3 cloves garlic, minced
- 2 tablespoons grated lemon peel
  About ½ cup mesquite, apple, or hickory wood chips
- 3 to 3½ pounds small (about 1½-inch diameter) red thin-skinned potatoes, scrubbed
- ½ cup balsamic or red wine vinegar
- 3 tablespoons Dijon mustard
- 1 tablespoon salad oil

With a long, sharp knife, cut a horizontal pocket about ¾ of the way through meat on a long side. Combine parsley, garlic, and lemon peel; spread mixture evenly in meat pocket. If assembling ahead, wrap airtight and chill up to 6 hours.

Herb-stuffed London broil and small red thin-skinned potatoes share space on the barbecue. Peak-season red and yellow tomatoes make the salad.

Pour enough warm water over wood chips to make them float; let soak at least 15 minutes.

In a 5- to 6-quart pan, combine potatoes and 3 quarts water. Cover, bring to a boil over high heat, and then simmer until potatoes are just barely tender when pierced, about 20 minutes. You can keep potatoes warm in water, off the heat, up to 45 minutes. Drain potatoes.

Stir together vinegar, mustard, and oil. Add half the vinegar mixture to potatoes in pan; mix well. Put potatoes in a grilling basket or thread on long (at least 12-in.) metal skewers; use a fork to guide hot potatoes. Push a second skewer through potatoes, parallel to and about ½ inch from the first, to keep potatoes from spinning.

Drain wood chips; scatter them over a solid bed of medium-hot coals (you can hold your hand at grill level only 3 to 4 seconds). Place a lightly greased grill 4 to 6 inches above coals. Lay meat on grill. Turn steak as needed to brown evenly, and cook until a thermometer inserted into thickest part registers 135° for rare (or meat is still red in center—cut to test), 12 to 15 minutes per side.

After meat has cooked 10 minutes, lay potatoes on grill; turn and baste often with remaining vinegar mixture

THE DETAILS

Smoking chips. *Soaked mesquite, hickory, or apple wood chips smolder on coals for flavor.*

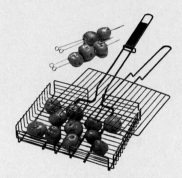

Grill control. *Hinged basket or double skewers control small potatoes on barbecue.*

Functional decor. *Citronella candles cast soft light, discourage flying nighttime bugs.*

Ripe tomatoes. *Keep tomatoes at room temperature to ripen; chilling halts process.*

---

until potatoes are browned and tender when pierced, about 20 minutes. Put meat on a platter; push potatoes from skewers onto platter. Slice meat through filling. Makes 6 to 8 servings.

PER SERVING: 382 calories, 34 g protein, 32 g carbohydrates, 12 g fat (3.9 g saturated), 87 mg cholesterol, 188 mg sodium

MIXED TOMATO SALAD WITH ARUGULA & SAGE

    3 to 3½ pounds firm-ripe tomatoes,
      equal parts red and yellow, or all
      red, rinsed and cored
    ½ pound *each* red and yellow cherry
      tomatoes, stemmed and rinsed
    ¼ pound arugula or watercress,
      rinsed and crisped
    2 tablespoons minced fresh or
      2 teaspoons dried rubbed sage
      leaves
    ⅓ cup balsamic or sherry vinegar
    2 tablespoons extra-virgin olive oil
      or salad oil
      Fresh sage sprigs
      Salt

Cut large tomatoes into ¼-inch-thick slices onto a large platter. Arrange cherry tomatoes and arugula on slices; sprinkle with minced sage. Mix vinegar and oil; pour over salad. Garnish with sage sprigs. Season to taste with salt. Makes 6 to 8 servings.

PER SERVING: 79 calories, 2 g protein, 11 g carbohydrates, 4.2 g fat (0.6 g saturated), 0 mg cholesterol, 20 mg sodium

---

LUNCH FOR A HOT AFTERNOON

Curried Corn & Shrimp Soup
Mixed Green Salad
Giant Breadsticks
Sparkling Cider   Gewürztraminer
Sliced Nectarines
Cinnamon Cream
Gingersnaps

Start the soup several hours ahead, or the day before; it takes only a few minutes to make but needs time to chill.

For a quick salad, purchase ready-to-use mixed greens, such as mesclun, and season the tender leaves with a dressing of oil and lemon juice.

Corn kernels, tiny shrimp, and bell pepper strips swim in lean, refreshingly cool soup.

As a whimsical touch, buy extra-long breadsticks, often sold at Italian bakeries and specialty food shops. If the long breadsticks are unavailable, regular breadsticks work as well.

Allow 1 to 2 ripe nectarines for a dessert serving; offer with cinnamon-flavored whipped cream, an indulgence you can afford with the low-fat soup. Buy gingersnaps or bake your favorite ginger-flavor cookies.

CURRIED CORN & SHRIMP SOUP

    2 cups regular-strength chicken
      broth
    2 medium-size (about 1 lb. total)
      tart apples, peeled, cored, and
      chopped
    1 large (about 10 oz.) onion,
      chopped
    ½ teaspoon curry powder
    1 large (about ⅔ lb.) red bell
      pepper, stemmed and seeded
    4 cups cold buttermilk
    ¼ cup lime juice
    1½ cups cooked corn kernels
    ½ cup minced fresh cilantro
      (coriander)
    ⅓ pound tiny cooked shrimp
      Cilantro sprigs (optional)

(Continued on next page)

In a 4- to 5-quart pan over high heat, combine broth, apples, onion, and curry. Cover, bring to a boil, and simmer until apples mash easily, about 30 minutes. Let cool, then cover and chill until cold, at least 3 hours or up to a day. Smoothly purée mixture in a blender or food processor.

Cut a few thin slivers from bell pepper and set aside; dice remaining pepper. Put diced pepper in a tureen with apple purée, buttermilk, lime juice, 1¼ cups corn, and minced cilantro. If making ahead, cover and chill soup, pepper strips, and extra corn up to a day.

Ladle soup into bowls and top with equal amounts of shrimp, remaining corn, bell pepper strips, and cilantro sprigs. Makes 6 servings.

PER SERVING: 213 calories, 14 g protein, 36 g carbohydrates, 3.1 g fat (1.2 g saturated), 55 mg cholesterol, 257 mg sodium

CINNAMON CREAM

½ cup whipping cream
2 tablespoons powdered sugar
½ teaspoon ground cinnamon
¼ teaspoon vanilla

In a bowl, whip cream, sugar, cinnamon, and vanilla until soft peaks form. If making ahead, cover and chill up to 2 hours; whisk to fluff before serving. Makes about 1 cup, 4 to 6 servings.

PER TABLESPOON: 26 calories, 0.2 g protein, 1.2 g carbohydrates, 2.3 g fat (1.4 g saturated), 8.3 mg cholesterol, 2.5 mg sodium

---

COOL SALMON SUPPER

**Poached Salmon with
Blackberry Cream
Tender-crisp Carrots & Peas
Crusty Rolls
Dry Chenin Blanc
Frozen Vanilla Yogurt**

Serve chilled poached salmon steak, tender-crisp carrots, and crunchy snap peas for supper on a warm evening. This cool meal can be completed the day before.

POACHED SALMON WITH BLACKBERRY CREAM

½ cup dry white wine
3 tablespoons lemon juice
2 dried bay leaves
1 tablespoon peppercorns
4 salmon steaks (each about ¼ lb. and 1 in. thick)
1½ cups blackberries, rinsed and drained (or unsweetened frozen blackberries)
1 cup regular-strength chicken broth
½ cup chopped fresh or 3 tablespoons crumbled dried mint
3 tablespoons raspberry vinegar or red wine vinegar
2 teaspoons sugar
3 tablespoons whipping cream
Mint sprigs (optional)

In a 5- to 6-quart pan, combine 2 quarts water, wine, lemon juice, bay leaves, and peppercorns. Cover and bring to a boil over high heat; simmer 15 minutes. Add salmon, cover, and remove from heat. Let stand until salmon is still moist-looking but opaque in thickest part (cut to test), about 8 minutes. Do not disturb until it is time to test; if not done, cover and let stand until it tests done.

Drain salmon well. Set on a platter, wrap airtight, and chill until cool or cold, at least 1 hour or up to a day.

In a 1- to 1½-quart pan, combine 1 cup berries, broth, chopped mint, vinegar, and sugar. Bring to a boil over high heat. Cover and simmer until berries fall apart, about 5 minutes; stir often. Press through a fine strainer into a bowl; discard residue. Rinse pan and return sauce to it. Boil on high heat, stirring often, until reduced to about ½ cup. Stir in cream. Let cool, then cover and chill until cold, about 1 hour or up to a day. Cover and chill (or keep frozen) remaining berries.

Arrange salmon on plates. Spoon sauce over portions; garnish with reserved berries (partially thawed, if frozen) and mint. Makes 4 servings.

PER SERVING: 224 calories, 21 g protein, 11 g carbohydrates, 10 g fat (3.2 g saturated), 67 mg cholesterol, 62 mg sodium

TENDER-CRISP CARROTS & PEAS

½ pound baby carrots
½ pound sugar snap peas
Raspberry vinegar and salt

Peel carrots. Remove ends and strings from peas. Rinse vegetables.

In a 5- to 6-quart pan over high heat, bring about 3 inches water to boiling. Add carrots; cook until barely tender when pierced, about 1 minute. Add peas; when just brighter green, in about ½ minute, drain and immerse vegetables in ice water. When cold, drain. Serve, or cover and chill up to a day. Season to taste with vinegar and salt. Makes 4 servings.

PER SERVING: 59 calories, 2.1 g protein, 13 g carbohydrates, 0.1 g fat (0 g saturated), 0 mg cholesterol, 24 mg sodium

Olive oil with crusty bread (page 200)

What's so great about
olive oil? What's behind its health claims? Is it worth
the price? This month we learn how the experts evaluate
California and imported oils and offer suggestions for
choosing your own favorite. If you find school lunches
a challenge, turn to our selection of student-tested
and approved menus, each designed to be packed the night
before and transported in a colorful, insulated container.
Other October treats include reader favorites ranging
from artichoke pesto pasta to chocolate torte and a
picnic for hungry pumpkin hunters.

School Lunches for a Week

MEET THE CHALLENGE *of back-to-school lunches with this student-tested and approved week-long plan. The featured foods can be packed the night before to travel in containers designed to keep foods at safe temperatures. (*If making these dishes ahead, refrigerate them, packed and ready to go, up to a day.) Below, we survey colorful, practical lunch containers now available; a small collection of them brings flexibility to lunch menus.*

MONDAY

Begin the week with bean dip and guacamole to scoop onto pocket bread or crunchy vegetables. Bring cold milk in a small insulated bottle. Tuck in jelly candy.

COOL BEAN DIP

¾ **cup canned pinto beans**
2 **tablespoons regular-strength chicken broth**
½ **to 1 teaspoon chili powder**
¼ **cup drained canned corn kernels**

Rinse, drain, and mash beans with broth and chili powder to taste. Stir in corn. Seal in a 1-cup plastic container.* Makes 1 serving.

PER SERVING: 183 calories (8.4 percent from fat), 11 g protein, 33 g carbohydrates, 1.7 g fat (0.2 g saturated), 0 mg cholesterol, 552 mg sodium

CRUNCHY GUACAMOLE

Children on our taste panel who liked avocado and apple liked them together, despite some pretaste doubts.

1 **small (about 5 oz.) ripe avocado, peeled and pitted**
1 **tablespoon lemon juice**
½ **cup chopped tart green apple**
   Salt and pepper

Mash avocado with lemon juice; stir in apple and add salt and pepper to taste. Seal in a 1-cup plastic container.* Makes 1 serving.

PER SERVING: 214 calories (67 percent from fat), 2.3 g protein, 20 g carbohydrates, 16 g fat (2.6 g saturated), 0 mg cholesterol, 14 mg sodium

POCKET BREAD CHIPS OR VEGETABLE DIPPERS

Cut each **pocket bread round** into 6 wedges. Lay in a single layer in a pan that is just big enough to hold all the pieces. Bake in a 350° oven until crisp and toasted, about 10 minutes. Let cool. Pack each serving airtight in a plastic bag up to a day; freeze to store longer.

For vegetable dippers, cut at least 6 to 8 slices (per person) of rinsed and drained **jicama,** cucumber, celery, or carrots. Pack each portion airtight in a plastic bag.*

TUESDAY

Pack this lunch in an insulated lunch box to keep the roll-up ingredients and juice cool. Wrap the ham slices around vegetables, cheese, or breadsticks; or just munch as you like, while sipping juice from a single-serving package.

Bright, Durable Lunch Carriers

SNAPPY STYLES AND cool colors turn lunch carriers into a fashion statement, sort of. And because different carriers work well for different kinds of foods, you might want more than one bag or box.

Boxes and bags for lunch come insulated and nonbreakable in bright colors.

Insulated bags or boxes come as soft fabric packs or rigid plastic containers; they'll keep chilled foods cool enough to prevent any likelihood of food spoilage between morning departure and lunch (particularly if the lunch box has been chilled overnight, too).

Small units of leakproof frozen coolant can be tucked in to keep foods cooler, also.

Rigid plastic boxes will protect foods if lunch is carried with books in a backpack; some boxes have compartments to keep hard foods from squishing soft fruits and foods.

The old standby, the brown paper bag, is now duplicated in bright washable fabrics.

Insulated bottles and cups, and bowls and boxes with tightly sealing lids, all of break-resistant plastic, are available in ½- to 2-cup sizes.

MONDAY

**Cool Bean Dip   Crunchy Guacamole
Pocket Bread Chips
Milk   Fruit Jelly Candy**

TUESDAY

**Ham Rolls with String Cheese, Carrots,
Celery   Breadsticks
Fruit Juice   Brownie**

HAM ROLLS WITH STRING CHEESE, CARROTS, CELERY & BREADSTICKS

- 3 thin slices (about 2 oz. total) cooked ham
- 1 piece (about 1 oz.) string cheese
- 4 baby carrots, scrubbed and ends trimmed
- 4 pieces celery, each about 3 inches long, rinsed and drained
- 3 or 4 breadsticks, 6 to 8 inches long

Cut ham slices in half. In a shallow 2-cup plastic container, layer ham, cheese, carrots, and celery; put on tight-fitting lid.* Seal breadsticks in a plastic bag up to a day ahead. At lunchtime, roll ham around other foods to eat. Makes 1 serving.

PER SERVING: 292 calories (24 percent from fat), 23 g protein, 28 g carbohydrates, 7.8 g fat (1.9 g saturated), 49 mg cholesterol, 1,250 mg sodium

WEDNESDAY

A brown paper bag, or one made of pretty, bright paper or fabric, works well for this lunch. The dried fruit sandwiches, grapes, and honey for dipping don't need to be chilled. But they will be kept cool by the yogurt shake that leaves home frozen. By noon, the shake is thawed enough to drink but still frosty.

DRIED FRUIT & PEANUT BUTTER SANDWICHES

- 8 moist-pack dried apple slices
- 8 dried apricot halves
- 4 teaspoons smooth or chunk peanut butter

On each of half the apple slices and apricot halves, put ½ teaspoon peanut butter. Press a matching fruit piece firmly onto peanut butter. Seal in a 1-cup plastic container.* Makes 1 serving.

PER SERVING: 263 calories (38 percent from fat), 7.3 g protein, 39 g carbohydrates, 11 g fat (1.8 g saturated), 0 mg cholesterol, 128 mg sodium

(Continued on next page)

WEDNESDAY

Dried Fruit & Peanut Butter Sandwiches
Frosty Yogurt Shake
Grapes   Honey

THURSDAY

Chef's Salad   Snack Croutons
Red Apple   Milk
Peanut Butter Cookie

Frosty Yogurt Shake

1 container (8 oz.) nonfat strawberry-flavor yogurt
1 cup cranberry juice cocktail

Scoop fruit-flavor yogurt into a 1-pint plastic bottle with tight-fitting lid (with pop-up straw, if desired); add cranberry juice cocktail. Seal shut with lid. Freeze at least 4 hours or up to 1 month.

Wrap bottle in paper napkin (to absorb moisture that forms as shake thaws) and pack in lunch. Serve within 4 to 5 hours, when thawed but still cold; shake to mix, then drink. Makes 1 serving.

PER SERVING: 244 calories (1.1 percent from fat), 9 g protein, 53 g carbohydrates, 0.3 g fat (0 g saturated), 4 mg cholesterol, 135 mg sodium

Other shake combinations. Guava-papaya flavor nonfat yogurt with orange juice; peach-flavor nonfat yogurt with apple juice.

Thursday

Be sure to include a plastic fork so you can mix and eat the big salad. To keep salad cool, set the container on a small frozen coolant pouch in your lunch box, or use an insulated lunch box. Buy milk at school, or bring in an insulated bottle.

Chef's Salad

1 cup rinsed, crisped bite-size pieces iceberg or romaine lettuce
3 or 4 thin cucumber slices
3 or 4 cherry tomatoes, rinsed, drained, and stemmed
3 or 4 sugar snap peas, ends and strings removed, rinsed and drained (optional)
About 1 ounce Swiss cheese, cut into thin sticks
About 1½ ounces sliced cooked turkey (or turkey sandwich slices), slivered
About 2 tablespoons prepared salad dressing (choose a favorite)
Snack croutons (recipe follows)

FRIDAY

**Kid's Choice—French Bread Pizza
Orange Wedges   Fruit Soda
Chocolate Wafer Cookies**

FRIDAY

The last day of the week deserves something special, like pizza on a crusty roll that's good cold. You can make one-serving portions in a toaster oven.

At home, cut orange into wedges and pack them snugly in a small plastic bag, or pack the whole fruit and peel it when ready to eat. Crisp chocolate wafers are good with the fruit.

KID'S CHOICE—
FRENCH BREAD PIZZA

> 1 **crusty roll, about 6 inches long**
> 3 **tablespoons prepared pizza sauce**
> **About ½ cup shredded mozzarella cheese**
> **About ¼ cup thinly sliced pepperoni**
> 6 **thin slices yellow or red bell pepper**

Cut roll in half horizontally. Set in an 8- to 10-inch-wide pan. Bake in a 400° oven until toasted, about 6 minutes. Spread cut sides with pizza sauce, then top with mozzarella cheese, pepperoni, and bell pepper.

Bake until cheese melts enough for toppings to stick securely to the cheese. Let cool. Package airtight in a plastic bag or foil.* Makes 1 serving.

PER SERVING: 484 calories (45 percent from fat), 21 g protein, 45 g carbohydrates, 24 g fat (10 g saturated), 54 mg cholesterol, 1,326 mg sodium

In a 2-cup plastic container with a tight-fitting lid, layer lettuce, cucumber, tomatoes, snap peas, cheese, and turkey; put on lid.*

Put dressing in another, smaller plastic container with tight-fitting lid.* Seal croutons in a small plastic bag. To eat, pour dressing over salad. Munch croutons with salad. Makes 1 serving.

PER SERVING WITHOUT CROUTONS: 319 calories (56 percent from fat), 22 g protein, 13 g carbohydrates, 20 g fat (7.2 g saturated), 66 mg cholesterol, 324 mg sodium

Snack croutons. Cut 1 slender, small (about ¼-lb.) **baguette** or crusty roll into ½-inch-thick rounds. In a plastic bag, mix 2 tablespoons **olive** or salad **oil,** ½ teaspoon **garlic salt,** and 1 teaspoon *each* **dried basil leaves** and **dried oregano leaves.** Add bread slices; shake to coat evenly with seasonings.

Arrange slices in a single layer in a 10- by 15-inch pan. Bake in a 350° oven until tops are golden, 10 minutes; turn slices over and bake until golden on top, 5 to 6 minutes more. Let cool; wrap airtight and store up to 1 week. Freeze croutons to store longer. Makes 4 servings.

PER SERVING: 145 calories (47 percent from fat), 2.7 g protein, 16 g carbohydrates, 7.6 g fat (1.1 g saturated), 0.9 mg cholesterol, 305 mg sodium

Second graders rate box lunches for this story.

What's So Great about Olive Oil?

"**O**F ALL THE GIFTS of heaven to man, it is ... most precious," wrote Thomas Jefferson of the olive during a 1787 tour of southern France and northern Italy. Since before written history, man has husbanded the olive tree for its fruit and oil—or fat—which along with carbohydrates and protein is one of our three food essentials. In many lands in many times, olives were the basic source of oil in volume.

Olives came to California in 1769 with the Franciscan fathers, who planted the trees as they established the missions. These trees produced seed that gave us the Mission variety, which is still grown today.

For well over a century, olives continued to be produced for oil; by 1900 some 400 commercial olive mills were at work in California. Then inexpensive edible oils from corn, cottonseed, and other plants came on the scene and began to push olive oil into the background.

But in the last few years, California olive oil has been reappearing. It's highly

Proliferation of olive oils, from $3 to 10 times more for the same amount, is standard in markets.

touted along with imported oil for its nutritional and health benefits; it has been popularized by the current interest in Italian and other Mediterranean cuisines; and, at a time when locally produced foods are prized, excellent-quality (and costly) olive oil by California makers is much sought after and holding its own alongside pricey imported oils.

In a well-stocked supermarket or fancy food store, you're likely to be able to choose from a dozen or more California olive oils.

WHAT'S BEHIND THE HEALTH CLAIMS?

In the 1960s at the University of Minnesota, Ancel Keys studied typical diets of people in seven countries, seeking clues to explain the diverse rates of coronary heart disease.

One of the principal differences he pinpointed was the type of fat consumed. In Italy and Greece, where coronary heart problems were much less common than they were in the United States, the total amount of fat eaten was about the same as it was in this country, but the fat consumed there was primarily monounsaturated olive oil.

At that time, the simplistic response in the United States was to switch from saturated animal fat to unsaturated vegetable ones. Polyunsaturated vegetable oils, already established in American households, seemed the ideal alternative.

But more recent research indicates that monounsaturated fats are better than polyunsaturates at transporting cholesterol out of the body.

THE PRESSURE IS ON

During the time that interest in olive oil was on the wane, several California families quietly carried on their oil-making traditions—Nick Sciabica & Sons of Modesto and Jerry Padula in Porterville for more than half a century, and Marino Garbis of Orland Olive Oil Company in Orland for more than three decades.

The Sciabicas and Padula both label and sell some of their own oil. All three pressers custom-produce oils for firms like Corti Brothers Market in Sacramento, Kimberley Wine Vinegar Works, Neiman Marcus, Oakville Grocery Co., Trader Joe's, and Williams-Sonoma.

The pressers also make oil from fruit grown and harvested by others, such as Lila Jaeger's Napa Valley extra-virgin olive oil and Oro Fino Lucque (an olive variety) from Wente Bros., in Livermore.

For limited production, Fritz Maytag, who grows olives, and Tra Vigne restaurant (Olio Santo) in St. Helena both have acquired small presses.

WHAT GIVES OIL ITS FLAVOR?

In California, olives grow primarily in the Sacramento and San Joaquin valleys. Varieties used for oil in Europe are being test-grown in Napa and Sonoma counties.

Each variety has its own subtle flavor and percentage of oil. Fleshy olives favored for eating, like Manzanillo and Sevillano, have lower oil content than the small Mission.

An olive oil's character and quality are determined by the variety of fruit (and, in the minds of many experts, where it's grown), and how the fruit is cultivated, harvested, handled (olives are fragile), and pressed.

Olives for oil can be harvested over several months. Mature green fruit picked in early fall yields oil that is typically green with a slightly sharp to very sharp raw flavor often described as acrid, beany, bell pepperish, grassy, herbaceous, leafy, or woodsy.

Riper fruit (mottled purple-green to black-purple color) is harvested from early winter to early spring, depending on variety. It yields more oil, proportionately, than greener olives. The oil is usually golden in color, fruitier, smoother, and more velvety in flavor and mouth feel than early-harvest oils.

Olive oil made exclusively from a specific harvest period may have this information on the label. Producers often make oil from several harvests through a season, then blend them to achieve a spectrum of flavors. To many, the softening effect of late-harvest oils benefits early-harvest oils, and late-harvest oils are enlivened by the vigor of early oils.

(Continued on page 202)

Olive oil replaces butter as a partner for bread at Il Fornaio and other contemporary restaurants.

HOW IS OLIVE OIL MADE?

Olives are crushed with their pits to make a thick paste called mash, which is either pressed or centrifuged to separate the oil. Traveling with the oil are solids and some watery liquid. The pressed mixture stands until the oil floats to the top and is removed. Centrifuged oil is centrifuged a second time. This oil is then aged three to six months to mellow a natural bitterness that comes from oleuropein phenolic (a glucoside that produces a bitter taste similar to that found in raw artichokes and walnuts).

HOW EXTRA IS EXTRA?

Legal definitions for olive oil grades come from the International Olive Oil Council in Madrid. There are no regulatory agencies, however, so the definitions are often compromised.

Oil is evaluated by two subjective measures, smell and taste, and by the scientific measure of free oleic acids (the predominant fatty acid in olive oil). Grade differences are based on the latter. When fatty acids break away from the oil structure (which happens, for example, if water gets in the oil) they have an unpleasant taste.

If olive oil has 1 percent or less free oleic acids, it is *extra virgin*—the top grade. If it has more than 1 but no more than 3.3 percent of these acids, it's *virgin* olive oil. *Pure* olive oil is a blend, with no more than 3.3 percent acidity. Oils with more than 3.3 percent acidity are *refined* with a process that uses heat

Almost colorless *"light" pure imported olive oil has body and neutral taste of vegetable oil.*

Yellow-gold *extra-virgin oil, made in Napa Valley from ripe, late-harvest fruit, has a subtle olive taste that's delicate, fresh, fruity.*

Olive Oil	Color	Aroma	Flavor	Aftertaste
Wesson pure (imported)	Clear	Neutral	Neutral	Neutral
Bertolli pure, X, L (Italy)	Pale yellow	Neutral	Neutral	Neutral
James Plagniol pure (France)	Yellow	L fruity-grassy	L fruity-grassy	Mild pepper
Bertolli Classico pure (Italy)	Golden yellow	L fruity	L fruity-grassy	Neutral
Lila Jaeger's X (Calif.)	Golden yellow	L fruity-grassy	M fruity–L grassy	Biting
Nuñez de Prado X (Spain)	Gold	L fruity-herbal	M fruity-grassy	Biting
Sciabica's Sevillano X (Calif.)	Gold	M fruity-grassy	M fruity–L grassy	Pepper
Peloponnese X (Greece)	Deep gold	M fruity-grassy	L fruity-herbal	Biting
Colavita X (Italy)	Deep gold	L fruity-grassy	L fruity-grassy	Biting

Note: X = extra virgin; L = light; M = medium.

Deep gold *extra-virgin Sevillano oil (late harvest or blend, Central Valley) has a mellow olive taste.*

Green-gold *extra-virgin Mission oil balances herbal flavor of early-harvest with smoother late-harvest oil.*

Pale gold-green *extra-virgin oil from southern Italy has faint olive flavor that indicates blending—or addition of refined olive oil.*

Green *extra-virgin Mission oil has hallmarks of early-harvest oil: deep color, grassy flavor, peppery aftertaste.*

Olive Oil	Color	Aroma	Flavor	Aftertaste
Roselle X (Italy)	Deep gold	L fruity-grassy	L fruity-grassy	Pungent
Wente Bros. Oro Fino Lucque X (Calif.)	Deep gold	L fruity-grassy	M fruity	Mild pepper
Star X (Italy)	Green-gold	M fruity-grassy	M fruity-herbal	Pungent
Sciabica's Mission X (Calif.)	Green-gold	L fruity-herbal	L fruity-grassy	Biting
Badia a Coltibuono X (Italy)	L green	M fruity-grassy	L fruity-herbal	Biting
Williams-Sonoma X (Calif.)	L green	M fruity-grassy	M fruity-grassy	Biting
Olio Santo X (Calif.)	L green	L fruity-grassy	M fruity-grassy	Pungent
Neiman Marcus X (Calif.)	L green	M fruity-herbal	M fruity-grassy	Pungent
Kuleto X (Calif.)	Green	M fruity-herbal	M fruity-herbal	Pungent

and makes them neutral in color, flavor, and aroma. To give such oils more personality, they are blended with extra-virgin or virgin oil and sold as pure olive oil or, more frequently, as just olive oil.

Because extra-virgin oil delivers the best flavors, it commands the best price. There is much unregulated temptation internationally to dilute extra-virgin with refined oils, labeling the results extra virgin. Of California olive oils, only extra virgin is presently sold at retail.

What about olive oils with *light* on the label? They have the same number of calories as any olive oil, but they are refined specifically to make them taste like mild vegetable oils.

WHICH OLIVE OIL TO BUY?

As in selecting wine, only your own preferences really count. The chart on pages 202 and 203 will help you choose. Of our taste panelists, about half were food professionals, half novices; their reactions were remarkably similar, though preferences differed.

For the clearest impression, dip a chunk of bread into the oil and taste. For seasoning salads, vegetables, sauces, and breads, any olive oil with a taste you like is the obvious choice.

For cooking, pure or refined olive oil works well; using extra-virgin oil is extravagant, as heat lessens its flavor.

Good-quality olive oil is quite stable compared with polyunsaturated oils. Kept airtight in a cool, dark place, unopened olive oil stays fresh-tasting up to two years; refrigerated, it turns cloudy and solidifies. At room temperature, the oil clears, but frequent chilling and warming start a breakdown that leads rapidly to rancidity.

Once opened, olive oil keeps longer than polyunsaturated oils because it doesn't bind as easily with oxygen atoms, which cause rancidity. Tightly close oil for storage and keep in a cool, dark place; it should stay fresh for six months to a year. Don't add new oil to a used oil container or to a clean, damp one. Old oil and water both speed deterioration.

Where olives were grown. On imported oils, may identify where oil was bottled.

Cream of the crop, with 1 percent acidity or less. Next is virgin, then pure (a blend of refined and virgin oils), then refined olive oil.

Redundant if extra-virgin or virgin olive oil, which are never refined.

Again, redundant if extra-virgin or virgin olive oil.

To distinguish from refined olive oil, which is treated with heat and chemicals. Only pomace oil (pomace is residue of pressed olives) is chemically extracted.

CALIFORNIA
First Cold Pressing
NO CHOLESTEROL

EXTRA VIRGIN
Olive Oil
Mission Olives
Early Harvest

Unrefined
All Natural - No Preservatives

Less than 1% acidity

No heat or chemicals
used to extract oil

Store away from heat and light

Confusing, as no heat is used when crushed olives are pressed (or centrifuged) for oil. Heat is used only if oil is refined.

Unnecessary hype. Like all fruits and vegetables, olives and their oil have no cholesterol.

Variety of olives used. In California, Manzanillo or Sevillano are often used for oil.

Mature green olives picked in fall make green early-harvest oils. Fruit can be picked anytime until fully ripe and almost black. Late-harvest oils are golden.

Amount of free oleic acids in olive oil. International standard for extra-virgin olive oil is 1 percent or less.

Good advice. Both hasten deterioration (rancidity).

More October Recipes

OTHER OCTOBER ARTICLES *offer an intriguing Mexican sweet, a salmon and spinach dinner pie, and homemade seasoning salts using dried chilies or peppercorns.*

POACHED APRICOTS WITH CHONGOS

An intriguing Mexican sweet called chongos, widely available canned in Latin markets, is the delicious secret of this quick dessert. Use the sweet, caramel-flavored chongo liquid to plump tart dried apricots, then serve with chongos.

Chongos, or chongos zamoranos (named for the city where they originated), are essentially simple, tender lumps of cheese much like cottage cheese.

- 1 **cup dried apricots**
- 1 **can (about 2 lb.) chongos**

Combine apricots and liquid drained from chongos in a 2- to 3-quart pan. Bring to a boil on high heat; simmer, stirring often, until apricots are plump, 10 to 15 minutes. Use warm or cool. Spoon chongos, apricots, and syrup into bowls. Makes 6 to 8 servings.

ESTIMATED PER SERVING: 460 calories (16 percent from fat), 8.6 g protein, 91 g carbohydrates, 8.2 g fat (5.1 g saturated), 34 mg cholesterol, 222 mg sodium

SALMON & SPINACH PIE

Good-looking and easy to make, this dinner pie is delicious hot, at room temperature, or chilled. If you make it a day ahead, cover when cool, then chill.

- 2 **packages (10-oz. size) frozen chopped spinach, thawed**
- 1 **large egg**
- 2 **cups cooked rice**
- 2 **teaspoons dried tarragon leaves**
- ¼ **teaspoon ground nutmeg**
- ¾ **teaspoon pepper**
- 1⅓ **pounds boned and skinned salmon fillets, cut ½ inch thick**
  No-fat duxelles (recipe follows)
- 1 **sheet (9 in. square, about 8 oz.) frozen puff pastry, barely thawed**
  Salt, sour cream, and lemon wedges

Squeeze liquid from spinach. In a bowl, beat egg to blend; save 1 tablespoon. Mix remaining egg with spinach, rice, tarragon, nutmeg, and pepper; pat half into an oiled 9-inch-diameter shallow casserole.

Lay salmon in casserole; cover with duxelles, then top with remaining rice mixture.

On a floured board, roll pastry into an 11-inch square. Cut an 11-inch round and drape over pie. Snip rim and fold decoratively; brush pastry with egg. Top pie with cut-out pastry scraps; brush with remaining egg. Bake in a 375° oven until top is golden brown, 35 to 40 minutes. Scoop from dish. Add salt, sour cream, and lemon to taste. Makes 6 to 8 servings.

PER SERVING: 351 calories (36 percent from fat), 22 g protein, 31 g carbohydrates, 14 g fat (1 g saturated), 68 mg cholesterol, 243 mg sodium

No-fat duxelles. In a 10- to 12-inch frying pan over medium-high heat, frequently stir 3½ cups (¾ lb.) chopped **mushrooms,** ¼ cup minced **shallots,** and ¼ teaspoon **ground nutmeg** until vegetable juices evaporate and mixture browns and sticks, 10 to 12 minutes. Add ¼ cup **dry white wine;** stir often until vegetables brown, about 3 minutes. Remove from heat. Stir in ⅓ cup more dry white wine to loosen browned bits. Use warm or cool.

CHILI PEPPER SALTS

Tingling, hot, or mellow, these seasoned salts are playful on the palate and make intriguing flavorings for simple foods. You start with dried chilies with a heat level you like, or use unrelated peppers—pink peppercorns, Sichuan peppercorns, or ground sansho pepper.

Pink peppercorns (with fancy foods in supermarkets) add more aroma than heat; perfumed Sichuan peppercorns and sansho pepper (sold in Asian markets) salts seem to sparkle in your mouth.

For starters, sprinkle chili pepper salts onto cooked meats, poultry, fish, or shellfish; also offer lime wedges to squeeze onto foods. Try rubbing salts liberally onto roasts before cooking. Use salts to season salads of greens, grains, or shellfish. Or use to season boiled corn, raw jicama sticks, citrus fruits, pineapple, and melons such as honeydew or cantaloupe.

Pink salmon, layered with cooked rice and spinach, fills this savory pie.

Ground chilies or pepper (choices follow)
1 **tablespoon salt**

Mix chilies or pepper with salt. Put in a shaker or small dish. Use as suggested, preceding. Mixture keeps indefinitely; store tightly covered. Makes 3 tablespoons.

PER ¼ TEASPOON: 3.8 calories (47 percent from fat), 0.1 g protein, 0.7 g carbohydrates, 0.2 g fat (0 g saturated), 0 mg cholesterol, 183 mg sodium

Ground chilies. For mild salt, use dried California, New Mexico, ancho, or pasilla chilies. For hot salt, use dried chipotle or small red chilies.

Wipe dust from 1½ ounces **dried chilies** (choices above) with a damp towel. Place chilies in a 10- by 15-inch pan. Bake in a 300° oven until chilies smell toasted and are flexible, 2 to 4 minutes. Discard stems, seeds, and membrane. Chop chilies; finely grind in a blender. Makes about 2 tablespoons.

Pepper. In a blender, finely grind 3 tablespoons dried pink or Sichuan **peppercorns;** or use 2 tablespoons sansho pepper.

ARTICHOKE PESTO PASTA

½ cup pine nuts
1 can (10 oz.) artichoke hearts in water, drained; or 1½ cups cooked edible-parts artichokes
½ cup grated parmesan cheese
1 small package (3 oz.) cream cheese
¼ cup diced white onion
1 tablespoon Dijon mustard
1 clove garlic, minced or pressed
⅛ teaspoon ground nutmeg
About 1 cup regular-strength chicken broth
¾ pound dried fettuccine
¼ cup minced parsley
¼ teaspoon crushed dried hot red chilies

In an 8- to 10-inch frying pan, stir pine nuts over medium heat until golden, 5 to 7 minutes. Pour into a small bowl.

Season hot cooked pasta with artichoke pesto and pine nuts.

In a food processor or blender, purée artichokes, parmesan, cream cheese, onion, mustard, garlic, nutmeg, and ½ cup broth (¾ cup with fresh artichokes).

Bring about 4 quarts water to a boil in a 6- to 8-quart covered pan on high heat. Add pasta; cook, uncovered, just until tender to bite, about 8 minutes. Drain well. Return to pan over medium heat; at once add ¼ cup broth. Lift pasta with 2 forks until broth is hot, about 30 seconds. Pour pasta mixture into a warm wide bowl. Pour artichoke mixture onto pasta. Sprinkle with parsley, nuts, and chilies; lift with forks to mix. Makes 6 to 8 servings.—*Kathryn Murdock, Moss Beach, Calif.*

PER SERVING: 290 calories (37 percent from fat), 12 g protein, 36 g carbohydrates, 12 g fat (4.4 g saturated), 56 mg cholesterol, 213 mg sodium

VINEGAR BEAN SOUP

3 large (about 1½ lb. total) onions
2 dried bay leaves
1 tablespoon olive or salad oil
4 cans (15 to 17 oz. each) butter or lima beans
3½ cups or 2 cans (14½ oz. each) regular-strength beef broth
½ cup firmly packed brown sugar
6 tablespoons cider vinegar or rice vinegar
2 tablespoons dry mustard
1 teaspoon grated lemon peel
¼ cup minced parsley

Hearty sweet-and-sour soup of canned butter beans makes a quick main dish.

Chop onions. In a 5- to 6-quart pan over medium-high heat, combine onions, bay leaves, and oil; stir often until onions are limp, about 10 minutes.

Meanwhile, in a blender or food processor, smoothly purée 2 cans of beans and their liquid. Add to pan, along with remaining beans and their liquid, broth, sugar, vinegar, mustard, and lemon peel. If making ahead, cover and chill up to a day. Bring to simmering on high heat; stir often. Ladle into bowls and top with parsley. Makes 7 or 8 servings.—*B.C. Flannery, Spokane, Wash.*

PER SERVING: 263 calories (11 percent from fat), 12 g protein, 51 g carbohydrates, 3.2 g fat (0.2 g saturated), 0 mg cholesterol, 675 mg sodium

ITALIAN OVEN-FRIED POTATOES

These potatoes take little attention.

2 pounds red-skinned potatoes, scrubbed, cut into 1-inch chunks
1 to 2 tablespoons olive oil
2 tablespoons minced fresh or 2 teaspoons dried oregano leaves
2 tablespoons minced fresh or 2 teaspoons dried basil leaves
1 clove garlic, minced or pressed
⅓ cup grated parmesan cheese
Fresh oregano and basil sprigs (optional)
Salt

Cube potatoes and oven-fry. Season with herbs, garlic, and grated cheese.

In a 10- by 15-inch pan, mix potatoes with oil. Bake in a 475° oven until they are a rich brown, 35 to 45 minutes; do not disturb until potatoes begin to brown, then use a wide spatula to turn pieces over several times.

Pour potatoes into a warm bowl and sprinkle with minced oregano, minced basil, garlic, and about ⅔ of the cheese. Mix, then sprinkle with remaining cheese; garnish with herb sprigs. Season to taste with salt. Makes 4 servings.—*Mickey Strang, McKinleyville, Calif.*

PER SERVING: 249 calories (21 percent from fat), 7.3 g protein, 42 g carbohydrates, 5.9 g fat (1.7 g saturated), 5.2 mg cholesterol, 141 mg sodium

STRAWBERRY CHICKEN

- 1 small can (8 oz.) tomato sauce
- 1 cup strawberry jam
- 2 tablespoons vinegar
- 1 tablespoon chili powder
- ½ teaspoon *each* dried thyme leaves and ground ginger
- 10 to 12 skinned chicken thighs (2 to 2½ lb. total), fat discarded
- ½ cup thinly sliced green onions Salt

In a shallow 3-quart casserole, mix tomato sauce, jam, vinegar, chili powder, thyme, and ginger. Roll chicken in the sauce.

Bake, uncovered, in a 400° oven until meat is no longer pink at bone (cut to test), about 45 minutes; baste chicken occasionally. Sprinkle with onions; add salt to taste. Makes 5 or 6 servings. —*Linda Salisbury, Reno.*

PER SERVING: 357 calories (30 percent from fat), 21 g protein, 42 g carbohydrates, 12 g fat (3.4 g saturated), 72 mg cholesterol, 315 mg sodium

Chicken thighs, baked in strawberry sauce, have extra sauce for rice.

IRISH SODA BREAD

- 3 cups all-purpose flour
- ½ cup sugar
- 1 tablespoon baking powder
- 1 teaspoon baking soda
- 1½ cups currants or raisins
- 1¾ cups buttermilk
- 2 large eggs
- 3 tablespoons melted butter or margarine
- ½ teaspoon vanilla

In a large bowl, mix flour, sugar, baking powder, baking soda, and the currants. In a small bowl, beat to blend butter-

milk, eggs, 2 tablespoons butter, and vanilla. Add to flour mixture and stir until evenly moistened.

Spread in a buttered 10-inch-diameter ovenproof frying pan or cheesecake pan with removable rim; drizzle with remaining butter.

Bake in a 350° oven until bread is well browned and pulls from pan sides, about 45 minutes. Serve warm or cool. Makes 1 loaf, about 2½ pounds.—*Louise Galen, Los Angeles.*

PER OUNCE: 75 calories (16 percent from fat), 1.8 g protein, 14 g carbohydrates, 1.3 g fat (0.7 g saturated), 13 mg cholesterol, 76 mg sodium

Soda bread, studded with tiny currants, bakes in an ovenproof frying pan.

CHOCOLATE TORTE

- ½ cup corn syrup
- 4 ounces unsweetened chocolate, coarsely chopped
- 3 large eggs, separated
- ¾ cup sugar
- ½ cup (¼ lb.) butter or margarine
- ½ cup all-purpose flour
- ½ cup minced pecans
- ½ teaspoon baking powder
- ½ teaspoon ground cinnamon
- ½ cup raspberry jam
  Glaze (recipe follows)

In a 1- to 1½-quart pan over medium heat, stir syrup until hot. Add chocolate and remove from heat; stir often until chocolate is melted. Cool slightly.

In a deep bowl, whip egg whites on high speed until frothy; gradually beat in ½ cup sugar. Whip whites until they hold soft, distinct peaks.

With the unwashed beaters, in another bowl beat remaining sugar and butter

until smoothly mixed. Stir in chocolate mixture, yolks, flour, pecans, baking powder, and cinnamon; beat to blend thoroughly. Stir about ¼ of the whites into batter; gently fold in remaining whites until well mixed.

Scrape batter into a buttered and floured 9-inch-diameter cheesecake pan with removable rim; smooth batter. Bake in a 350° oven until cake is firm when lightly touched in center, about 30 minutes. Cool in pan. Remove pan rim. Spread jam on top of cake. Drizzle glaze over top and sides. Serve or, if making ahead, cover airtight up to 2 days. Makes 10 to 12 servings.—*Roxanne E. Chan, Albany, Calif.*

PER SERVING: 375 calories (48 percent from fat), 4 g protein, 50 g carbohydrates, 20 g fat (10 g saturated), 74 mg cholesterol, 144 mg sodium

Glaze. In a 1- to 1½-quart pan over medium heat, stir ¼ cup **corn syrup** until hot. Add 4 ounces chopped **semisweet chocolate;** remove at once from heat and stir until melted. Use warm.

Glossy chocolate glaze coats dense cake; top with pecans, if desired.

Chefs of the West®

Adventures with Food

THE TRIO OF SWEET onions—*Maui, Vidalia, and Walla Walla—has become a quintet with the arrival of Sweet Imperials from Southern California's Imperial Valley and Rio Grande Golds from Texas. All are bred to mature during short days and relatively cool weather. They are milder and sweeter than the long-day types and are sold primarily for immediate use. Each region claims superiority for its product, and each region is right. Frank Holder, of Rocky Ford, Colorado (a town noted more for its melons than for its onions), likes Sweet Imperials for his steak and onion sandwich, but, to be honest, any onion, slowly cooked, is sweet.*

These open-faced sandwiches are spectacular as well as delicious; the onion rings are a lovely pinky golden color, the result of gentle cooking with butter and paprika. (True onion fanciers may object to the use of steak and the other trimmings; they believe that a thick slice of onion between two slices of bread is paradise enow.)

STEAK & SWEET ONION SANDWICH

- 1 **beef flank steak, about 1½ pounds**
- 1 **cup beer**
- ½ **teaspoon freshly ground pepper**
- ¾ **cup light sour cream**
- 3 **tablespoons prepared horseradish**
- 4 **drops liquid hot pepper seasoning**
- 3 **large (about 2 lb. total) sweet onions, such as Walla Walla, Maui, or Sweet Imperial**
- 1 **tablespoon butter or margarine**
- ½ **teaspoon paprika**
- 6 **slices French bread cut about 1 inch thick**

Trim and discard fat from flank steak. Lay meat flat in a 9- by 13-inch pan. Pour beer over meat and sprinkle with pepper. Cover and chill at least 4 hours or up to a day; turn the meat over several times.

Mix sour cream, horseradish, and hot pepper seasoning. If making ahead, cover and chill up to a day.

Slice onions. Melt butter in a 10- to 12-inch frying pan over medium heat; add onions and sprinkle with paprika. Stir often until very limp and pale gold color, about 25 minutes.

Meanwhile, on fire grate in a barbecue, ignite about 50 briquets. When briquets are dotted with ash, 25 to 30 minutes, spread in a single layer. Set grill 4 to 6 inches above coals; lightly oil grill. Lift meat from marinade, drain briefly, and place on grill; reserve marinade. Turn meat as needed to brown evenly; baste with remaining marinade. Do not baste after turning meat over for the last time. For medium-rare (red-pink in center; cut to test), cook about 10 minutes. The last 2 to 3 minutes, toast bread on grill.

On a board, cut meat across the grain into thin, slanting slices. Spread bread with horseradish mixture; pile meat, then onions, equally onto slices. Makes 6 servings.

PER SERVING: 361 calories (32 percent from fat), 24 g protein, 36 g carbohydrates, 13 g fat (6.1 g saturated), 57 mg cholesterol, 299 mg sodium

Frank Holder

Rocky Ford, Colo.

"True onion fanciers believe that a thick slice of onion between two slices of bread is paradise."

CHARCOAL, SALTPETER, *and sulfur aren't remarkable individually, but combined they form an explosive mixture —gunpowder. Kimiko Bigelow's Korean-style salad works on the same principle; here beef, lettuce, and some seasonings produce a main-course salad that resembles Chinese chicken salad in the same way a Marine band resembles a string quartet.*

Salads like this are ideal for important lunches or for dinners when your appetite calls for something significant in flavor.

KOREAN-STYLE SALAD

    2 tablespoons soy sauce
    1 tablespoon oyster sauce
    1 tablespoon rice vinegar
    1 teaspoon sake (or 1 more teaspoon rice vinegar)
 1½ teaspoons sugar
    1 teaspoon Oriental sesame oil
    1 teaspoon minced or pressed garlic (optional)
    1 pound thinly sliced, fat-trimmed cooked roast beef, shredded
    1 small (1 lb.) iceberg lettuce, rinsed, crisped, and shredded
    1 cup thinly sliced celery
    2 green onions, including tops, thinly sliced
    1 large (¼ lb.) carrot, finely shredded
      Fresh cilantro (coriander) sprigs

In a bowl, stir together soy sauce, oyster sauce, vinegar, sake, sugar, sesame oil, garlic, and beef.

In a large bowl, mix lettuce, celery, green onions, and carrot.

If making ahead, cover both containers and chill up to 4 hours.

"Ingredients in Kimiko's salad work on the same principle as gunpowder."

Pour beef mixture onto vegetables, mix well, and sprinkle with cilantro sprigs. Makes 4 to 6 servings.

PER SERVING: 182 calories (31 percent from fat), 24 g protein, 7.3 g carbohydrates, 6.2 g fat (2 g saturated), 61 mg cholesterol, 532 mg sodium

Kimiko Bigelow

San Jose, Calif.

NO KAFFEEKLATSCH *is possible without some sort of coffee cake. Doughnuts, brioches, or croissants, unless they are homemade, indicate lack of preparation for the event.*

Ruth Watson has the right idea with her Walnut Coffee Roll, an overnight refrigerator yeast dough that enfolds a not-too-sweet filling of walnuts, graham cracker crumbs, and brown sugar. A bit of effort, to be sure, but the reward is three sweet rolls, not just one—her way of being prepared.

WALNUT COFFEE ROLL

    1 cup (½ lb.) butter or margarine
    ¼ cup granulated sugar
      About 4 cups all-purpose flour
    1 package active dry yeast
    1 cup warm (110°) water
    2 large eggs
    2 cups firmly packed brown sugar
    1 cup chopped walnuts
    1 cup graham cracker crumbs
    ¾ cup powdered sugar
    1 tablespoon cool water

In a large bowl, cut butter into granulated sugar and 4 cups flour with a pastry blender or 2 knives until fine crumbs.

Meanwhile, in a small bowl, sprinkle yeast over warm water; let stand until softened, about 5 minutes. Add eggs and beat to blend, then pour into flour mixture and stir until moistened. Cover airtight and chill at least 12 hours or up to a day.

In another bowl, combine brown sugar, walnuts, and graham cracker crumbs.

Divide dough into 3 equal parts. On a lightly floured board, roll 1 portion of dough into a 12-inch square. Spread square with ⅓ of the crumb mixture, pressing into dough. Snugly roll dough into a log; pinch ends to seal shut. Repeat with remaining dough and crumbs.

Place rolls, seams down, at least 2 inches apart on an ungreased 12- by 15-inch baking sheet. Cover with plastic wrap and let stand until slightly puffy, about 1 hour. Uncover and bake in a 350° oven until richly browned, about 35 minutes. Transfer to a rack.

In a small bowl, smoothly stir together powdered sugar and cool water. Drizzle evenly over warm rolls. Slice and serve warm or cool. To store, cool, wrap airtight, and hold up to a day or freeze to store longer. Makes 3 rolls, each about 1¼ pounds.

PER OUNCE: 117 calories (36 percent from fat), 1.5 g protein, 18 g carbohydrates, 4.7 g fat (2.1 g saturated), 15 mg cholesterol, 48 mg sodium

Ruth Elaine Watson

Littleton, Colo.

October Menus

THE CRISPNESS OF FALL *brings a sharper edge to October days, making way for menus—from picnics to cozy meals—that bridge the change of seasons. Turn the pumpkin patch search for perfect candidates for Halloween jack-o'-lanterns into a two-family outing, with a portable feast that appeals to young and not-quite-so-young tastes—chicken drumsticks and wing drumettes, and more.*

At home, consider a scramble of eggs, vegetables, and sausage for breakfast or supper. Soup from scratch makes another fast meal.

PUMPKIN PICNIC

Jack-o'-lantern with Vegetables
**Honey Mustard Chicken
Drumsticks & Drumettes**
Roasted Red Pepper Dip
Crusty Bread
Pomegranates, Lady Apples,
Muscat Grapes
Pumpkin-Cheese Cakes
Hot or Cold Spiced Apple Cider
Brandy or Calvados

Pack this no-utensils, hands-on picnic to take with you on your hunt for the great pumpkin. If you like, buy an extra pumpkin and carve it to use as a basket for the vegetables; later use it as a jack-o'-lantern. For vegetables, long sticks of celery, carrots, cucumber, and green onions work well; allow 3 to 4 pounds untrimmed vegetables for 8 servings.

Bring baked chicken drumsticks for the adults in your party and wing drumettes for the little ones; you can bake the chicken in advance and chill it, or bake it just before leaving. The vegetables and chicken share the mild roasted red bell pepper dip.

Offer cider to drink; adults can add calvados or brandy.

Bring moist towels for the cleanup.

HONEY MUSTARD CHICKEN DRUMSTICKS & DRUMETTES

12 chicken drumsticks (about 2¾ lb. total)

16 to 24 chicken wing drumettes (shoulder wing sections; 1½ to 2 lb. total)

Picnic awaits as Halloween pumpkins are selected: big and little chicken legs, dip and vegetables, pumpkin cupcakes. No utensils are needed for this easy-to-eat menu.

¼ cup balsamic vinegar (or red wine vinegar plus 1 teaspoon sugar)

2 tablespoons honey

2 tablespoons Dijon mustard

2 tablespoons soy sauce

Rinse chicken; pat dry. Place drumsticks and drumettes in separate foil-lined 10- by 15-inch pans. Mix vinegar, honey, mustard, and soy; brush over chicken.

Bake in a 425° oven, basting occasionally with any remaining honey mixture, until chicken is browned and no longer pink at bone (cut to test), 30 to 35 minutes for drumsticks, 20 to 25 minutes for wings. (If using 1 oven, switch pan positions halfway through baking.) Serve chicken warm or cool. Makes 8 servings.

PER SERVING: 302 calories (48 percent from fat), 31 g protein, 6 g carbohydrates, 16 g fat (4.4 g saturated), 101 mg cholesterol, 469 mg sodium

ROASTED RED PEPPER DIP

Use hollowed squash or bell pepper to hold this easy dip.

1 large (about 10 oz.) red bell pepper

1 clove garlic

¼ cup unflavored nonfat yogurt

**3 tablespoons reduced-calorie mayonnaise
Salt**

Broil bell pepper in an 8- or 9-inch-wide pan about 4 inches from heat until charred on all sides, turning as needed, 15 to 20 minutes total. Cool. Pull off skin, stems, and seeds. In a blender or food processor, purée bell pepper, garlic, yogurt, and mayonnaise. Add salt to taste. (If making ahead, cover and chill up to a day.)

Use preceding serving suggestion or scrape dip into a small bowl. Makes about 1 cup, enough for 8 servings.

PER TABLESPOON: 14 calories (51 percent from fat), 0.4 g protein, 1.4 g carbohydrates, 0.8 g fat (0.2 g saturated), 1 mg cholesterol, 18 mg sodium

THE DETAILS

Fall fruits. *Seasonal fruits with messy seeds or staining juices suit casual ambience.*

Vegetable bowls. *Hollowed-out pepper, squash, and pumpkin serve as containers.*

Cupcake carrier. *To protect cupcakes, tote them in baking pan; cloak with towel.*

Trick-or-treat bags. *For another picnic, pack kids' lunches in bags for easy handling.*

PUMPKIN-CHEESE CAKES

  1 **cup all-purpose flour**
1¼ **teaspoons baking powder**
1¼ **teaspoons ground cinnamon**
  1 **teaspoon ground ginger**
  ½ **teaspoon baking soda**
  ½ **teaspoon ground nutmeg**
  ¼ **teaspoon salt**
  ⅓ **cup salad oil**
  ⅓ **cup firmly packed brown sugar**
  1 **large egg**
  ¾ **cup canned pumpkin**
  ½ **cup unflavored nonfat yogurt**
    Filling (recipe follows)
 12 **unblanched almonds**

In a bowl, mix flour, baking powder, cinnamon, ginger, baking soda, nutmeg, and salt. In another bowl, beat to blend oil, brown sugar, egg, pumpkin, and yogurt. Stir oil mixture into flour mixture until batter is evenly moistened.

Place a paper liner in each of 12 muffin cups (2½-in. size). Fill each cup about ⅓ full with batter. Top equally with cheese filling. Spoon equal portions of remaining batter over filling; top each with an almond.

Bake in a 350° oven until top of cake (not cheese) springs back when gently pressed, 25 to 30 minutes. Serve warm or cool. If making ahead, cool, cover, and chill up to a day. Makes 12 cakes.

PER PIECE: 223 calories (48 percent from fat), 4.2 g protein, 24 g carbohydrates, 12 g fat (4.2 g saturated), 51 mg cholesterol, 186 mg sodium

Filling. Beat together 2 small packages (3 oz. each) **cream cheese,** 1 **large egg,** and ⅓ cup **sugar.** Stir in ⅓ cup chopped **dried apricots.**

JOE'S SPECIAL BREAKFAST

Joe's Special 1992
Sliced Tomatoes
Toasted Pocket Bread
Orange Juice   Coffee

This updated version of a scrambled egg classic called Joe's Special replaces ground beef with Italian turkey sausage, and spinach with Swiss chard.

Eggs get scrambled with Swiss chard, turkey sausage, and mushrooms for breakfast or supper. Serve sliced tomatoes alongside.

JOE'S SPECIAL 1992

  ¼ **pound mild Italian turkey sausage**
  1 **tablespoon olive oil**
  1 **large (about ½ lb.) onion, chopped**
  ½ **pound mushrooms, thinly sliced**
  4 **cups (about ½ lb.) shredded Swiss chard**
  6 **large eggs**
  4 **small Swiss chard leaves, rinsed and dried (optional)**
    Grated parmesan cheese
    Salt and pepper

Remove sausage casings; crumble meat into a 10- to 12-inch frying pan; add oil. Stir over high heat until meat is browned;

add onion and mushrooms. Stir often until onions are lightly browned, about 5 minutes.

Add shredded chard; stir often until liquid evaporates, 3 to 5 minutes. Reduce heat to medium-low. Beat together eggs and ¼ cup water. Add eggs to pan. With a wide spatula, gently stir until eggs are softly set, 2 to 3 minutes. Spoon onto chard leaf–lined plates. Add cheese, salt, and pepper to taste. Makes 4 servings.

PER SERVING: 286 calories (63 percent from fat), 16 g protein, 11 g carbohydrates, 20 g fat (6 g saturated), 340 mg cholesterol, 427 mg sodium

SPEEDY SOUP SUPPER

Curried Lentil & Lamb Soup
Red Slaw
Caramel Apples
Zinfandel   Milk

Start with fast-cooking, red hulled lentils to make curry base for a thick, satisfying soup in which lamb meatballs simmer. Look for the lentils in supermarkets, Indian markets, and health food stores.

CURRIED LENTIL & LAMB SOUP

   1 **large (½ lb.) onion, chopped**
   1 **teaspoon cumin seed**
   1 **tablespoon minced fresh ginger**
   1 **tablespoon curry powder**
   2 **quarts regular-strength chicken broth**
   1 **pound (about 2¼ cups) decorticated red lentils or regular lentils with hulls, sorted for debris and rinsed**
   1 **pound ground lean lamb**
   1 **teaspoon ground coriander**
   1 **teaspoon chili powder**
   ¼ **cup fresh cilantro (coriander) leaves**
      Unflavored nonfat yogurt
      Salt

In a 4- to 5-quart pan, combine onion, cumin, ginger, and ¼ cup water. Cook on high heat, mixing often, until liquid evaporates and mixture begins to stick. Add 2 tablespoons water; stir to free the onion pieces.

Boil onion until dry and sticking again; stir to free with 2 tablespoons water. Repeat until onion is light brown, about 10 minutes total. Turn heat to low and add curry powder; stir until fragrant, about 1 minute. Add broth and lentils.

Bring to a boil on high heat. Cover and simmer just until lentils are almost tender to bite, about 10 minutes for decorticated lentils, 25 to 35 minutes for lentils with hulls.

Meanwhile, mix lamb, ground coriander, and chili powder. Form into 1-inch balls and drop as made into simmering soup; cover and simmer until lamb is no longer pink in center (cut to test), about 5 minutes. Ladle into bowls. Sprinkle with cilantro. Add yogurt and salt to taste. Makes 6 servings.

PER SERVING: 531 calories (36 percent from fat), 38 g protein, 50 g carbohydrates, 21 g fat (8.4 g saturated), 55 mg cholesterol, 130 mg sodium

RED SLAW

   4 **cups finely shredded red cabbage**
   ½ **cup shredded carrot**
   ½ **cup chopped red onion**
   ½ **cup seasoned rice vinegar (or red wine vinegar and 1 tablespoon sugar)**
   1 **teaspoon mustard seed**
      Salt and pepper

In a bowl, mix cabbage, carrot, onion, vinegar, and mustard seed. Add salt and pepper to taste. Makes 6 servings.

PER SERVING: 41 calories (6.6 percent from fat), 1.1 g protein, 9.2 g carbohydrates, 0.3 g fat (0 g saturated), 0 mg cholesterol, 406 mg sodium

Harvest pies (page 232)

Welcome in the festive
season with a leisurely look at our holiday entertaining
section, filled with ideas to enrich your gatherings of
family and friends. You'll find menus and recipes
for a holiday appetizer party, a bountiful Thanksgiving
dinner, and a Christmas feast. Included are fabulous
first courses, showpiece side dishes, tangy relishes, elegant
desserts, and festive beverages. Sharing is part of the
joy, so you'll find cookies to give and dishes that
travel well for communal feasts. Happy holidays!

A SPONTANEOUS INVITATION *extended with a request to bring along nibbles —for a designated number of guests—is a popular way busy people make parties happen. This is just such a party. The recipes use ingredients found in almost any market, so guests assigned (by fax, perhaps) to prepare them won't have to make special shopping trips. The dishes also can be made ahead, a boon for those coming from the office—or for the hosts, should they decide to take on the whole party menu.*

Beverages can be handled in the same relaxed fashion. These foods go with a wide range of wines, beers, fruit juices, or bottled waters. Invite guests to bring what they like, or provide a variety of beverages they will enjoy.

HOLIDAY APPETIZER PARTY FOR 10 TO 12

Baked Beans & Sausage Bites
Hominy Hummus   Couscous Sushi
Hot Fajita Wings with Guacamole
Escargot Tumble
Golden Fruits with Chèvre
Selection of
Wines, Beers, Juices & Waters

BAKED BEANS & SAUSAGE BITES

- 1 can (16 oz.) pinto beans, drained
- 1 can (16 oz.) baked beans
- 1 small (about 6 oz.) red onion, chopped
- 1 tablespoon mustard seed
- ¼ pound Polish sausage, sliced ¼ inch thick
- 2 cans (16 oz. each) Boston brown bread or 1 pound sliced raisin bread

In a shallow 1- to 1½-quart casserole, mash pinto beans. Stir in baked beans, all but 2 tablespoons of the onion (wrap remainder airtight and chill up to a day), and mustard seed. Scatter sausage over beans. (If assembling ahead, cover and chill up to a day.)

Cut brown bread in half lengthwise, then crosswise into ⅓-inch-thick slices; if desired, cut slices in half. Or cut raisin bread slices into quarters. Lay pieces close together on 12- by 15-inch baking sheets. Bake in a 400° oven until bread is toasted, about 15 minutes; turn slices after 6 minutes. Serve warm or cool; wrap cool bread airtight up to a day.

Bake beans, uncovered, in a 400° oven until bubbly, 30 to 40 minutes. Sprinkle reserved onion over beans. Serve hot or warm; spoon beans and sausage onto bread. Makes about 4 cups, 10 to 12 appetizer servings.

PER SERVING: 259 calories (16 percent from fat), 9.3 g protein, 47 g carbohydrates, 4.5 g fat (1.1 g saturated), 9.3 mg cholesterol, 502 mg sodium

HOMINY HUMMUS

For every 8 to 10 servings, offer about 2 pounds rinsed, trimmed raw vegetables such as bell peppers, jicama, and celery.

- 1 can (14½ oz.) golden hominy
- 1 can (8 oz.) creamed corn
- 2 tablespoons lemon juice
- 1 clove garlic
- ½ teaspoon ground cumin
- ¼ teaspoon cayenne
- ¼ cup chopped radishes
  Crisp raw vegetables

Drain the hominy. In a food processor or a blender, combine the hominy, creamed corn, lemon juice, garlic, cumin, and cayenne. Whirl until smooth. Mound hummus into a bowl. (If making ahead, cover and chill up to a day; let warm to room temperature.)

Sprinkle hummus with chopped radishes and offer crisp raw vegetables to scoop up the mixture. Makes about 1⅔ cups hummus, 8 to 10 appetizer servings.

PER TABLESPOON: 18 calories (10 percent from fat), 0.4 g protein, 4 g carbohydrates, 0.2 g fat (0 g saturated), 0 mg cholesterol, 59 mg sodium

(Continued on page 216)

Effort shared by guests divides the work to simplify this party. On the table (from left foreground) are couscous sushi, hominy hummus with raw vegetables, baked beans and sausage bites, fajita chicken wings with guacamole, escargot tumble, and fruit with cheese.

COUSCOUS SUSHI

- ½ cup couscous
- ½ teaspoon Oriental sesame oil
- ⅓ cup minced carrots
- ¼ cup seasoned rice vinegar (or ¼ cup distilled white vinegar plus 1½ tablespoons sugar)
- 2 ounces shelled cooked tiny shrimp
- ¼ cup thinly sliced green onion
- 2 tablespoons shredded pickled ginger
  About 3 dozen toasted nori (dried seaweed) squares, about 4-inch size
  Soy sauce
  Wasabi (directions follow) or prepared horseradish

In a 1- to 1½-quart pan, bring 1 cup water to a boil. Stir in couscous and oil; cover pan tightly and remove from heat.

All the appetizers hold up well, so the party can focus on conversation, songs, and games with foods to nibble all through the event.

Munch a fajita wing, then try couscous, seasoned like sushi, on seaweed square.

Let stand until couscous absorbs water, about 5 minutes. Transfer to a bowl. Lightly stir in carrots; let cool. Gently mix in vinegar, shrimp, and onion. Spoon into a serving bowl; top with ginger. (If making ahead, cover and chill up to 6 hours.)

To eat, spoon couscous mixture onto nori; add soy and wasabi to taste. Makes about 2⅓ cups, 8 to 10 appetizer servings.

PER TABLESPOON: 21 calories (4.3 percent from fat), 1.2 g protein, 3.9 g carbohydrates, 0.1 g fat (0 g saturated), 3 mg cholesterol, 39 mg sodium

Wasabi. To make each tablespoon, mix about 2 tablespoons **wasabi powder** (green horseradish) to a firm paste with about 2 teaspoons **water.**

HOT FAJITA WINGS WITH GUACAMOLE

- ¼ cup honey
- 2 tablespoons lime juice
- 2 tablespoons chili powder
- 2 tablespoons soy sauce
- 2 to 2½ pounds chicken wings, shoulder and midsection only, cut apart
- 1 carton (6 oz.) frozen avocado dip, thawed; or 1 cup homemade guacamole

In a large plastic bag, mix honey, lime juice, chili powder, and soy sauce. Add wings; seal bag and mix to coat. Chill, turning occasionally, at least 1 hour or up to a day.

Lift out wings and place in a single layer on racks in 2 broiler pans, each about 10 by 15 inches. Bake in a 450° oven 15 minutes. Turn pieces over and continue baking until browned, 25 to 30 minutes. (If making ahead, let cool, wrap airtight, and chill up to 1 day; serve at room temperature or reheat in a single layer in pans in a 350° oven for about 10 minutes.) Put wings on a platter.

Place avocado dip in a bowl set on platter with the wings. Makes 8 to 10 appetizer servings.

PER SERVING: 170 calories (53 percent from fat), 10 g protein, 10 g carbohydrates, 10 g fat (2.4 g saturated), 29 mg cholesterol, 363 mg sodium

ESCARGOT TUMBLE

½ pound firm chorizo sausage,
  coarsely chopped
1 can (4½ oz.) extra-large snails,
  rinsed and coarsely chopped
  (or omit snails and use ¼ lb.
  more firm chorizo sausage)
2 cloves garlic, pressed or minced
1 can (5 oz.) sliced water chestnuts,
  drained and chopped
¼ cup finely chopped parsley
  Fresh parsley sprigs
  About 3 dozen small (about ¼ lb.
  total) butter lettuce leaves, rinsed
  and crisped

Combine chorizo, snails, and garlic in a
10- to 12-inch frying pan. Stir over
medium-high heat until sausage is
lightly browned, about 8 minutes. Drain
fat. Stir in water chestnuts and chopped
parsley.

Pour mixture into a bowl; garnish
with parsley sprigs. Serve warm (keep
hot on an electric warming tray or in a
hot water jacket over a low flame). Spoon
mixture, a portion at a time, into lettuce
leaves. Makes about 2⅔ cups filling, 10
appetizer servings.

PER SERVING: 120 calories (67 percent from fat), 7.6 g protein, 2.5 g
carbohydrates, 8.9 g fat (3.3 g saturated), 5.7 mg cholesterol, 64 mg
sodium

GOLDEN FRUITS WITH CHÈVRE

2 tablespoons hazelnuts
8 to 10 ounces fresh or ripened
  chèvre cheese (or chèvre fromage
  blanc)
3 small (about 1⅓ lbs. total) Golden
  Delicious apples or firm-ripe Bosc
  or Comice pears

Place nuts in a 9- to 10-inch-wide pan.
Bake in a 350° oven until nuts are toasted
under the skin, about 10 minutes. Pour
nuts onto a towel and rub to remove
loose skin. Lift nuts from towel; discard
the skins. Coarsely chop the nuts.

Arrange cheese on a board or platter.
Sprinkle with toasted nuts. Mound
apples or pears alongside. Offer an apple
wedge cutter or a knife to slice whole
fruit, 1 piece at a time. To eat, spread
cheese and nuts onto fruit slices. Makes
8 to 10 appetizer servings.

PER SERVING: 107 calories (56 percent from fat), 4 g protein, 9.3 g
carbohydrates, 6.6 g fat (0.1 g saturated), 0 mg cholesterol, 224 mg
sodium

*Hazelnut bits stud swirl of fresh goat cheese; spread onto apple wedges. Firm-ripe
Bosc or Comice pears also go well with chèvre cheese.*

HOLIDAY ENTERTAINING: A Bountiful Thanksgiving Dinner

THE BEAUTY *of this handsome table is much more than the eye beholds. With the exception of the turkey and gravy, the dishes travel well—should friends or family volunteer to lend a hand. Subtly worked into many recipes are fat-cutting steps obvious only in preparation, but definitely not hinted at by the dishes' taste or look.*

To enhance festivities, domestic sparkling wines complement the menu's range of flavors. Choices include Culbertson Blanc de Noir; Domaine Chandon nonvintage reserve or nonvintage Blanc de Noirs; Iron Horse brut or Blanc de Blancs; Domaine Mumm vintage reserve brut, cuvée Napa; and Roederer Estate brut nonvintage. Cost is $15 to about $30 a bottle.

THANKSGIVING DINNER FOR 16 TO 20

Artichokes with Thai Shrimp Salsa
(page 224)
Roasted or Barbecued Turkey
Port Gravy
Wild Rice & Sourdough Dressing
with Almonds (page 228)
Cranberry Relish (page 230)
Sweet Potato–Fennel Gratin
(page 228)
Green Pea Pods with Red Onions
(page 226)
Persimmon-glazed Pumpkin
Cheese Pie (page 232)
Sparkling Wine or Champagne

Settle the annual debate about how to cook the turkey by evaluating competition for oven space against the enthusiasm of the barbecue chef.

THE TURKEY TWO WAYS: ROASTED OR BARBECUED

To prepare turkey to roast or barbecue, select the size of fresh or frozen bird you want; allow at least ½ pound raw turkey (including bone and skin) for each person. If leftovers are intended, get a bigger bird.

If turkey is frozen, thaw in its plastic wrapper in the refrigerator; this may take 2 to 3 days.

(Continued on page 220)

Artichokes with Thai-seasoned shrimp start this meal; next come turkey and port gravy, sweet potato and fennel casserole (far left), pea pods with red onions (center), wild rice and sourdough dressing (top right), and cranberry relish.

If you're rushed, immerse frozen turkey in its wrapper in a basin of cool (not warm) tap water. As the water gets icy cold (once or twice an hour), drain and cover bird generously with more cool tap water. A 30-pound turkey takes about 7 hours to thaw.

When turkey breast is thawed to feel soft when pressed, unwrap. If legs are trussed, release them. (If giblets packed in body cavity are still frozen, wiggle them free, rinsing cavity with cool tap water as you work.)

Pull off and discard lumps of fat and remove giblets. Rinse bird inside and out, then pat dry. Rinse giblets, drain, and start simmering for port gravy (directions follow).

To season turkey, start from tail end of bird and ease your fingers beneath skin, up and over breast, to loosen, but keep in place. Slip rinsed and drained **fresh sage leaves** and **thyme sprigs** between skin and meat; you'll need ⅓ to ⅔ cup *total*, depending on bird size. Rub bird all over with 1 to 3 tablespoons **olive oil.**

Insert thermometer straight down through the thickest part of the breast to the bone.

ROASTED TURKEY

Prepare and season **turkey,** and insert thermometer as directed (preceding). Set turkey, breast up, on a V-shaped rack in a rimmed pan at least 2 inches deep and at least 1 inch wider on all sides than bird (if you don't have a pan quite big enough, use foil to keep drips from spilling out of pan).

Roast as directed in chart (below). If

desired, baste turkey every 30 minutes with **pan drippings** (or olive oil or melted butter if bird is small and has very few drippings).

Remove turkey from oven; let rest in a warm place (or tent with foil) for 10 to 15 minutes, allowing juices to settle. If desired, present at the table. Turkey cooked according to the chart will have moist breast meat, but thighs are often still pink at hip joint. Cut off the legs and disjoint; if meat at the hip joint is pinker than you like, put thighs in a 9- to 10-inch-wide pan and return to 450° oven until meat at joint is no longer pink, 10 to 20 minutes.

Meanwhile, carve and serve remaining turkey.

PER 3-OUNCE PORTION COOKED TURKEY, MEAT ONLY, HALF WHITE, HALF DARK: 144 calories (26 percent from fat), 25 g protein, 0 g carbohydrates, 4.2 g fat (1.4 g saturated), 67 mg cholesterol, 64 mg sodium

BARBECUED TURKEY

Prepare and season **turkey,** and insert thermometer as directed (preceding). .

In a barbecue with lid, mound and ignite 60 charcoal briquets on fire grate. When briquets are dotted with gray ash, about 30 minutes, divide in half and push to opposite sides of fire grate. Place a drip pan between coals. Add 5 briquets (10 total) to each mound of coals now and every 30 minutes while cooking.

Set grill 4 to 6 inches above fire grate; rub lightly with oil and set turkey, breast up, on grill over drip pan. Cover and cook with vents open; for cooking time, see chart below. If parts of the turkey begin to get darker than you like before the bird is done, drape browned areas with foil.

AND THE GRAVY

You can start the gravy a day ahead. If your turkey is 18 pounds or less, be sure to start gravy before you put the bird on to cook. If your turkey is more than 18 pounds, double the recipe, using a 6- to 8-quart pan. If the roasting pan isn't large enough to hold liquid, finish the gravy in the saucepan.

PORT GRAVY

Giblets from 10- to 18-pound turkey
1 medium-size (about 6 oz.) onion, quartered
1 large (about ¼ lb.) carrot, cut into chunks
⅔ cup sliced celery
4 cups regular-strength chicken broth
At least 1 cup ruby or tawny port
¼ teaspoon black peppercorns
Turkey drippings from roasted or barbecued turkey (preceding)
⅓ cup cornstarch
Salt and pepper

Rinse giblets; chill liver airtight. In a 2- to 3-quart pan, place remaining giblets, onion, carrot, celery, broth, 1 cup port, and peppercorns. Bring to a boil; cover and simmer until gizzard is tender when pierced, 1¼ to 1¾ hours. If making ahead, let mixture cool, cover, and chill up to a day; reheat to simmering.

Add liver; cook for 10 minutes.

Pour broth through a fine strainer into a bowl; save giblets for gravy or other uses. Discard residue.

If using giblets, pull meat off neck, and chop neck meat and giblets; set aside. Measure broth; if needed, add water to make 4 cups.

Spoon and discard fat from turkey drippings in roasting pan (if barbecue drippings aren't too charred, skim and discard fat, then scrape drippings into the 2- to 3-qt. pan).

Smoothly mix cornstarch with ¼ cup water; add to broth and mix with turkey drippings, scraping browned bits free. Add chopped giblets and stir over high heat until boiling, about 5 minutes.

Season to taste with more port and salt and pepper. Makes 4 to 5 cups.

PER ¼ CUP WITH GIBLETS: 41 calories (24 percent from fat), 2.7 g protein, 4.5 g carbohydrates, 1.1 g fat (0.3 g saturated), 23 mg cholesterol, 22 mg sodium

Roasted or Barbecued Turkey

Turkey weight with giblets	Oven temperature*	Internal temperature**	Cooking time
10 to 12 lb.	350°	160°	1¾ to 2¼ hr.
14 to 20 lb.	325°	160°	2½ to 3 hr.
24 to 26 lb.	325°	160°	3 to 3¾ hr.
28 to 30 lb.	325°	160°	3½ to 4½ hr.

*To barbecue, follow recipe above; cooking time is about the same as for roasting.
**Insert thermometer to bone through thickest part of breast.

Holiday Entertaining: Centerpieces from the Produce Market

The old masters loved to paint still lifes of fruits and vegetables. But why not turn the tables and make such masterpieces come to life as centerpieces?

Designers Dennis W. Leong and Françoise Kirkman took their keen eyes to the produce market and came back with the makings for the artfully simple, easy-to-duplicate arrangements shown. The beauty of this approach is that no skill is required, it's fast, and, once the scene has been played, the foods can go to the kitchen for use or be left for snacks.

Candles and their soft light add beauty to these centerpieces. If you want to vary candles' heights, set them on small, steady objects of different heights.

Pine-cone clusters and evergreens accent an alignment of apples and candles. Cubes cut from florist's foam anchor candles.

Brilliant liquidambar leaves and persimmons show up magnificently on blue moiré tablecloth. Wired silk ribbon, the color of leaves, scrolls gracefully through the arrangement.

Pomegranates, tangerines, and apples fill basket lined with aromatic juniper; dusty miller rises at base of candles.

THE FIRST COURSE IS *a lot like a pretty ribbon on a gift. It sets up anticipation for good things to come. The aim of such an offering is to bring not only satisfaction but attention, too. Not unexpectedly, therefore, much consideration is often devoted to appearance as well as taste in creating artful tidbits such as these: caviars as fine as your purse permits triangulated on crisp pastry, wild mushrooms daringly perched on crunchy polenta boards, artichokes cut to show off with shrimp, and pink smoked salmon draped beside a golden citrus sauce. Sound complex? It's more show than effort.*

ART DECO CAVIAR

In a hurry? Skip the pastry and use 8 toasted white-bread triangles as the base for these appetizers; the results aren't quite as fancy, but you'll feel more relaxed.

- ½ **pound (½ of a 1-lb. package) puff pastry, thawed if frozen**
- **About 3 ounces (⅓ cup) salmon or other red caviar**
- **About 2 ounces (¼ cup) sevruga or other dark caviar**
- 3 **ounces (about ½ cup) neufchâtel cheese**
- 2 **tablespoons light sour cream or unflavored nonfat yogurt**
- 1 **tablespoon instant toasted onion**
- 30 **to 40 chive spears (about 12 in. long), rinsed and drained**
- **Lemon wedges**

On a lightly floured board, roll puff pastry until it is slightly larger than 4 by 16 inches. Trim edges, cutting straight down with a sharp, floured knife, to make a 4- by 16-inch rectangle. Cutting the same way, divide rectangle into 4 squares (4 in. each). Cut each square in half diagonally to make 8 triangles.

Carefully (to avoid crumpling edges) place pastry pieces well apart on a 12- by 15-inch baking sheet. Pierce each all over with the tines of a fork. Bake in a 375° oven until a rich golden brown, about 20 minutes. Transfer to racks to cool. As soon as the pastries are cool, use them or pack them airtight and let stand at room temperature up to a day.

If caviars taste quite salty (or are dyed), place them individually in a fine strainer and rinse gently with cool water. Pat bottom of strainer with a towel to remove excess moisture; cover and chill caviar while assembling appetizers.

In a small bowl, smoothly mix together cheese and sour cream. Stir in onion. Spread mixture evenly on tops of pastry triangles.

Cut 16 chive pieces, each 1½ inches long. Finely chop remaining chives. On each cheese-topped triangle, position 2 chive pieces to divide surface into 3 equal areas; press down lightly to hold in place.

Using a small spoon and a slender skewer or toothpick to guide, fill 1 area on each pastry with chopped chives; fill another with red caviar, and the last with dark caviar. Serve at once, adding lemon to taste. Makes 4 to 8 servings.

PER PIECE: 196 calories (60 percent from fat), 7.2 g protein, 12 g carbohydrates, 13 g fat (1.4 g saturated), 111 mg cholesterol, 461 mg sodium

WILD MUSHROOM POLENTA BOARDS WITH ROASTED GARLIC

- 1 **medium-size head garlic**
- 2 **tablespoons extra-virgin olive oil or salad oil**
- ½ **pound fresh shiitake mushrooms**
- ½ **pound fresh chanterelles**
- ½ **pound fresh oyster mushrooms**
- 1 **tablespoon minced fresh or 1½ teaspoons crumbled dried rosemary leaves**
- 1 **tablespoon minced fresh or 1½ teaspoons dried rubbed sage**
- 2 **teaspoons cornstarch mixed with ¾ cup regular-strength chicken broth**
- **Polenta boards (recipe follows)**
- 2 **tablespoons shredded parmesan cheese**
- **Fresh rosemary and sage sprigs (optional)**

Cut garlic head in half crosswise. Pour 1 tablespoon oil into an 8- or 9-inch-wide pan. Place garlic, cut sides down, in pan. Bake in a 350° oven until cut sides are golden brown, about 45 minutes. When cool enough to touch, squeeze cloves from skins; discard skins. Mash garlic.

Meanwhile, quickly immerse mushrooms in water to rinse. Lift from water; drain. Trim the shiitake stems and the discolored stem ends of chanterelles and oyster mushrooms. Thinly slice the shiitakes and chanterelles.

In a 5- to 6-quart pan, combine remaining oil, mushrooms, and minced rosemary and sage. Cover and cook over medium-high heat until mushrooms are juicy, about 8 minutes. Uncover; stir often until liquid evaporates and mushrooms are browned, 15 to 20 minutes. (If making ahead, cool, cover, and chill up to a day; reheat to continue.) Add garlic and cornstarch mixture; stir until boiling.

Lay polenta boards side by side on a 12- by 15-inch baking sheet; spoon hot mushroom sauce equally onto centers. Sprinkle mushrooms with cheese. Broil 4 to 6 inches from heat until sizzling, about 2 minutes. With a spatula, transfer to 6 plates; garnish with herb sprigs. Makes 6 servings.

PER SERVING: 212 calories (30 percent from fat), 7.7 g protein, 32 g carbohydrates, 7 g fat (2.2 g saturated), 7 mg cholesterol, 188 mg sodium

Polenta boards. In a food processor or a bowl, mix ½ cup **all-purpose flour,** ½ cup **polenta** or yellow cornmeal, ¼ cup **instant nonfat dried milk,** and 1½ teaspoons **baking powder.** Add 1 tablespoon **butter** or margarine; whirl or rub with fingers until coarse crumbs form. Add ⅓ cup **water;** whirl or stir with a fork until dough begins to form a ball. Pat into a ball and knead briefly on a lightly floured board until dough sticks together smoothly.

Divide into 6 equal portions; cover with plastic wrap. On a well-floured board, roll 1 piece at a time into a randomly shaped 6- to 7-inch round. Put on a 12- by 15-inch baking sheet and cover with plastic wrap. Repeat to shape remaining pieces, spacing slightly apart on sheet (you'll need to use 2 pans, or bake in sequence).

Bake in a 350° oven until crusts are lightly browned, 12 to 14 minutes. If making ahead, wrap cool crusts airtight and hold up to a day.

(Continued on page 224)

Colorful as nautical flags, puff pastry appetizers with black and red caviars and minced chives signal good dining ahead.

A cascade of spiced shrimp tumbles over fanned artichoke leaves.

ARTICHOKES WITH THAI SHRIMP SALSA

½ cup seasoned rice vinegar (or ½ cup rice vinegar and 1 tablespoon sugar)

1 tablespoon mustard seed

1 teaspoon black peppercorns

4 thin slices (each about the size of a quarter) fresh ginger

3 large (4 to 4½ in. wide, about ¾ lb. each) artichokes

¾ pound shelled cooked tiny shrimp

⅓ cup minced pickled scallions

¼ cup minced fresh cilantro (coriander)

¼ cup minced fresh or 2 tablespoons crumbled dried mint leaves

2 tablespoons fish sauce (nuoc mam or nam pla) or soy sauce

¼ to ½ teaspoon hot chili oil

Fresh cilantro and mint sprigs, rinsed and drained

In a 6- to 8-quart pan, combine ¼ cup vinegar, mustard seed, peppercorns, and ginger with 4 quarts water. Cover and bring to a boil over high heat.

Meanwhile, remove coarse outer leaves from artichokes and trim stems flush with bases. With a sharp knife, cut off top third of each artichoke. With scissors, trim thorny tips off remaining leaves.

Immerse artichokes in cold water and swish back and forth vigorously to release debris; shake out water.

Place artichokes in boiling liquid. Cover, reduce heat, and simmer until bottoms are tender when pierced, about 35 minutes. Drain, reserving liquid. Let artichokes stand until cool enough to touch (if making ahead, wrap airtight and chill up to a day).

Pour cooking water through a fine strainer and reserve seed.

In the strainer, rinse shrimp with cool water; drain and mix with reserved seed, remaining vinegar, pickled scallions, minced cilantro, minced mint, fish sauce, and chili oil to taste. If making ahead, chill airtight up to a day.

With a large, sharp knife, cut each artichoke in half vertically. Remove sharp pointed inner leaves and scoop out fuzzy centers. Set each half on a salad plate. Spoon shrimp mixture equally into artichoke cavities. Garnish with cilantro and mint sprigs. Makes 6 servings.

PER SERVING: 114 calories (11 percent from fat), 15 g protein, 11 g carbohydrates, 1.4 g fat (0.2 g saturated), 111 mg cholesterol, 657 mg sodium

SMOKED SALMON WITH CITRUS MÉLANGE

- 1 teaspoon *each* grated orange and grated lemon peel
- 2 tablespoons sugar
- 1¼ cups orange juice
- ¼ cup lemon juice
- 2 teaspoons cornstarch blended with 1 tablespoon water
- ¾ pound thinly sliced smoked salmon
- 4 to 5 cups (about 3¼ oz.) mixed salad greens or mesclun, rinsed and crisped
- 3 tablespoons finely chopped roasted, salted pistachios

In a bowl, combine orange and lemon peels with 1 tablespoon sugar; press with a spoon to mingle flavors.

In a 1- to 1½-quart pan, combine remaining sugar and the juices. Boil, uncovered, on high heat until reduced to 1 cup. Mix in peel with sugar and cornstarch mixture; stir until liquid boils again. Let cool; if making ahead, cover and chill up to 4 hours.

Fan salmon slices equally along 1 side of 8 salad plates, rippling them slightly. Tuck equal portions of salad greens beside fish, leaving about ¼ of plate empty; spoon cool sauce into empty area and a little over greens. Sprinkle with nuts. Makes 8 servings.

PER SERVING: 104 calories (30 percent from fat), 8.7 g protein, 9.7 g carbohydrates, 3.5 g fat (0.6 g saturated), 9.8 mg cholesterol, 362 mg sodium

Tart-sweet citrus sauce dresses up smoked salmon and greens.

TRIM COOKING PROCEDURES *keep these vegetable showpieces and dressings lean enough to provide wholesome balance for the roasts they accompany. Because tender vegetables often require last-minute attention—when that attention could be well used elsewhere—we've built in make-ahead steps and highlighted them with asterisks so you can spot them easily.*

The dressings are flavorful combinations of grains and nuts, plus one with sourdough bread. To comply with current food safety recommendations, dressings cook in casseroles rather than in the bird. We think the flavorful gravy on page 220 will adequately compensate those who love stuffing from the turkey. If you do stuff the bird, be sure to do so just before it goes into the oven, then remove the dressing while it's still hot.

GREEN PEA PODS WITH RED ONIONS

½ cup red wine vinegar
1 teaspoon mustard seed
1 teaspoon cumin seed
2 large (about 1 lb. total) red onions, thinly sliced
1 teaspoon sugar
2 pounds edible-pod peas, ends and strings removed
Salt

In a 5- to 6-quart pan, bring about 1 quart water to a boil on high heat. Add 5 tablespoons vinegar, mustard seed, cumin seed, and onions. Cook just until onions are limp, about 2 minutes. Drain in a fine strainer. Add onion-seed mixture to remaining vinegar and sugar.

(*If cooking ahead, cover and chill, stirring occasionally, up to a day.)

Rinse pan well and fill with about 2½ quarts water. Cover and bring to a boil on high heat. Add peas and cook, uncovered, just until brighter green, 2 to 3 minutes. Drain. Arrange peas in a shallow 3- to 4-quart casserole. (*If cooking ahead, immerse peas in ice water until cold, then drain. Arrange in a casserole, cover, and hold at room temperature up to 6 hours or chill up to a day.)

Serve from cold to room temperature. Just before serving, spoon onions onto peas; add salt to taste. Makes 8 to 10 servings.

PER SERVING: 60 calories (6 percent from fat), 3.3 g protein, 12 g carbohydrates, 0.4 g fat (0 g saturated), 0 mg cholesterol, 8.6 mg sodium

OAT PILAF WITH HAZELNUTS & SCOTCH

¾ cup hazelnuts
2 large (about 1 lb. total) onions, chopped
About 6½ cups regular-strength beef broth
3 cups oat groats (uncut grains)
About 6 tablespoons Scotch whisky
⅓ cup minced green onions

Place hazelnuts in a shallow 3- to 3½-quart casserole (about 9 by 13 in.). Bake at 350° until nuts are lightly browned under skins, about 15 minutes; shake pan occasionally.

Pour nuts onto towel; rub with towel to free as much of the skins as possible. Lift from towel; discard skins. Coarsely chop nuts; set aside.

In same casserole, combine chopped onions and ½ cup water. Bake in a 400° oven until liquid evaporates and onions are browned at edges, about 30 minutes. Add ¼ cup simmering hot broth; stir to free browned bits stuck to casserole. Continue baking, stirring occasionally, until liquid again evaporates and browned bits begin to stick. Add ¼ cup broth and repeat process. Each step takes about 20 minutes.

Bring remaining 6 cups broth and oats to a boil in a 2- to 3-quart pan over high heat. Add to casserole; stir to combine with onions. Cover casserole tightly

Red onions, turned cerise by dressing, are brilliant on edible-pod peas.

with foil. Bake in a 400° oven until oats are tender to bite, about 30 minutes.

Uncover; stir in Scotch to taste. Sprinkle with nuts and green onions. To each portion, add more Scotch. Makes about 6 cups, 6 to 8 servings.

PER SERVING: 352 calories (28 percent from fat), 13 g protein, 47 g carbohydrates, 11 g fat (1.2 g saturated), 0 mg cholesterol, 8.5 mg sodium

BROCCOLI WITH SHERRY-GLAZED ONIONS

 2 pounds broccoli
 1 package (1 lb.) frozen petite whole onions, thawed
 1 teaspoon olive oil
 1 cup dry sherry or dry madeira
 1 cup regular-strength chicken broth
 ¼ cup sherry vinegar or cider vinegar
 ¼ cup firmly packed brown sugar
 2 tablespoons currants
 1 tablespoon cornstarch
   Salt

Trim tough ends off broccoli. If skin on stalks is tough, peel. Cut broccoli into 3-inch lengths. Cut stalks lengthwise to make ⅓-inch-thick slices. Leave flowerets whole or cut in half if thicker than 1½ inches.

Fill a 5- to 6-quart pan with 2½ to 3 quarts water; cover and bring to a boil on high heat. Add broccoli and cook, uncovered, stirring occasionally, just until barely tender when pierced, 5 to 6 minutes; drain. Arrange on a platter or in a shallow 3- to 4-quart casserole. (*If making ahead, immerse in ice water until cool; drain. Arrange on platter, cover, and hold at room temperature up to 6 hours or chill up to a day.)

Drain pan and add onions and oil. Cook over high heat, shaking pan often, until onions brown, 6 to 8 minutes. Remove onions. (*If browning ahead, cover and chill up to a day.)

To pan, add sherry, broth, vinegar, sugar, and currants. Boil rapidly, uncovered, until reduced to 1⅓ cups, 6 to 8 minutes. Mix cornstarch with ¼

Broccoli provides nesting spots for petite sherry-glazed onions.

cup water. Stir into pan; bring sauce to a boil. (*If assembling ahead, cool, cover, and chill up to a day.)

To serve dish warm or at room temperature, combine hot sauce and onions and pour over broccoli. (*To reheat sauce, cook over medium heat, stirring, until hot. *To reheat broccoli in a microwave oven, cover with microwave-safe plastic wrap and cook at full power—100 percent—until hot, 4 to 7 minutes; rotate casserole ½ turn every 2 minutes. *To reheat broccoli in a conventional oven, cover with foil and bake at 400° until hot, 20 to 30 minutes.) Add salt to taste. Makes 8 to 10 servings.

PER SERVING: 80 calories (9 percent from fat), 2.4 g protein, 17 g carbohydrates, 0.8 g fat (0.1 g saturated), 0 mg cholesterol, 29 mg sodium

GREEN RICE WITH PISTACHIOS

 2 cups long-grain white rice
 5½ cups regular-strength chicken broth
 ½ teaspoon ground nutmeg
 1½ tablespoons canned green peppercorns in brine, rinsed and drained
 ¾ pound spinach leaves, rinsed, drained, and finely chopped (about 3 cups packed)
 1 cup minced parsley
 ½ cup roasted and salted pistachios, coarsely chopped

Spread rice in a shallow 3- to 3½-quart casserole (about 9 by 13 in.). Bake, uncovered, in a 350° oven until grains are toasted to a light brown, about 35 minutes; stir occasionally.

In a 2- to 3-quart pan, combine 5 cups broth with nutmeg and peppercorns. Bring to a boil. With casserole on oven rack, stir broth into rice. Cover dish tightly with foil.

Bake in a 350° oven until liquid is absorbed, about 20 minutes. Stir at 10 and 15 minutes; re-cover dish.

Uncover rice and stir in remaining ½ cup broth, spinach, and ¾ cup parsley; bake 5 minutes longer. Stir rice and sprinkle with remaining parsley and pistachios. Makes about 9 cups, 8 to 10 servings.

PER SERVING: 203 calories (20 percent from fat), 6 g protein, 34 g carbohydrates, 4.6 g fat (0.8 g saturated), 0 mg cholesterol, 111 mg sodium

(Continued on next page)

SWEET POTATO–FENNEL GRATIN

- 3 large (3- to 4-in.-wide) heads fennel
- 2 large (about 1 lb. total) onions, chopped
- 1 teaspoon fennel seed
  About 4½ cups regular-strength chicken broth
- ¼ cup all-purpose flour
- ¼ teaspoon ground nutmeg
- ½ cup whipping cream
- 2¾ pounds (about 4 medium-size) sweet potatoes or yams
- 1¼ cups (5 oz.) shredded reduced-fat or regular jarlsberg cheese
  Salt and pepper

Trim stems from fennel; reserve some of the feathery green leaves for garnish. (*If working ahead, rinse, wrap in towels, enclose in a plastic bag, and chill up to a day.) Discard stems. Trim off discolored parts of fennel. Finely chop heads.

In a 5- to 6-quart pan, combine chopped fennel, onions, fennel seed, and ⅓ cup broth. Cook over high heat, stirring occasionally, until liquid evaporates and browned bits stick in pan, about 15 minutes. Deglaze by adding ¼ cup broth and stirring browned bits free; cook until browned again. Repeat deglazing step 2 or 3 more times, until vegetables are a rich brown, adding

about ½ cup broth total. Reduce heat to low. Mix flour and nutmeg with vegetables, then stir in 3½ cups broth and cream. Stir over medium heat until mixture boils, 4 to 5 minutes.

Peel sweet potatoes and thinly slice crosswise.

Arrange about ¼ of the fennel mixture in an even layer in a shallow 2½- to 3-quart casserole. Cover with ¼ *each* of the potatoes and cheese. Repeat layers, ending with potatoes; reserve the remaining cheese. (*At this point, you can cover and chill casserole and cheese up to a day.)

Bake, tightly covered, in a 350° oven for 45 minutes. Uncover and sprinkle the vegetables with remaining cheese.

Bake, uncovered, until potatoes are tender when pierced and top is browned, about 45 minutes longer. Serve hot. Casserole holds well up to 45 minutes if kept covered and warm. Garnish with reserved fennel leaves. Add salt and pepper to taste. Makes 8 to 10 servings.

PER SERVING: 233 calories (27 percent from fat), 8.8 g protein, 32 g carbohydrates, 6.9 g fat (3.9 g saturated), 20 mg cholesterol, 193 mg sodium

Cheese glazes sweet potato slices baked with braised fennel.

WILD RICE & SOURDOUGH DRESSING WITH ALMONDS

- ½ pound (½ of a 1-lb. loaf) sourdough bread, cut into ½-inch cubes (about 6 cups total)
- ½ cup slivered almonds
- ¾ pound Italian turkey or pork sausage
- 2 large (about 1 lb. total) onions, chopped
- 1 tablespoon minced fresh or 1 teaspoon crumbled dried rosemary leaves
- 1 tablespoon minced fresh or 1 teaspoon dried rubbed sage
- 1⅓ cups wild rice, rinsed and drained
  About 6 cups regular-strength chicken broth
- 1 to 2 tablespoons melted butter or margarine
  Fresh rosemary or parsley sprigs
  Salt

Sourdough bread dressing contains wild rice, almonds, sausage.

Spread bread cubes in a 10- by 15-inch pan. Bake in a 350° oven, stirring occasionally, until dry and lightly browned, about 20 minutes. Pour from pan. (*If making ahead, package airtight when cool and hold up to 3 days at room temperature.)

In the same pan, spread almonds. Bake in a 350° oven until lightly toasted, 10 to 15 minutes; shake pan occasionally. Pour from pan. (*If making ahead, package airtight when cool and chill up to 3 days.)

Remove sausage from casings and crumble meat into same 10- by 15-inch pan. Mix sausage with onions, minced rosemary, and sage. Bake in a 450° oven until sausage and onions are well browned, about 50 minutes; stir often with a wide spatula. If mixture sticks before it browns, add ½ cup broth; scrape pan to free browned bits. Drain; discard any fat.

Meanwhile, in a 2- to 3-quart pan, combine rice and 4 cups broth. Bring to a boil over high heat; cover and simmer

until rice is tender to bite, 45 to 60 minutes; stir occasionally. Drain rice, reserving liquid. (*At this point, you can cover and chill sausage mixture, rice, and liquid up to 3 days.)

Measure reserved broth and add more broth to make 3 cups. Pour into a bowl with 5 cups of the bread cubes; stir occasionally, until bread softens and absorbs liquid, about 10 minutes. Squeeze bread with hands to pulverize. Add rice and sausage mixture; mix well. Spoon into a shallow 3- to 3½-quart casserole (about 9 by 13 in.) and pat to make level. Cover casserole tightly with foil.

Bake in a 350° oven until hot in center, about 40 minutes (50 minutes if ingredients are chilled). Mix remaining 1 cup bread cubes with melted butter. Uncover dressing; scatter cubes and nuts onto it. Bake until cubes are hot and crisp, about 5 minutes. Garnish with rosemary sprigs; add salt to taste. Makes about 8 cups, 8 to 10 servings.

PER SERVING: 261 calories (32 percent from fat), 12 g protein, 33 g carbohydrates, 9.3 g fat (1.3 g saturated), 30 mg cholesterol, 327 mg sodium

AROMATIC RICE WITH TOASTED PECANS

4¾ cups regular-strength chicken broth
1 tablespoon mustard seed
2 teaspoons grated lemon peel
½ teaspoon ground coriander
2 cups pecan or other aromatic rice such as basmati or Texmati
¾ cup pecan halves
2 to 3 tablespoons minced green onions or chives

In a 2- to 3-quart pan, combine 4½ cups broth, mustard seed, peel, coriander, and rice. Bring to a boil.

Set a shallow 3- to 3½-quart casserole on a rack in a 400° oven. Pour boiling rice mixture into casserole; cover very tightly with foil. Bake until broth is absorbed, about 20 minutes.

Uncover and stir ¼ cup broth into rice; scatter nuts onto rice. Continue to bake until nuts are lightly toasted, about 10 minutes.

Sprinkle casserole with green onions. Makes about 8 cups, 8 to 10 servings.

PER SERVING: 218 calories (28 percent from fat), 4.6 g protein, 34 g carbohydrates, 6.7 g fat (0.7 g saturated), 0 mg cholesterol, 26 mg sodium

Aromatic rice, pecans, and spices team up for a flavorful dressing.

FRESH INGREDIENTS *and flavors blend harmoniously in these simple relishes. In the first, cranberries stain water chestnuts red, so their crunch comes as a surprise. Cilantro, mint, and coconut suggest an Indian condiment, but jicama keeps the focus Western. The last relish combines pomegranate seeds and blood oranges.*

CRANBERRY RELISH

- 1 **bag (12 oz., 3 cups) cranberries, rinsed and drained**
- 1 **can (8 oz.) drained water chestnuts**
- 1 **cup lightly packed fresh cilantro (coriander)**
- 1 **tablespoon Dijon mustard**
- ¼ **to ⅓ cup sugar**

In a food processor (or a food chopper with coarse blade), coarsely chop cranberries, water chestnuts, and cilantro. Stir in mustard and sugar to taste. Serve, or cover and chill up to 2 days. Makes about 2 cups.

PER TABLESPOON: 15 calories (3 percent from fat), 0.1 g protein, 3.8 g carbohydrates, 0.1 g fat (0 g saturated), 0 mg cholesterol, 15 mg sodium

JICAMA-MINT RELISH

For a hotter relish, add 1 more fresh jalapeño chili.

- 6 **tablespoons lime juice**
- 1 **cup lightly packed fresh mint leaves**
- 1 **cup lightly packed fresh cilantro (coriander) leaves**
- 1 **fresh jalapeño chili, stemmed and seeded**
- 2 **cloves garlic**
- ½ **teaspoon ground cumin**
- 1 **cup sweetened shredded dried coconut**
- 1 **cup finely chopped jicama**
  Salt

In a blender or food processor, whirl lime juice, 2 tablespoons water, mint, cilantro, chili, garlic, and cumin until smoothly puréed. Stir in coconut and jicama. If making ahead, cover and chill up to a day. Add salt to taste. Makes about 2 cups.

PER ¼ CUP: 57 calories (49 percent from fat), 0.8 g protein, 7.3 g carbohydrates, 3.1 g fat (2.6 g saturated), 0 mg cholesterol, 28 mg sodium

Crimson cranberry relish gets its tender crunch from water chestnuts; cilantro and Dijon mustard add intriguing nuances to this holiday favorite.

POMEGRANATE-ORANGE RELISH

- 2 **medium-size (about 1 lb. total) pomegranates**
- 4 **or 5 medium-size (about 1¼ lb. total) blood or common oranges**
- ¼ **cup red wine vinegar**
- 4 **teaspoons sugar**
- 2 **teaspoons prepared horseradish**
  Crisped onions (recipe follows)
  Salt

Score sides of pomegranates with a sharp knife. Holding fruit under water in a large bowl, pull pomegranate apart into large chunks. With your fingers, separate seeds from membrane and skin. Skim off membrane and skin; pour out water and drain seeds well.

Finely shred 1 to 2 teaspoons peel from oranges; set aside. With a sharp knife, cut peel and white membrane from oranges. Holding oranges over a bowl to catch the juice, cut between the inner membranes to free segments. Squeeze juice from membranes into bowl; discard membranes.

Gently mix fruit with the vinegar, sugar, and horseradish; pour mixture into a shallow bowl. Sprinkle with pomegranate seeds and onions. If making ahead, cover and chill up to 8 hours. Add salt to taste. Makes about 3 cups.

PER ¼ CUP: 40 calories (2 percent from fat), 0.6 g protein, 10 g carbohydrates, 0.1 g fat (0 g saturated), 0 mg cholesterol, 2.7 mg sodium

Crisped onions. Coarsely chop enough **red onion** to make 1 cup. Put in a bowl with **water** to cover. Squeeze onions to bruise lightly; drain. Add 4 cups **ice cubes,** 2 cups water, and ¼ cup **raspberry** or red wine **vinegar.** Let stand until crisp, 20 to 30 minutes. Drain well and discard ice cubes.

Tiny Cookies to Give or Share

DAINTY, DURABLE, *and diverse accurately describe these handy cookies. You start with a basic dough, flavored by browned butter, then add other ingredients to create four different variations, including a hazelnut-chocolate combination that Italians call gianduia. Because the cookies are tiny, one batch makes many, and dozens of them take up little space; because they keep well, they make good gifts; and because there are so many flavor choices, tasters will be delighted.*

GOLDEN BUTTON COOKIES

½ cup (¼ lb.) **butter or margarine**
¾ cup **sugar**
1 teaspoon **baking soda**
1 large **egg white**
1 teaspoon **vanilla**
    Flavor options (choices follow)
1 cup **all-purpose flour**

In an 8- to 10-inch frying pan over medium heat, melt butter and heat just until it begins to smell and look lightly browned, about 10 minutes.

Pour into a bowl with sugar and soda. Beat to mix. Add egg white and vanilla; beat to blend well.

If desired, add flavor option.

Add flour and stir to mix well. If making ahead, cover airtight and chill up to 3 days.

Measure dough in ½-teaspoon portions and drop about 1 inch apart on lightly oiled 12- by 15-inch baking sheets (use 2 or 3 pans and bake in sequence).

Bake in a 350° oven until cookies are golden brown, about 10 minutes. (If you have 1 oven, alternate pan positions after 5 to 6 minutes.) Transfer to racks; when cookies are cool, serve or package airtight up to 3 days. Freeze to store longer. Makes about 9½ dozen.

PER COOKIE: 17 calories (48 percent from fat), 0.1 g protein, 2.1 g carbohydrates, 0.9 g fat (0.5 g saturated), 2.2 mg cholesterol, 16 mg sodium

FLAVOR OPTIONS

Gianduia buttons. Place ½ cup **hazelnuts** in an 8- to 9-inch-wide pan. Bake in a 350° oven until nuts are browned under their skins and smell toasted, about 15 minutes. Pour nuts onto a clean towel. Rub vigorously with towel to remove as much of the brown skin as possible. Lift nuts from towel; discard skins. Whirl nuts in a food processor or blender until finely ground.

Exceptionally crisp, two-bite-size golden button cookies come in five flavors. Each batch makes at least 9½ dozen cookies, ample for holiday gifts or tasting.

Make **golden button cookies,** preceding, adding as flavor options the nuts, 2 tablespoons **unsweetened cocoa,** and 2 teaspoons **instant coffee powder.** Reduce **flour** to ¾ cup, add to dough, and continue as directed. Bake cookies until tops begin to look dry and slightly cracked, about 10 minutes. Makes about 11 dozen.

PER COOKIE: 17 calories (58 percent from fat), 0.2 g protein, 1.9 g carbohydrates, 1.1 g fat (0.5 g saturated), 1.9 mg cholesterol, 14 mg sodium

Bizcochitos buttons. Coarsely crush ½ teaspoon **cardamom seed** and ¼ teaspoon **anise seed** with a mortar and pestle or flat-bottomed glass. Make **golden button cookies,** preceding, adding seed as the flavor option. Makes about 9½ dozen.

PER COOKIE: 17 calories (48 percent from fat), 0.1 g protein, 2.1 g carbohydrates, 0.9 g fat (0.5 g saturated), 2.2 mg cholesterol, 16 mg sodium

Lemon buttons. Coarsely crush enough **hard lemon drop candies** to make ½ cup; grate 1 teaspoon *each* **lemon** and **orange peel.** Make **golden button cookies,** preceding, adding candy and peel as the flavor option. Makes about 11 dozen.

PER COOKIE: 16 calories (39 percent from fat), 0.1 g protein, 2.3 g carbohydrates, 0.7 g fat (0.4 g saturated), 1.9 mg cholesterol, 14 mg sodium

Peppermint buttons. Coarsely crush enough **hard peppermint candies** to make ½ cup. Make **golden button cookies,** preceding, adding candy as the flavor option. Makes about 11 dozen.

PER COOKIE: 16 calories (39 percent from fat), 0.1 g protein, 2.3 g carbohydrates, 0.7 g fat (0.4 g saturated), 1.9 mg cholesterol, 14 mg sodium

IT TAKES A DESSERT *of stellar character to woo appetites at the conclusion of a holiday dinner. Here you have not just one but three picture-pretty pies equal to the task. Making the pies in shallow tart pans shows off fillings best, with a subtle side benefit—portions are thinner, therefore less filling, than traditional pie wedges. Each pie makes 8 to 10 servings; for a large party, you might want to offer more than one kind.*

GINGER-CARAMEL MACADAMIA PIE

 Pastry for a single-crust 9-inch-diameter pie
1½ **cups salted, roasted macadamia nuts**
 3 **large eggs**
 1 **cup firmly packed brown sugar**
 ½ **cup minced candied ginger**
 1 **tablespoon minced fresh ginger**
 1 **teaspoon vanilla**
 Warm chocolate sauce (recipe follows)
 Vanilla ice cream or sweetened whipped cream (optional)

Fit pastry over bottom and press against sides of a plain or fluted 9-inch tart pan with removable bottom; fold any excess pastry down to make flush with rim of pan.

Pour nuts onto a towel and rub lightly to remove salt. Lift nuts from towel and put in pastry.

In a bowl, beat to blend eggs, sugar, candied ginger, fresh ginger, and vanilla. Pour evenly over nuts.

Bake on lowest rack of a 325° oven until filling jiggles only slightly when pie is gently shaken, about 40 minutes. Cool on a rack. If making ahead, wrap airtight and chill up to a day. Offer warm chocolate sauce to spoon onto wedges to taste; accompany with ice cream. Makes 8 to 10 servings.

PER SERVING: 381 calories (52 percent from fat), 4.7 g protein, 43 g carbohydrates, 22 g fat (4.2 g saturated), 64 mg cholesterol, 230 mg sodium

Warm chocolate sauce. In the top of a double boiler, combine 1¼ cups **semi-sweet chocolate baking chips** and ¾ cup **half-and-half** (light cream). Place over simmering water and stir often until chocolate is smoothly melted. (Or put chocolate and cream in a micro-wave-safe bowl and heat on full power—100 percent—in a microwave oven; stir at 1-minute intervals, until chocolate is smoothly melted.)

Use chocolate sauce warm; if making ahead, cover and chill up to 3 days. Reheat over simmering water or in a microwave oven. Pour into a small pitcher. Makes 2¼ cups.

PER TABLESPOON: 34 calories (58 percent from fat), 0.4 g protein, 4.1 g carbohydrates, 2.2 g fat (1.3 g saturated), 1.9 mg cholesterol, 2.2 mg sodium

PERSIMMON-GLAZED PUMPKIN CHEESE PIE

 Pastry for a single-crust 9-inch pie
 1 **can (16 oz.) pumpkin**
 1 **cup nonfat or low-fat cottage cheese**
 1 **cup sugar**
 2 **large eggs**
 1 **tablespoon grated orange peel**
 1 **teaspoon grated lemon peel**
 ½ **teaspoon ground cinnamon**
 Persimmon glaze (recipe follows)

Fit pastry over bottom and press against sides of a plain or fluted 2-inch-deep and 9-inch-wide tart pan with remov-able bottom; fold any excess pastry down to make flush with the pan rim. Pierce pastry all over with a fork. Bake in a 350° oven until lightly browned, about 15 minutes.

Meanwhile, in a blender or food pro-cessor, whirl pumpkin, cottage cheese, sugar, eggs, orange and lemon peel, and cinnamon until mixture is very smooth.

Pour mixture into hot or warm pie shell. Bake in a 350° oven until filling barely jiggles in center when gently shaken, 35 to 40 minutes. Cool on a rack. Spoon persimmon glaze onto pie, then spread evenly to the pastry rim.

Rivulet of warm chocolate sauce flows onto ginger-caramel macadamia pie; if you like, serve ice cream or whipped cream alongside.

Help for the Holiday Cook

"IS IT OKAY TO ROAST *a turkey that's been in my freezer for two years?" "What can I do to make the cookie dough less crumbly?"*

Questions like these inundate consumer service hotlines, particularly around the holidays when both novice and experienced cooks run into trouble. Toll-free lines can save the day if you need help with holiday cooking problems.

The area code is 800, and most lines are closed on Thanksgiving, Christmas, and New Year's. P (i.e., Pacific), C, and E are time zones. (Dates are for 1992.)

American Seafood Institute: 328-3474; 9 to 5 E Mondays through Thursdays.

Butterball Turkey Talk-Line: 323-4848; 8 to 8 C weekdays November 2 through 25 (except 8 to 6 November 21 and 22, 6 to 6 Thanksgiving), 8 to 6 weekdays November 27 through December 23. In Canada, also call 323-4848; hearing impaired can call TDD-3848.

Dole Food Company: 232-8888 for grocery products, 356-3111 for fresh vegetables; 541-2349 in Canada; 8 to 5:30 P weekdays.

Frieda's, Inc. (specialty produce): 241-1771; 8 to 4 P weekdays.

Land O'Lakes Holiday Bakeline: 782-9606; 8 to 6 C daily November 1 through December 24, including Thanksgiving.

National Center for Nutrition and Dietetics: 366-1655; 9 to 4 C weekdays.

The Pillsbury Company: 767-4466; 8 to 6 C weekdays.

Reynolds Metals Company (about turkey): 745-4000; 24 hours from November 1 through 30, including Thanksgiving.

Specialty Brands (Fleischmann's Yeast; about baking): 777-4959; 7 to 5 P weekdays.

USDA Meat and Poultry: 535-4555; 10 to 4 E weekdays year-round (except 9 to 5 weekdays November 1 through 30 and the weekend of November 21 and 22, and 8 to 2 Thanksgiving).

Chill until glaze is set, at least 2 hours; to store up to a day, cover pie airtight without touching glaze. Makes 8 to 10 servings.

PER SERVING: 281 calories (23 percent from fat), 6.1 g protein, 48 g carbohydrates, 7.3 g fat (1.9 g saturated), 45 mg cholesterol, 206 mg sodium

Persimmon glaze. Rinse 3 medium-size (about 1 lb. total) ripe and jelly-soft **Hachiya-type persimmons;** cut in half lengthwise and use a spoon to scoop flesh from skin. Put persimmon pulp in a fine strainer over a bowl; discard skin.

Firmly rub pulp through strainer; discard residue. Measure 1 cup pulp (save extra for other uses); mix in 1 tablespoon **lemon juice.**

In a 3- to 4-cup pan, sprinkle 1 teaspoon (½ envelope) **gelatin** over 2 tablespoons **water.** Let stand about 5 minutes to soften. Stir over medium heat until gelatin melts. Off the heat, add ¼ cup **orange-flavor liqueur.**

At once, stir gelatin mixture into persimmon pulp. Chill (to speed, set bowl in ice water), stirring often, until mixture just begins to thicken. Spoon onto pumpkin filling.

HAZELNUT, PEAR & APRICOT PIE

- 1 **cup hazelnuts**
- ½ **cup sugar**
- 2 **tablespoons all-purpose flour**
- ¼ **cup (⅛ lb.) butter or margarine, cut into pieces**
- 2 **large eggs**
- 2 **teaspoons vanilla**
  Pastry for a single-crust 9-inch pie
- 1 **large (about ½ lb.) firm-ripe pear, such as red or regular Bartlett or Comice**
- 2 **tablespoons lemon juice**
- ¼ **cup apricot jam**

Place hazelnuts in an 8- or 9-inch-wide pan. Bake in a 350° oven until the nuts are lightly browned under skins, 15 to 20 minutes. Pour onto a towel; rub with towel to remove as much of the brown skins as possible. Lift nuts from towel; discard the brown skins.

In a food processor or blender, whirl nuts with sugar and flour until finely ground. Add butter, eggs, and vanilla, and whirl until thoroughly blended.

Fit pastry over bottom and press against sides of a plain or fluted 9-inch tart pan with removable bottom; fold any excess pastry down to make flush with pan rim. Pour nut mixture into pastry; spread smooth.

Core pear and cut into ¼-inch wedges. Sprinkle with lemon juice. Arrange pear slices, overlapping, on nut filling. Bake in a 350° oven until filling is richly browned, about 40 minutes.

In a 3- to 4-cup pan over low heat, stir apricot jam until warm (or warm jam in a microwave-safe bowl on full power—100 percent—in a microwave oven; stir every 10 seconds). Spoon jam onto warm pie, then gently spread to pastry rim. Serve warm or at room temperature. If making ahead, cover airtight and chill up to 1 day. Makes 8 to 10 servings.

PER SERVING: 300 calories (57 percent from fat), 4.2 g protein, 30 g carbohydrates, 19 g fat (5.2 g saturated), 55 mg cholesterol, 172 mg sodium

SHIMMERING ICE-CLAD BOTTLES of vodka or other spirits, with decorations sealed in the ice, make an amusing way to offer liquors that are syrupy and flavorful when super-chilled—like aquavit, vodka, or gin. To avoid dissipating the cold quickly, serve these beverages in tiny glasses for sipping "neat."

In heated contrast, eggnog lattes are a seasonal derivation of caffelatte (or cappuccino) to enjoy after dinner or as dessert. This brew is particularly popular in the Northwest, where coffee has long been a passion. For an especially luxurious refreshment, add a favorite liqueur to the hot eggnog latte to taste. Try some of the variations we describe here, or experiment to create some of your own.

Use leaves, evergreen sprays, flowers, citrus slices, or small chilies to decorate ice decanters molded in empty milk cartons.

DECORATED ICE DECANTER

To make a mold, cut triangular top from a clean ½-gallon milk carton. Check bottle shape of the liquor you want to freeze. There should be at least ¼ inch between milk carton and bottle all the way around. If bottle is too large, choose one that does fit and pour liquid into it; chill.

On the carton, fold in ½ inch of top edge at a 45° angle to make a rim. Tape the corners to secure.

Lay carton on its side in a rimmed pan. Arrange the decorations (see suggestions in photo caption, at left). Set pan level in freezer. Add about ⅛ inch water to carton; if decorations float, rearrange. Freeze solid. Tip carton onto another side, and repeat to line wall with ice; repeat with remaining sides.

Stand carton upright, put liquor bottle in carton, fill carton with water, and freeze until solid. After 8 hours, package for freezer storage so ice won't evaporate.

To serve, peel carton away from bottle. Use a towel to hold bottle; it will be cold and slippery. Return bottle to freezer or set it in a shallow bowl to catch drips when not serving.

Eggnog for lattes develops a thick, creamy head of foam when steamed, beaten, or whirled in a blender. Garnish with cinnamon sticks and freshly grated nutmeg.

The Beverage Dilemma

WITH WATERS COMPETING as a beverage of choice, fruit drinks proliferating like hybrids (and cross-pollinating with waters), wines made in more styles and places, the explosion of microbreweries, and the evolution of nonalcoholic wines and beers, hosts who hope to please the expanding tastes of their guests at large holiday parties are often in a state of confusion.

Variety is the easiest answer for events like open houses, where people come and go.

Set up the bar as self-service, with a collection of beverages. Then let guests make their own selections. Be sure to have a generous supply of waters or fruit juices for those who prefer nonalcoholic beverages or are acting as designated drivers.

Bar sink works well for chilling beverages; melting ice drains and bottles won't float.

FROTHY EGGNOG PLUS

Eggnog lattes are delicious on their own and can be served at brunch, as dessert, or mixed with liqueurs to make luxurious refreshments.

Liqueurs you might choose to serve in coffees, like brandy or cognac, work well. Amaretto and frangelico are pleasing, as are chocolate and coffee liqueurs. Add to taste to hot eggnog lattes.

EGGNOG LATTE

2 cups purchased eggnog
2 cups hot strong coffee or espresso
Cinnamon sticks (optional)
Freshly grated nutmeg (optional)

Pour eggnog into a 1½- to 2-quart pan. Sir often over medium heat until eggnog is hot, about 6 to 8 minutes. To make frothy, whip with a mixer at high speed while on the heat, or whirl in a blender. (Or heat and froth with steam jet of an espresso maker.)

Immediately divide coffee among 2 or 4 cups or among heat-resistant glasses (1 cup or 2 cups each), then add eggnog and foam, distributing equally. Add a cinnamon stick and a dusting of nutmeg to each cup. Makes 2 or 4 servings.

PER SERVING: 174 calories (49 percent from fat), 4.9 g protein, 18 g carbohydrates, 9.5 g fat (5.6 g saturated), 75 mg cholesterol, 71 mg sodium

HOLIDAY ENTERTAINING: A Christmas Feast

MEMORIES OF THE *holidays are crowded with images of special events, special times, and most especially, meals like this Christmas dinner featuring an imposing crown roast.*

To go with this meal, serve a chardonnay with ample acid and no more than moderate oak flavor. Wineries producing this style of chardonnay include Beringer Vineyards, Chalk Hill Winery, Dehlinger Winery, De Loach Vineyards, E & J Gallo Winery, Ferrari-Carano Vineyards, Fetzer Vineyards (Sundial has no oak), Grgich Hills Cellar, Husch Vineyards, and Wild Horse Winery. Many of these wineries also make oakier chardonnays, so read labels carefully.

CHRISTMAS MENU FOR 10 TO 12

Smoked Salmon with Citrus Mélange (page 225)
Pork Crown Roast with Brown Rice Filling & Baked Tomatoes
Jicama-Mint Relish (page 230)
Broccoli with Sherry-glazed Onions (page 227)
Ginger-Caramel Macadamia Pie (page 232)
Chardonnay   Mineral Water

Select two center-cut pork loin roasts to make a crown large enough for this recipe. At the market, have roast backbones (but not the meat) cut with a saw (cracked) before the roast is shaped so it will be easy to carve. The well of the cooked roast makes a cozy serving container for the brown rice filling, which cooks separately. The tomatoes bake in the oven with the roast.

PORK CROWN ROAST WITH BROWN RICE FILLING & BAKED TOMATOES

1 **center-cut pork loin crown roast (9 to 10 lb.), fat trimmed and backbone cut for carving**
Soy-wine marinade (recipe follows)
Brown rice filling (recipe follows)
Baked tomatoes (recipe follows)
1 **or 2 green onions, ends trimmed**
Salt and pepper

Rinse pork and pat dry. Pour marinade into a deep bowl, about 3-quart size, add pork, and rotate to coat with marinade. Cover and chill at least 3 hours, or up to a day; baste occasionally with marinade.

Lift roast from marinade; save liquid. Set roast, narrow end up, on a rack in a roasting pan about 11 by 14 inches. Bake in a 350° oven until a thermometer inserted against bone in thickest part of meat registers 155°, about 1¾ hours.

Meanwhile, bring reserved marinade to a boil, let simmer 1 to 2 minutes, then set aside to season rice.

With wide spatulas, transfer roast to a platter. Mound hot rice filling into center of roast; put remainder in a dish. Surround roast with tomatoes; garnish with onions.

Cut between ribs to serve; allow 1 or 2 ribs per portion. Spoon rice and tomatoes onto plates with sliced roast. Season to taste with salt and pepper. Makes 10 to 12 servings.

PER SERVING WITH RICE: 516 calories (33 percent from fat), 39 g protein, 44 g carbohydrates, 19 g fat (6.4 g saturated), 113 mg cholesterol, 791 mg sodium

Soy-wine marinade. Combine ½ cup *each* **soy sauce** and **dry red wine**; ¼ cup **honey;** 4 cloves **garlic,** minced or pressed; and 1 teaspoon **ground cinnamon.**

Brown rice filling. In a 4- to 5-quart pan, combine 3 cups **short-grain** or long-grain **brown rice,** 3 cups *each* **water** and **regular-strength chicken broth,** and ¼ cup minced **fresh ginger.** Cover; bring to a boil over high heat. Simmer gently until rice is tender to bite, about 45 minutes. Off the heat, stir in ½ cup of the reserved boiled **soy-wine marinade.** (If cooking ahead, drain and save any liquid. Cover rice and liquid; chill up to a day. Return rice and liquid to pan. Stir often over medium-low heat until hot; or, in a microwave oven, heat at half-power—50 percent—in a microwave-safe bowl, stirring every 1 to 2 minutes until hot, 10 to 15 minutes.) Mix in 1½ cups sliced **green onions.** Use hot.

Baked tomatoes. Rinse 10 to 12 large (about 2 lb. total) firm-ripe **Roma-type tomatoes;** cut in half lengthwise. Set cut side up in a 10- by 15-inch pan. Mix together ½ cup shredded **parmesan cheese,** 2 tablespoons minced **parsley,** 1 teaspoon **dried rubbed sage,** and ¼ teaspoon **pepper;** sprinkle mixture evenly onto tomatoes. Drizzle 1 to 2 tablespoons **olive oil** (total) over tomato halves.

Bake in a 350° oven (on rack beneath the pork) until tomatoes begin to soften slightly, 15 to 20 minutes. Makes 10 to 12 servings.

PER SERVING: 42 calories (51 percent from fat), 2 g protein, 3.7 g carbohydrates, 2.4 g fat (0.8 g saturated), 2.6 mg cholesterol, 69 mg sodium

Easy-carve roast yields thick pork chops to go with brown rice, cheese-topped baked tomatoes, and make-ahead broccoli with tiny onions (see page 227).

Warm glow of candlelight illuminates majestic presence of two pork loin roasts joined to form a crown. Brown rice filling, baked Roma-style tomatoes, broccoli and onions, and jicama-mint relish round out the main course.

Day-after-Thanksgiving Turkey Sandwiches

FRIENDLY COMPETITION *is as American as Plymouth Rock and discussing what makes the best Thanksgiving menu. But the fray heated up last November 29 in Seattle.*

Four connoisseurs of turkey and trimmings entered the great annual debate: whose day-after-Thanksgiving turkey sandwich is best? Each contestant claimed years of hands-on experience as competition credentials.

Though bread is the undisputed base, it's a foundation challenged. Steve Graham announced, ''Rye!'' Aki Takeda waved a baguette, Greg Malley defended sliced white, and Dave Cator scrambled the issue with egg bread.

The only standard ingredients were turkey and mayo, but even then there were preferences for dark or white meat, regular or reduced-calorie.

We aren't taking sides, or attempting to settle disputes.

But we do think the following combos might inspire further evolution, in your hands, of a post-Thanksgiving turkey sandwich that will become a winner with your family.

ANYTHING-GOES SEATTLE TURKEY SANDWICH

Following are the essentials of the sandwich presentation. Measuring of ingredients was for the faint-hearted; eye and appetite, it was mutually agreed, are the best guides.

Rye Graham. For the foundation of the sandwich, use sliced **light caraway rye bread.** For the fixings, spread bread lightly with **reduced-calorie mayonnaise,** add 1 or 2 thick slices **canned jellied cranberry sauce** (plain, not whole berry), top with slices of **dark turkey meat,** and add a few crisp **iceberg lettuce leaves.**

Baguette Takeda. Start with a long, thin **baguette** sliced lengthwise. Spread bread lightly with **margarine** followed by **mustard,** then generously with **mayonnaise.** Add sliced **white turkey meat;** slather it with **cream cheese.**

Top meat with thin slices of **smoked salmon** and drained **canned capers.** Next add thinly sliced **cucumber, tomato,** and **mild onion,** and finally a tangle of **alfalfa sprouts.** Cut crosswise into manageable hunks.

White Malley. The base is **thick-sliced white bread.** Spread lightly with **creamy Dijon mustard** and **reduced-calorie mayonnaise.** Top with slices of **dark** and **light turkey meat.** Sprinkle meat with **salt** and **pepper** to taste, then cover meat with thin slices of **smoked gouda cheese** (or jack cheese).

Put meat-topped piece of bread in a microwave oven and heat just until cheese begins to melt. Let sit until cool enough to touch, then add a slice of **canned pineapple,** several slices of crisply cooked **bacon,** and some **butter lettuce leaves.** Finally, top with another slice of white bread.

Egg Cator. Start with sliced **egg bread.** Spread with enough **mayonnaise** to ooze, add several layers of thinly sliced **white turkey meat,** and cover the meat with paper-thin slices of **Granny Smith apple. Salt** lightly and **pepper** heavily.

Cator got the last word: "Don't let the simplicity fool you. This one is to die for!"

Turkey sandwiches on the line: Everyone came out a winner in Seattle turkey tasting—and no one shared. Competitors enjoy their entries (left to right): Egg Cator, Rye Graham, White Malley, and Baguette Takeda.

Cooking with Quince

RESEMBLING A LUMPY, *sometimes fuzzy golden apple, quince doesn't convey its merits overtly. Raw quince is tough, dry-tasting, and generally unappealing. But cooking transforms this fruit. It becomes tender, aromatic, and slightly bittersweet—provocative with meats and grand in desserts.*

Here we pair quince with lamb stew; for dessert, it bakes in an orange syrup and in a pie.

LAMB STEW WITH CARAMELIZED QUINCE

  2 **tablespoons butter or margarine**
 ¼ **cup sugar**
  5 **large (about 3-in.-diameter, 2½ lb. total) quinces, peeled, cored, and cut into ¾-inch wedges**
2½ **pounds boned lamb shoulder, fat trimmed, cut into 1½-inch chunks**
  2 **large (about 1¼ lb. total) onions, chopped**
  3 **cups regular-strength beef broth**
 ¼ **cup minced fresh cilantro (coriander)**
  3 **tablespoons honey**
  2 **tablespoons minced fresh ginger**
  1 **teaspoon ground cinnamon**
 ¼ **teaspoon cayenne**
  1 **tablespoon cornstarch mixed with ¼ cup water**
  3 **to 4 cups hot cooked couscous or rice**
   Cilantro sprigs

In a 5- to 6-quart pan, melt butter and sugar over medium-high heat; add quince. Turn fruit often until richly browned, about 15 minutes; remove slices as browned. Put quince in a 9- by 13-inch pan. Cover the pan tightly with foil. If making ahead, chill up to a day.

To the 5- to 6-quart pan, add lamb and onion. Cover and cook over high heat until mixture is juicy, about 5 minutes. Uncover; stir often until liquid evaporates and browned bits form in pan. Add ¼ cup broth and scrape browned bits free. Boil until liquid evaporates and browned bits form again. Add another ¼ cup broth; repeat step.

When liquid evaporates, stir in remaining broth, minced cilantro, honey, ginger, cinnamon, and cayenne. Bring to a boil over high heat. Cover; simmer until meat is very tender when pierced, about 1½ hours. (If making ahead, cool, cover, and chill up to a day. To continue, stir over medium heat until simmering.)

Meanwhile, place covered quince in a 300° oven until hot to touch, about 20 minutes (about 25 minutes if chilled). With a slotted spoon, lift meat from pan. Skim and discard fat from broth. On high heat, stir in cornstarch; stir until broth boils. Return meat and any juices to pan.

On a platter, mound couscous and spoon stew onto it. Arrange quince around stew; garnish with cilantro sprigs. Makes 6 to 8 servings.—*Florence Goguely, Menlo Park, Calif.*

PER SERVING: 440 calories (26 percent from fat), 32 g protein, 50 g carbohydrates, 13 g fat (5.3 g saturated), 101 mg cholesterol, 141 mg sodium

BAKED QUINCE

  4 **large (about 3-in.-diameter, 2 lb. total) quinces, quartered, cored, and peeled**
  1 **tablespoon grated orange peel**
1½ **cups orange juice**
 ⅔ **cup sugar**
  3 **tablespoons lemon juice**
   About ¼ cup sour cream (optional)
 ¼ **cup coarsely crushed gingersnap cookie crumbs (optional)**

Place quince in a shallow 1½- to 2-quart baking dish. Mix orange peel, orange juice, sugar, and lemon juice; pour over quince. Cover tightly with foil. Bake in a 375° oven until quinces are just tender when pierced, 35 to 45 minutes. Uncover and baste quince often until very tender when pierced, 20 to 30 minutes longer.

Serve hot, warm, or chilled. Offer sour cream and gingersnap crumbs to spoon onto portions to taste. Makes 4 to 6 servings.

PER SERVING: 169 calories (0.7 percent from fat), 0.8 g protein, 44 g carbohydrates, 0.1 g fat (0 g saturated), 0 mg cholesterol, 6.2 mg sodium

Caramelized quince lends aromatic touch and provocative flavor to lamb stew.

QUINCE STREUSEL PIE

  5 **large (about 3-in.-diameter, 2½ lb. total) quinces, peeled, cored, and thinly sliced**
  1 **tablespoon grated orange peel**
1¼ **cups orange juice**
 ½ **cup raisins**
  2 **tablespoons cornstarch**
  1 **unbaked single-crust 9-inch pie shell**
   Streusel (recipe follows)

In a bowl, mix quince with orange peel, orange juice, raisins, and cornstarch. Pour into pie shell. Top fruit mixture with streusel. Bake in a 375° oven until juices bubble and quinces are tender when pierced, 50 to 55 minutes; if streusel darkens, drape with foil. Serve warm or cool. Makes 8 or 9 servings.

PER SERVING: 328 calories (41 percent from fat), 2.8 g protein, 49 g carbohydrates, 15 g fat (5.2 g saturated), 14 mg cholesterol, 185 mg sodium

Streusel. In a bowl, combine ⅓ cup **all-purpose flour**, ½ cup firmly packed **brown sugar**, ⅓ cup chopped **pecans** or walnuts, ¼ cup (⅛ lb.) **butter** or margarine, and 1 teaspoon **ground cinnamon.** With a pastry blender or your fingers, cut or rub mixture until coarse crumbs form. Squeeze to form into lumps, then break apart.

Eggnog Desserts

IF AN ABUNDANCE OF *purchased eggnog remains after a holiday party, here are two festive ways to put it to work: in a smooth white chocolate mousse laced with rum, and in a bread pudding. The pudding has a choice of toppings—one dresses it for dessert, the other for breakfast.*

EGGNOG & WHITE CHOCOLATE MOUSSE

- 1 **teaspoon unflavored gelatin**
- ¼ **teaspoon ground cinnamon**
- ⅛ **teaspoon ground nutmeg**
- 2 **cups purchased eggnog**
- 3 **ounces finely chopped white chocolate or white chocolate chips (suitable for melting)**
- 3 **tablespoons dark rum or brandy (optional)**
- 1 **teaspoon vanilla**
   Whipped cream (optional)

In a 1½- to 2-quart pan, sprinkle gelatin, cinnamon, and nutmeg over eggnog. Stir often over medium heat until eggnog is steaming, 7 to 8 minutes.

Remove from heat and stir in chocolate, rum, and vanilla; stir occasionally until chocolate is smoothly melted, about 5 minutes.

Pour mousse mixture into 6 small (about ½-cup-size) pôts de crème, demitasse, or dessert cups. Cover with plastic wrap (do not let wrap touch mousse); chill mousse until softly set, at least 4 hours or up to a day. Garnish each serving with a small spoonful of whipped cream. Makes 6 servings.

PER SERVING: 196 calories (51 percent from fat), 4.3 g protein, 21 g carbohydrates, 11 g fat (3.8 g saturated), 52 mg cholesterol, 58 mg sodium

EGGNOG BREAD PUDDING

Serve pudding with hard sauce for dessert, or with the fruit topping for breakfast.

- ½ **cup chopped pecans or walnuts**
   About ⅔ of a 1-pound baguette, cut into ¾-inch-thick slices
- ⅓ **cup raisins**
- 2 **cups purchased eggnog**
- 4 **large eggs**
- ½ **cup sugar**
- ½ **teaspoon ground cinnamon**
- ¼ **teaspoon ground nutmeg**
- ¼ **cup dark rum or brandy (optional)**
- 2 **teaspoons vanilla**
   Hard sauce or fruit topping (recipes follow)

Puff of whipped cream tops tiny pot of elegant white chocolate mousse made with purchased eggnog and lightly laced with rum.

In a 7- to 8-inch frying pan over medium heat, stir nuts occasionally until lightly browned, about 6 minutes. Pour from pan; let cool.

Arrange bread slices slightly overlapping in a lightly buttered shallow 3- to 3½-quart baking dish. Sprinkle with nuts and raisins.

Beat eggnog with eggs, sugar, cinnamon, nutmeg, rum, and vanilla. Pour mixture evenly over bread; press bread into liquid to saturate. Cover; chill at least 1 hour or up to 4 hours.

Bake pudding in a 350° oven until the center jiggles only slightly when dish is gently shaken and the top is golden brown, about 35 minutes. Spoon hot or warm pudding into small bowls; top with hard sauce or fruit topping to taste. Makes 8 servings.

PER SERVING: 349 calories (34 percent from fat), 9.7 g protein, 49 g carbohydrates, 13 g fat (4.2 g saturated), 145 mg cholesterol, 287 mg sodium

Hard sauce. Beat together until fluffy ¼ cup (⅛ lb.) **butter** or margarine (at room temperature), 1½ cups **powdered sugar,** ¼ cup **purchased eggnog,** 1 tablespoon **brandy** or dark rum, and 1 teaspoon minced **lemon peel** (yellow part only). If sauce is made ahead, cover and chill up to 1 week. Makes 1 cup.

PER TABLESPOON: 78 calories (38 percent from fat), 0.2 g protein, 12 g carbohydrates, 3.3 g fat (2 g saturated), 10 mg cholesterol, 33 mg sodium

Fruit topping. In a 10- to 12-inch nonstick frying pan, melt 1 tablespoon **butter** or margarine over medium-high heat. Add 2 large (about 1¼ lb. total) firm-ripe **pears,** cored and sliced; 2 large (about 1 lb. total) **apples,** cored and sliced; ¼ cup **sugar;** and 2 tablespoons **lemon juice.**

Cook fruit, turning occasionally, until liquid evaporates and fruit is slightly browned, 10 to 15 minutes. Makes 8 servings.

PER SERVING: 107 calories (16 percent from fat), 0.9 g protein, 24 g carbohydrates, 1.9 g fat (0.9 g saturated), 3.9 mg cholesterol, 15 mg sodium

CRÊPES EDINBURGH DO *not take their name from the Scottish capital known to its citizens as the Athens of the North, but rather from the Edinburgh Lodge, a bed-and-breakfast establishment in Ashland, the Athens of southern Oregon and site of the Oregon Shakespeare Festival. Graham Lewis tells us that the crêpes are a favorite of the playgoers who stay at the lodge. Although any berries will do, Lewis prefers blueberries.*

He also tells us that the recipe has been evolving and may not yet have reached his ultimate goal. We can't suggest improvements, but you are welcome to try.

CRÊPES EDINBURGH

- 1 **large package (8 oz.) cream cheese**
- 3 **tablespoons powdered sugar**
- 2 **cups blackberries, raspberries, or blueberries, or 3 cups hulled strawberries, rinsed and drained**
- 3 **large eggs**
- ½ **cup** *each* **milk and water**
- 1 **tablespoon granulated sugar**
- 1 **tablespoon vanilla**
  About 1 tablespoon melted butter or margarine
- 1 **cup all-purpose flour**
  Sour cream
  Edinburgh berry sauce (recipe follows)
  Slivered almonds

In a bowl, beat cream cheese with powdered sugar until cheese is soft. If using strawberries, slice fruit. Gently stir half the fruit into the cream cheese mixture; set aside.

In a blender or food processor, smoothly whirl eggs, milk, water, granulated sugar, vanilla, 1 tablespoon butter, and flour.

Place a 6- to 7-inch crêpe pan or other flat-bottomed frying pan over medium heat. When pan is hot, coat lightly with more butter or cooking oil spray. At once, pour in about 3 tablespoons batter, tilting pan so batter flows quickly over entire flat surface. Cook crêpe until

edge is lightly browned and surface looks dry. Turn and brown lightly on second side. Tip crêpe out onto a plate. Repeat to cook remaining batter; stack crêpes.

Divide cream cheese mixture equally among crêpes; roll to enclose filling and set crêpes seam down on individual plates or a platter. Top with dollops of sour cream and remaining berries, then pour Edinburgh berry sauce over the dessert. Sprinkle with almonds. Makes 14 to 16 crêpes, 7 or 8 servings.

PER SERVING: 363 calories (37 percent from fat), 7.2 g protein, 49 g carbohydrates, 15 g fat (8.9 g saturated), 121 mg cholesterol, 146 mg sodium

Edinburgh berry sauce. In a 1- to 1½-quart pan, combine ¾ cup **sugar**, 2 tablespoons **cornstarch**, and 1 cup **orange juice.** Stir over high heat until boiling. Remove from heat and mix in 1 tablespoon **lime juice**, 1 tablespoon **butter** or margarine, 1 cup **berries** (same as used in filling), and 3 tablespoons **orange-flavor liqueur.** Serve warm or cool. Makes 2⅓ cups.

Graham Lewis

Ashland, Oreg.

THE ELEMENTS IN THIS *soup, seemingly disparate, blend to produce a surprisingly good flavor. If you think that apple, onion, water chestnuts, honey, and pumpkin pie spice seem a bit odd together, just consider the ingredients in mincemeat pie. Neither sweet nor savory, Lori Cloninger's Cream of Water Chestnut Soup is a blend of both.*

She serves it hot or cold, but prefers it hot, with a cinnamon stick garnish. She also swirls it with carrot soup for a two-color holiday first course.

CREAM OF WATER CHESTNUT SOUP

- 1 **medium-size (6 to 7 oz.) Golden Delicious apple, peeled, cored, and minced or grated**
- 1 **small (¼ lb.) onion, chopped**
- 2 **cans (8 oz. each) water chestnuts, drained**
- 2 **cans (10½ oz. each) condensed chicken broth**

- 1 **tablespoon honey**
- ½ **teaspoon pumpkin pie spice (or ¼ teaspoon ground cinnamon and ⅛ teaspoon** *each* **ground allspice and nutmeg)**
- 2 **cups half-and-half (light cream)**
  Ground nutmeg or ground cinnamon (optional)

In a 3- to 4-quart pan over medium heat, combine apple, onion, and 2 tablespoons water. Simmer until onion is very soft, about 15 minutes. In a blender or food processor, smoothly purée onion mixture and water chestnuts; add a little of the broth to keep mixture fluid.

Pour purée back into pan; add broth, honey, pumpkin pie spice, and half-and-half. Cook, uncovered, over medium heat for about 15 minutes to blend flavors; stir occasionally. Ladle into bowls and dust with nutmeg. Makes about 7 cups, 6 or 7 servings.

PER SERVING: 175 calories (46 percent from fat), 6.5 g protein, 19 g carbohydrates, 8.9 g fat (5.2 g saturated), 26 mg cholesterol, 566 mg sodium

Lori Cloninger

Los Angeles

"Crêpes are a favorite of Ashland playgoers."

Red pear wedges with ginger dressing make colorful splash on spinach salad.

FALL PEAR SALAD

6 slices (about ¼ lb.) bacon
3 large firm-ripe red pears (about 1½ lb. total)
3 tablespoons lemon juice
1 package (10 oz.) washed fresh spinach (or 1½ lb. spinach, stems and wilted leaves discarded), rinsed and crisped
½ pound mushrooms, rinsed and thinly sliced
Ginger dressing (recipe follows)

In a 10- to 12-inch frying pan over medium-high heat, cook bacon until brown and crisp, turning often. Drain on towels. When cool, crumble.

Core pears and cut each into 16 wedges; mix fruit with lemon juice.

On a platter or 8 salad plates, arrange spinach and mushrooms; top with pear slices and juice. Moisten with dressing; top with bacon. Makes 8 servings.—*Louise Ross, Elk Grove, Calif.*

Ginger dressing. Mix ½ cup minced **crystallized ginger,** ¼ cup *each* **extra-virgin olive oil** and **red wine vinegar,** and ½ teaspoon **pepper.**

PER SERVING: 201 calories (43 percent from fat), 3.2 g protein, 29 g carbohydrates, 9.5 g fat (1.7 g saturated), 3.4 mg cholesterol, 103 mg sodium

---

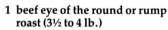

Lentils and lots of vegetables simmer to make a thick and satisfying soup.

WHOLESOME LENTIL SOUP

1 package (12 oz. or 2 cups) lentils
2 large (about 1¼ lb. total) onions, chopped
6 cups regular-strength chicken broth
4 cups water
2 pounds carrots, thinly sliced
2 cups sliced celery
1 can (28 oz.) Italian-style tomatoes
2 teaspoons *each* dried basil leaves and dried thyme leaves
3 dried bay leaves
1 teaspoon *each* fennel seed and pepper

Sort lentils for debris; rinse and drain lentils. In an 8- to 10-quart pan over high heat, boil onions with ½ cup broth until liquid evaporates and onions begin to brown. Add remaining broth; stir to free browned bits. Add lentils, water, carrots, celery, tomatoes and their liquid, basil, thyme, bay, fennel seed, and pepper.

Cover, bring to a boil, and simmer until lentils are soft to bite, about 1 hour. Serve, or if making ahead, let soup cool, cover, and chill up to 3 days. Makes 10 to 12 servings, about 5 quarts.—*Karen Meter, Aurora, Colo.*

PER SERVING: 185 calories (6.3 percent from fat), 11 g protein, 34 g carbohydrates, 1.3 g fat (0.3 g saturated), 0 mg cholesterol, 279 mg sodium

---

Oven-pot-roasted beef bakes with tiny onions and cranberries; serve with port sauce.

CRANBERRY-PORT POT ROAST

1 beef eye of the round or rump roast (3½ to 4 lb.)
1 tablespoon salad oil
1 can (14½ oz.) regular-strength beef broth
1¾ cups port
⅓ cup firmly packed brown sugar
2 packages (10 oz. each) frozen petite onions
2 cups fresh or frozen cranberries
6 cups hot cooked egg noodles
2 tablespoons cornstarch
Parsley sprigs
Salt and pepper

Rinse meat, pat dry, and rub with oil. Place in a 10- by 14-inch roasting pan. Bake in a 450° oven until meat is well browned, about 45 minutes; turn often. Add broth and port. Cover tightly; reduce oven to 400° and bake 1½ hours.

Mix sugar and onions into pan; cover and bake 1 hour. Add cranberries; cover and bake until meat is tender when pierced, about 30 minutes longer.

Put meat and noodles on a platter. With a slotted spoon, ladle onions and berries onto noodles; keep warm. Skim fat from pan juices. Mix cornstarch with 3 tablespoons water. Bring pan juices to boiling over high heat. Stirring, add cornstarch mixture until sauce is as thick as you like. Pour sauce into a small bowl; serve with meat and noodles. Garnish with parsley sprigs. Add salt and pepper to taste. Makes 10 to 12 servings.—*Dorothy B. Rosenthal, Pacific Palisades, Calif.*

PER SERVING: 363 calories (20 percent from fat), 33 g protein, 38 g carbohydrates, 8 g fat (2.3 g saturated), 98 mg cholesterol, 87 mg sodium

Baked Zucchini with Mushrooms

- 1 pound mushrooms, rinsed
- 1 medium-size (about 6 oz.) onion
  About 1⅓ cups regular-strength chicken broth
- 3 large eggs
- 4 large (about 2 lb. total) zucchini, ends trimmed, shredded
- ½ cup fine dried bread crumbs
- ¼ cup grated parmesan cheese
- ¼ teaspoon *each* dried oregano leaves and pepper
- 2 tablespoons minced green onion

Thinly slice mushrooms and chop onion; combine in a 10- to 12-inch frying pan with ½ cup water. Stir often on high heat until liquid evaporates and browned bits stick to pan. To deglaze pan, add ⅓ cup broth; stir browned bits free. Boil dry and stir often until onion begins to brown. Repeat deglazing step until onion is golden brown, 2 or 3 more times, using ⅓ cup broth each time.

In a bowl, beat eggs to blend; stir in zucchini, crumbs, cheese, oregano, pepper, and mushroom mixture. Pour into a buttered 10- by 12-inch shallow oval casserole (or 9- by 13-in. rectangle). Bake in a 325° oven until mixture is set in center when shaken, about 45 minutes; top with green onion. Makes 8 servings.—*Betty Risse, San Jose, Calif.*

PER SERVING: 106 calories (30 percent from fat), 7.1 g protein, 13 g carbohydrates, 3.5 g fat (1.2 g saturated), 82 mg cholesterol, 129 mg sodium

Zucchini and mushroom casserole makes a good vegetable main dish.

Mideastern Lamb Shanks with Couscous

- 4 lamb shanks (about 4 lb. total)
- 2 large (about 1¼ lb. total) onions
- 2 tablespoons paprika
- 2 teaspoons dried thyme leaves
- 1 teaspoon pepper
- 1 can (28 oz.) tomatoes
- 1 cup dry red wine
- ⅓ cup calamata olives
- 1 package (10 oz.) frozen petite Brussels sprouts
  About 4 cups hot couscous
  Salt

Rinse shanks; place in a 4- to 5-quart casserole. Bake in a 450° oven for 30 minutes. Chop onions; mix with lamb juices. Sprinkle shanks with paprika, thyme, and pepper. Bake 30 minutes.

Add tomatoes and their liquid, wine, and olives. Cover tightly. Bake until meat is very tender when pierced, about 1½ hours. Add sprouts, cover tightly, and bake until sprouts are hot, about 15 minutes. Serve with couscous and salt to taste. Makes 4 servings.—*Robin Warren, Fort Bragg, Calif.*

PER SERVING: 638 calories (17 percent from fat), 60 g protein, 72 g carbohydrates, 12 g fat (3.8 g saturated), 145 mg cholesterol, 584 mg sodium

Slow-baked lamb shanks are meltingly tender; serve with juices and couscous.

Fall Leaf Bars

- 1¾ cups all-purpose flour
- 1½ cups sugar
- 1½ teaspoons ground cinnamon
- 1 teaspoon baking soda
- ½ teaspoon *each* baking powder and ground nutmeg
- 2 large eggs
- 1 cup canned pumpkin
- 6 tablespoons butter or margarine, melted
- ⅓ cup water
  Cheese leaf filling (recipe follows)

In a large bowl, mix flour, sugar, cinnamon, soda, baking powder, and nutmeg. Add eggs, pumpkin, butter, and water; beat well. Spread batter in a buttered and floured 10- by 15-inch pan. Drop cheese filling in 24 equal portions (each about 1 tablespoon) evenly spaced over surface of batter. With a knife tip, pull edges of cheese into leaf shapes.

Bake in a 350° oven until center of cake (not cheese) springs back when lightly touched, about 30 minutes; let cool. Cut pieces so cheese is in center of each. Serve warm or cool, or cover and chill up to 3 days. Makes 24.—*Renée Murdock, Kent, Wash.*

Cheese leaf filling. Smoothly mix 1 large package (8 oz.) **cream cheese,** 1 **large egg,** and ¼ cup **sugar.**

PER PIECE: 161 calories (39 percent from fat), 2.6 g protein, 23 g carbohydrates, 6.9 g fat (4.1 g saturated), 45 mg cholesterol, 109 mg sodium

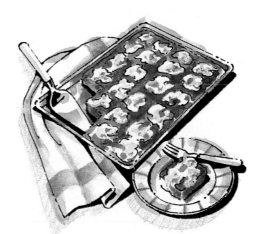

Cream cheese filling makes moist centers for pumpkin cake squares.

November Menus

NEVER ENOUGH *drumsticks? Never enough breast? Love turkey but hate to carve? Such quandaries have a simple solution: buy turkey parts and create your ideal "bird." Buy more drumsticks than a single turkey can offer, and get a boneless breast—slicing is quick and easy. This meal is planned to allow ample leftovers, but without a carcass to crowd the refrigerator.*

With all the football games this month, our second meal accommodates fans who are hard to get from the TV to the table. Great-tasting Reuben sandwiches will keep them well nourished.

BEST-OF-THE-BIRD DINNER

Mixed Salad with Feta Cheese
Roast Turkey Breast & Four Drumsticks
Dried Tomato Couscous
Green Beans with Toasted Almonds
Pecan-Cranberry Pie
Dry Chenin Blanc

If you have just one oven, the pecan-cranberry pie can be made a day ahead or baked before the turkey.

While turkey parts roast, cook beans and assemble the salad and couscous makings. Follow package directions for couscous, using 3 cups; season to taste with chopped, oil-drained dried tomatoes and a little sage and oregano.

ROAST TURKEY BREAST & FOUR DRUMSTICKS

Make a triangular mound of couscous on platter to lean drumsticks against. Or serve in a bowl alongside.

  4 turkey drumsticks, each about 1 pound
  1 boned turkey breast half, 3 to 3½ pounds
  ⅔ cup apple jelly
  2 tablespoons raspberry vinegar or wine vinegar

Best-of-the-bird dinner features roast turkey breast and extra drumsticks, served with dried tomato couscous. Dinner starts with mixed salad, finishes with pecan-cranberry pie.

  ½ teaspoon ground sage
  2 tablespoons cornstarch
  About 2 cups regular-strength chicken broth
  Salt and pepper

Rinse drumsticks and breast; pat dry. Trim fat from breast. Set skin side up and fold narrow end under breast to make an evenly thick piece; pull skin to cover as much breast as possible. Tie breast snugly with cotton string at 1-inch intervals lengthwise and crosswise.

In a 1- to 1½-quart pan over medium heat, stir the jelly with the vinegar and sage until jelly melts.

Lay drumsticks slightly apart in an 11- by 17-inch roasting pan and brush with part of jelly mixture. Bake in a 375° oven for 15 minutes.

Set breast in pan and baste with more of jelly mixture. Bake breast until a thermometer registers 160°, and the

---

Drumstick finials. On 3- by 10-inch paper, cut slits ¼ inch apart; fold lengthwise; tape.

Menu card. Fall fruits, gold-sprayed leaves and nuts hold dinner menu card upright.

Harvest decor. For table, golden fabric and cord provide nests for natural treasures.

Napkin loops. Use more golden cord to loop around napkins, show off knot know-how.

drumsticks until thermometer registers 185° at bone in the thickest part, about 2 hours longer. (If one part cooks faster, remove from oven and keep warm.)

As turkey roasts, baste with drippings and jelly mixture, using it all. If drippings start to scorch, add ⅓ cup water and scrape browned bits free.

Transfer meat to a warm platter; keep warm and let stand 5 to 10 minutes. As juices accumulate on platter, drain into roasting pan.

To make gravy, skim and discard fat from drippings. In a 1-quart or larger glass measure, blend a little of the drippings smoothly with cornstarch; add remaining drippings and enough broth to make 2½ cups. Return gravy to pan; stir over high heat until boiling. Pour into a bowl.

Slice breast; slice drumsticks or serve whole. Serve meat with gravy, salt, and pepper to taste. Makes 12 to 16 servings, or 8 to 10 with leftovers.

PER SERVING WITH ½ CUP GRAVY: 299 calories (33 percent from fat), 37 g protein, 10 g carbohydrates, 11 g fat (3.4 g saturated), 101 mg cholesterol, 98 mg sodium

PECAN-CRANBERRY PIE

- 3 large eggs
- 1 cup corn syrup
- 1 cup sugar
- 1 teaspoon vanilla
- 1¼ cups fresh or frozen cranberries, rinsed
- 1 cup pecan halves
  Unbaked pastry for a 9-inch single-crust pie
  Vanilla ice cream (optional)

In a large bowl, beat to blend eggs, corn syrup, sugar, and vanilla. Stir in cranberries and pecans.

Line pan with pastry and crimp rim decoratively; pour in cranberry filling. Bake in a 350° oven until filling is set when pan is shaken, 55 to 65 minutes. Let cool at least 30 minutes; serve warm or cool. If making ahead, cool, cover, and let stand up to a day. Cut into wedges; offer with ice cream. Makes 8 to 10 servings.

PER SERVING: 365 calories (37 percent from fat), 3.9 g protein, 56 g carbohydrates, 15 g fat (2.5 g saturated), 64 mg cholesterol, 177 mg sodium

Split baguettes surround Reuben filling that peeks from sides. Olives anchor subs.

GAME-DAY REUBEN SUBS

Beef or Chicken Noodle Soup
Reuben Submarines
Ice Cream Sandwiches
Beer   Water

This menu needs no utensils. Sip soup from mugs. Provide plates for the sandwiches because they drip; pass ice cream sandwiches.

(Continued on next page)

REUBEN SUBMARINES

2 slender (½ lb. each) baguettes
About 3 tablespoons Dijon
  mustard
Russian slaw (recipe follows)
¾ pound thinly sliced cooked
  corned beef
⅓ pound thinly sliced Swiss cheese
1 small (about ¼ lb.) mild onion,
  thinly sliced

Cut baguettes in half lengthwise; pull bread from bottom sections to make shallow trenches. Spread cut sides of bread with mustard.

With a slotted spoon, mound slaw into trenches. Top with beef, cheese, and onion. Press down tops of sandwiches. Cut each into 3 portions. Makes 6 servings.

PER SERVING: 514 calories (37 percent from fat), 27 g protein, 53 g carbohydrates, 21 g fat (8.5 g saturated), 81 mg cholesterol, 1,546 mg sodium

Russian slaw. In a bowl, combine ½ cup **nonfat** or regular **sour cream**, 3 tablespoons **tomato-based chili sauce**, 2 tablespoons **sweet pickle relish**, 1 tablespoon **prepared horseradish**, and 6 cups finely shredded **napa cabbage**; mix. Use or, if making ahead, cover and chill up to a day.

DECEMBER

Christmas dinner (page 248)

One secret of a
successful holiday season is to simplify your entertaining,
keeping it easy and relaxed. Our splendid Christmas
feast needs a minimum of last-minute effort as the
beef roast cooks together with vegetables in the same oven.
The flexible holiday buffet is quickly assembled and
easily expanded if your guest list grows; it combines
purchased, ready-to-eat foods with make-ahead dishes.
You'll also find Christmas tree bread and holiday
sweets to make for serving or giving and a
comprehensive look at the newest cookware.

A Christmas Feast from the Oven

JUST HOW EASY CAN CHRISTMAS *dinner be? Let this splendid meal be your measure. The main course is a handsome, succulent beef roast surrounded by a colorful, aromatic array of vegetables. As they roast together in the same oven, mingling meat and vegetable juices collect; these juices, enhanced by the dazzle of flaming brandy, become a memorable and exquisitely simple sauce.*

You can bake and frost the cake a day ahead.

What do you do while dinner cooks? Devote yourself to enjoying the day.

CHRISTMAS DINNER

Greens with Vinaigrette
**Peppered Beef Rib Roast
with Roasted Vegetables
& Brandied Juices**
Prepared Horseradish
Hot Buttered Rolls
Chocolate-Chestnut Star Cake
Cabernet Sauvignon
Black Muscat Dessert Wine

While the roast rests for carving, sit down to a salad of crisp mixed greens.

To go with the main course, dust off a mature, smooth Cabernet Sauvignon that you've been hoarding for a special occasion.

Centerpiece is a natural mix of fruits and nuts nested among evergreen branches.

A fruity dessert wine made of black or other muscat grapes is a splendid complement to the cake.

PEPPERED BEEF RIB ROAST WITH ROASTED VEGETABLES & BRANDIED JUICES

- 2 **tablespoons black peppercorns**
- 2 **tablespoons fennel seed**
- 3 **large cloves garlic**
- 1 **center-cut beef standing rib roast, about 10 pounds**
- 12 **medium-size (about 2¼ lb. total) carrots, peeled**
- 6 **small (2½-in.-wide, 2 lb. total) onions, unpeeled**
- 2 **dozen small (2-in.-wide, about 3 lb. total) red thin-skinned potatoes, scrubbed**
- 6 **small (about 2 lb. total) red bell peppers, cut in half lengthwise, stemmed, and seeded**
- ⅔ **cup brandy or regular-strength beef broth**
- 1¾ **cups regular-strength beef broth**
    Salt

In a blender or food processor, coarsely grind peppercorns and fennel. Add garlic and whirl until finely chopped; rub mixture over beef.

Set roast, fat up, in a V-shaped rack in a deep 12- by 17-inch roasting pan. Place carrots under and around roast. Place onions in a 9- by 13-inch pan. Bake beef on bottom rack and onions above in 325° oven (or use 2 ovens); cook 30 minutes.

Add potatoes to meat pan, peppers to onion pan. Bake until a thermometer inserted in center of thickest part of meat reads 130° for rare, 2½ hours longer; 140° for medium, about 3 hours longer; or 150° for well done, about 3½ hours longer.

Put meat on a platter (remove strings if roast is tied). Cut onions in half lengthwise; add vegetables to platter. Keep warm. Tilt roasting pan and skim off and discard fat. Add brandy to pan. Place over high heat and carefully ignite (not beneath a vent or near flammable materials). When flame dies, add broth and bring to a boil, stirring to loosen browned bits; add to pan juices that have drained from roast. Pour into bowl; serve with meat and vegetables. Add salt to taste. Makes 12 servings.

PER SERVING WITH FAT-TRIMMED COOKED MEAT: 604 calories (36 percent from fat), 51 g protein, 40 g carbohydrates, 24 g fat (9.6 g saturated), 139 mg cholesterol, 164 mg sodium

CHOCOLATE-CHESTNUT STAR CAKE

Look for the sweetened chestnut spread or purée (ingredient list must include sugar) in specialty food stores, European delicatessens, and supermarkets.

- 1 **chocolate cake baked in a 9- by 13-inch pan (use a favorite recipe or a cake mix)**
    Chestnut butter cream (recipe follows)
    Chocolate icing (recipe follows)
    Gold-color sugar (optional)

Let cake cool, then invert from pan, centering on a platter or board at least 12 by 15 inches. Cut cake in half horizontally. Supporting top layer with 2 wide spatulas, lift off and set aside. Spread chestnut butter cream evenly on cut side of cake base. Set cake top on butter cream; pat gently to adhere cake to filling.

If you want a star-shaped cake, make a 3-inch-long cut into the center of cake from each narrow end. Align knife with cut end and corner of a narrow end of cake; cut wedge free. Repeat to cut free remaining 3 wedges. Butt pan-end edges of each pair of wedges together. Center 1 triangle on each long side of cake.

Swirl icing over top and sides of cake. Decorate with colored sugar. Serve, or let stand until icing is firm, about 4 hours; cover airtight up to a day. Makes 12 to 16 servings.

NUTRITIONAL INFORMATION NOT AVAILABLE BECAUSE OF VARIABLES IN CAKE.

Chestnut butter cream. Beat to smoothly blend ½ cup (¼ lb.) **butter** or margarine (at room temperature) and about 1½ cups (1 large can, 17½ oz., or 2 small cans, each 8¾ oz.) **sweetened chestnut spread** or purée.

Chocolate icing. In a 1- to 1½-quart pan over low heat, stir 1½ cups **whipping cream** and ½ pound chopped **semi-sweet chocolate** until chocolate is melted. Let cool, stirring occasionally, until thick enough to spread, about 1 hour. To speed thickening, set pan in ice water and stir icing until thick enough to spread.

The main event awaits: succulent seasoned beef rib roast with brandied juices and roasted vegetables. As the meat roasts, you add the carrots, onions, potatoes, and red bell peppers in sequence so they will all be ready at the same time.

Easy, Expandable Buffet

BUY YOUR WAY TO SUCCESS? *That's the secret of this quickly assembled buffet. It expands easily if the guest list multiplies. The Belleville family heartily endorses the built-in flexibility because it leaves time to catch up on news of family and friends. Ready-to-eat purchased foods are the meal's backbone; simple make-ahead dishes round it out.*

The buffet is also geared to look fresh over a period of several hours, so guests can arrive at staggered times and dine comfortably at their own pace.

All of the recipes have make-ahead steps or start with ready-to-serve ingredients that go together rapidly.

HOLIDAY BUFFET FOR 10 TO 12

Buy & Serve Appetizers
Garden Vegetables
Curry Yogurt Dip
Sugar-crusted Baked Ham
Mustard
Basket of Assorted Breads
Marinated Vegetable Salad
Bulgur Salad
Christmas Rose Trifle
Dry Red Wine   Hot Cider Bar

Sliced smoked salmon, bite-size appetizers from the freezer case, and fresh vegetables with curry yogurt dip are nibbles to enjoy leisurely before dipping into the heart of the meal, which features a purchased sweet-crusted cooked, sliced-on-the-bone ham. To go with the ham, there are a quickly assembled marinated vegetable salad of canned roasted red peppers and marinated artichoke hearts, a bulgur salad, and a basket of assorted breads.

A day ahead, assemble the dessert trifle (using purchased cake); you can also make the bulgur salad and the curry yogurt dip and rinse the raw vegetables (wrap in towels, enclose in plastic bags, and chill). Shortly before serving time, heat the frozen appetizers and warm the cider to serve all evening.

This menu has a useful bonus: extras keep well for at least a week in the refrigerator, at the ready for sandwiches and snacks for an expanded household of family and guests.

What to do next? Just relax like the Bellevilles—sharing the season's good cheer and good food.

BUY & SERVE APPETIZERS

Plan on 4 or 5 appetizer portions per person.

The key offering is **sliced smoked salmon;** for buffet serving, a 1-ounce portion is adequate, but a whole fillet looks festive, and extras can be used later. With the salmon, offer **sour cream, capers, lemon wedges,** and chopped **chives** or green onions.

Also use purchased **frozen bite-size appetizers** such as tiny tacos, individual spanakopitas, dim sum, or miniature quiches; follow package instructions to thaw or heat. You can keep several extra packages of these foods in your freezer, just in case the guest list gets bigger.

GARDEN VEGETABLES

To serve 10 to 12, you need at least 2 pounds of fresh vegetables such as **small carrots with tops, baby squash, edible-pod peas, cucumbers, bell peppers,** and **cherry tomatoes;** rinse well. Leave small vegetables whole; cut larger vegetables into chunks. If making ahead, wrap in towels, enclose in plastic bags, and chill up to 48 hours.

Arrange vegetables attractively, perhaps with a just-harvested look from a basket. Nibble plain, season with **salt,** or dunk into the **curry yogurt dip** (recipe follows).

SUGAR-CRUSTED BAKED HAM

For 10 to 12, buy at least a 5-pound portion (or half) of a **cooked, seasoned, sliced-on-the-bone ham.** Serve cold ham and **breads** (following) with a pot of **mustard** or mustards of your choice. You can also offer **chutney, prepared horseradish,** or other relishes.

BASKET OF ASSORTED BREADS

Buy at least 10 **crusty rolls** or 30 **breadsticks,** as well as 2 **whole-grain loaves** (1 lb. each) to slice.

(Continued on page 252)

This home-for-the-holidays party welcomes the gang with an easy, expandable buffet that uses ready-to-eat purchased foods to supplement make-ahead dishes. Extras keep well in the refrigerator, ready for sandwiches and snacks for family and guests.

MARINATED VEGETABLE SALAD

For 10 to 12, drain 24 ounces (1 or more jars to equal this weight) **roasted red peppers.** Slice peppers and put on a platter. With a slotted spoon, lay 14 ounces (1 or more jars to equal this weight) **marinated artichoke hearts** on peppers; moisten salad with about ½ cup of the artichoke marinade, or to taste.

CURRY YOGURT DIP

- 2 **cups unflavored nonfat yogurt**
- 2 **teaspoons curry powder**
- 2 **teaspoons cumin seed**
- 1 **teaspoon pepper**
  Salt

Mix yogurt, curry, cumin, pepper, and salt to taste. Pour into a small bowl and serve, or cover and chill up to 1 week. Makes 2 cups, 10 to 12 servings.

PER TABLESPOON: 9 calories (10 percent from fat), 0.8 g protein, 1.2 g carbohydrates, 0.1 g fat (0 g saturated), 0.3 mg cholesterol, 11 mg sodium

BULGUR SALAD

- 4 **cups (about 1½ lb.) bulgur (cracked wheat)**
- 5 **cups boiling water**
- ¾ **cup balsamic vinegar (or ¾ cup red wine vinegar plus 1½ teaspoons sugar)**

Christmas trifle is cake layered with jam, raspberries, and a delicate custard.

- 1 **tablespoon grated orange peel**
- 1¼ **cups orange juice**
- 3 **tablespoons olive oil**
- 1 **teaspoon crushed dried hot red chilies**
  Salt
  Romaine lettuce spears, rinsed and crisped
  Thin orange slices

In a large bowl, combine bulgur and boiling water. Let stand until most of the liquid is absorbed, 15 to 20 minutes. Drain and discard liquid.

Mix vinegar, orange peel, orange juice, oil, and chilies; mix with bulgur. Season mixture to taste with salt. (If making ahead, cover and chill up to a week.) Stir and pour into a serving bowl; garnish with romaine and orange slices. Makes 10 cups, 10 to 12 servings.

PER SERVING: 241 calories (16 percent from fat), 7.2 g protein, 47 g carbohydrates, 4.2 g fat (0.6 g saturated), 0 mg cholesterol, 10 mg sodium

CHRISTMAS ROSE TRIFLE

- 2½ **cups nonfat or regular milk**
- ¾ **cup sugar**
- 1 **vanilla bean, 5 to 6 inches long, split lengthwise**
- 3 **tablespoons cornstarch**
- 1 **large egg**
- 2 **to 4 tablespoons rose flower water (available in specialty food and liquor stores)**
- 2 **cups whipping cream**
- 1 **pound cake (1 lb.), thawed if frozen**
- 1½ **cups orange juice**
- ¼ **cup black raspberry–flavor liqueur (optional)**
- ½ **cup black cherry or raspberry jam**
- 2 **cups raspberries, rinsed and drained**
  Sweetened whipped cream (optional)
  Candied rose petals or fresh rose petals (free of pesticides and herbicides), rinsed and drained (optional)

In a 2- to 3-quart pan over medium heat, combine 2¼ cups milk, sugar, and vanilla bean. Stir often until milk is steaming, 5 to 8 minutes. Remove milk from heat and let stand 20 minutes. Holding an end of the vanilla bean, use the tip of a small knife to scrape the tiny seeds into milk. Rinse vanilla bean and let dry thoroughly; store airtight to reuse.

Smoothly mix remaining milk and cornstarch; add egg and beat to blend. Pour into warm milk. Stir over medium-high heat until sauce bubbles, about 5 minutes. Let cool, then chill, covered, until cold, about 2 hours; to speed chilling, set pan in ice water and stir often. Add rose water to taste to cold sauce.

Whip the 2 cups cream until soft peaks form. Fold cream into sauce, blending gently. Cover and chill until needed to assemble trifle.

Cut cake into ¼-inch slices. Line bottom of a 3½- to 4-quart bowl (glass, to show off filling) with ⅓ of cake slices, overlapping if necessary. Mix orange juice and liqueur. Spoon ⅓ of the liquid evenly over cake. Spread cake gently with ⅓ of the jam, sprinkle with ⅓ of the raspberries, and pour in ⅓ of the whipped cream mixture. Repeat to make 2 more layers.

Cover trifle and chill at least 4 hours or no more than 2 days before serving (up to 1 week after assembling, any extra trifle will taste fine but look tired). If desired, garnish with additional whipped cream and rose petals. Makes 10 to 12 servings.

PER SERVING: 437 calories (49 percent from fat), 5.7 g protein, 51 g carbohydrates, 24 g fat (11 g saturated), 119 mg cholesterol, 89 mg sodium

HOT CIDER BAR

Offer a selection of spirits for guests to add to cups.

- 1 **pound lady apples or other tiny apples, rinsed**
- 1 **tablespoon whole cloves**
- 5 **quarts apple cider or juice**
  About 15 cinnamon sticks, each about 3 inches long
- 3 **strips (each about 10 in.) lemon peel, yellow part only, cut with a vegetable peeler**
  Orange-flavor liqueur, bourbon, brandy, rum, or cognac (optional)

Stud apples with cloves. In an 8- to 10-quart pan, combine apples, cider, 5 cinnamon sticks, and peel. Cover and bring to steaming over high heat, about 20 minutes. Keep cider warm on very low heat. Ladle cider into cups, adding a cinnamon stick to each. Add liqueur to taste, if desired. Makes 20 cups, 10 to 12 servings.

PER CUP WITHOUT ALCOHOL: 110 calories (2.5 percent from fat), 0.2 g protein, 27 g carbohydrates, 0.3 g fat (0.1 g saturated), 0 mg cholesterol, 7 mg sodium

What's New in Cookware?

LOOKING FOR NEW *cookware? These days, there's a pan to suit every need and style, from flashy to functional, heavy-duty "professional" to lightweight budget. And there are finishes and coatings to consider. What's the best choice? It all depends on you. The perfect pan for one cook may drive another cook crazy.*

EVALUATING YOUR NEEDS

Every pan has pros and cons. Appearance and price may be your starting point, but you should also consider materials and construction. To help you select pans that will best suit your needs, consider these questions:

What type of cooktop do you have? Not all pans work well on all cooktops. You can use any kind of cookware on electric coil and gas ranges (glass-ceramic cookware, however, performs best on gas cooktops). Electric radiant, halogen, and solid-element ranges need heavy, flat-bottomed pans, while induction ranges require magnetic pans —cast iron, carbon steel, or some types of stainless. (Before choosing pans, check the individual range manufacturer's recommendations.)

Match pans to burner sizes for the most even cooking and to safeguard cooktops and pan handles.

Lid options include glass with replaceable phenolic fingerguard (this one's ovenproof to 425°) and handle, and metal with stay-cool hollow loop handle.

How important are durability and heat conductivity? How long do you want your pans to last—a lifetime, or just until you're tired of the way they look? Are you willing to pay more for good materials and construction?

For many cooks, the most important consideration is a pan's heat conductivity—that is, its ability to quickly and evenly transfer heat from a burner throughout the pan. Materials, especially those that are used in the pan's bottom, are key in determining this quality.

What about design? Do shape, balance, and weight work together for good function? Does the pan sit steadily when empty—or does it tip? Are the handles heat resistant and easy to grip? Does the pan feel balanced and comfortable in your hands? Will a filled, heavy pan be a burden to maneuver?

How do you cook? Do you want a pan for every chore, or will a few standard pans suffice? Do you need a pan with a nonstick finish? Do you prefer a pan with sensitive heat response, say for cooking delicate fish, or a fairly heavy pan that browns meat and cooks pancakes evenly?

What are you willing to spend? Materials, construction, and design influence cost. Pans made to last generally cost more. Warranties on less expensive pans may exclude a key component, like a nonstick coating.

MATERIALS

Cookware is made from a variety of materials, sometimes used singly, sometimes in combination. Here we detail the properties of the five most common pan materials.

Aluminum

Basics. Aluminum's heat conductivity is second only to copper's. Aluminum pans are versatile and come in a wide range of prices and styles.

On the down side, aluminum is soft and scratchable. If salty or acidic foods have long contact with aluminum, they can pit it and pick up a metallic flavor. Therefore, most aluminum pans have a nonstick (see pages 256–257) or anodized surface.

Handles may be permanent or replaceable (screwed on). Some stay cool on the range or are ovenproof. Heavy pans may have a helper handle to make lifting easier.

Anodizing is an electrochemical process that permanently changes the pan surface, making it harder and abrasion resistant and sometimes less reactive (depending on the brand). Calphalon and Magnalite Professional are anodized pans.

Does uncoated aluminum cookware have any connection to Alzheimer's disease? Both the Alzheimer's Association and the Food and Drug Administration say there is no conclusive evidence of any direct effect. Most experts agree that aluminum intake from pans is small; we ingest more aluminum from things like antacids and buffered aspirin.

Use and care. To reduce scratching, avoid using sharp-edged metal utensils.

Remove salty or acidic foods right after cooking, and wash pans. Don't use uncoated or anodized pans for food storage.

Wash anodized pans by hand; over time, chlorine-based automatic dishwashing cleaners can cause surface deterioration.

(Continued on next page)

Cast iron

Basics. Whether you're buying old-fashioned uncoated, preseasoned, or bright enamel–coated cast-iron pans, they're durable enough to last a lifetime—given the proper care.

Cast iron is heavy and a relatively poor heat conductor. It heats up and cools down slowly but retains heat for a long time—which means it's great for even browning, for braising and simmering, and for keeping food hot—but poor if you need precise heat control.

Use and care. Uncoated pans (such as Lodge and Wagner's brands) need to be seasoned to discourage rusting and sticking. This means developing an oily patina by cloaking the pores with a thin, oily film before using the pans for the first time.

To season, lightly rub clean pans and metal lids with salad oil or shortening and bake in a 325° oven for 1 hour; let cool. If pans rust, scour with steel wool, dry, then repeat seasoning.

Manufacturers recommend that, when cooking with cast iron, you heat the pan slowly before adding food. Don't store food in uncoated pans. Cast iron reacts with acidic foods and gives them a metallic flavor.

Clean cast iron by hand with hot water and a nonabrasive pad, and dry immediately. A little dish soap is fine for coated pans. Manufacturers disagree on whether soap removes seasoning from uncoated pans. Lightly rub uncoated pans with salad oil before storage to prevent rusting.

Copper

Basics. Copper's burnished glow and its superb ability to conduct heat quickly and evenly make it attractive to many cooks. Copper pans perform well for a wide range of cooking chores, from slow-simmering stews and delicate sauces to browning foods quickly.

The drawbacks of copper? For many, one is the high price. And copper is heavy and requires frequent polishing.

Copper reacts with acidic foods and can form off-tastes or colors and leach into food (toxic at high levels). Therefore, most pans are lined.

Tin is the traditional lining choice. But pans lined with tin need retinning often; the metal is not durable and eventually wears off—and it can melt above 450°.

Today, stainless steel is a popular pan liner. It's permanent, improves the pan's toughness, and is easy to care for. (Bourgeat and All-Clad produce copper pans with stainless steel linings.)

Use and care. Copper dents and scratches easily; thick, heavier pans are stronger and hold up better. Hand-wash with nonabrasive cleaners. Automatic dishwashers that reach high temperatures may stain the metal and damage the tin lining. To remove tarnish, polish regularly with a commercial cleaner or ½ cup vinegar and 1 tablespoon salt.

Glass-ceramic

Basics. Glass-ceramic, first used for rocket nose cones, withstands extreme temperature changes; it goes from freezer straight to rangetop or microwave.

Glass-ceramic cookware (such as Visions Cookware by Corning) conducts heat poorly but retains heat well.

Lower temperatures are recommended for cooking with glass-ceramic. Water-based foods like soups or sauces cook successfully; other foods may take longer and can stick. Pans with special nonstick finishes help reduce this problem.

Use and care. Although glass-ceramic cookware can break from impact, it won't break from thermal shock. Avoid metal utensils, which may scratch the material. Wash by hand or machine.

Stainless steel

Basics. Exceptional durability and good looks make stainless steel very popular for cookware. Unlike other metals, it does not react with foods, and it resists scratching. Because it's strong, pans can be thin and lightweight.

On its own, stainless is a poor heat conductor. And pans can develop hot spots (where scorching occurs) when they are in direct contact with a heat source like an electric coil. To improve heat distribution, Revere Cookware and Farberware combine stainless with metals that are better heat conductors. (See cores and disks section, following.)

Most stainless steel is 18/10: 18 percent chromium, 10 percent nickel, and the rest iron and other elements.

FIVE BASIC MATERIALS

Copper (top left)
- Best heat conductor
- Beautiful, expensive, heavy
- Must be hand-washed
- Requires frequent polishing
- Pictured pan's stainless steel liner adds durability

Stainless Steel (top center)
- Poor heat conductor alone
- Shiny, low-maintenance, lightweight, dishwasher-safe
- Wide price range
- Pictured pan has an aluminum disk that improves heat conduction

Glass-Ceramic (top right)
- Poor heat conductor but, once hot, retains heat well
- Can go from freezer to rangetop and back
- Can chip. Dishwasher-safe
- Pictured pan has a nonstick coating

Aluminum (bottom right)
- Excellent heat control
- Lightweight to heavy
- Wide price range. Most are nonstick or anodized
- Pictured anodized pan is abrasion resistant. Must be hand-washed

Cast Iron (bottom left)
- Poor heat conductor but, once hot, retains heat well
- Heavy. Wide price range
- Must be hand-washed
- Pans come uncoated, preseasoned, or enameled
- Pictured uncoated pan must be seasoned

Use and care. The advantage of stainless steel over other pan materials is that it requires so little attention. It can go into the dishwasher, although dishwasher temperatures and detergents may mar the sheen over time.

(Continued on page 256)

Cookware comes in five basic materials (clockwise from top left): copper, stainless steel, glass-ceramic, aluminum, and cast iron. For characteristics of each (heat conductivity, appearance, maintenance, other features), see screened box on facing page.

... What's New in Cookware?

CORES, DISKS, PLATING

To improve heat conductivity, some cookware incorporates highly conductive inner cores or disks attached to the pan base. Plating (lining pan bottoms with conductive materials) is also done. To identify a pan's construction, read the manufacturer's information.

Stainless steel typically gets these improvements. But manufacturers of conductive copper and aluminum pans may rely on these techniques simply to lower their cost.

Cores. A core is a highly conductive metal used between layers of less conductive materials to improve a pan's overall heat conductivity. Some pans may have three layers, with stainless on the inside and outside and a different metal sandwiched in between as the core. Five-ply pans are stainless on the inside and outside, with three layers of highly conductive metal in between.

Copper is the most conductive core material, followed closely by aluminum, and far behind by steel. Since copper is expensive and heavy, aluminum, which is cheaper and lighter, is often the material of choice.

Many believe a core's thickness is as important as the material itself. The thicker the core, the faster, more uniform the heating. Unfortunately, comparisons between different constructions are difficult, because many manufacturers don't indicate thicknesses.

The core diameter usually equals that of the pan bottom. Sometimes the core continues partway up the pan sides. If it continues all the way up the sides, the pan is called a clad pan. A clad pan improves conduction and discourages hot spots. All-Clad is one manufacturer. Because these pans add more highly conductive materials, they may be heavier and more expensive.

Starter set makes a great gift. Include a 1- to 2-quart saucepan, 3- to 4-quart saucepan, 10-inch frying pan (uncoated or nonstick), and 5- to 6-quart pan, all with lids. You'll pay from $40 for budget aluminum to as much as $850 for copper. If retailers' sets don't include pans you want or need, mix and match brands from open stock (as above). It is likely to increase your cost.

Disks. Pans with this feature have a metal disk attached to the bottom of the pan, where heating is focused, to improve conductivity. It may be copper, aluminum, or a combination. You may see the disk, or it may be covered with metal to protect it from scratching and uneven wear.

Plating. Some manufacturers deposit copper on the outside of pans to boost heat conduction. Watch out, however, for pans that have extremely thin plating, which doesn't improve conductivity.

FINISHES & COATINGS

Cookware may have three types of finishes and coatings.

Nonstick

Basics. Nonstick cookware is the answer for the health-conscious and those wanting easy cleanup—and certainly appeals to most of us!

Gone are the days when nonstick meant inexpensive pans that would last only a couple of years. Now, you'll find durable, high-performance nonstick models. How to tell a short-lifer from a long-lifer? Check the warranty and the price—basically, you get what you pay for. A 10-inch frying pan can cost as little as $8 (Regal) to $35 (Berndes's Granit line) or as much as $100 (Le Creuset's Castoflon line).

Part of nonstick's performance comes from the pan beneath the coating—it can be any of the materials already discussed.

Coatings usually fall into three categories. Manufacturers Du Pont and Whitford describe their products as good (Teflon 2 and Xylan), better (SilverStone and Xylan Plus), and best (SilverStone Supra and Xylan Eterna). Although service life varies according to individual use, coatings in the good category are likely to perform well for 5 years or less, those in the better category for 5 to 10 years, and coatings in the best category for 10 or more years.

Textured surfaces are the biggest news in nonstick cookware. These recently introduced pans have bumps or grooves in different configurations; wear occurs on the peaks, and the nonstick coating remains in the valleys, continuing to provide food release. The texture may be visibly imprinted (T-Fal Resistal and Circulon) or nearly invisible, as in the case of LeCook's-Ware Steelon and Farberware Millennium with Excalibur (which comes with a 20-year coating warranty).

Use and care. Before the first use but after washing, lightly wipe pans with oil for optimum food release.

Most nonstick pans are dishwasher-safe. In most cases, you must use wood or nylon tools if you want the pans to last. Some pans that have reinforced textured coatings are unaffected by metal tools.

Leaving an empty nonstick pan on high heat may break down some coatings. For longevity, some manufacturers suggest cooking on medium to low heat. Even with the best care, a coating's releasing effect will diminish over time. You can keep using the pan—just add a little oil to prevent sticking.

Porcelain enamel

Basics. A coating of porcelain enamel is hard and durable; it comes in a wide range of attractive colors; and it is impervious to moisture, most foods, and high heat. It can be fused to the inside or outside of cast iron (like Le Creuset), aluminum (such as Regal), and carbon steel pans (like Chantal).

Use and care. If food tends to stick or scorch, try cooking at a lower heat. Remove acidic foods from pans right after cooking; they can dull the surface. Enamel may chip if it's hit sharply or

dropped on a hard floor. Cleaning needs vary with pan type.

Acrylic

Basics. An acrylic coating adds a colorful exterior to inexpensive aluminum pans, but it scratches fairly easily, and fat and other foods may leave permanent stains.

Use and care. Don't bang pans against other utensils or sharp objects. Wipe spills off coating as soon as possible. Wash by hand or in the dishwasher.

THREE OPTIONS FOR COOKWARE FINISHES

Acrylic (top)

- Used on inexpensive aluminum pans
- Scratches easily, can stain
- Pictured pan has colorful acrylic finish

Porcelain Enamel (right)

- Colorful and durable (but it can chip)
- Goes on cast iron, carbon steel, or aluminum
- Pictured cast-iron pan is enameled inside and out

Nonstick (bottom)

- Pan base can be any material and can range from lightweight to heavy
- Short- to long-life coating (see discussion, beginning on facing page)
- Wide price range. Many are dishwasher-safe
- Pictured pan's barely visible textured coating withstands wear from metal utensils

Cookware finish options include (clockwise from top) acrylic, porcelain enamel, and nonstick.

A Trio of Holiday Sweets

NUT-TOPPED BUTTER *cookie triangles, iced ginger cookies, and creamy hazelnut truffles are sweets to suit holiday merrymaking.*

NUT MOSAIC TRIANGLES

1¾ cups all-purpose flour
¾ cup sugar
2 teaspoons baking powder
1 cup (½ lb.) butter or margarine
2 large eggs
3 tablespoons honey
1 cup sliced almonds
½ cup shelled pistachios
1 teaspoon almond extract

In a food processor or bowl, mix flour, ½ cup sugar, and baking powder. Whirl or rub in ½ cup butter until fine crumbs form. Add eggs; whirl or stir until dough holds together. With floured fingers, press dough evenly in bottom of a buttered rimmed 10- by 15-inch pan.

Stir honey and remaining sugar and butter in a 1- to 2-quart pan over medium-high heat until bubbling. Add almonds, pistachios, and extract. Spoon over dough.

Bake in a 350° oven until topping is deep gold, 18 to 20 minutes. Let cool in pan. Cut into 3-inch triangles (plus a few small pieces). Serve, store airtight up to 2 days, or freeze. Makes about 35.

PER COOKIE: 122 calories (58 percent from fat), 1.9 g protein, 12 g carbohydrates, 7.9 g fat (3.6 g saturated), 26 mg cholesterol, 82 mg sodium

CHRISTMAS GINGERSNAPS

¾ cup (⅜ lb.) butter or margarine
About 1 cup granulated sugar
½ cup dark molasses
1 large egg
1 tablespoon ground ginger
2 teaspoons ground cinnamon
1½ teaspoons baking soda
¼ teaspoon *each* ground allspice, ground nutmeg, and ground cloves
2½ cups all-purpose flour
Icing (recipe follows)
¼ cup colored sugar

In a food processor or bowl, whirl or beat butter, 1 cup granulated sugar, and molasses until smoothly mixed. Add egg, ginger, cinnamon, soda, allspice, nutmeg, and cloves; whirl or beat to blend. Thoroughly mix in flour.

Shape dough into 1-inch balls and set about 2 inches apart on buttered 12- by 15-inch baking sheets. With a flat-bottomed glass dipped in granulated sugar, press cookies to ½ inch thick. Bake in a 375° oven until a cookie springs back when gently pressed in center, about 12 minutes.

Transfer cookies to racks to cool. Spread with icing and sprinkle decoratively with colored sugar; let stand until icing hardens. Serve, store airtight up to 3 days, or freeze. Makes about 45.

PER COOKIE: 104 calories (28 percent from fat), 0.9 g protein, 18 g carbohydrates, 3.2 g fat (1.9 g saturated), 13 mg cholesterol, 64 mg sodium

Icing. Stir 2 cups **powdered sugar** and 3 tablespoons **water** until smooth.

HAZELNUT TRUFFLES

26 shelled hazelnuts
12 ounces bittersweet or semisweet chocolate, chopped
½ cup whipping cream
¼ cup hazelnut- or chocolate-flavor liqueur
¼ cup unsweetened cocoa

Place hazelnuts in an 8- to 9-inch-wide pan. Bake in a 350° oven until nuts are golden under skins, 10 to 12 minutes. If desired, rub nuts in a towel to remove most of the skins; lift off towel. Let cool.

In a 2- to 3-quart pan, stir chocolate and cream often over low heat until smoothly melted, 6 to 7 minutes. Stir in liqueur. Let cool, then chill until firm enough to shape, about 1½ hours.

Shape chocolate mixture into 1¼-inch balls; roll in cocoa to coat. Press a nut into each ball. If desired, place in small decorative paper cups. Serve, or chill airtight up to a week. Makes 26.

PER TRUFFLE: 95 calories (74 percent from fat), 1.4 g protein, 7.6 g carbohydrates, 7.9 g fat (4.1 g saturated), 6.3 mg cholesterol, 2.2 mg sodium

Festive touches for holiday sweets include powdered sugar icing and colored sugars, unsweetened cocoa, hazelnuts, and glazed nuts.

Fruit-filled Bread for Christmas Morning

IN THE MIDST OF THE *Christmas morning excitement, offer this showy bread. Slice it to display the spiraled fruit filling, and accompany with thin slices of gouda cheese (buy a 2- to 3-pound wedge) or another favorite cheese such as jarlsberg or cheddar.*

With a compote of fresh fruit—perhaps a mixture of sliced oranges and kiwi fruit with grapefruit wedges—hot chocolate, and coffee, you have the makings of a fine breakfast.

CHRISTMAS TREE BREAD

  2 **packages active dry yeast**
  ½ **cup warm (110°) water**
  ½ **cup (¼ lb.) butter or margarine,**
      cut into chunks
  1 **cup milk**
  3 **large eggs**
  ¼ **cup sugar**
  2 **teaspoons vanilla**
  1 **teaspoon grated lemon peel**
  ½ **teaspoon ground cardamom**
      or mace
  ½ **teaspoon salt**
      About 5½ cups all-purpose flour
      Fruit filling (recipe follows)
  1 **large egg yolk mixed with**
      1 tablespoon water
      Glaze (recipe follows)
      Fresh cranberries and holly
      leaves, rinsed and drained dry
      (optional)

Spiraled into a Christmas tree, glazed bread holds center stage at breakfast.

In a large bowl, soften yeast in warm water, about 5 minutes. In a 1- to 1½-quart pan, combine butter and milk. Warm over medium heat just until milk is 110°; butter does not need to melt. (Or heat butter and milk in a microwave-safe bowl, uncovered, in a microwave oven until milk is 110°.)

Add milk mixture, whole eggs, sugar, vanilla, lemon peel, cardamom, salt, and 3 cups flour to yeast mixture. Beat with a mixer at medium speed until dough is stretchy and shiny, 5 to 8 minutes. Stir in 2¼ cups flour.

To knead with a dough hook, beat at high speed until dough pulls cleanly from sides of bowl, 5 to 8 minutes. If dough still sticks, add flour, 1 tablespoon at a time, until dough pulls free.

To knead by hand, scrape dough onto a lightly floured board. Knead until smooth and elastic, adding as little flour as possible to prevent sticking, about 10 minutes. Return dough to bowl.

Cover bowl with plastic wrap. Let dough rise in a warm place until doubled, about 1 hour. Punch dough down; reserve ⅓ cup of it.

On a floured board, roll the large portion of dough into a 10- by 36-inch rectangle. Spread fruit filling over dough to within ½ inch of long sides. Roll from a long side, jelly roll–style.

On an oiled 14- by 17-inch baking sheet, zigzag dough (like stacked S's), seam down, to make a tree that's narrow at top and broad at base (see photo at left). Form reserved ⅓ cup dough into a ball and attach to the base of tree as the trunk.

Cover with plastic wrap; let rise in a warm place until puffy, about 25 minutes. Brush tree with yolk mixture.

Bake in a 350° oven until golden brown, 40 to 45 minutes. Let bread stand on pan until warm.

(If making ahead, let bread cool, then wrap airtight. Store at room temperature up to 1 day, or freeze up to 1 month. Allow at least 4 hours to thaw at room temperature. Reheat thawed loaf, lightly covered, in a 350° oven until warm, 15 to 20 minutes.)

Spoon glaze over warm bread; transfer to a board and garnish with cranberries and holly leaves. Slice when warm

When cut into thick, tender slices, bread displays filling of nuts and fruits.

or cool. Makes 1 loaf, about 4¼ pounds, 12 to 16 servings.—*Barbara Bochner, Ross, Calif.*

PER SERVING: 382 calories (26 percent from fat), 8.6 g protein, 62 g carbohydrates, 11 g fat (4.7 g saturated), 71 mg cholesterol, 151 mg sodium

Fruit filling. Bake ¾ cup **slivered almonds** in a 9-inch-wide pan in a 350° oven until golden, about 10 minutes.

Soak 1 cup **golden raisins** in 3 tablespoons **orange juice** and 2 tablespoons **brandy** or vanilla until plump, about 30 minutes.

In a food processor, finely chop raisin mixture, almonds, 1 cup coarsely chopped peeled **apple,** 1 cup coarsely chopped **dried apricots,** 2 teaspoons **ground cinnamon,** and 1 teaspoon grated **orange peel.** (Or, reserving raisin liquid, finely chop mixture with a knife, then add liquid.)

Glaze. Mix 1¼ cups **powdered sugar** with 2 tablespoons **orange juice** until smooth.

Brazilian Bonbons

THESE SPEEDY CONFECTIONS *start with an ingredient popular in their native Brazil, sweetened condensed milk. Its caramel-like taste forms a backdrop for the more intense flavor of peanut butter or chocolate.*

Just heat milk with peanut butter or cocoa to thicken it and develop a chewy texture. Then shape candies and coat with sugar or chocolate shot.

CASHEW FRUIT CANDIES
(Cajuzinho)

1 **can (14 oz.) sweetened condensed milk**
1 **cup peanut butter**
  About ½ cup sugar
  About 64 (¼ lb.) small roasted cashews, salted if desired

Place milk and peanut butter in a 2- to 3-quart pan. Stir over medium-high heat until mixture is warm to touch and holds together in a soft mass, about 3 minutes; fat will separate from mixture if overcooked. Remove from heat.

To shape each candy, roll about ½ tablespoon peanut-butter mixture between your palms into a 1-inch log, then roll it in sugar. Press pointed end of a cashew partway into 1 end of log, squeezing log gently to taper slightly (see picture).

Serve, or chill airtight up to 1 week; freeze to store longer. Makes about 64.— *Eliana Woodfort, Perris, Calif.*

PER PIECE: 67 calories (48 percent from fat), 2.1 g protein, 7.3 g carbohydrates, 3.6 g fat (1 g saturated), 2.8 mg cholesterol, 30 mg sodium

CHOCOLATE TAFFIES
(Brigadeiro)

1 **can (14 oz.) sweetened condensed milk**
1 **cup unsweetened cocoa**
  About 1 tablespoon butter or margarine
3½ **ounces (½ cup) chocolate shot (sprinkles)**

In a 2- to 3-quart pan over medium-low heat, stir milk, cocoa, and 1 tablespoon butter until mixture starts to bubble,

Chocolate taffies and cashew fruit candies (shaped like fruit from which cashews grow) are easy to make.

then stir until mixture holds together as a soft mass when pushed to side of pan, 3 to 5 minutes. Remove from heat and let stand until cool enough to touch.

With lightly buttered hands, shape mixture into 1-inch balls and roll 4 or 5 at a time in shot to coat. If desired, place each candy in a small paper or foil bonbon cup.

Serve at room temperature. If making taffies ahead, chill airtight up to 1 week; freeze to store longer. Makes about 34.

PER PIECE: 71 calories (28 percent from fat), 1.7 g protein, 13 g carbohydrates, 2.2 g fat (1.3 g saturated), 6.3 mg cholesterol, 24 mg sodium

Why? Answers to Your Cooking Questions

WHY DO SOME OF THE SIMPLEST *cooking tasks occasionally produce bizarre results? It could be because you use a different tool or technique—one that seems like it should produce the same results but in fact radically changes the end product. Here we give three such cases.*

If you've encountered similar kitchen mysteries and would like solutions, send your questions to Why? Sunset Magazine, 80 Willow Rd., Menlo Park, Calif. 94025.

For help in unraveling culinary puzzles, we call on Dr. George York, extension food technologist at UC Davis's Department of Food Science and Technology.

WHY DO POTATOES GET GLUEY IF YOU MASH THEM IN A FOOD PROCESSOR?

When the food processor was new, mashing potatoes was one of the first things many of us tried to do with it. After all, an electric mixer does the job well, and a food processor should do it easier and better. Right? Wrong.

The reason has to do with the starch in potatoes—it's distributed in structures called starch buds (also called starch grains or starch granules). In a food processor or blender, the blade is so fast and forceful it cuts open the starch buds, allowing the gluey starch to leak out.

Why doesn't this happen when you break up potatoes with a masher or electric mixer? Because these tools aren't forceful enough to break the starch buds by the time the potatoes are fluffy and ready to eat. But if you keep on mashing or mixing, you can make any potato gummy.

In thin-skinned potatoes, the structure that holds the starch buds together is fragile, making buds easy to break; these potatoes are not good mashers. Russet potatoes mash best because their large starch buds tend to separate easily from each other rather than break.

WHY DOESN'T WHIPPING CREAM ALWAYS WHIP?

It's the fat emulsified in cream that allows it to whip and stay whipped. As you beat the cream, tiny fat globules suspended in liquid stretch around air bubbles whipped into cream and hold them for several hours. Given sufficient agitation, milk with as little as 3½ percent fat will get quite foamy, but the foam rapidly fizzles because there is not enough fat to sustain it.

Heavy whipping cream (36 to 40 percent fat) whips most readily and at best can double in volume (depending on which whipping tool you use). Richer cream won't hold as much air. Light whipping cream (the kind most available, and usually labeled just "whipping cream") has less fat—a minimum of 30 and up to 36 percent—but whips satisfactorily.

To whip well, cream must be cold (35° to 45°). If it's warmer, the fat globules in the cream are so soft that, as the whipping action takes place, they run together rather than stretch. You get either no foam or a curdled mess. If the bowl and beaters are chilled, they help cream stay cold while it develops good volume.

The shape of the beater or whipping utensil also affects the amount of air beaten into the cream. A food processor (or blender) with a metal blade pulls in little air, producing a dense, thick foam with little volume; the process is also so fast you can easily end up with butter instead of whipped cream.

Balloon-shaped whips (with multiple wires) and electric or rotary beaters do the best job of incorporating air into cream for the lightest, fluffiest results.

For stiffest foams, whip the cream by itself. Stir in sugar or flavorings last.

Cream beaten to hold distinct peaks stays whipped longer than softly whipped cream. But if you softly whip cream ahead and chill it, covered, until ready to use, you can perk up its texture with a few last-minute whisks.

Gluey potatoes? Potatoes whirled in food processor turn into a gummy mass. Hand-mashed, they stay fluffy. Why? It's all in how you handle the starch buds.

WHY WON'T JELLY JELL WHEN YOU MULTIPLY THE RECIPE?

Pectin, which makes jelly set, is heat sensitive. This is particularly true of pectin sold for home jelly making.

If you multiply ingredients for a jelly recipe, you're asking for trouble. The mixture must cook longer than the recipe (or pectin) is designed for, and the pectin in the bottom of the pan stays hot long enough to lose its jelling properties before the top of the mixture reaches the jell point. This is why directions that come with pectin should be followed exactly.

Then how do commercial makers cook large batches? They use steam-jacketed kettles, which bring heat uniformly and quickly to all sides of the containers.

More December Recipes

OTHER RECIPES *for the holidays include a spicy chili snack and cranberry-flavored salad dressing and vinegar.*

CRISP CHILI RINGS

Crisp rings of fried pickled jalapeño chilies tingle palates with their zippy sour-hot flavor.

Because they start as purchased pickled chilies, they're easy to make. Just drain, dust with flour, and fry. They taste best freshly cooked but can be made ahead and reheated.

- 1 **jar (16 oz.) sliced jalapeño chili rings**
- **About ½ cup all-purpose flour**
- **Salad oil**

Rinse and drain chili rings; pat dry. Pour flour into a bag. Add about half of the chili rings and shake to coat evenly with flour.

In a deep 2- to 3-quart pan, bring 1 inch oil to 300°. Shake excess flour from chilies and add them to oil. Stir often until light gold and crisp, 6 to 8 minutes. Regulate heat, as needed, to maintain oil at 300°.

With a slotted spoon, lift out chilies and drain on towels. Repeat to cook remaining chilies. Serve warm or cool. Or, when chilies are cool, package airtight and chill up to 3 days. To reheat, spread in a single layer in a 10- by 15-inch pan and bake in a 350° oven until warm and crisp, 3 to 4 minutes. Makes about 1½ cups.

PER ¼ CUP: 136 calories (64 percent from fat), 1.7 g protein, 12 g carbohydrates, 9.6 g fat (1.2 g saturated), 0 mg cholesterol, 1,106 mg sodium

CRANBERRY HONEY VINAIGRETTE

Fresh cranberries add a fruity tartness that rounds out the flavor balance in this oil-free dressing of cranberry juice cocktail, balsamic vinegar, and honey.

The dressing goes well with mild salad greens such as leaf or butter lettuce. Allow about 1 tablespoon vinaigrette for each cup of salad greens.

Or, for a change of pace, serve the dressing as a sauce with simply prepared poultry, lamb, or pork.

- ½ **cup cranberry juice cocktail**
- 3 **tablespoons balsamic vinegar (or red wine vinegar and 2 teaspoons honey)**
- 2 **tablespoons honey**
- ½ **cup fresh or frozen cranberries, rinsed, drained, and finely chopped**

In a bowl or jar, mix cranberry juice, vinegar, honey, and cranberries. Use or, if making ahead, cover airtight and chill up to 4 days. Makes about 1 cup.

PER TABLESPOON: 17 calories, 0 g protein, 4.5 g carbohydrates, 0 g fat, 0 mg cholesterol, 0.4 mg sodium

Chili chips' heat demands cold contrast—icy beer or fruit juice.

Cranberries give mild rice vinegar a snap that celebrates salads.

CRANBERRY VINEGAR

Clear vinegar boiled with cranberries turns bright red and absorbs the fruit's flavor. The blend makes attractive holiday gifts in decorative bottles.

Splash the vinegar over salad greens, orange slices, raw or cooked red cabbage, and turkey salad.

- 2 **cups fresh or frozen cranberries, rinsed**
- 3 **cups rice vinegar**
- **About 3 tablespoons sugar**

In a 2- to 3-quart pan on high heat, bring to boiling cranberries, vinegar, and 3 tablespoons sugar. Simmer, covered, until cranberries pop and are soft, about 5 minutes. Add more sugar to taste, if desired. Let stand until cool. Pour vinegar through a fine strainer into a container with a pouring lip; discard residue. Pour vinegar into decorative bottles, using a funnel if necks are narrow. Seal with lids.

Use, or store at room temperature up to 4 months. If an opaque film develops on surface, spoon it off or, to preserve clarity of vinegar, pour vinegar through a fine strainer into a 2- to 3-quart pan and bring to boiling. Wash bottle, then refill with vinegar. Store as before. Makes about 3 cups.

PER TABLESPOON: 7.4 calories, 0 g protein, 1.9 g carbohydrates, 0 g fat, 0 mg cholesterol, 2.5 mg sodium

CAJUN CUISINE PAYS *little attention to the number of ingredients it employs and none at all to calorie count. This insouciance is nowhere better displayed than in jambalaya, which might be described as the condemned prisoner's last meal-in-a-pot. Martin Le Masters, who learned to make jambalaya from his chef father, continues to use all the spices, vegetables, and aromatics of the original stew, but he has substituted lower-fat bacon, ham, and sausage made from turkey for the regular bacon, ham, and andouille sausage. The turkey products are remarkably similar to the originals, and in a spicy dish such as this no one is likely to notice the switch.*

Of course, you can use the original meats at the cost of a higher fat content. However, if cholesterol rather than fat is your concern, note that oysters and shrimp, though low in fat, are both high in cholesterol.

EASY-ON-YOUR-HEART JAMBALAYA

- 1 large (about ½ lb.) onion, chopped
- 1 medium-size (6- to 7-oz.) green bell pepper, stemmed, seeded, and chopped
- ¼ cup diced celery
- 1 teaspoon minced or pressed garlic
- ¼ pound turkey sausage, thinly sliced
- 2 slices turkey bacon, diced
- ¼ pound turkey ham, cut into ½-inch cubes
- 1 dried bay leaf
- ¼ teaspoon cayenne
- ½ teaspoon *each* dried thyme leaves, dried basil leaves, and pepper
- ¼ cup chopped parsley
- 1 cup long-grain white rice
- 1 can (1 lb.) cut-up tomatoes
- 3 cups regular-strength chicken broth
- 1 jar (10 oz.) shucked fresh small Pacific oysters
- 1 pound medium-size (45 to 50) shrimp, shelled and deveined
  Salt

In a 5- to 6-quart pan over high heat, combine onion, bell pepper, celery, garlic, and ½ cup water. Stir often until moisture evaporates and vegetables

begin to stick to pan, about 10 minutes. Stir free with 2 tablespoons water. Add turkey sausage, bacon, and ham; stir often until mixture begins to brown, 8 to 10 minutes.

Stir in bay leaf, cayenne, thyme, basil, pepper, parsley, rice, tomatoes and their liquid, broth, and juices drained from oysters. Bring to a boil over high heat; cover and simmer until rice is tender to bite, 30 to 40 minutes. Stir occasionally.

Add shrimp and oysters (cut in half if large) and cook, uncovered, just until shrimp turn pink, about 8 minutes; stir often. Season to taste with salt. Makes 8 servings.

PER SERVING: 249 calories (20 percent from fat), 21 g protein, 28 g carbohydrates, 5.4 g fat (1.5 g saturated), 111 mg cholesterol, 502 mg sodium

Martin Le Masters

Concord, Calif.

THE BLACK SWAN WAS *once thought to be an impossibility (it was the original rara avis, or rare bird, of poetry and folk wisdom), but the discovery of Australia led also to the discovery of real black swans.*

The moral of this tale is that the world is an unending source of marvels. One of these is a white white–chocolate chip cookie invented by Gerry Cutler. Unable to obtain the recipe from the proprietor of a Washington coffee shop, Cutler produced this superior version by research, experimentation, and the use of a fine palate.

White chocolate is not chocolate that has been bleached. It is a blend of essentially colorless cocoa butter (separated from chocolate), sugar, and flavorings. It is milder in flavor than regular chocolate.

WHITE WHITE CHOCOLATE COOKIES

- 1¼ cups all-purpose flour
- 3 tablespoons cornstarch
- ¼ cup sugar
- 1 teaspoon baking powder
- ½ cup (¼ lb.) butter or margarine, cut into chunks
- ¼ cup coarsely chopped almonds
- 2 tablespoons unsweetened dried flaked coconut
- ½ cup coarsely chopped white chocolate
- ¼ cup milk

In a food processor or bowl, mix flour, cornstarch, sugar, and baking powder. Add butter; whirl or rub with your fingers to form fine crumbs. Stir in almonds, coconut, and chocolate. Then add milk and stir until mixture is moistened.

With floured hands, roll dough into 1½-inch balls. Place balls 2 inches apart on ungreased 12- by 15-inch baking sheets. Press each ball to ⅜-inch thick.

Bake in a 300° oven until cookies are a rich golden brown, about 35 minutes. If using 1 oven, alternate pan positions after 15 minutes. Transfer cookies to racks; serve warm or cool. To store, seal airtight and hold at room temperature up to a day; freeze to store longer. Makes about 2 dozen.

PER COOKIE: 101 calories (53 percent from fat), 1.3 g protein, 11 g carbohydrates, 5.9 g fat (2.7 g saturated), 11 mg cholesterol, 61 mg sodium

Gerry Cutler

Redmond, Wash.

"Cajun cuisine pays little attention to the number of ingredients it employs."

Start the day with egg and bean burrito topped with yogurt and salsa.

BREAKFAST BURRITOS

- 1 can (1 lb.) refried beans
- 1 can (4 oz.) diced green chilies
- 6 large eggs
- ¾ cup purchased green salsa, mild to hot
- ⅓ cup chopped fresh cilantro (coriander), plus cilantro sprigs
- 6 flour tortillas (7 to 8 in.)
- ¾ cup shredded jack cheese
- 1 cup unflavored nonfat yogurt
  Lime wedges

In a 10- to 12-inch frying pan over medium heat, stir beans and chilies often until bubbling, 3 to 4 minutes.

Meanwhile, beat eggs to blend with 3 tablespoons salsa and chopped cilantro. Push beans to 1 side of the pan; pour egg mixture into cleared area and stir often until set, about 3 minutes.

Concurrently, wrap tortillas in a towel and heat in a microwave oven at full power (100 percent) until hot, about 3 minutes. (Or seal tortillas in foil; bake in a 350° oven until hot, about 10 minutes.)

For each burrito, spoon ⅙ of beans, eggs, and cheese in center of a tortilla; roll to enclose. Serve, seam down, on warm plates with additional salsa, yogurt, lime, and cilantro sprigs. Makes 6 servings.—*Suzanne Soulé, Vista, Calif.*

PER SERVING: 312 calories (35 percent from fat), 19 g protein, 33 g carbohydrates, 12 g fat (1.9 g saturated), 226 mg cholesterol, 924 mg sodium

Golden bread spirals are filled with cheddar, horseradish, and mustard.

CHEESE TWISTS

- 1 large egg white
- 1 tablespoon dry mustard
- ⅓ cup prepared horseradish
  All-purpose flour
- 1 loaf (8 oz.) frozen white or whole-wheat bread dough, thawed
- 2 cups (½ lb.) shredded sharp cheddar cheese

In a bowl, beat egg white to blend well with mustard and horseradish.

On a floured board, roll dough with a floured rolling pin into a 12- by 15-inch rectangle. (Let dough rest 5 minutes if it's too springy to stay in place.) Spread with ⅓ cup of the egg mixture. Sprinkle half the dough lengthwise with all but ½ cup cheese. Fold plain dough over cheese; pinch edges to seal. Gently expel air with rolling pin.

With floured knife, cut dough crosswise into 16 to 18 equal strips. Brush with remaining egg mixture; sprinkle with remaining cheese. Lift 1 strip, make 4 twists, and lay on a greased 12- by 15-inch baking sheet; repeat with remaining strips, placing about ½ inch apart. Lightly cover with plastic wrap. Let stand in a warm place until puffy, 20 to 25 minutes; remove wrap.

Bake in a 375° oven until deep golden, 25 to 30 minutes. Transfer to rack with a spatula.

Serve hot or cool. Cool on a rack; store airtight up to 2 days or freeze to store longer. To reheat, place on baking sheet and bake in a 400° oven for about 5 minutes. Makes 16 to 18.—*Joyce Fellingham, Porterville, Calif.*

PER PIECE: 85 calories (48 percent from fat), 4.5 g protein, 6.5 g carbohydrates, 4.5 g fat (2.7 g saturated), 13 mg cholesterol, 159 mg sodium

Crisply cook pepperoni strips; add escarole to wilt, then stir in cannellini.

ESCAROLE ITALIAN-STYLE

- 1½ pounds (2 large heads) escarole
- 3 ounces thinly sliced pepperoni, cut into matchstick pieces
- 2 large cloves garlic, minced or pressed
- 1 can (about 1 lb.) cannellini (white kidney beans), rinsed and drained
  Lemon wedges
  Salt and pepper

Trim and discard core and tough stems from escarole. Rinse leaves, drain well, and tear into 2-inch pieces.

In a 5- to 6-quart pan over medium-high heat, stir pepperoni until it sizzles and begins to brown, about 4 minutes. Add garlic and stir for 30 seconds. Add escarole, a portion at a time, stirring often until wilted, about 3 minutes total. Gently stir in cannellini.

Pour into a shallow bowl and offer with lemon wedges and salt and pepper to add to taste. Makes 6 servings.—*Donna Parla, Glendale, Calif.*

PER SERVING: 137 calories (45 percent from fat), 7.8 g protein, 12 g carbohydrates, 6.8 g fat (2.3 g saturated), 11 mg cholesterol, 396 mg sodium

Warm Cioppino Salad

½ pound extra-large shrimp (26 to 30 per lb.), shelled and deveined
3 tablespoons olive oil
2 cups ¼-inch-thick slices mushrooms
2 cups ¼-inch-thick slices zucchini
1 can (14½ oz.) tomatoes, drained and coarsely chopped
1½ cups drained pitted black ripe olives
   Dressing (recipe follows)
3 quarts lightly packed, rinsed and crisped fresh spinach leaves
½ pound shelled cooked crab

In a 10- to 12-inch frying pan over medium-high heat, stir shrimp in oil until pink, about 2 minutes. Lift out and set aside. Add mushrooms and zucchini to pan; stir often on medium-high heat until zucchini is tender-crisp to bite, about 3 minutes.

Return shrimp to pan; add tomatoes, olives, and dressing; stir often until hot. Put spinach in a wide bowl; pour hot mixture over greens, top with crab, and mix gently. Makes 6 servings.—*Linda Lum, Tacoma, Wash.*

PER SERVING: 231 calories (47 percent from fat), 20 g protein, 14 g carbohydrates, 12 g fat (1.7 g saturated), 85 mg cholesterol, 693 mg sodium

Dressing. Mix ¼ cup **lemon juice,** 1 tablespoon **Worcestershire,** and 1 teaspoon *each* **dried basil** and **oregano leaves** and minced **garlic.**

Cioppino elements (seafood and tomatoes) top greens in salad.

Hearty Baked Pork & Apple Stew

2 pounds pork shoulder (fat trimmed), cut into 2-inch chunks
1 large (¾ lb.) onion, chopped
½ cup water
1¾ cups regular-strength beef broth
¾ cup apple butter
1 large (½ lb.) bell pepper, stemmed, seeded, and sliced
1¾ cups sliced carrots
½ cup sliced celery
3 large (1½ lb. total) Granny Smith apples, peeled, cored, and sliced

Place pork, onion, and water in an ovenproof 5- to 6-quart pan over high heat. Cover, bring to a boil, and boil for 10 minutes. Uncover and stir often until moisture evaporates and pan drippings are dark brown, about 5 minutes.

Add broth and apple butter; stir to free browned drippings. Bake, covered, in a 350° oven for 30 minutes. Stir in bell pepper, carrots, celery, and apples. Continue to bake, covered, until meat is very tender when pierced, about 1 hour longer. Makes 6 servings.—*Betty Maesner, Tacoma, Wash.*

PER SERVING: 316 calories (23 percent from fat), 20 g protein, 42 g carbohydrates, 8.2 g fat (2.6 g saturated), 63 mg cholesterol, 97 mg sodium

Tart apples stew with pork, adding flavor and thickening the sauce.

Cream Cheese Mincemeat Cookies

1 cup (½ lb.) butter or margarine
1 large package (8 oz.) cream cheese
2 cups powdered sugar
   About 3 cups all-purpose flour
¾ cup prepared mincemeat
1 teaspoon grated lemon peel

In a food processor or with a mixer, whirl or beat butter, cream cheese, and ½ cup sugar until smoothly blended. Thoroughly mix in 3 cups flour. Cover and chill dough until firm enough to handle, about 1 hour.

On a floured board, roll half the dough (keep remainder cold) ⅛ inch thick. Cut into 2½-inch rounds with a floured cutter; place rounds slightly apart on 2 ungreased 12- by 15-inch baking sheets. Reroll scraps and cut.

Combine mincemeat and peel; drop ½ teaspoon of mixture in center of each round. Fold each round over filling and press edges to seal.

Bake in a 375° oven until golden, 18 to 20 minutes; if using 1 oven, switch pan positions after 10 minutes. Transfer a few hot cookies at a time to a paper or plastic bag with remaining sugar; shake to coat well. Cool on racks. Repeat to use remaining dough and filling. Serve, or store airtight up to 2 days or freeze. Makes about 5 dozen.—*Margaret Pache, Mesa, Ariz.*

PER COOKIE: 87 calories (47 percent from fat), 1 g protein, 11 g carbohydrates, 4.5 g fat (2.8 g saturated), 12 mg cholesterol, 53 mg sodium

Powdered sugar–coated half-moon cookies make a holiday treat.

December Menus

*S*EASONAL EXCITEMENTS *inevitably make this month one of the year's busiest. Holidays, school breaks, frenzied shopping, travel plans, and special meals all compete for our time.*

Hearty meals featuring robust flavors and plenty of make-ahead steps are not only appealing, they're essential. Take a warm break on a snow hike with an easy-to-carry meal of hot sausage and vegetable sandwiches. Be ready for drop-in guests with flaky fila-wrapped chicken packets to bake. And turn meat from leftover roasts into tempting hash.

For a snow picnic at the lake, serve roasted sausage-vegetable sandwiches heated with tomato sauce from thermos. Bring cheese, fruit, and cookies, too.

SNOW PICNIC AT THE LAKE

Italian Sausage & Vegetable Sandwiches with Tomato-Porcini Sauce
Tiny Bonbel Cheeses
Red & Green Grapes   Apples
Zinfandel
Boxed Fruit Juices
Giant Cookies

Up to three days before outing, make sauce. The day before, roast sausage and vegetables. Reheat and assemble sandwiches just before you depart.

Bake or buy cookies that are 4 or 5 inches wide.

ITALIAN SAUSAGE & VEGETABLE SANDWICHES WITH TOMATO-PORCINI SAUCE

- 4 **(about 1 lb. total) mild Italian sausages**
- 2 **large (about 1½ lb. total) onions, cut into eighths**
- 2 **large (about 1¼ lb. total) yellow or red bell peppers, stemmed, seeded, and cut into 1-inch pieces**
- 4 **sourdough French rolls (each about 3 by 5 in.)**
  Tomato-porcini sauce (recipe follows)

Place sausages, onions, and peppers in a 12- by 17-inch pan; pierce meat all over. Bake in a 425° oven until vegetables' edges look almost charred but aren't burned, about 1 hour; stir occasionally. Use hot; or cool, cover, and chill up to 1 day. Reheat in a 350° oven for about 10 minutes.

Cut ½ inch off top of each roll. Pull bread from roll base and top to make a shell ¼ inch thick; reserve scraps for another use.

Set roll pieces, cut sides up, on a 12- by 15-inch baking sheet. Bake in a 400° oven until golden, 10 to 12 minutes. Place 1 sausage and ¼ of the vegetables in each roll. Top with roll lid.

If transporting, seal each roll in foil, then wrap in several thicknesses of newspaper to insulate; tie securely and carry in an insulated pack. Serve within 2 hours.

At picnic, untie packets. Spoon sauce into the sandwiches. Makes 4 servings.

PER SERVING: 713 calories (56 percent from fat), 24 g protein, 54 g carbohydrates, 44 g fat (14 g saturated), 88 mg cholesterol, 1,166 mg sodium

Tomato-porcini sauce. In a small bowl, soak ½ ounce **dried porcini mushrooms** (about ½ cup) in 1 cup hot **water** until soft, about 20 minutes. Lift mushrooms from water and squeeze dry; chop finely and set aside. Without disturbing sediment in bottom of bowl, pour soaking liquid into a measuring cup. Discard remainder.

In a 3- to 4-quart pan on medium-high heat, cook ¼ pound finely chopped **pancetta** or bacon until brown and crisp, about 5 minutes; stir often. Finely chop 1 small **onion** (about ¼ lb.), 1 small **carrot** (2 to 3 oz.), and 1 large (about 12-in.-long) stalk **celery;** add to pan. Stir in 1 clove minced **garlic** and 2 tablespoons minced **parsley.**

Stir often until vegetables begin to brown, about 5 minutes. Add 1 can (8 oz.) **chopped** or puréed **tomatoes,** 1 cup **regular-strength beef broth,** the chopped mushrooms, and reserved

THE DETAILS

Picnic carriers. *Carry foods in backpacks or fanny packs. Many have insulated pockets.*

Insulator. *To keep sandwiches warm, wrap in foil, then newspaper and insulated bags.*

Food holders. *Thermos keeps sauce hot; rigid containers protect fruit, cookies.*

Beverage caddies. *Boxed drinks, bota, or insulated holder simplify beverage transport.*

---

soaking liquid. Bring to a boil; simmer, uncovered, until sauce is reduced to 2 cups, 10 to 15 minutes. If making ahead, cool, cover, and chill up to 3 days; reheat to use. Add **salt** to taste.

To pack, pour sauce into a preheated wide-mouth 1-pint to 1-quart thermos (sauce keeps hot up to 2 hours).

PER TABLESPOON: 25 calories (72 percent from fat), 0.5 g protein, 1.2 g carbohydrates, 2 g fat (0.8 g saturated), 2.4 mg cholesterol, 38 mg sodium

IMPROMPTU COMPANY DINNER

Tricolor Winter Salad
Chicken Fila Packets with Dried Tomatoes, Basil & Prosciutto
Peas with Toasted Hazelnuts
Pinot Grigio
Sparkling Water
Grasshopper Sundaes

Make-ahead chicken breasts baked in fila packets are an elegant entrée for spur-of-the-moment entertaining. Packets can be made up to a month ahead and stored in the freezer. They thaw in 1 to 2 hours at room temperature, but keep them well wrapped so fila doesn't dry out.

While chicken bakes, make salad. Dress up the peas with chopped hazelnuts; to toast the nuts quickly, stir them in a frying pan over medium heat until they are lightly browned, 4 to 6 minutes.

For an easy, elegant dessert, drizzle scoops of vanilla ice cream with equal parts crème de menthe and white crème de cacao liqueurs; tuck a chocolate wafer into each serving of ice cream.

TRICOLOR WINTER SALAD

2 small oranges or tangerines, about ¼ pound total
3 cups radicchio leaves, rinsed and crisped
6 cups butter lettuce leaves, rinsed and crisped
2 teaspoons Dijon mustard
3 tablespoons balsamic vinegar
2 tablespoons olive oil
Salt and pepper

Using a sharp knife, cut peel and membrane from oranges. Cut between membranes to separate into segments; discard seeds. Put fruit in a wide bowl, squeezing any membrane

---

Golden fila packet conceals moist chicken breast seasoned with prosciutto, basil, and dried tomatoes.

juice over fruit. Add radicchio and lettuce leaves. In a small bowl, mix mustard, vinegar, and olive oil; pour over salad and mix. Add salt and pepper to taste. Makes 6 servings.

PER SERVING: 61 calories (71 percent from fat), 1.1 g protein, 4.2 g carbohydrates, 4.8 g fat (0.6 g saturated), 0 mg cholesterol, 55 mg sodium

CHICKEN FILA PACKETS WITH DRIED TOMATOES, BASIL & PROSCIUTTO

3 whole chicken breasts (about 1 lb. each), skinned, boned, and split
¾ cup mayonnaise
3 tablespoons drained and finely chopped dried tomatoes packed in oil
2 tablespoons minced fresh or 2 teaspoons dried basil leaves
⅛ pound thinly sliced prosciutto, finely chopped
3 cloves garlic, minced or pressed
½ cup freshly grated parmesan cheese
6 tablespoons butter or margarine, melted
12 sheets fila dough (thawed if frozen), each about 11 by 17 inches
¼ teaspoon pepper

(Continued on next page)

Rinse chicken breasts and pat dry.

In a small bowl, stir together mayonnaise, tomatoes, basil, prosciutto, 2 cloves garlic, and parmesan cheese.

Stir remaining garlic into butter.

To make each packet, lay 1 fila sheet flat; brush lightly with butter. (Keep remaining fila covered with plastic wrap to prevent drying.)

Top buttered fila with another fila sheet; brush lightly with butter. Lightly sprinkle pepper on 1 side of each chicken piece, then spread 1 side of the chicken with about 1½ tablespoons mayonnaise mixture.

Lay chicken, coated side down, on 1 corner of fila. Spread top of chicken with 1½ more tablespoons mayonnaise mixture. Lift corner of fila over chicken; roll chicken with fila over once. Fold 1 side of fila over chicken and roll again. Fold opposite side of fila over chicken, then roll to use all the fila. Place packets seam side down. Repeat steps to wrap remaining pieces of chicken in the remaining fila.

Brush packets with remaining butter. (At this point, you can arrange packets in a single layer in a container with a tight-fitting lid and freeze up to 1 month. Thaw completely, covered, before baking.)

To bake, arrange fila packets at least 2 inches apart in a rimmed 12- by 17-inch pan. Bake, uncovered, in a 375° oven until packets are golden brown on all sides, 20 to 25 minutes. Makes 6 servings.

PER SERVING: 673 calories (55 percent from fat), 45 g protein, 30 g carbohydrates, 41 g fat (13 g saturated), 145 mg cholesterol, 905 mg sodium

---

ONE-PAN HASH BREAKFAST

Holiday Hash
Toasted English Muffins
Pineapple Wedges with Warm Cranberry Coulis
Sparkling Cranapple Cider

Leftover meats from holiday gatherings star with potatoes, onions, parsley, and eggs in this flavorful breakfast hash.

While hash ingredients are browning, cut up the pineapple and heat the cranberry sauce. Be sure to offer some of the sauce with the hash, too.

HOLIDAY HASH

 3 tablespoons butter or margarine
 2 pounds russet potatoes, peeled and diced
 1 large (about ½ lb.) onion, chopped
 ½ pound *each* cooked ham and roast beef (or all of 1 kind), finely diced
 ¼ cup minced parsley
 3 large eggs, slightly beaten
   Freshly ground pepper
   Parsley sprigs
   Salt

In a 12- to 14-inch nonstick frying pan on medium-high heat, melt 2 tablespoons butter. Add potatoes; stir often until golden brown, 20 to 25 minutes. Remove from pan and set aside.

To pan, add remaining butter, onion, meats, and minced parsley. Stir often until onion and meats begin to brown, 10 to 12 minutes.

Return the potatoes to the pan; stir to heat, about 2 minutes. Add the eggs and stir just until eggs are softly set, 1½ to 2 minutes. Sprinkle with pepper.

Serve hash from frying pan, garnished with parsley sprigs; add salt to taste. Makes 6 servings.—*Gail A. Reiss, Mendocino, Calif.*

PER SERVING: 351 calories (38 percent from fat), 26 g protein, 28 g carbohydrates, 15 g fat (6.4 g saturated), 175 mg cholesterol, 695 mg sodium

PINEAPPLE WEDGES WITH WARM CRANBERRY COULIS

 1 small (about 2 lb.) pineapple
 1 can (1 lb.) whole cranberry sauce

Cut pineapple into 6 lengthwise wedges; leave leaves or discard, as desired.

In a small, microwave-safe bowl, heat 1 can whole cranberry sauce, uncovered, on full power (100 percent) until warm. (Or stir sauce in a 1- to 1½-qt. pan over medium-high heat.)

Spoon sauce over pineapple. Makes 6 servings.

PER SERVING: 146 calories (2.5 percent from fat), 0.4 g protein, 37 g carbohydrates, 0.4 g fat (0 g saturated), 0 mg cholesterol, 21 mg sodium

Articles Index

Index of Recipe Titles

General Index

Photographers

Glenn Christiansen: 55. **Peter Christiansen:** 1, 7, 11, 13, 20, 21, 23, 33, 38–39, 40, 41, 53, 58, 59, 61, 62, 63, 68, 69, 71, 72, 74, 75, 76, 79, 80, 81, 84, 87, 92, 93, 95, 96–97, 98, 99, 100, 105, 111, 113, 114, 115, 116, 117, 118, 121, 122, 123, 127, 133 (right), 135, 136, 137, 138, 142, 143, 148, 149, 151, 152, 153, 154, 155, 156, 157, 159, 162, 163, 164, 168, 172, 173, 175, 177, 182, 183, 186, 192, 193, 195, 197, 198, 199 (top), 200, 201, 202–203, 205, 213, 221 (top right), 223, 229, 232, 234, 235 (top), 239, 240, 244, 245, 247, 248, 249, 250–251, 253, 255, 256, 257, 259, 261, 262, 266, 267. **Patrick Cone:** 161 (top). **Stephen Cridland:** 158. **Bob Daemmrich:** 180 (bottom). **Jerry Anne DiVecchio:** 10 (left). **Hawaii Department of Business, Economic Development, and Tourism:** 73. **Jim McHugh:** 32 (right). **Alan Huestis:** 161 (center, bottom). **Renee Lynn:** 178. **Kevin Miller:** 140, 141. **Richard Morgenstein:** 86. **Don Normark:** 160, 176. **Norm Plate:** 2, 15, 26, 36 (left), 103, 110, 165, 166, 167, 179, 180 (top), 181, 184, 185, 187, 196, 199 (bottom), 211 (right), 214–215, 216, 217, 218–219, 221 (left), 224, 225, 226, 227, 228, 230, 231, 235 (bottom), 236, 237, 258. **Joel Rogers:** 32 (left). **Teri Sandison:** 125 (top). **Chad Slattery:** 221 (bottom right), 252. **W.D.A. Stephens:** 5. **Darrow M. Watt:** 9, 10 (right), 14, 16, 24, 25, 27, 28, 29, 30, 31, 36 (center, right), 42–43, 44, 45, 50, 51, 56, 57, 77, 82, 83, 101, 102, 104, 124, 126, 128, 132, 133 (left), 144, 210, 211 (left), 260. **Charles West:** 4. **Doug Wilson:** 85, 125 (bottom), 238.